Politics and Ecology

Politics and Ecology

Edited by

Phillip O. Foss

Colorado State University

Duxbury Press, A Division of
Wadsworth Publishing Company, Inc.
Belmont, California

Duxbury Press
A Division of Wadsworth Publishing Company, Inc.

L.C. Cat. Card No.: 72-075108
ISBN 0-87872-025-1
Printed in the United States of America

1 2 3 4 5 6 7 8 9 10——76 75 74 73 72

Be fruitful, and multiply, and
replenish the earth, and subdue it:
and have dominion over the fish of
the sea, and over the fowl of the
air, and over every living thing
that moveth upon the earth.

Genesis 1:28

And I brought you into a plentiful
country, to eat the fruit thereof
and the goodness thereof; but when
ye entered ye defiled my land, and
made mine heritage an abomination.

Jeremiah 2:7

Foreword

Environmental problems cannot be realistically compartmentalized; they form a single entity. Nevertheless, it is difficult to grasp this wholistic view of the world; so, in this book, I have tried to go both ways. Some chapters attempt to view the whole thing—the "big picture," while other chapters concentrate on particular aspects of the environmental problem.

Wherever possible, I have tried to present different or conflicting viewpoints to give the reader a broader basis of understanding. This has been difficult to do, because the pros and cons, unlike those of an issue such as Viet Nam, are not obvious or easy to identify. Since no one is in favor of dirty air, dirty water, or hazardous pesticides, the objections to environmental restoration are likely to be in the "yes, but" category.

In the chapters that follow I have tried to provide enough technical information so that the basic ecological problems can be understood by readers who have not been trained in the biological sciences. At the same time I have tried to choose political selections that I believe can be understood by nonpolitical scientists. I hope these efforts have not produced a superficial treatment of the most pressing problems of this, or any other, time.

Phillip O. Foss

Contents

Politics and Ecology

1 Prologue

Man: An Endangered Species

The most pervasive and important set of policy issues during the 1970's will be man's efforts to survive in the ravaged environment that is his creation. The policy decisions which are formulated in the next decade will largely determine the fate of the eco-system within the foreseeable future, because we have now reached a crisis period in which man himself is an endangered species.

Large scale environmental changes do not occur without cause nor do they occur without warning. And the warnings are both clear and ominous.

The supply of oxygen in the atmosphere is neither infinite nor inexhaustible. Oxygen is formed by land plants and by minute marine plants called phytoplankton. The oceans produce about twice as much oxygen as do land-based plants. The industrialized nations of the world are indiscriminately dumping into the oceans millions of tons of oil, sewage, poison gas, pesticides, and nuclear wastes. This garbage, unless checked, will eventually kill the oceans—and when the oceans die, we all die—choking.

In the summer of 1970 deadly mercury compounds were found in Vermont's isolated Silver Lake. Further investigation established the presence of mercury in 20 states. Mercury residues may remain in the environment for up to 100 years. We have consumed some 160 million pounds of mercury during this century.

Responsible scientists have become alarmed at the rapid buildup of carbon dioxide and other assorted garbage in the atmosphere. Some of them theorize that this "envelope" will trap the heat like a greenhouse, and that as a result the polar icecaps will melt and flood the coastal cities. Others contend that the thick cloud cover will screen out enough sunlight to cause a new ice age. Take your choice.

Pesticide residues have been found in the tissues of polar bears and Antarctic penguins—far from any known application point. Some American women carry milk in their breasts with DDT concentrations higher than the Federal government allows in dairy milk.

Despite the expenditure of several billion dollars, the quality of America's water is still deteriorating (and the incidence of water-borne diseases is increasing). As could be expected, the most heavily polluted waters are those closest to high population concentrations. The Cuyahoga River in Ohio became so loaded with industrial effluent in the summer of 1969 that it caught fire and burned down two railroad trestles. Increasingly, more water is used more times.

Already the entire flow of the massive Ohio River is used an estimated 3 1/2 times before it enters the Mississippi. If population continues to expand, and if per capita use of water continues to grow, most of us will be drinking water that several other people upstream have already used.

On November 20, 1967 an applauding crowd watched the hands of the census clock move to 200 million Americans. By the year 2000 there will be twice as many people in the world as there are now. That means at least twice as much food, fibre, and other natural resources. It means at least twice as much garbage and air and water pollution. It means more than twice as much fertilizer and pesticides. And it means a still wider gap between the "have" and "have-not" nations.

Stewart Udall summarized our current situation this way:

> The change in attitude began when we observed that we had not just conquered Nature—we had achieved overkill. We saw supine forests, exhausted rivers, sullen air, and realized that to the victor belonged only the spoiled.[1]

How Did We Get in This Mess?

First of all, we are not alone in having environmental problems. All the industrialized nations of the world have the same problems in varying degrees. The Rhine River may be the most heavily polluted major river system in the world. Tokyo's air pollution is apparently worse than that of Los Angeles. Norwegian skiers complain of "black snow"—soot from British industrial plants. Russian paper mills are killing fish. However, the fact that we are not alone is no excuse for inaction. Actually, its worldwide proportions make the problem more formidable and frightening.

Perhaps the basic reason we "got into this mess" (along with the rest of the world) is that man has historically thought of the world as being infinite, or at least as holding infinite resources. When resources were exhausted in one area, he could always move on. There was always a new horizon, a new frontier. Even though we now understand that the world is not infinite, we still behave as if it were—particularly with regard to air and water.

It seems reasonable to believe (and the evidence suggests) that man has always thought nature existed to be exploited to satisfy his wants. It seems very doubtful if there has ever existed a "land ethic" or a "conservation ethic" in any human society of any size. Those societies that "learned to live with nature" probably were simply incompetent exploiters, whose depredations therefore had little effect. After all, primitive life was in large part a battle against nature, so the conquerors or super exploiters became the legendary folk heroes. Paul Bunyan and Buffalo Bill have counterparts throughout the world.

A third reason commonly advanced to explain man's destruction of the environment is that he didn't know any better—that he did not understand the ecological consequences of his actions. This argument is only partially valid. Even primitive man must have recognized that if he killed off a particular group of animals, he must move on to a new hunting ground. He must have noticed that when he burned off forests, they were replaced by other types of vegetation. In more recent times men have understood that deforestation and overgrazing cause an accelerated rate of erosion. "Cut out and get out" was not invented in the United States. There is a long recorded history of such tactics. The dreary record includes China, all of the Middle East, Northern Africa, Greece, Italy, and Spain, as well as the American West. The historical evidence is clear. The causes and effects were obvious but they went unheeded. From ignorance? More likely foresters and herdsmen simply didn't care—and why should they? There was always more over the horizon.

Modern man appears to be no different from his ancestors. Either he doesn't know or he doesn't care. We blow poisons into the atmosphere without knowing what the consequences will be. We dump anything we don't want into the water without asking what the results will be. We spread millions of tons of pesticides (including DDT) around the world with little apparent regard for their effects except on the "target population." We build huge dams on the simplistic premise that such impoundments do nothing but store water. We play with atomic energy despite known (and unknown) dangers. In Barry Commoner's words,

> Like the sorcerer's apprentice, we are acting upon dangerously incomplete knowledge. We are, in effect, conducting a huge experiment on ourselves.[2]

Throughout most of our history, American politics has been mainly concerned with territorial expansion and with the exploitation of, and competition for, natural resources. Westward expansion and "manifest destiny" were for years the dream and the driving force of American government. The exploitation of nature meant settlement and increased production. The folk heroes were those who "conquered the wilderness."

Government policies moved the borders of the United States from the Appalachians to the Pacific Coast to Alaska and Hawaii. *Progress* meant *more* and *bigger*. "Science" was mainly concerned with improving the methods used to exploit nature. These attitudes, life styles, and views of the world have been built into governmental institutions and practices. These institutions and practices have been designed mainly to protect individual and private property rights, with little attention given to their ecological consequences.

The United States, we say, is a pluralistic society where people can freely choose a specialty and follow their individual destiny. This concept has had many labels. Among them are: freedom, rugged individualism, everybody for himself, the right to choose, the American Way, and doing your own thing. Whatever the virtues of this life style (and they are many), an individualistic and pluralistic society leaves something to be desired where feelings of responsibility towards society as a whole are concerned. As Kenneth Boulding puts it, "The principle of the public be damned is the secret vice of practically everybody."

The American Way includes more than individualism. It also encompasses the work ethic, a commitment to progress and growth, and a drive to produce—more, better, faster, cheaper. This is the way we "built a great America." This is the way we built the biggest and the best of almost everything (including universities). In the process of this fabulous production we inevitably used, and used up, incredible quantities of raw materials and produced equally incredible amounts of pollution and garbage. The Affluent Society produces more, consumes more, wastes more, and pollutes more. It also creates greater stresses and disturbances in the eco-system.

The historical trends and general attitudes outlined above have produced a highly advanced technology. This technology has been directly responsible for creating the most effective instruments of ecological disturbance. Improved technology has developed more efficient methods for "harvesting" fishes, birds, and wildlife, with the result that some species are nearing extinction. Technology has developed machines and methods which have expedited the decimation of forests and the clearing of land for farms, factories, highways, and suburbs. Agricultural technology has encouraged specialized crop production, and the consequent simplification of the ecology has produced an increased need for pesticides and fertilizers—and a reduction in numbers of birds and wildlife. Advances in transportation technology have given us millions of smog-producing automobiles. To accommodate them, we have paved over a total land area larger than the state of Maine. The technology of power production has created water and air pollution, hazards from the production of atomic energy, and devastated landscapes from strip mining. Chemical technology has created hazards both known and unknown. Production technology has encouraged the concentration of people into large urban centers where environmental degradation is also most concentrated. Medical technology has sharply reduced the death rate with the consequent "population explosion." This suggestive listing could be extended for several pages. It seems evident, however, that the products of technology are the most efficient agents of environmental destruction. Whether this same technological skill can be redirected to correct the mistakes of the past and improve future environments has yet to be tested.

Perhaps, at bottom, we have got into "this mess" because we have behaved like human beings, for whom the basic drive is individual self-preservation. We now call it "rational self-interest." People, now and in the past, strive for individual security and a better life for themselves and their immediate families. Other considerations and values come second. Individual, rational, short term self-interest may be long run suicidal madness. But after all, we are all here on a short run, and posterity has never done anything for us.

Solutions?

Once we have recognized a problem, we begin to cast about for solutions. All of us prefer quick, easy, simple ones. But ordinarily, complex problems are not amenable to simple solutions. Moreover, the cost of some solutions makes them questionable or prohibitive—even if they accomplish their purpose. Thus a prohibition on "no deposit-no return" containers would reduce (but not solve) the littering and solid waste problem, but the time costs for both processor and consumer would be very high.

In this section, we will consider some of the more common proposals that have been advanced to solve the environmental problem.

Back to Nature.

Backpack sales have gone up sharply; a "Whole Earth" mail order catalog has been produced and widely distributed; and numerous "nature communes" have been established. Is this the answer? Is a return to the primitive life the way out? We can probably agree that most of us would benefit from more frequent experiences in wild or primitive areas. We can probably also agree that many of us eat too much and exercise too little. But return to nature for a whole population on a permanent basis? Back to nature as a solution to environmental problems means back to ignorance, back to poverty, back to drudgery, back to filth, disease, and early death.

Search Out the Villains.

Perhaps the oldest method for resolving social problems is to search for villains and, having found them, eliminate them. This approach assumes that the problems of the world are caused by "bad guys" who sin against their neighbors. This scapegoating process may have some temporary cathartic value, but it is not likely to do much toward solving the problem. Currently, the most serious threat to the environment may be rapid population growth. Who are the villains in this scenario? Apparently the arch-villains have been scientists who developed methods and serums to control disease and the medical personnel who have saved millions of lives by administering such treatments.

"Industry" is another villain in the public mind. There is no doubt that some large industries produce high concentrations of air and water pollution and that they are, in fact, responsible directly and indirectly for much of the environmental degradation that has occurred. However, as will be reiterated several times throughout this book, careless use of the environment tends to reduce the cost of doing business. Therefore any control devices must be applied equally throughout the nation, or a firm in one location will have a competitive advantage over firms located elsewhere. Furthermore, nation-wide controls may not be enough. American firms who operate internationally may be placed at a disadvantage if they are forced to use expensive control devices or methods. But these are not the only problems. Probably most industrial products have substitutes, or at least such substitutes can be developed. If high-cost controls are levied against one product, it may not be able to compete with a less-controlled substitute product. Nor is this all. Persons whose livelihood depends upon the continued success of a given industry will quickly lose interest in the environment if their livelihood is threatened. Thus employees at the ITT Rayonier pulp paper mill in Fernandina Beach, Florida are worried about efforts to force the mill to clean up its discharges or close down. In the words of one typical plant workman, "I've got to feed my kids. Let me keep my job and to hell with the environment."

Finally, all of us benefit more or less from the low-cost products of industry, and not many of us are willing to boycott such products because they add to air or water pollution. As Pogo says, "We have met the enemy and they are us."

Having said all this, let us reverse the field. It is true that the enemy is us. It is true that we are all polluters, *but not of the same magnitude.* The housewife with her backyard incinerator pollutes the air, but only infinitesimally so as compared with the Consolidated Edison Company. A childless couple does not put as much pressure on the environment as a couple with a dozen children. The SST will spew infinitely more chemical and noise pollutants into the air than will a student on his bicycle. Perhaps it is unfair to thus personalize the examples. Nevertheless there are practices, processes, devices, and compounds that *are* villains and that *do* sin against the environment. These are the villains that can be hunted down and eliminated.

"Science" Will Find a Way.

There exists a mystical belief in the magic of science. The physical scientists especially have come to be the shamans of modern industrial society. And for good reason: their record has been most impressive. However, the record of "Science" in terms of ecological consequences rates an "F" grade. It seems safe to say that most damage to this planet has occurred as a result of technological developments. So "Science as usual" will not find a way unless scientific endeavor is directed toward the restoration of the world's eco-system.

Stop Growth, Reduce Consumption.

This solution advocates that people live more simply, consume less, and consequently pollute less. As an example, we could drive cars with lower horsepower, or better yet, ride bicycles. From an environmental point of view such a change would be desirable, but most Americans would think of it as going backwards. Furthermore, a reduction in the growth rate would most immediately affect people in the lower half of the income scale. Jon Margolis puts it this way:

> Stop growing? But growing is the secret of our success. We have mass affluence, to the extent we have it, not because we took from the rich and gave to the poor but because we became—*we grew*—so much richer that even most of the poor live tolerably. They still get the short end of the stick, but the stick is so long now that one can get at least a fingerhold on that end. To stop growing is to stop elongating the stick, and since most people are still clinging to that short end, this presents some problems.[3]

Attempts to limit growth are probably not politically feasible, but there are, fortunately, some other alternatives. Much of the material we now discard can be reprocessed, recycled, and reused. By so doing we could reduce the strain on resources and also reduce pollution. Secondly, an increasing proportion of Americans can be employed in so-called "service industries" such as education, health, communications, and entertainment. Such endeavors put little stress on the environment. This shift from consumer goods to services is already taking place.

Salvation Through the Courts.

The courts still command considerable respect and confidence among the American people, and they *may* provide one of the few mechanisms by which an individual citizen can act to prevent, or remove, a specific environmental hazard.

The courts have long been involved in pollution abatement in nuisance proceedings, and public agencies have also used the courts to obtain judicial enforcement of their orders. Increasingly, however, the courts have consented to hear suits brought by private individuals against other individuals or corporations, and against government agencies, on environmental grounds. Common actions have been suits against a highway department challenging a proposed road location or against a proposed new airport or airport extension. In the past the courts have been reluctant to allow "public interest litigation" because plaintiffs were not considered to have "standing." A litigant was thought to have standing only if he had been injured in some way differently from the rest of the public—otherwise his grievance was considered to be a political matter. Thus it is understood that a citizen cannot bring suit against the President because he is opposed to the Viet Nam War, nor can he sue because he doesn't like the way his tax money is being spent.

In the past the courts have invoked the doctrine of standing in air and water pollution questions on the grounds that the complainant suffered no distinguishably different harm from the rest of the society. In most cases this was not actually true. A Manhattan resident obviously suffers more from Consolidated Edison's smoke than does a Wyoming cowboy.

It is likely that a continuing number of environmental cases will be heard by the courts with probable beneficial effects. However, the adversary proceedings of a courtroom, with judgments based on existing statutory or common law, do not lend themselves to decision making on the basis of ecological principles. We might also note in passing that the damage suit as a legal remedy in automobile accidents has produced overcrowded court dockets, a $7 billion annual charge for liability insurance—and no discernible reduction in auto accidents.

Develop an Ecological Conscience.

This, of course, is a basic requirement if any other measures are to succeed. We have come a long way in the last few years toward developing such a conscience, but so far we have not really had to face up to the cost of change. When we are confronted with hard choices that cost money, restrict our activities, or restrict our choices in the market, we may repress our new-found conscience.

Ecological Improvement through Political Action

What does politics have to do with ecology? Government is, and has been, the social mechanism for establishing rules and procedures which determine how men will use the environment. Past environmental exploitation and degradation has occurred with the concurrence and encouragement of governments in response to the commonly held values of society. Corrective and restorative actions will have to be undertaken by government because of the complexity and magnitude of the task. Partial, voluntary, and private efforts can have little real impact.

In the latter part of the 1960's there was apparently a significant shift in the attitudes and expectations of the American people regarding their natural environment. Various polls indicated that a majority of the public was concerned about environmental degradation; that they believed "something ought to be done"; and that they were willing to pay part of the costs of "cleanup." Numerous individuals, groups, and business corporations made voluntary efforts to improve the quality of the environment. But voluntaryism was not enough. It never can be, because ordinarily the noncooperators are rewarded. A paper mill that empties raw effluent into a river has a competitive advantage over a mill that spends money to treat sewage. The operation of the market system tends to reward pollution and environmental degradation.

If voluntaryism and the operation of the market do not produce the desired results, governmental action is the next logical alternative. When we have reached some kind of consensus on "ought to," we must next move to "how to" through the political process. It is at this point that many people lose interest. For some of them, spelling out the "oughts" and "shoulds" is enough. For others, politics means "dirty politics" and they want no part of it. But in its most basic sense politics is the process of formulating government policy. Policy changes require political action.

When ecology and environment became popular terms, some politicians who had previously evinced little interest suddenly "climbed on the bandwagon." Such behavior should not be regarded as cynical or hypocritical. After all, the primary function of a politician is to represent his constituents and, in his role as political broker, to try to get them what they want. In this role the politician is a follower—a servant of the people. Are there no political leaders? Yes; perhaps most successful politicians are leaders in some areas of public policy, but it is important to recognize that political leaders cannot be too far out in front (or off to the side), or they will wind up all alone with no followers.

Even if a high proportion of Americans generally favor efforts to improve the environment, this does not mean that government policies will automatically change to accommodate their wishes. Some obstacles to action follow, but at this point we should notice that policy changes ordinarily take place as a result of highly organized interest group activity. If a small, tightly organized group with a direct personal interest is arrayed against a large, inchoate, unorganized mass, the small, organized group ordinarily wins. By 1972, no well organized group of "environmentalists" had yet emerged and for good reason. Most successful interest groups have very narrow objectives, so that the members need only agree on one or a few matters. But the environmentalists have no such single focus. Some of them are mainly interested in vanishing wildlife, others in air quality, water pollution, population control, pesticidal effects, esthetics of urban structures—to mention only a few of their various concerns. The older conservation organizations such as the Audubon Society, the Izaak Walton League, and the Wilderness Society do have definite and restricted objectives, but saving the environment means more than saving birds or fishes or wilderness.

It does not seem likely that all the interests under the environmental umbrella can be effectively represented by a single organization. It does seem possible, however, that temporary coalitions of specialized groups can be highly effective on specific policy questions.

Obstacles to Action

If practically every person in the United States is generally in favor of a better natural environment, why don't we have it?

Recognition of the problem has come late—perhaps too late to correct it. Even today, millions of Americans are really unaware of the environmental problem. Until people recognize that a problem exists, obviously they won't try to solve it.

A generalized, positive attitude toward improving the environment does not necessarily involve a personal commitment. Persons who are genuinely concerned about air pollution may drive old cars with big engines and continue to use back-yard incinerators. Housewives may continue to use high phosphate content detergents, even though they may deplore the death of fresh water lakes. Industrial firms may unwillingly continue to pollute streams because adequate treatment costs would reduce profits. In most cases, rational short term self-interest leads to environmental destruction.

Ignorance is an important deterrent to action. As we have previously noted, large segments of the population know little about the environmental crisis. In addition, even though we may recognize a problem and be prepared to do something about it, we may not know what to do or the best way to do it. However, we cannot wait until we have perfect knowledge. The only sensible course is to proceed on the basis of what is known while at the same time seeking to expand that knowledge.

Administrative methods or organizational structures can be obstacles to action. Any large scale effort requires an organized bureaucracy. After all the talking is done, somebody finally has to do something. The task of restoring the environment may require new organizations or a regrouping of present agencies. Governmental reorganization is ordinarily difficult to accomplish in a democratic system because it is resisted by the clientele groups which tend to surround and support existing structural arrangements.

Who will pay the cost of restoring the environment? Ordinarily we depersonalize this question by speaking of funding methods and devices, but let us be clear about this—only people can pay taxes, fees, or charges. Politics is not only concerned with Lasswell's "who gets what, when, and how," but with who pays for it. Sloganized thinking such as "we are all polluters so we all must pay for the cost of cleaning up" does not help to solve the real problem of who pays what proportion of the costs. While all of us presumably want an improved environment, we would prefer that someone else pick up the check.

A final obstacle to action is the question of priorities. Many serious matters are clamoring for the attention and resources of the nation: Southeast Asia and the Middle East, the space program, highways, housing, education, and poverty come to mind. Each of these programs is supported by a substantial segment of the voters. Which has priority? What proportion of the country's brainpower, energy, and dollars should be allocated to each one?

Prologue
[1] U.S. Department of the Interior, *The Third Wave* (Washington, D.C.: U.S. Government Printing Office, 1966), p. 3.
[2] Barry Commoner, *Science and Survival* (New York: The Viking Press, Inc., 1966), p. 28.
[3] Jon Margolis, "Our Country 'Tis of Thee, Land of Ecology . . . ," *Esquire,* LXXIII, No. 3 (March 1970), 180.

2 What's the Problem?

We travel together, passengers on a little spaceship, dependent on its vulnerable resources of air and soil; all committed for our safety to its security and peace; preserved from annihilation only by the care, the work, and I will say the love we give our fragile craft.

Adlai Stevenson

In typical American fashion, we have lately begun to sloganize environmental problems. Bumper stickers, editorial writers, and public speakers carry the message:

Be eco-logical.
We have met the enemy and they are us.
You're the solution to all the pollution.
Population is everyone's baby.
Who will pay for cleaning up the environment? All of us.
Can we afford to pay the costs of improving the environment? We can't afford not to.

While such slogans and glib answers may help draw attention to the pervasive nature of environmental concerns, they oversimplify and thus tend to obfuscate the many-faceted complexities of the environmental problem. Unless we can correctly identify and define "the problem," it is most unlikely that we can develop workable solutions.

The basic problem is that mankind is rapidly destroying the ecological system of the earth, which sustains all life. The earth *is* like a space capsule. Its resources are limited and finite. We will not get any more on this "flight." Neither can we jettison our refuse by throwing it over the side.

On this limited sphere that is our home we survive as part of a cycle which is commonly called the eco-system. The eco-system consists of all living and nonliving matter which enters into the cycle or "web of life." In oversimplified terms, the cycle works something like this: (1) Sunlight, water, oxygen, carbon dioxide, and various other elements and compounds are used as nutrients by plants; (2) the plants convert these nutrients, through photosynthesis, into food for herbivores (cattle, sheep, antelope, etc.); (3) some of the herbivores are consumed by carnivores (predators) and some die for other reasons; (4) bacteria, fungi, and other organisms break down the dead herbivores and carnivores (and also unused plants) and recycle the chemical compounds back for reuse by plants.

This eco-system is thus interdependent, interrelated, and fragile. Garrett Hardin quotes the verse:

"Thou canst not stir a flower
Without troubling of a star."

The point is, Hardin goes on to say, "We can never do merely one thing, because the world is a system of fantastic complexity. Nothing stands alone. No intervention in nature can be focused exclusively on but one element of the system."[1]

But men have been insulting their environment for thousands of years. Why the sudden concern? When population was sparse and tools were primitive, man did little permanent damage except by overgrazing pastures and burning off woodlands. In recent years, however, world population has been growing much more rapidly than in the past, and the rate of technological advancement has given men equipment, devices, and compounds which multiply many times over their ability to disrupt the eco-system. Atomic power is only one of the natural forces that man has supposedly "harnessed" for his own use. As a consequence of high population concentrations combined with advanced technology, the industrial nations of the world, in particular, have contaminated their air and water, have reduced and degraded areas available for the enjoyment of nature, have increased hazards to health by various chemical compounds, and have endangered the life of the oceans and thus the quantity of the thin layer of oxygen which enshrouds the earth.

The ecological problem is further complicated by its world-wide dimensions. Some problems can be approached unilaterally, but others require the combined efforts of many nations.

Add to all of this the apparently inexorable continuation of population growth, which can overwhelm the resources of the earth if it continues unchecked.

Many of the "solutions" to the ecological problem run contrary to the age-old folkways and mores of most of the people in the world, who have traditionally believed that nature existed to be exploited. Policies of exploitation have produced systems of property rights, taxation, banking, insurance, and business practices which will require extensive revision. In the process of such change some persons and corporations will inevitably suffer financial loss. It is also probable that efforts to restore the environment may reduce human liberty and freedom of choice in the market. So while it is politically safe to be against pollution, it may be politically hazardous to support specific measures aimed at reducing pollution.

When we speak of programs to improve the environment, we are by definition speaking of political (governmental) programs. Restoring environmental quality will necessarily involve social controls and government intervention into the personal habits and business practices of most Americans. This means that the overriding problem is how to achieve ecological balance and an improved environment through the political system.

. . .

This chapter begins with a selection by George P. Marsh which was written more than a century ago. Marsh begins by asserting that the earth was given to man for "usufruct alone" and not for consumption or waste. According to Marsh, man has "subverted the relations and destroyed the balance which nature had established." Marsh warns that the earth is "fast becoming an unfit home" for man and that "another era of human improvidence" could result in barbarism or perhaps even in the extinction of the species.

The second selection is an article by Senator Edmund Muskie, one of the leaders in the fight to restore environmental quality in the United States. Muskie briefly reviews the nature of the problem and past and current efforts at solution, and concludes ". . . that man's ability to survive depends upon what he himself does to and about his environment; that the continuation of his current behavior patterns means a daily reduction in the prospects for healthy life on this planet; and that the present deterioration may already be irreversible in some vital respects."

Economist Kenneth Boulding examines the concepts of economic abundance and continued growth in relation to the limited capacities of the globe. Boulding says that we are walking a "tightrope over an enormous chasm" and that "jiggling the tightrope is absolutely out" for the next hundred years, which may be the most dangerous to mankind in the history of the planet. But Boulding hopes "that God is *not* just and that we will *not* get what we deserve."

In a wide-ranging article, Roger Revelle admits that technology has created new problems in the process of solving old ones. The answer, he says, is not to abandon technology but to use more of it. In his words, "Once man has bitten into the fruit of the tree of knowledge, there can be no return to Eden."

The articles by Marsh, Muskie, Boulding, and Revelle describe and define "the problem" in general terms. The specific problem of how to manage and improve the environment through the political process is considered in the next two selections, which are by Harvey Wheeler and Norman Wengert.

Wheeler states the problem thus—"How can we transmit ecological wisdom to the average citizen for rational and deliberate application at the polls?" The old politics of sectional competition, with its reliance on piecemeal efforts and pressure-group tactics, cannot cope, says Wheeler, with the "architectonic" problems of ecology. What is needed is a new politics which can not only preserve ecological balances but also "calculate hidden social costs so as to determine how much is really being spent on side effects" of such things as a new freeway or the SST. Wheeler hopes that such analyses can be obtained through the use of computers and that the results can be so presented that the average citizen can "comprehend and cope" with them.

In Wengert's view, the problem is one of reconciling facts, values, and interests. "The issues of environmental protection and enhancement," he says, "are ultimately issues of social policy or social control, in one way or another involving governmental action." Governmental action necessarily involves political choices based upon value preferences. However, these value preferences are as yet ill-defined, partly because the costs of change are as yet unknown. In addition, Wengert says, "environmental decisions involve complex relationships among governments and between governments, individuals and groups. Most significantly, environmental policy decisions must be made under conditions of high uncertainty, and inevitably result in a differential distribution of benefits and costs." Finding the "answers" will be difficult and "fraught with hazards."

Destructiveness of Man*
George P. Marsh**

Man has too long forgotten that the earth was given to him for usufruct alone, not for consumption, still less for profligate waste. Nature has provided against the absolute destruction of any of her elementary matter, the raw material of her works; the thunderbolt and the tornado, the most convulsive throes of even the volcano and the earthquake, being only phenomena of decomposition and recomposition. But she has left it within the power of man irreparably to derange the combinations of inorganic matter and of organic life, which through the night of aeons she had been proportioning and balancing, to prepare the earth for his habitation, when in the fulness of time his Creator should call him forth to enter into its possession.

Apart from the hostile influence of man, the organic and the inorganic world are, as I have remarked, bound together by such mutual relations and adaptations so as to secure, if not the absolute permanence and equilibrium of both, a long continuance of the established conditions of each at any given time and place, or at least, a very slow and gradual succession of changes in those conditions. But man is everywhere a disturbing agent. Wherever he plants his foot, the harmonies of nature are turned to discords. The proportions and accommodations which insured the stability of existing arrangements are overthrown. Indigenous vegetable and animal species are extirpated and supplanted by others of foreign origin, spontaneous production is forbidden or restricted, and the face of the earth is either laid bare or covered with a new and reluctant growth of vegetable forms and with alien tribes of animal life. These intentional changes and substitutions constitute, indeed, great revolutions; but vast as is their magnitude and importance, they are, as we shall see, insignificant in comparison with the contingent and unsought results which have flowed from them.

The fact that, of all organic beings, man alone is to be regarded as essentially a destructive power, and that he wields energies to resist which Nature—that nature whom all material life and all inorganic substance obey—is wholly impotent to resist, tends to prove that, though living in physical nature, he is not of her, that he is of more exalted parentage, and belongs to a higher order of existences, than those which are born of her womb and live in blind submission to her dictates.

---

*George P. Marsh, *The Earth as Modified by Human Action* (New York: Charles Scribner's Sons, 1864), pp. 33-34, 37-38, 42-43.

**Mr. Marsh was an attorney, member of Congress (1842-1849), and minister to Italy (1861-1882).

There are, indeed, brute destroyers, beasts and birds and insects of prey—all animal life feeds upon, and, of course, destroys other life,—but this destruction is balanced by compensations. It is, in fact, the very means by which the existence of one tribe of animals or of vegetables is secured against being smothered by the encroachments of another; and the reproductive powers of species which serve as the food of others are always proportioned to the demand they are destined to supply. Man pursues his victims with reckless destructiveness; and while the sacrifice of life by the lower animals is limited by the cravings of appetite, he unsparingly persecutes, even to extirpation, thousands of organic forms which he can not consume.

. . .

In short, without man, lower animal and spontaneous vegetable life would have been practically constant in type, distribution and proportion, and the physical geography of the earth would have remained undisturbed for indefinite periods, and been subject to revolution only from slow development, from possible unknown cosmical causes, or from geological action.

But man, the domestic animals that serve him, the field and garden plants the products of which supply him with food and clothing, cannot subsist and rise to the full development of their higher properties, unless brute and unconscious nature be effectually combated, and, in a great degree, vanquished by human art. Hence, a certain measure of transformation of terrestrial surface, of suppression of natural, and stimulation of artificially modified productivity becomes necessary. This measure man has unfortunately exceeded. He has felled the forests whose network of fibrous roots bound the mould to the rocky skeleton of the earth; but had he allowed here and there a belt of woodland to reproduce itself by spontaneous propagation, most of the mischiefs which his reckless destruction of the natural protection of the soil has occasioned would have been averted. He has broken up the mountain reservoirs, the percolation of whose waters through unseen channels supplied the fountains that refreshed his cattle and fertilized his fields; but he has neglected to maintain the cisterns and the canals of irrigation which a wise antiquity had constructed to neutralize the consequences of its own imprudence. While he has torn the thin glebe which confined the light earth of extensive plains, and has destroyed the fringe of semi-aquatic plants which skirted the coast and checked the drifting of the sea sand, he has failed to prevent the spreading of the dunes by clothing them with artificially propagated vegetation. He has ruthlessly warred on all the tribes of animated nature whose spoil he could convert to his own uses, and he has not protected the birds which prey on the insects most destructive to his own harvests.

. . .

The ravages committed by man subvert the relations and destroy the balance which nature had established between her organized and her inorganic creations, and she avenges herself upon the intruder, by letting loose upon her defaced provinces destructive energies hitherto kept in check by organic forces destined to be his best auxiliaries, but which he has unwisely dispersed and driven from the field of action. When the forest is gone, the great reservoir of moisture stored up in its vegetable mould is evaporated, and returns only in deluges of rain to wash away the parched dust into which that mould has been converted. The well-wooded and humid hills are turned to ridges of dry rock, which encumber the low grounds and choke the watercourses with their débris, and—except in countries favored with an equable distribution of rain through the seasons, and a moderate and regular inclination of surface—the whole earth, unless rescued by human art from the physical degradation to which it tends, becomes an assemblage of bald mountains, of barren, turfless hills, and of swampy and malarious plains. There are parts of Asia Minor, of Northern Africa, of Greece, and even of Alpine Europe, where the operation of causes set in action by man has brought the face of the earth to a desolation almost as complete as that of the moon; and though, within that brief space of time which we call "the historical period," they are known to have been covered with luxuriant woods, verdant pastures, and fertile meadows, they are now too far deteriorated to be reclaimable by man, nor can they become again fitted for human use, except through great geological changes, or other mysterious influences or agencies of which we have no present knowledge and over which we have no prospective control. The earth is fast becoming an unfit home for its noblest inhabitant, and another era of equal human crime and human improvidence, and of like duration with that through which traces of that crime and that improvidence extend, would reduce it to such a condition of impoverished productiveness, of shattered surface, of climatic excess, as to threaten the depravation, barbarism and perhaps even extinction of the species.

Fighting for Survival*
Senator Edmund S. Muskie**

Eighty-six years ago, the physicist Henry Augustus Rowland observed that "American science is a thing of the future, and not of the present or past." Today we may well ask if science—which has contributed to much of our past and present—has prevented the future, or whether it will make possible a worthwhile future for man. Until very recently the question of human destiny was related to the threat of nuclear war. That menace remains, of course, but it has been joined by the specter of environmental contamination. We have so misused the fruits of scientific endeavor, we now imperil our own existence.

Some dangers come piecemeal, the by-products of our industrial economy, as noted by the Nobel prize-winning geneticist Joshua Lederberg in the Washington *Post* of last December 20: "The modern industrial economy is dependent upon hazardous materials that are shipped throughout the country . . . in the last five years, over 50 cities and towns have had to be evacuated as a result of accidents involving hazardous materials." The very next

---

*Reprinted with permission from *The New Leader,* February 16, 1970. Copyright (c) The American Labor Conference on International Affairs, Inc., pp. 16-19.
**Mr. Muskie is a United States Senator from Maine.

day, the national Sunday supplement magazine *Parade* carried the following item: "When the sulfur dioxide content of the air in New York City rises above .2 parts per million, 10 to 20 people die as a result. In the past five years, sulfur dioxide has reached this level at least once every ten days."

Still other threats derive from defense projects designed to protect national security. Again the Washington *Post* of December 20: "The President's statement [on germ warfare] has not ruled out the production of toxins. The Department of Defense does not find in the President's directive any specific prohibition to the production of toxins."

A third source of contamination is the result of efforts to dispose of waste from the conversion of materials and energy. Outside Denver, for example, a farmer's well emits the weed killer 2,4-D, while his neighbor's well flows gasoline. In Ponca City, Oklahoma, springs bubble refined motor oil into residential basements. The culprit in these cases is called deep well disposal, a system that continually pumps billions of gallons of salt water mixed with oil and other liquid wastes back into the ground. Texas alone has 30,000 such wells.

On the East Coast, one scientist has proposed the construction of a 48-inch, 80-mile-long pipeline to carry municipal and industrial wastes from the lower Delaware River basin out into the Atlantic Ocean. The discharge of up to 4 million gallons a day would be beyond the continental shelf. This scheme, to be sure, would reduce pollution in the Delaware basin—but at the expense of the ocean. Like so many other control programs, it proposes to dump the load on someone else, downstream.

We are learning, however, that there is no one else downstream from us; that having made the world smaller through population increases and advances in transportation, we contaminate the very land we use, the air we breathe, with wastes of our own making. We have gone past the point where the question of conservation is limited to those who want to protect a stream or forest or stretch of shore. Such preservation is still needed, but it is no longer the central issue. The central issue today is the health of man, wherever he lives and whatever his station.

The young people understand this. That is why the topic is now a major campus concern, second in importance only to the Vietnam war. Indeed, this is the single issue that cuts across economic, social and racial lines, and binds the suburbs to the cities in a common life-related problem. Touching as it does the lives of the young and the old, the rich and the poor, it is deeply and strongly political. It is real, and therefore susceptible to emotional appeals. It is broad, and therefore subject to many uses.

When an issue of this kind arises it attracts would-be leaders and voters looking for scapegoats, and scapegoats will not be hard to find. There are those in business and industry who reject any liability for pollution or its clean-up. There are public officials who avoid the unpleasant encounters so necessary for change, who dismiss environmental complaints as "uninformed demagoguery." There are managers of public programs, civil and military, too "mission-oriented" to admit any responsibility for protecting the surroundings. And there are scientists whose commitment to their own projects has been so complete they have ignored the consequences of their work.

But pollution is not the fault of a small band of men; neither is it the consequence of our particular economic system. It is, rather, the special product of any society that places the consumption of goods and services high on its scale of values, and which has the means to provide them in abundance. For what determines the impact of an industrial-technological culture on the environment is not who owns the means of production but how they are managed. The problem is worldwide and will not give way to political code words. It can be exorcised only through intelligent public action based on understanding of its causes, and appreciation of its constantly changing aspect, and a comprehension of its implications.

From the preceding it might appear that nothing has been done to protect man from his own follies, but that would be an inaccurate and misleading appraisal. Since the latter part of 1940's, we have been chipping away at the indisputable municipal and industrial sources of water pollution. The greater part of the limited success in this area has come in the last six years, with the development of a water quality standards program, a substantial increase in our commitment to build sewage treatment plants, and attacks on such specific problems as oil, thermal and vessel pollution.

Work on air contamination came later, because its threats were not as evident and we did not make the ready connection between it and public health. Nevertheless, we have launched a program designed to achieve high standards of air quality in all parts of the nation by dealing with both moving and stationary pollution sources. Most important, the plan is organized to stimulate the gathering of scientific data, to build upon it and apply it to public health.

Finally, we are in the process of converting the solid waste control program from a mere exercise in disposal. The goal is to reduce the volume of refuse in our society and encourage the more efficient use and reuse of materials and energy.

These programs all deal with the obvious, straightforward problems of pollution: the physical by-products of our activities and production, the first stage, if you will, of environmental protection. The next stage will involve the more subtle and pervasive questions of land and resource use, hazardous substances, population distribution and industrial location, noise and esthetic pollution, ecological balances and urban design. How we cope with them will inevitably affect the organization of Federal, state and local government, as well as our systems of taxation, public works projects, support of research and development, and defense policies. Increasingly, too, these matters will influence our relations with other countries, not just in this hemisphere, but in Europe, Africa and Asia.

Efforts on the Federal level are already under way to lay a foundation for this second-stage effort. Thus on January 1, President Nixon approved the National Environmental Policy Act of 1969, which presents a statement of policy and directs all Federal agencies to comply with it; provides for a Council on Environmental Quality; and requires the President to submit to Congress and the people an annual pollution report. In addition, the Water Quality Improvement Act of 1969, now in House-Senate conference, seeks to complement the new measure in two important respects: It would expand the requirements for Federal compliance with water quality standards to include activities and projects supported or authorized by Washington; and it would establish an office to furnish staff support to the President, the newly created Council on Environmental Quality, and the older Cabinet-level Environmental Quality Council. (Those who are sensitive to the implications of words have probably noted the shift from "pollution control and abatement" to "environmental quality.")

The object of the proposals for expanding the President's capacity to deal with Federal environmental responsibilities is in part a recognition of the past confusion that has hampered various control efforts. Similarly in Congress, members of the Senate and House of Representatives, recognizing the need to expand their own understanding and coordinate their endeavors more closely, are proposing the creation of a nonlegislative joint committee on environmental quality. This is an outgrowth of my recommendation for a select committee on technology and the human environment. Because pollution control cannot be isolated from other concerns, membership would be drawn from the several legislative committees whose activities affect our natural surroundings. These include Public Works, Agriculture, Interior, Government Operations, Banking and Currency, and Labor in both Houses; Commerce in the Senate; Merchant Marine and Fisheries and Interstate and Foreign Commerce in the House. The new group is intended to develop a body of knowledge which would guide the legislative committees in their activities, and give more visibility to ecological matters on a day-to-day basis. It would, moreover, provide a forum and clearinghouse for those who question, those who want change, and those who have ideas for the betterment of man's place in the universe.

In the Executive branch, a more formal reorganization is required to insure proper status for environmental protection. I am not the first to note that pollution control and abatement programs are scattered through several departments and agencies. The Federal Water Pollution Control Administration, for instance, is housed in the Department of Interior, while the Air Pollution Control and Environmental Control administrations are part of the Consumer protection and Environmental Health Service program in the Department of Health, Education and Welfare.

Congress has assigned responsibilities for pesticide control to the Department of Agriculture, which also promotes the use of the chemicals for increased farm production. The Atomic Energy Commission supervises radiological protection from nuclear energy, the use of which it encourages. The Army Corps of Engineers shares some responsibility for pollution control of the same navigable waters it dredges and into which it authorizes the dumping of refuse. And certain parts of the solid waste programs are lodged in the Department of Interior's Bureau of Mines, which has as its primary mission the furthering of mineral resource development and use. We have also given authority to the Department of Housing and Urban Development and the Farmers Home Administration in the Department of Agriculture to make grants and loans for the construction of sewage systems.

Proliferation of activities and overlapping of responsibilities are not, of course, unique to environmental protection programs in the Federal government. But the condition is becoming increasingly intolerable in the face of the adverse effects it has on our efforts at improvement. We must, therefore, create an independent, watchdog agency to exercise the regulatory functions associated with environmental protection. Bureaus, divisions, and administrations housed in separate departments cannot marshal the forces required to combat the interlocking assaults on our air, water and resources. They have neither the status nor the manpower to deal with one of the most fundamental, insidious threats to our society, even with the new staff support we hope to provide the President.

I am not talking about a new department of natural resources or of conservation; for environmental protection is not the same as conservation, although the one certainly enhances the other. Some projects developed and promoted by the Soil Conservation Service, the Bureau of Reclamation or the Corps of Engineers, though, are not at all consistent with broader societal needs: Consider what we have done to southern Florida and the Everglades with our conservation measures in the south-central part of the state. Then, too, the traditional concerns of conservation have been too closely identified with the preservation of resources separated from population centers. Our primary interest must be man where he lives.

An independent agency, charged with responsibility for developing and implementing Federal environmental quality standards, supporting basic research, stimulating investigation of control techniques, and providing technical assistance to state, interstate and local operations, would reflect the national commitment necessary to avoid ecological disaster. Establishment of such an agency must in turn be backed up by a commitment to employ all available assets to eliminate the discharge of municipal and industrial wastes into our public waterways, to reduce drastically air pollution emissions, to prevent the distribution of materials and products which threaten man and other species, and to insure the reconstruction and development of our metropolitan areas. This requires money and manpower, and hard decisions on where—and where not—to allocate resources. Above all, it means making environmental protection and improvement much more than a conventional political issue.

In the final analysis, the Administration, Congress, and state and local governments will move to improve the environment in direct proportion to the degree of public awareness of the problem, the determination of the people to be heard, and the amount of informed opinion brought to bear on the matter. This is particularly true of those subtle threats to man's health and well-being that do not result in immediate death and obvious damage, but lower our resistance to diseases and accidents and interfere with our ability to live up to our full potential.

It is here that scientists have a special responsibility to society. We have relied on science for generations to teach us more about our world and the universe, and to increase our capacity to use our planet's resources. Now we have found that in exploiting this knowledge and the secrets it has unlocked, we have been exploiting ourselves. It is imperative, then, for us to adapt our scale of values, our approach to the uses of technology, to the long-term survival of the species. The object of basic and applied research should not be to multiply man's creature comforts and to overcome the natural environment, but to free him from unnecessary hazards and to enable him to live in harmony with his surroundings.

As we look to the future, the so-called policy-makers are confronted by two realities. First, it is clearer than ever before that man's ability to survive depends upon what he himself does to and about his environment; that the continuation of his current behavior patterns means a daily reduction in the prospects for healthy life on this planet; and that the present deterioration may already be irreversible in some vital respects. And second, the threshold of public patience with our failure to come to grips effectively with the problem is lower than ever before, and the level of public demand that we do what needs to be done is rising rapidly. To put it bluntly: The crisis is here; the people are ready—but what will the leaders do?

When I say that the people are ready, I mean that they are aware of the danger and receptive to a call to action. Although many of them may be inclined to believe that someone else's behavior is at fault, and that the problems can be licked if someone else makes the appropriate sacrifices, most, I am sure, can be persuaded to accept restraints upon their own activities and share the necessary costs. And an entire new generation, disturbed by what *we* are doing to *their* world, is demanding that steps be taken now to protect and enhance the environment, to safeguard and improve man's health, to restore the balance in man's relationship to other species.

At the recent 13th National Conference of the U.S. National Commission for UNESCO, Pennfield Jensen, a graduate student at San Francisco State College, made the following apt remarks: "We don't want to merely survive; we want to live. There is only one place in which to live and that is on this planet, and we must live here together."

I welcome Mr. Jensen and all others of like mind in both his generation and mine to our continuing struggle. It is one we must win if science is to be worth advancing and man is to have a future. Despite all obstacles, I think the current prospects for victory are excellent: The goal of a healthy environment is an idea whose time is come.

The Prospects of Economic Abundance*
Kenneth E. Boulding**

As, then, we look at the world of the future, I think we have to ask ourselves three critical questions from the point of view of the future of economic abundance. The first is, how long can the developed world keep it up; that is, how long can we go on doubling per capita income in whatever period we now succeed in doing this, whether every generation or every seven years? At some point, it is clear that affluence becomes excessive, even ridiculous. If for instance in the United States we even continue to grow at our present rather modest rate of, say, doubling our per capita income every generation, this carries us to $10000 per head in two generations and to $80000 per head by the end of the next century. One thing we know about any process is that growth at a constant rate cannot go on for very long in nature or anywhere else. So we have to ask ourselves what are the factors which are going to slow down the rate of growth. We may run into these factors fairly soon. We are going to have to face the fact, for instance, certainly within a couple of generations, that Earth has become a 'space ship' and a very small, crowded space ship at that, destination unknown. Up to now the human race has behaved and acted as if it lived on an illimitable plane. Now the earth has become a sphere, and we have to think of society as a

---

*In *The Control of Environment,* ed. John P. Roslansky (Amsterdam, Netherlands: North-Holland Publishing Company, 1967), pp. 51-57. Reprinted by permission.

**Kenneth E. Boulding is a Professor of Economics and Director of the program in General Social and Economic Dynamics at the Institute of Behavioral Science, University of Colorado. He is a past president of the American Economics Association and the author of several books on economic theory.

sociosphere, that is, a sphere of all human interaction; and in this respect a sphere is very different from a plane. The great plains are gone for good; that was an episode, and a very brief episode, in human history, and we will probably never be able to go through it again.

In the space ship there are no mines, no ores, no fossil fuels, no pollutable reservoirs, and no sewers. Everything has to be recycled, the water to go through the kidneys and the algae to the kidneys and the algae, and so on indefinitely. Everything has to go from man to his environment, from the environment back to man. This is a very different kind of economics from that with which we are familiar. It is an economy in which the overriding consideration is parsimony in consumption, not the expansion of consumption. From now on the space ship is going to begin to close in on us. From the point of view of pollution, this may be much closer than we think.

We are already producing irreversible changes in the atmosphere which are causing alarm among the meteorologists, and it is clear also that we know very little about what we are really doing, that we do not understand the earth at all well, and that the earth sciences, even the physical sciences, are shockingly backward. It may be, of course, that for the present generation or two this is simply a problem in economics. We have to manipulate the rewards of the system so that pollution is not rewarded. It is a problem, however, which may easily go beyond economics, simply because man has not yet learned to develop a technology which is really stable in the sense that he could live comfortably in the midst of a self-perpetuating cycle. Our present technology is suicidal. We will certainly run out of ores and fossil fuels in historic time, and we may run out of pollutable reservoirs before we run out of mines. The growth of affluence, that is, may be limited sharply by the growth of effluence. There are subtle questions also about the transmission of culture and values which are worrying and about which we know very little. All societies produce effluents of people as well as of sewage, the criminals, the mentally sick, the self-perpetuating poverty subcultures, and so on. The more complex a society, the more prone it may become to human effluence; and we may learn that values have to be recycled just the way nitrogen does.

The second question is, even supposing that the process which is going on in the rich countries continues, how long is it going to take the poor countries to catch up with the rich? That is, can the great gap be narrowed or even eliminated? I do not know the answer to this question. There are certainly extraordinary difficulties in the way of any rapid elimination of the gap. Today, for instance, we face an appalling demographic crisis in the poor countries, partly a result of the World Health Organization, which went round the world about 1950 eliminating malaria, thereby almost eliminating infant mortality, without affecting the birth rate. As a result of this, most of the poor countries today have enormous generations of teenagers and almost 50% of the total population under the age of twenty. There is no place for this enormous generation of teenagers in the traditional society; they will almost have to go to the cities, where they will contribute to the already unbearable strain of explosive urban growth. At the moment, therefore, the poor countries are faced with an almost insoluble problem, with a small proportion in the labor force and an enormous generation of children to feed, educate, and bring into the modern world. I am inclined to think that unless we have a birth reduction campaign of major magnitude in the next five years, the situation in many of these countries is almost hopeless for the next fifty years. We will have anarchy, famines, disorganization, and perhaps a nightmarish retrogression from poverty into destitution.

For the long run, I am prepared to be more optimistic, simply because I think the processes of increase of knowledge are almost irreversible. Once we have wised up, it is very hard to wise down, particularly once knowledge becomes widespread. Knowledge, in fact, reproduces itself even more efficiently than the gene. I have a great deal of confidence, therefore, that the growth of knowledge will eventually enable us to overcome these difficulties and create a universal and stable high-level society. Nevertheless, we may be in for a very rough hundred years, or even more. One of the critical problems is that we do not really know how large a population a space ship earth could support. If it can manage a crew of ten billion, we have time, and we may be able to make the adjustment without great catastrophes. If it can only support one billion in a stable high-level economy, we are in for a rough time; for the reduction of human population has never come about except by catastrophe. It may well be, therefore, that the critical question of the present age is how do we get through catastrophes and how do we learn from them, so that we can at least emerge on the other side.

The third question is how does the nature of the international system affect these various processes? In these days we are all sensitive to the fact that the international system has built into it a positive probability of almost irreversible disaster in major nuclear war. Another generation of military research and development will unquestionably produce the Doomsday Machine, after which the destruction of the planet will only be a matter of time. As long as the present international system continues, therefore, we are living in a society under sentence of death. We have a little reprieve; we are in the condemned cell, but we can still work at escape. This is the kind of world in which each day the hand of fate reaches down into a bag in which there is one black ball among the white. Every day up to now, she has brought up a white ball, and the world goes on; but the black ball is still there and until we get it out of the bag, nobody can breathe easily. For some strange reason, since the Cuban crisis nobody believes in nuclear war any more; and though its probability may have diminished, it is very far from having vanished.

In my more optimistic moments, I think that quite a small change in the character of the international system is all that is necessary to make it tolerable and to produce something approaching stable peace. We find that within the international system there are certain subsections of it which exhibit stable peace right now, that is, countries among which the probability of war is almost negligible. One thinks especially of the Scandinavian countries and of the United States and Canada or even Mexico. This was not always the case. Under Gustavus Adolphus, for instance, the Swedes were not very nice people, and were, in fact, the scourge of Europe. The Scandinavian countries fought among themselves almost continuously until the eighteenth century. Since that time, however, there has clearly been a learning process; and the Scandinavian countries at any rate have learned how to be both independent and peaceful among themselves. They have given up being 'great' nations, which is a very good thing, as national greatness is incompatible with human welfare. Perhaps one of the most significant events in recent history was the peaceful separation of Norway from Sweden in 1904, which I am sure Gustavus Adolphus would never have permitted. Now, however, we do better than Gustavus Adolphus; and the Scandinavians have achieved a degree of maturity in conflict behavior which is an example to the world. With a little bit of luck the United States may be on the road to achieving a maturer security community with the Russians, as we have with the British. The Test Ban agreement was perhaps the corresponding event in this process to the Rush-Bagot agreement of 1817, which initiated the process of development of stable peace between Britain and the United States.

I would not suggest that the slow maturation of national behavior is the only road to stable peace, or that it can be relied on. We also need the development of third party organization, as represented, for instance, by the United Nations or by the limited world government which ought to succeed it. At the moment we put very little into world organization. The ordinary budget of the United Nations, for instance, is less than that of the University of Michigan, and in a table of national incomes it lies between Barbados and the Fiji Islands. We put so little into the achievement of peace, it is not surprising that we get so little out.

There is a very fundamental principle in all systems which my spy at IBM calls the GIGO principle, that is, garbage in, garbage out. A corollary of this I have called the NINO principle, that is, nothing in, nothing out. Our investment in the system of peace is dangerously close to this, and it is high time we realized it. We have put enormous resources into preparing for world destruction and practically nothing into developing the systems of behavior which are necessary to our salvation. One hopes that God is not just and that we will not get what we deserve. We are still living under the illusion of the great plains; we still think we can play cowboys and Indians; yet the fact is the world is a space ship right now, and in a space ship you cannot play cowboys and Indians. You cannot afford to horse around. The first prerequisite in a space ship is peace, that is, the ability to resolve conflicts without unreasonable cost. The idea of greatness is the most appalling mental disease of mankind, and unless we awake to the folly of our delusions of grandeur, the future is indeed dark.

The picture which I now have of man is that he is walking a tightrope over an enormous chasm to a promised land. I think there is a promised land, in the sense that built into the human organism itself there is a covenant, a potentiality, a promise which is capable of redemption. There is a state of the world which is much better than what we have now, which is both possible and achievable; but it is achievable only across the tightrope. We may fall off it, and this part of the universe will have to be written off as an unsuccessful experiment. Jiggling the tightrope is absolutely out; we need to concentrate all our energies on getting across this next dangerous hundred years, perhaps the most dangerous hundred years in the history of the planet. What lies on the other side, however, looks very nice; and being a human being, I can't help having some optimism about it. This is a lovely planet, and it deserves to fulfil its potential. I recommend it to you earthlings. Tend it with loving care.

Technology and Human Environment*
Roger Revelle**

We all know we live in an age of science and technology, which is in many ways almost an age of miracles. But in recent years we have come to realize that technical developments usually create new problems in the very process of solving old ones.

What is not so generally appreciated is that in the modern world the realistic answer to a problem created by technology will itself usually be in part a technological one. To solve the problem we must not abandon our technology but use more of it. One way to state this proposition is that once men start down the technological road they cannot turn back. This is in accordance with the conventional wisdom of our race. Once man has bitten into the fruit of the tree of knowledge, there can be no return to Eden.

To change the metaphor, ever since men began to modify their lives by using technology they have found themselves in a series of technological traps.

The first clear-cut example of such a technological trap was the invention of agriculture, about 8,000 years ago probably by some bright woman in the hills of what is now Iraq or Iran, who noticed that when seeds fell off a plant she was gathering, the same kind of plant grew up in the spring, and she decided to try to see if by planting these seeds she could get plants to grow up where she wanted them.

Prior to that time, men were very scarce animals; there were probably more lions than there were men. They made their living by hunting and food gathering. This may have been a rather happy Eden-like existence, but it resulted in very high infant and child mortalities. Probably, to keep the race going, the average woman had to give birth to all the children she was capable of having.

As soon as agriculture was invented and human beings could have a more assured food supply, the population grew for a while, so fast that it was quite impossible to go back to the simple life of hunting and gathering. It became necessary for men and women to work for their living, earn their bread by the sweat of their brows. For 8,000 years human beings were condemned to the hard and brutalizing toil of hand agriculture, simply to keep their families going.

It wasn't until very recently that we have been able to climb out of this technological trap. We have done it, of course, by a series of developments in agricultural technology, almost technological miracles. These have changed farming from harsh and continuously demanding labor to an industry in which only 6 percent of our people are able to grow more than enough food for all the rest of us in the United States, and hardly get their hands dirty in the process. Pretty much the same thing is true in Western Europe.

*U.S. Congress, Senate, Hearings before the Subcommittee on Intergovernmental Relations of the Committee on Government Operations, 90th Cong., lst Sess., on S. Res. 68, *Establish a Select Senate Committee on Technology and the Human Environment,* 1967, pp. 329-338.
**Mr. Revelle is the Director of the Harvard University Center for Population Studies and former Science Adviser to the Secretary of the Interior.

But today as their technology has burgeoned and multiplied we have gotten ourselves caught in a set of new traps. At least in many cases, it seems to me, the way to extricate ourselves is through still further technological changes. And some of these changes will be rather large and we are liable to be frightened even to think about them.

For example, metropolitan air pollution could be eliminated if we had the capital, the courage, and the skill to make two basic technological changes. One of these would be the substitution of automobiles powered by electrical batteries or fuel cells for the present automobiles driven by internal combustion engines. The reason why this seems like the most realistic way to solve the problem of air pollution resulting from automobiles is that internal combustion engines by their very nature combine atmospheric oxygen and nitrogen into nitrogen oxide, just because of the high temperatures of combustion. This looks like the kind of physical chemistry which is very hard to get around by anything that you can do to an internal combustion engine except abandon it, not use it.

Another change would be to eliminate sulfur dioxide fumes from coal burning in metropolitan air by the generation of electric power near coal mines, so-called mine mouth generation, and the transportation of electric energy to metropolitan areas by high-voltage, direct-current transmission lines. Both of these technologies are quite feasible, of course.

The Swedes have been using long-distance, direct-voltage transmission for 20 years. So far we haven't had the courage and the capital to do that in this country.

Other alternatives are, of course, possible. Conceivably we might be able to keep most of the automobiles out of our cities by the development of high speed, convenient mass transportation systems. But I myself feel this would require a real technological miracle, and is very unlikely to happen. We may be able to break through the atmospheric inversion layers that press down stagnant air on our cities, if we can learn enough about the weather, and how to change it.

An unforeseen development could occur which would make it possible to remove nitrogen oxides from autombile exhausts. As far as power generation is concerned we may be able to eliminate sulfur compounds from our coal and oil before burning them, or to filter out sulfur dioxide from the flue gases. We could almost certainly substitute atomic energy for sulfur-containing coal, and fuel oil in metropolitan electric power-generating plants.

Whatever the solution, however, it is likely to be at least in part a technical one involving technological invention and change, and we can be even more certain that these new technical developments will bring a train of new problems in their wake which will be at least as difficult and perhaps more disagreeable than those that face us now.

It is quite clear, for example, in the case of atomic energy, that we will have a very serious problem of getting rid of the radioactive wastes.

When I was a boy in Pasadena there were a good many little old ladies who used to drive around in electric automobiles. Those were completely silent contraptions, and really quite dangerous especially to us children when we played in the streets. In the future, new dangers may arise from electric automobiles because of their peculiar characteristics.

An entirely new set of problems will be raised when computers become more widely used and closely linked to communications systems.

We can see that the technological consequences, or rather the social consequences of the developments of computers that lie just ahead of us are really very great. Of course, there will be some quite satisfactory things about these developments. Nobody will have to write checks any more. You won't have to pay bills, you won't get a paycheck, all your finances will be handled automatically. You will just carry a card around with you which you slip into a machine and that will immediately enable you to charge or to pay at all stores. Similarly, the handling of many of the problems of industrial organizations—inventory, accounting, and management—will be tremendously improved.

We can see that in education every child will be able to talk back to a computer, which he can't do with a television set. Every student will have immediately available to him all the resources of all the libraries in the United States and possibly in the world by computerized coding and long-distance satellite transmission. It may be unnecessary to print newspapers and distribute them. Every home will have its own newspaper printed right in the home, and newsboys will become archaic. These are all things which we can see as possible benefits from the technological development of communications and computers.

But at the same time, also, we can see many social problems that will be raised by these new developments. Perhaps the principal one will be the tremendous potential loss of privacy. When every fact of everybody's life is on the tapes of a computing machine it will be very difficult for the average citizen to keep himself to himself.

Beside questions of privacy, the problems of control, control of persons, simply by the enormous amount of information that will be available to the people who want to exercise control, will undoubtedly be a serious development in our democracy. In terms of voting, for example, instead of having a Gallup poll or a Harris poll, one may be able to push a button on any question at any time and have 200 million people reply.

This is not necessarily going to help the democratic process. It is difficult enough with the Gallup poll.

And the question is what kinds of technological solutions will we be able to invent to solve the problems that will be created by the new computerized technology?

There are many other examples of the problems created by technical change and of the role of technology in their solution. For example, I have spoken about the miracles of modern agriculture.

One of these is the control of insects and other varmints in crops by pesticides which make it possible to grow a lot more per acre.

Pesticides and related substances have been one of the major developments that have helped American agriculture. At the same time they have killed the birds and many of the fish and the wild creatures in much of the area of the United States.

Nobody would suggest that we abandon attempts to control insect pests, but what we can do is to improve our methods of control, and we can do this by more technology, not less.

A case in point may be the application of something that has recently been done by one of my colleagues at Harvard, Prof. Carrol Williams. He has found that the front page of the *New York Times* is capable of killing something like a million bugs if you just persuade them to walk across it. The reason this is so is that the *New York Times* is made out of Canada balsam, a Canadian fir tree, and this fir tree long ago invented a means of killing its own insect pests. It did it by producing a substance that looked ike a growth hormone. The caterpillar, the insect larvae, would get close to the ree and ingest some of this pseudohormone, and they were never able to mature into adults and reproduce. The result was that the bugs against which the tree invented this natural pesticide have become completely extinct.

However, it still works very well against Indian bugs, insects that attack cotton and other crops in India, and it is very likely that similar substances produced by Asiatic trees are capable of killing American bugs that have never been subjected to them. Professor Williams and his colleagues have now been able to synthesize one of these substances, and here we may have a sharply focused pesticide that won't kill birds and bees and fish and deer.

Another example of the potential role of technology in solving a problem produced by the technology concerns the very serious, worldwide problem of rapid population growth. I said that up until the time of the invention of agriculture there probably weren't as many people as there were lions on the earth, and until a very short time ago human populations increased very slowly. It is only within the last few decades that on a worldwide basis human populations have started to grow at an unprecedentedly rapid rate.

In 1940, for example, the world's population was increasing at about 1 percent a year—in other words, doubling about once every 70 years. This was, of course, very rapid compared to what its doubling time was, say a few tens of thousands years ago. In those days the world population doubled every 20,000 to 30,000 years. Between 1940 and 1960 the rate of growth went up from 1 percent to 2 percent, which means the world population will double before the year 2000.

This great increase in population growth rates has been brought about almost entirely by the great lowering of death rates in the poor countries of the world during the past three decades resulting from technical improvements in sanitation, nutrition, food distribu ion and disease control through antibiotics and other public health measures.

One can state the problem th way: on a worldwide basis we human beings have radically changed part of ou biology, that is, our average life expectancy. Unlike other animals we are learni g to control our own biology. But we have so far controlled only part if it, our death rates. The only possible long-term solution is to change an equally fundamental aspect of our biology; namely, our birth rates; and here one of the key problems, although by no means the only one, is the development of a set o satisfactory techniques for family planning and birth control.

Some of my colleagues have said that the new birth control pills and the new intrauterine devices will change the history of the world. I myself am far less sanguine about these particular inventions but I am convinced that major technical changes, major technical innovations, will be absolutely necessary. They will be a necessary condition, although not a sufficient condition, to solve the enormous problem of rapid growth of human populations that hangs over our heads today.

Although we have already modified part of the biology of our human species, this is only the barest beginning, for biology is the great new realm of technological change. The average lifespan of adults in the United States has hardly increased over the last 15 years but we can expect that very considerable improvements may be just around the corner. We can look forward to a very marked increase in longevity in the future, as our knowledge of the aging process improves. Techniques are already being developed for replacements of wornout hearts, kidneys, and other organs with new artificial ones. Here will be another technological trap, particularly when a very marked increase in longevity is combined with the necessity to limit the numbers of children to just about two per family.

What will people do with most of their lives when the average lifespan is a hundred years, and the average married couple can have only two children who will grow up and leave home before their parents' lives are even half completed? How shall we help women fulfill their lives when they are empty of children throughout most of the long years?

As a matter of fact, it seems to me that among the lost souls in our modern technological world are our American women. They are perhaps the loneliest, hardest working, most isolated women who ever lived. All of the laborsaving devices like the dishwasher and the washing machine, the vacuum cleaner and the automatic oven, have resulted in our young middle-class women staying by themselves all day with young children, and there is no conversation duller than that of young children when it goes on for too long. This is in contrast to the older days when families were much bigger, when in every home there were several women, who talked together, and worked together. No wonder our women are worrying about what their education should be and what their roles should be.

Every wife now has to be an engineer, but in many ways, technology has emptied her life rather than filled it.

Some biological modifications are just around the corner. Already, of course, we are capable of genetic manipulation of other animals. I think this is unlikely with people for a couple of reasons: In the first place man is in a real sense a wild animal. He can tame other animals but he can't tame himself. How are men going to decide what kind of men they want? What are the qualities we want to breed into human beings, and who is going to decide?

In the case of domestic animals we have usually bred for one characteristic, speed in racehorses, more milk in cows, peculiar appearances in dogs.

The great thing about human beings is their diversity, their adaptability, the fact they are generalized, they are wild animals, who can adapt themselves to many different situations and to rapid changes, and this is a much more complicated thing to change than to breed animals for more speed or more milk production.

However, it will undoubtedly be possible to change individuals. One of the people who has written on this subject recently is Joshua Lederberg, the Nobel Prize winning biologist of Stanford University.

I feel reasonably certain we will be able to increase the intelligence of individual children. By careful attention to their environment when they are very young, we will be able to increase their health and physical fitness and their emotional stability. Many properties of individuals will be markedly changed by biological inventions.

But we have always the question of who is going to decide what changes are desirable.

One area with which perhaps you are particularly concerned is the relationship of technology to our human environment.

When I was a young man about to become a geologist we were all oppressed by the approaching depletion of natural resources, minerals, fuels, lumber, and land. But as time has receded, natural resources are playing a smaller and smaller role in our time. Advancing technology has made it possible for us to win them more cheaply and to use and reuse them more effectively. We have invented new substitutes for old scarce resources—aluminum for copper, plastics for wood and metal.

Today some natural resources are almost a drug on the market, with the serious consequence that the terms of trade have turned against the poor countries that produce and sell raw materials, and thereby have added to their poverty and almost destroyed their hopes for economic improvement.

In our own country we have seen a great decline in the importance of resources. A hundred years ago resource industries made up about half of our gross national product. Now they make up about 10 percent.

We have come more and more to realize that the real natural resources are those the Greeks talked about, earth, air, fire, and water, the totality of our environment, and this is a resource in the sense that it is a scarce commodity, one that we have to cherish and to protect and to pay for.

It has economic value and economic meaning, and this is what we mean by a natural resource.

We are here involved with the deepest kind of human values, values that come right out of our biology. We spent a million years living in the forests, living by wild rivers in the wilderness, among the green and brown hills and the tall grasses, living with other creatures, and in some sense communing with them and with the natural world. Our need for nature and our love of nature is built into our genes. One of the most important things that needs to be done in the United States, and in the world for that matter, is to preserve, to cherish, and to develop our abilities to be close to and be inspired by the world of nature.

Technology can help us or hurt us in our relationships with the natural world depending in part at least on the ways in which we use substitutes for resources. Many people are concerned today about the destruction of the California redwoods, those ancient giants that link us to the distant past and thrill us because of their wonderful size and beauty.

We can use technological substitutes for the redwoods in two ways. Conceivably we could cut down all the living trees and replace them with plastic imitations after the manner of Disneyland, or we can develop cheaper and better substitutes for redwood lumber, and thereby remove the economic justification for destroying these irreplaceable trees.

In this way, technology can help us or hurt us in maintaining the natural world.

I have already spoken about the fact that technological developments of pesticides, sharply focused pesticides, can help us to preserve the birds and our other fellow creatures that live on this continent with us.

We can also improve the natural world and our relationships to it through technology.

One clear-cut example is evident to anyone who visits Chicago, that wonderful adventurous and pioneering city. The people of Chicago have carefully guarded their Lake Michigan shoreline. But they have realized it is too short, because it is a straight coastline, and they have begun to stretch it by wrinkling it, by building peninsulas and carving bars out from the shore, just simply to make more of it so more people can enjoy it.

The same thing can be done on our seacoasts, with offshore islands and offshore bars, but this requires a good deal of technology to do this in such a way that you don't lose the sand you have got and don't set up wave and current patterns which destroy the structures along the shore.

One of the characteristic things about our shorelines in the United States is that everybody wants to live near them. The center of our country has been pretty much emptying and people have been moving to the coasts. Yet our shorelines are so short at the present time that we can easily see that within a few decades—even if all the beaches were available for public use and recreation, and most of them are now used for other purposes or are in private hands—we will have two people for every foot of shoreline trying to get from the land to the sea and back again.

Along many stretches of our American shoreline the water is too cold for swimming, or at least not very satisfactory for swimming. The Maine shoreline . . . is, of course, a case in point. Surprisingly enough, so is my State of California. About four-fifths of the coastal waters of California are really too cold to swim in. Here, again, technology may conceivably help us a good deal.

Very large power generating plants using sea water for cooling have to use enormous quantities of it. This is particularly true, if, as in California, electric power generation can be combined with sea water conversion. The amount of warm water that can be produced in this way could be very great. This water could be poured along the shoreline and maybe create whole new stretches of resort beaches—where people could use this priceless natural asset of ours for maximum benefit.

Technology has already helped us in enjoying the ocean in many other ways. The development of scuba diving is a marvelous case in point. The man-in-the-sea program, which may enable people to live underwater for weeks on end, will have great entertainment and recreational value in times to come.

One desirable thing to do, particularly in the modern world which tends to be so relatively uniform and tends to keep people from participating in events themselves, is to develop risk and adventure, variety and excitement in our recreation. Here such things as sky diving and scuba diving, two entirely different technological kinds of recreation, and many other technological developments can help us to stretch and to diversify our recreational possibilities.

We have national parks on land, why shouldn't we have national underwater parks of a great variety of kinds?

I have spoken about the role of new technological developments in solving the problems created by technology, but it is characteristic of most problems of the real world, at least the real world of our times, that they can't be solved by technology alone.

In almost every case we need to bring to bear a wide range of human knowledge, understanding and experience. Sociologists, economists, businessmen, public administrators, and politicians, the scientists and the artists of human behavior are needed, and if the problems are to be solved sensibly and well, these various kinds of specialists need to work together not only with each other but with the scientists, engineers, and inventors.

One of the most difficult aspects of the pollution problem is the multiplicity of local jurisdictions. Smoke and smog and water pollutants pay no attention whatever to political boundaries, and particularly not to small political boundaries; you have to deal with watersheds and air sheds.

We must make new political inventions to give political entities which correspond to the natural realities sufficient authority, and effective operational techniques so that they can work.

This is very difficult because of our long tradition of local control of zoning, planning, and establishment of standards, let alone our traditions of private property and private rights.

The problems of pollution always involve problems of economics, who is going to pay the bill; how much can he afford to pay; what will the cost be; what will the benefits be. Clearly the benefits are very hard to quantify. It will take a new kind of economics.

To find out what the benefits are, will be, in many cases, the task of the sociologist, the person who understands people and the behavior of people in groups.

We need a battery of computer-aided analyses. One of the important things that has happened in the field of water resources has been the development of new methods of analysis using computers, such as numerical simulation of river basin systems, not hydraulic models like those at Vicksburg but modeling with numbers in an electronic computing machine. It turns out that, for many purposes, the computer can do a better and faster job than a hydraulic model. One interesting thing about computers is that they help the engineers, scientists, and inventors to talk with the economists, sociologists, and public administrators. They can find a common language through this mechanical contraption.

The modern problems of urbanization have been created by technology, primarily by our agricultural technology that has driven so many people off the land into the cities, but partly by our technology of transportation and communication. Modern cities would be impossible without automobiles. They would break down if it weren't for the new methods of communication.

The problems of today's cities are the problems of the ghettoes and the slums, of water and air pollution, of getting supplies in and getting waste out, problems of political control, of raising taxes, problems which involve very largely the social sciences and the social arts, the arts of the politician and the administrator.

Yet, nevertheless, new building materials, new ways to make buildings, new kinds of transportation, and other technological changes may be the essential means to the city of the future. With our new communication systems we may be able to abandon the development of megalopolises and create many smaller entities where today's urban problems don't exist.

The universities of the United States are great reservoirs of talent in all of these fields of the social sciences and the natural sciences. But unfortunately the different kinds of specialists are usually organized inside the more or less water- and air-tight walls of departments, each responsible for a special field of discipline. It is only within the last few years that university professors and administrators have realized the necessity to cut across departmental barriers and to bring different kinds of specialists together if our universities are to attack the problems of our time at the levels where they can be effective; namely, the levels of analysis, research, development, and planning. Many universities have recently created new interdisciplinary institutions such as the joint center for urban studies between MIT and Harvard, the new centers for water resources research in each State university, and centers for population studies in several universities including my own.

It turns out that very few of the great problems of the real world can be solved within one discipline. They have to be solved by people from many different disciplines working together. This is just as true of the world food problem as it is of the problem of smog in New York City.

Of course, we have to think seriously not only about the interdisciplinary problems that now exist but also about the new problems that may appear in the future.

The three major industries in the United States 20 to 30 years from now will probably be education, health and recreation, and entertainment. The technological problems that will arise in these new industries will be enormous. In the case of education, I would guess that most people will be in school most of their lives—not preparing for a job but learning how to do their job better, and especially learning how to be better and happier human beings. People will go and return over and over to the school and university. We will give a quite different character to the schools themselves.

The development of computerism will change the character of education in ways we can't even foresee. It may be that we will end up with everybody studying at home and communicating with the school through the computer-communications network.

I have spoken already about the problems of recreation. The problems of health will also require great developments in technology. These will all be real problems of the real world and in most cases, as I have said, it will be possible to solve them only if people from different disciplines work together. Through their new interdisciplinary institutions, and in other related ways, the American universities are returning to an old tradition, the great tradition of the land-grant universities during the 19th century, perhaps the most important educational invention ever made. The land-grant universities, with their close relationships to the U.S. Department of Agriculture through the agricultural experiment stations, and their effective concern, in teaching, research, and public service, with all aspects of farming, were the primary creators of the marvelous agricultural revolution in the United States during the past 25 years, one of the most profound changes that has ever occurred in any human society.

Perhaps our modern universities will be able to play an equally significant role in solving the problems of our time, the problems of urbanization and transportation, of poverty and deprivation in the midst of abundance, of education and health, of the waste of human resources and the destruction of the natural world.

The Politics of Ecology*
Harvey Wheeler**

Until little more than six months ago, "new politics" referred to either the protest movement or late-model mass-media campaigning. Today, however, a third new politics is springing up. It is being given urgency by a growing public alarm over all varieties of pollution. War protest has yielded to demonstrations against the rape of the environment. Youth is turning away from Marxists like Herbert Marcuse and flocking to ecologists like Paul Ehrlich. The message is ecocide, the environment being murdered by mankind. Each day brings to light a new ecological crisis. Our dense, amber air is a noxious emphysema agent; farming—anti-husbandry—turns fertile soil into a poisoned wasteland; rivers are sewers, lakes cesspools, and our oceans are dying.

The early warning signals seemed unrelated and were easily ignored. Five hundred Londoners died of a summer smog attack. New York, blacked out and turned out, became dysfunctional. Union Oil's Platform A sprang a leak and converted Santa Barbara's postcard beaches into a sludge swamp. Traffic congestion made driving slower than walking. Airways threatened to become as dangerous as freeways. Cities, unable to function, closed schools and reduced public services. As power blackouts became seasonal, power demands rose and pushed pollution levels—thermal and hydrocarbon—to higher readings. Mathematical ecologists, such as Kenneth Watt, estimate that the United States is approaching the point where the interstitial energy required to keep the system going is greater than the energy it employs productively: Overhead costs overwhelm output. Our entire social order faces an ecosystem "depression" that will make 1929 look like a shower at a garden party.

It is imperative to correct one common fallacy—one especially popular among the young. Technology is not the culprit. Admittedly, the misuse of technology is part of the problem, but the essence of the real problem is what Watt calls the ecocidal asymptote. It is to the new politics of ecology what $E = mc^2$ was to the thermonuclear era.

The ecocidal asymptote runs as follows: Statistical studies of the pattern of exploitation of every natural resource can be plotted as two curves. One represents the rate of depletion of a resource, the other represents the technological capacity for its exploitation. Both curves are exponential; that is, in the beginning they rise very gradually. But their rate of increase is always rising, pushing their curves up ever more steeply until they reach a vertical explosion. Both follow the same pattern at the same rate, exploding, asymptotically, at the same time.

As an illustration, consider the ocean's fisheries—the blue whale, the salmon, the tuna. In the beginning, the supply is virtually unlimited, and harvesting

*Saturday Review, March 7, 1970, pp. 51-52, 62-63, 64. Copyright 1970 Saturday Review, Inc. Reprinted by permission of the publisher and author.

**Harvey Wheeler is a senior fellow at the Center for the Study of Democratic Institutions, Santa Barbara, California.

techniques make little or no dent in the available supply. Soon fishing techniques improve, and, as they do, they gradually overtake reproduction rates; supplies decline as techniques improve. As this situation becomes apparent, it spurs on competition to get more and more while the getting is good. Ever more efficient fishing techniques are invented, and their rate of efficiency rises in direct ratio to the depletion of the resource until the point arrives when the ultimate in fishing technology coincides with the extinction of the species. This "falling together" of the technology and resource depletion curves is the ecocidal asymptote. It is the inimical process that characterizes our age, the enemy of the new politics of ecology. The death of one resource leads to the depletion of another; one technological fix begets another. Each of our ecocidal crises is interconnected with all the others, and none can be solved in isolation. The politics of ecology is architectonic.

The new politics of ecology, however, is not merely an outgrowth of the old politics of conservation. Conservation has a long and revered history, tracing back to such men as John Muir and Gifford Pinchot. This conservationist tradition, somewhat ineffectual in the past, is acquiring a new vitality today. In fact, entire states, largely in the American Northwest, are known for their being officially conservation-minded. Washington, Oregon, and Montana are prominent examples. Conservationist slogans gain in popularity each day: "Keep Arizona Clean"; "Preserve Washington's Water" (and keep it out of California); "Stamp Out Billboards"; "Save Lake Tahoe." Rotarians and Yippies unite in "GOO"— "Get Oil Out of Santa Barbara"; and the cry of that great conservationist Howard Hughes is voiced: "Don't let the AEC shake down Caesar's Palace." These are laudable examples of conservationist politics, but all share the basic characteristics of the conservationism of the past; all are local, piecemeal efforts, and all rely upon traditional pressure-group tactics.

Today, we can count approximately 126 Congressmen who have publicly identified themselves as a conservationist bloc. A new bill introduced by Congressman Richard L. Ottinger and others proposes to guarantee all citizens the right to enjoy a healthful environment. Yet, such efforts are still in the mode of the old politics. They have a new twist, a new power base, and a new constituency. This new lease on life for the old mode of conservationist politics is not difficult to understand. It is an outgrowth of the leisure industries spawned by our affluent society. It is, to oversimplify, the politics of tourism. Conservationism is a gut issue in the West. It means preserve our state as an enclave of natural beauty and tourist attractions.

But the new politics of ecology means something quite different. A few examples will sharpen these differences. The essential political problem of the future is, first, to figure out how to preserve general ecological balances, and, second, how to calculate hidden social costs so as to determine how much is really being spent on side effects such as a new freeway, the three-car family, and the SST. Complete ecological harmony is impossible to achieve, but the "trade-offs" necessary to approach it as closely as possible must become known.

There is no such thing as an atmosphere without any pollution. However, it is obvious that certain kinds of air pollution deriving from fossil fuels already have reached perilous levels. This is not merely a question of unsightliness nor even of the threat of a rise in lung cancer and emphysema. Even more serious hazards may develop if pollution particles are carried by superjets from the lower atmosphere into its upper, turbulence-free layers. Scientists warn that these jet contrails may not be dispersed and could act as an insulation layer between Earth and sun, cooling the earth and leading to a new Ice Age. Of course, no one is certain what will really happen. We are in much the same position as when DDT was introduced; nobody knew for certain what its cumulative effects would be. Today, it does not seem inconceivable that pollution particles could quickly clog the upper atmosphere, and before we knew it utter havoc would be upon us.

Obviously, pollution must be reduced, but again we are not dealing in absolutes. We must know what levels are tolerable, and we must know the conveniences or desires that must be sacrificed to maintain these levels. New mass transit systems may be required. Individual desires to own several automobiles will have to be curtailed. And this is but the beginning. Ecologists tell us we shall have to mount a revolution of declining expectations. Gadgets will have to go. Creature comforts will have to give way to culture comforts. Americans today are at 1788. Never again will they or their children enjoy as many material conveniences. This is the real revolution implicit in the new politics of ecology.

What level of public education should we and can we maintain? How much are we willing to pay for it? How can we finance that level? Can we continue to support schools from state land taxes? Is it just to do so? Must we institute a national educational system? To answer these questions we must know the optimum size of an urban community, and how population should be distributed in our clustered communities. In short, we shall have to find out exactly what life in a megalopolis really costs, and whether or not we are getting our money's worth.

What degree of smog is created by population density? Perhaps the same number of people could live in roughly the same area, and even own the same number of cars if they displayed different density patterns with lower ratios of travel between residence and work. Simple freeway tariff schedules could alter traffic patterns immediately by penalizing over-powered and under-occupied vehicles. But we don't know. We don't know how much interstitial overhead energy we waste in a city like New York, merely trying to hold its parts together and keep it operating. We shall have to learn how to calculate the interstitial requirements of cities of different types and sizes to determine the optimum balance between urban amenities and overhead costs. We have no real measures of the price we pay for slums in all sorts of ways—poor health, substandard living conditions, crime, and so on. We do know that slums are high statistics areas; in them are concentrated most of everything bad, and at the end of each statistic lies a dead body.

Automation reduces the number of people required for factory and office operations, making huge cities unnecessary as well as uneconomic. Industrialists have known this for a long time. But what about the city as a cultural center? If we reduced cities to the size of fifty thousand or even a hundred thousand people, wouldn't we have to sacrifice our great cultural centers, our theaters, our museums, our libraries? The answer is no, we would expand them, improve them, and make them more widely available to all. We speak already of the museum without walls, meaning that the treasures of the entire world can now be exhibited everywhere. Microfilm libraries plus computer terminals make it possible for everybody everywhere to use the Library of Congress as well as the British Museum and the Bibilothèque Nationale.

What of the theater, the symphony, the ballet? Of course, recordings and television spread them to all, in one sense. Even great "living" theaters and symphonies are possible in very small cities. Vienna was relatively small when it reached its musical apex. Our greatest cultural traditions have been produced in very small cities. Seventeenth-century London abounded with genius; by modern standards it was but a mini-town. Ancient Athens was even smaller, and Plato and Aristotle thought it far too large at that. There is no reason why the same thing cannot be done again. At least, failure would not be due to smallness. All we really need is to decide to produce the cultural conditions necessary to elicit similarly high achievements. Gross size, far from a prerequisite, is an insuperable hindrance.

To answer such questions and to implement the answers will be one of the chief tasks of the politics of the future. We've never asked these questions of politics in the past. But today, we can have everything that is really valuable about our large cities, and at the same time avoid the disagreeable and expensive side effects due to size. These are ecological questions, and, even though we may be able to answer them soon, there will still be no way to transmit this ecological wisdom to the average citizen for rational and deliberate application at the polls. Yet, this is exactly what we must be able to do in the near future. We shall require a new kind of party system with a new kind of participational democracy seeking solutions to ecological problems. Finally, we shall require a new kind of deliberation or legislative process to grow out of the new politics of ecology, and we shall have to relate to it in something like the way the existing legislative process related to our traditional party system.

Let us take the second problem first, for although it is generally understood that our party system is inadequate, the deficiencies of our legislative system have received scant attention. Reflect for a moment on the fact that our legislatures and our party system are well-tailored to each other. Our parties are, as the textbooks say, loose confederations of state and local boss systems. The key element is "state and local." This means that the representatives selected through our present electoral system arrive at our legislative chambers representing the interests of their local districts. An implicit assumption is that all our primary problems and conflicts will arise from the clash of local interests—conflicts relating to the interests people acquire because they live in one place rather than another. Since before James Madison—the man who provided the underlying rationale for this system of politics—we have trusted that this pluralistic, territorially based expression of interests would produce the general interest almost as if guided by an unseen hand.

But the issues described earlier are not related to any specific territory as such. Nor are they capable of solution through the expression of local interests. On the contary, the critical problem—the source of our indictment of the old politics—is that its foundation is too restricted and particularistic to cope with the characteristic problems of our times. Technology-related problems know no territorial bounds, and they defy locally based efforts to deal with them. The same is true for science-related issues. Our present political system is unable to bring all such problems together for resolution within an ecological framework. Yet, this is what we must do.

The characteristic political problems of the present arise from disorders of the entire ecological order. Their solutions are to be found, not through the traditional interaction of local interests and pressure-group politics, but through a new politics of the whole—politics considered architectonically, as the ancients called it. This requires a politics that is more speculative and less mechanistic; it requires us to do our lobbying in the realm of thought as well as in the corridors of power. Our most pressing political problems now have their origins in science and technology. Their solutions will require a new politics especially designed to cope with science and technology, a politics based on what Teilhard de Chardin called the "noösphere," instead of our accustomed politics based on real estate. It follows that entirely new policy-forming institutions will be needed to deal with the ecological politics of the noösphere. Legislatures must be redesigned accordingly. But, of course, before all this can happen, the popular base from which representatives are chosen must be given a new foundation. The scientific-biological-technological revolution that awaits us around the corner of post-industrial time demands entirely new ecological parties.

One portent of the new politics occurred in California in 1969. Over the decades, the Sierra Club—a tradition-oriented pressure group of the Pinchot type—had grown into a potent political force. An internal crisis resulted in the defeat of its activist wing. Shortly thereafter, the deposed leadership forming around the John Muir Society, announced the establishment of a new political movement to be devoted to ecological concerns. Of course, this was not thought of as a new political party, but, nonetheless, it used language that looked ahead to something like the new politics called for above. Whether or not this particular movement prospers, ecological parties promise to be the wave of the future, providing the underpinning required to produce the novel legislative institutions the future will require.

How would such a party system actually operate? How would it differ in essential structure and mode of operation from the electoral and precinct organizations of the past? Again, in California, a technological breakthrough occurred in 1969 that may provide the informational and educational components required to enable voters to make intelligent ecological choices as they function politically in the future.

A team of multidisciplinary experts headed by Kenneth Watt designed a model that would ultimately contain mathematical expressions for almost every conceivable problem concerning the state of California. All these expressions will be programed into a complex computerized analytical system whose formulas alone will run to 5,000 pages. When finished some five years hence, it will be capable of revealing the multifarious interrelationships of each part of the model. The result will be an architectonic mathematical model of California considered as a complete ecological system. Watt calls this the "Model of a Society." Such computer programs will help us to find out how any given problem relates to all others. Suppose we must decide whether to vote for or against a bond issue to raise funds for a new school system. At the present, our choice is determined largely by whether or not we favor public education. But countless other considerations are involved. How would residential patterns be affected? How would traffic on streets and freeways be changed? What new public utilities would be required? How about other services such as fire and police? Would these changes lead to a relocation of shopping centers? What would all these changes add up to? Would they produce the kind of future we want? Computers are not foolproof, and computer models are even less so. We don't expect perfection from either people or machines. All we expect is a device to help us make our decisions on a somewhat more systematic basis. Not only politics would be affected, planning would also change. Those who make new proposals would have to calculate their full ecological consequences well in advance of offering them to the public. The result would be a profound shift in the terms on which political deliberation occurs. The voter would be able to visit computer terminals with multimedia display consoles where the foreseeable implications of alternative policies would be portrayed in pictures, figures, and graphs.

Mathematicians, ecologists, and social scientists working together can lay the beginnings of a new participatory democracy that will be as well-suited to the conditions of the post-industrial era as was the old, grass-roots democracy to the simpler conditions of the nineteenth century.

* * *

All this is technologically possible today. It is only necessary for us to devote our scientific resources to bringing it about. If that is done, we can move toward the realization of one of man's oldest dreams. All our citizens, the most lowly as well as the most favored, can enjoy the highest fruits of civilization. The optimistic conclusion is that we no longer need despair of democracy's future prospects because of the increased complexity of the problems of the post-industrial world. The very technological advances that are bringing about this new world will also make it possible to produce a citizenry able to comprehend and cope with them, ushering in a new era in the history of democracy.

Environmental Policy and Political Decisions: The Reconciliation of Facts, Values, and Interests*
Norman Wengert**

Enhancement and protection of the environment has become one of the great issues of the day. Concern is being expressed throughout the world. In the United States, in addition to substantive concerns based on the merits of the situation, a growing number of politicians, academics, publicists, and others are seeking to ride the wave of environmental fervor for reasons which include

---

*A paper presented at the *Third International Seminar for Hydrology Professors,* Purdue University, Lafayette, Indiana, July 18-30, 1971, sponsored by National Science Foundation, UNESCO, U.S. National Committee for the International Hydrological Decade, Universities Council on Water Resources, and the Department of Agricultural Engineering and Water Resources Research Center of Purdue University, in cooperation with American Geophysical Union, American Society of Civil Engineers, American Society of Agricultural Engineers, American Society of Agronomy, Society of American Foresters, and the Division of Conferences and Continuation Services, Purdue University.

**Mr. Wengert is a Professor of Political Science at Colorado State University, Fort Collins, Colorado.

possible election to the Presidency, as well as more modest rewards of fame or fortune.

Reviewing these trends, two authors recently commented:[1]

"By the later 1960's, the environmental bandwagon had begun to roll. Survival had become an issue.

"Environmental pollution, ecological disarray, and urban decline are excellent subjects for illustration. They provide the mass media with ideal copy. . . . Pollution became a major social issue. The tempo of the debate was increased by the extensive coverage it received from the major radio and television networks. . . .

". . . . All over the country, meetings and activities—sometimes involving many thousands of people—made it seem that this was the major issue in the public mind. . . . Such mass exhibitionism was not limited to the United States; similar demonstrations occurred in Europe and Canada. Everywhere overexaggeration was the order of the day."

Environmental problems continue to be identified and solutions proposed with a zeal that can only be compared to "old-time religion." We are in the midst of an "environmental revival," accompanied, as are religious revivals, with deep guilt feelings and remorse, as well as commitments to reform. Perhaps evidence of "back-sliding" will also ultimately appear. As in the case of religion, so in the environmental movement, dogmatic assertions are common. Proposals for action often assume that opinion is fact, that knowledge is certain, and in any case, that solutions are unquestionable, values unchallengeable, and that the advocate's course is the only way to protect the "public interest."

In this mood opposition and criticism are not tolerated, because they obviously represent the forces of evil and exploitation. Compromises and accommodation are rejected as morally reprehensible. Since the cause is right and just, authoritarian implications are ignored.

This paper, in modest contrast, advances the proposition that proper courses of action in order to protect and enhance the environment are less certain, and that the decisions needed require societal choices with respect to both ends and means, and that such decisions are uniquely political. It argues that to understand the decisions which are made (as well as those which may not be made), it is necessary to understand the American political process and the way in which individuals and groups behave in that process.

Although some of the more strident rhetoric seems to deal with wolves, bison, wilderness, fish, landscapes, and other aspects of nature as ends in themselves, most of these concerned would recognize that these natural features have no meaning separate from people. Thus, the issues of environmental protection and enhancement are ultimately issues of social policy and social control, in one way or another involving governmental action. But environmental policy is political not only because societal or public sector decisions are involved. It is political because it is concerned with value choices and preferences. Action generates conflicts over facts, and among interests and conflict resolution is one of the functions of politics. In addition, environmental decisions involve complex relationships among governments and between governments, individuals and groups. Most significantly, environmental policy decisions must be made under conditions of high uncertainty, and inevitably result in a differential distribution of benefits and costs—non-economic as well as economic. Choosing, in this context, is difficult and fraught with hazards.

In introducing a perceptive and stimulating issue of the journal *Environment and Behavior,* the issue editor, Professor W. R. Derrick Sewell, has written:[2]

"The birth of a new national objective is an important event, and especially so if it seems incompatible with other objectives already being pursued. Such an event occurred recently in the United States when improvement of the quality of the environment was adopted as a major goal of public policy. . . .

"The approach so far has been the traditional one . . . —the quick administrative, financial, and technological fix. Almost predictably, the first step was administrative reorganization. . . .

"Appropriations have been made to finance construction of municipal sewage disposal systems and other depollution facilities. At the same time, the technologists are being urged to find better ways of disposing of wastes."

It might also be noted that reorganization is rarely neutral; it, too, reflects political power struggles and illustrates how people seek to exploit advantages of position and influence to achieve desired ends or frustrate those not desired.[3] Similarly, it might be noted that program content may be influenced by factors only indirectly related to program goals. With the prospect of public expenditures of several billion dollars a year for water pollution control, it is perhaps not surprising to find that some of the most insistent support for control programs comes from the sellers of equipment and the builders of facilities. The analogy to the interstate highway program is obvious; from its initiation during the Eisenhower years that program has received stalwart support from the sellers of gravel and cement, the manufacturers of earth-moving equipment, and the road builders—just as the Army Corps of Engineers has over many decades received strong support for its river works construction from the contractors who are likely to build such projects. Among the insistent advocates of President Johnson's "Poverty Program" were those who had or expected to get jobs, contracts, and other benefits—and not the poor! Public programs and policies are often influenced more by those who stand to gain what economists have tended to call "secondary" benefits than by those interested in and affected by the primary, stated purposes.*

Professor Sewell properly stresses that much more than administrative reorganization, finance, and technological advance is required to deal effectively with environmental problems. Of critical importance is a genuine recognition on the part of the public that environmental improvement is necessary and desirable, and a willingness to accept the possible sacrifices (costs) that its attainment might entail. To date in the United States, public programs have not

---

*Rejection of "secondary benefits" as irrelevant to national income calculations has falsely led to ignoring the political significance of such benefits.

infrequently been adopted as though they were cost free. Benefits have been touted, while burdens have been deliberately obfuscated. It could well be that the political crisis engendered by the wide-spread concern for environmental quality may force a confrontation in which conflicting goals will need to be reconciled, and really hard choices made. The "something for everyone" and "I want my share" *may* be in for searching examination.

Determination of environmental goals and objectives has been left to the technical and bureaucratic elite and to publicists drawing on them for information (or misinformation). To a large extent, present goals reflect the views of biologists, medical officers, foresters, engineers, planners, architects, and similar specialists. And although a variety of articulate interest groups have been very active, especially on certain issues, there is really no indication of *what kind* of environmental quality the public desires, nor *how much* improvement it is willing to support. Even more important, perhaps, is the absence of reliable data on consequences that may flow from particular actions, and of an awareness of the trade-offs that achievement of environmental goals may require. We really know far less about what constitutes a "proper" environment than the rhetoric of preservation and enhancement suggests; we know even less about how to achieve it.

Professor Sewell points out that the present approach has tended (wrongly) to assume that the appropriate level of environmental quality can be determined by how much the public is willing to pay for its attainment. But clearly more than money values are involved; and "willingness to pay" is a function of education, propaganda, and other socialization factors, as well as dollar costs and marginal utilities. Economic choice is not the sole nor even the important dimension. Issues of environmental policy involve not only aggregate data on economic costs and benefits, but require a rigorous analysis of who will benefit and who will pay the costs of protection and enhancement. And these benefits and costs usually involve more than dollars.

Environmental protection and enhancement necessarily is concerned with what economists have called "externalities, i.e., those effects and consequences the costs and benefits of which fall on others than those who initiate action and who may receive dollar gains from it. In some cases, "internalizing the externalities" may adequately deal with some environmental problems. But it is important to recognize that the essence of "community," of "society," and hence of government, is the equitable distribution of costs and benefits in terms of such non-monetary criteria as needs, welfare, and ability to pay.*

Constructing a pseudo-market built on shadow prices, premised on simulated interest rates and assuming individual transactions where each individual is supposed to pay for what he gets as measured by his own conception of his own marginal utilities, is just not adequate. Such a limited approach, despite its quantitative elegance, serves to mislead decision-makers by oversimplifying the nature of the decisions and giving them a false sense of precision. Wise environmental policies require hard societal choices in situations which abound with uncertainties. It is just in such situations that the political process functions most appropriately.

---

*Describing politics in Laswell's phrase "Politics: who gets what, when, and how" (to which I would add "where") accurately describes the focus of the American political process. Concern with that process has often led political scientists to ignore the normative questions of who should get what, when, how, and where. These are equitable and distributive questions—and it does make a great difference to society how they are answered.

A Classification of Decisions

By definition all decisions and for our purposes particularly public sector decisions involve choices—choices as to ends and choices as to means; choices at a grand level, and choices at a petty level. Even conditioned responses require earlier deliberate decisions.

As a heuristic device, the following classification of public sector decisions may serve to distinguish those types and kinds of decisions where politics and the political process might be expected to operate most appropriately:

In our complex society, there are, *first,* decisions which can be considered as *automatic* or *autonomous.* These are decisions where the facts are clear or undisputed, policies set, precedents well established, the consequences generally accepted. In such situations choices seem virtually non-existent. In law these are decisions in which a *writ of mandamus* would probably be available to require administrative action. By definition, these decisions are characterized by a minimum of conflict and controversy. An example might be a decision, based on current scientific knowledge, to destroy a diseased elm tree. It should be noted, however, that circumstances could change with the result that particular decisions which one day properly fall into this category could in other circumstances move to one of the other categories.

A *second* category of public sector decisions might be designated *pseudo-automatic* or *pseudo-autonomous* decisions. These are decisions in which decision-makers as well as the public, or segments of it, *assume* that the facts are clear and that no choices are involved. For a variety of reasons and for a period of time society tends to accept action, not recognizing that alternatives may be available, that choices could be made with differential consequences. It may be that neither information, nor technology, nor institutions are available for approaching the decision differently or challenging the way in which the decision is reached, and it may require a crisis to stimulate a re-examination of the decisional premises. Common examples of pseudo-automatic decisions are those made by scientists, engineers, planners, and other technical specialists where the factual basis for decision is presumed to be more reliable than is warranted, or where major premises for action are hidden and the decision-maker ascribes his own values to society at large and is thus not really aware of alternatives. These types of decisions frequently also reflect the fragmentation which results from specialization and which makes it easy to ignore factors that could alter the weighting of particular facts. Many decisions which seek to save the environment, as well as those which contribute to its degradation, fall into this category. (Systems analysis could contribute to minimizing these conflicts by identifying causal relationships, feedback, and linkages.)

The *third* category involves decisions characterized by varying degrees of uncertainty, where action is dependent on judgment, and the "proper" choice is not clearly evident. The uncertainties may be of various kinds. One type is the uncertainty inevitable in making decisions for the future, where unanticipated variables often alter the premised conditions. Even the best crystal ball is cloudy; and perhaps that is why discounting the future is such a common practice in our every-day lives as well as in the bureaucracies which serve us. Another type of uncertainty arises from the inadequacy of facts for decision. Unfortunately the loudness or frequency of an assertion does not convert it into fact. Still another type of uncertainty is a result of our need to simplify matters so that we can deal with them. Basically, this is a "span of attention" problem, and it must be recognized that our ability to simplify lies at the base of much scientific progress, but it also can contribute to uncertainty since the factors held constant or disregarded may be the ones of greatest social significance. Finally, since much human activity is value based, uncertainty is introduced into our decisions by the difficulty in assessing values or determining which ones to seek. Here we enter the complex field of human motivation and motives. Thus, where uncertainty is dominant, conflict and competition are common and power and influence come into play. No simple calculus is available to make the choices which action requires. It is the political process of bargains and negotiation that here must have its fullest sway, even though motives and motivations may range from those seeking the "public interest" to those based on self-seeking and personal gain and advantage rationalized as in the "public interest." To the problem of defining the "public interest" I will return below.

Characteristics of the Political Process

As implied above, an important function of the political process is making choices—among candidates, among policies and programs, among ways of accomplishing public goals and objectives, etc. For analysis, three focal points of the process may be identified: the *actors* in the process; the *institutions* which determine how they act, i.e., the framework for decisions; and the *substantive problems* with which the process deals. At each of these points ideas, ideals, and ideology—the values of the participants, of the institutions, and of those associated with the definition and solution of particular problems are important influences in what is done and how it is done.

The actors. Not infrequently the actors in the political process are portrayed as being in a kind of pyramidal, hierarchical relationship to each other. At the base of the pyramid are "the people"; in the middle are a variety of collectivities—communities, groups, agencies, and organizations; and at the apex are the leaders—the bureaucrats, government officials, and other influentials who are believed to "call the tune" on public policies.

The dominant view among political scientists tends to reject as simplistic this hierarchic portrayal, emphasizing, rather, the pluralistic structure of our society in which influence is widely spread, and its use is related to particular functional topics and interests. Dahl's study of *Who Governs*[4] in New Haven, Connecticut provides one of the best examples of this pluralistic view of the power structure. Political scientists have recognized that:

> "In all societies, and under all forms of government, the few govern the many.... Because the symbols and concepts of American politics are drawn from democratic political thought, we seldom confront the elemental fact that a few citizens are always called upon to govern the remainder.

> "It is somehow undemocratic to think of elites and masses and to differentiate between them.... [Yet] elite-mass interaction is the very heart of the governing process."[5]

Political scientists have emphasized, too, that there is not a single "public" but many publics, and that rarely on even the simplest issue can one truly speak of *majority* wishes or interests. Although it is often effective rhetoric to assert that a particular program is "what the majority of the people want," evidence to this effect is not convincing. Moreover, in our system dedication to majority rule tends to be balanced by an equally emphatic recognition of minority rights. Both emphases give rise to a concern for citizen education, for broadening the basis of public understanding of policy alternatives and choices. Although we are willing to accept Presidents and other officials chosen by 51% of the voters, we have been quite reluctant in most situations to decide policy issues on this basis. Plebiscitary democracy sounds fine so long as one is in the majority or has the power to draw voting district lines. But polarization may be dysfunctional and the real problems of citizen participation center around the multiplicity of interests and the difficulty in identifying whose interests are really involved and deciding which should be advanced and which curtailed; weighting interests once they have been identified; determining what to do about those who are silent, whether from ignorance, apathy, lack of interest or lack of time; deciding the time perspective for considering policy direction and content; and determining who can speak for whom. Too often, those who have demanded more participation have had particular motives ranging from satisfying their own ego needs, building their own political organizations, destroying the establishment and with it the system, or simply playing the power game so that they and their interests might secure some of the rewards.

Clearly, responsible democratic government must try to take all of the views and wishes of its citizens into account. This cannot mean simply counting noses or measuring clamor on a decibel scale. It must mean careful analysis of program consequences and an honest assessment of who benefits from and who bears the costs of public programs in the context of what is socially desirable and equitable.

Decisions in the political system almost always involve negotiations, bargains, and building of alliances and alignments to assure legitimation. And the major participants in the process are groups already in being or stimulated to "become involved" by particular issues or controversies. In the interactive process, moreover, the views and recommendations of technical specialists may be modified or even ignored not because they are "wrong" but because their premises or consequences are unacceptable. Not untypically specialists of many different points of view are called into the fray, espousing analyses of the situation more suitable to those who support them and creating uncertainty for the decision-makers. Although the issue may be one of professional integrity, more often than not it simply reveals the intricate interweaving of facts and values in policy decision-making and suggests that in the absence of definitive date (i.e., which may serve to reduce uncertainty) the process of conflict resolution by negotiation and bargaining may in fact be the best way of coming close to achieving the public interest in particular situations.

The institutions. Unfortunately, the effect which institutions have on political decisions has not received much research consideration. Yet, analytically, one may reason that societal institutions in various ways serve to constrain and condition action, as well as to determine *what* questions are presented for consideration and *how* they are dealt with. Reflection suggests that a web of both public and private institutions shape and influence the content of environmental policies. These institutions include such diverse structures as the legal system, the private corporation and other economic institutions, the family and its consumption patterns, schools, churches, various patterns of living and life styles such as the middle class suburban home with its 1/3 to 1 acre lot. But space does not permit an examination of this constraint on political decision-making. It is relevant to point out, however, that a dominant aspect of the governmental institutional structure is the American Federal system. Significant is not only the legal constitutional relationships among Federal, State and local levels, but more importantly the extent to which the norms of federalism have permeated our approach to problems requiring governmental action.

It is often forgotten that the federal system as it developed in the United States was initially a compromise among varying views as to how a stronger government might be provided. Instead, the patterns of relationship which resulted have been raised to a philosophy of government dogmatically defended as "best," if not God-given, even though the circumstances that gave rise to the system initially have drastically altered.

The *Federalist Papers* went to some lengths to justify the "utility of a superior power" (i.e., a stronger central government), and one may presume that this view reflected the dominant philosophy of the founding fathers. Nevertheless, in the first fifty years of the nation for a variety of reasons the philosophy of Federal-State relations was projected to State-local relationships with the result that we have ever since been saddled with entrenched localism which serves to protect numerous vested interests, and, with respect to environmental policies, encourages grave doubts as to whether the public interest is well served. Among the results has been the abrogation of State responsibility in many fields, and the necessity to resort to "buying" local compliance with State or National program goals by means of so-called grants-in-aid.

The situation we find ourselves in with respect to intergovernmental relations has not been the result of any sinister plot, but rather serves to suggest how institutions structure approaches to problems. The dominance of the local view is supported by and supports the political party system. It is often not recognized that our political decision makers in Congress and in State legislatures are almost entirely products of local political communities. Their roots are local and their political commitments are primarily to the local constituency that elects them. It is sometimes pointed out that the President (and Vice-President) is our only national official. But even the President must secure the nomination of his party by building up coalitions of local party organizations. The National party is largely a figurehead and in any case it has little influence and no sanctions over the Congress. The same decentralized structure exisits in most states. Hence the generalization that the federal structure permeates the way in which public problems, including those of the environment, are approached; the resulting institutional arrangements condition both how these problems are dealt with as well as which ones are dealt with at what levels.

The Substantive Problems. An adequate consideration of the way in which the substantive problems influence political decisions would require a careful review of many public programs and fields of government activity. Space will permit me only to suggest some of the kinds of effects that may be involved. First, those who identify and formulate the problem may play a large though often fortuitous role in determining how the problem will be dealt with. It is clear, for example, that the intense interest of Senator George W. Norris in electric hydro power and in public power policy generally contributed to electric power generation being a dominant aspect of the program of the Tennessee Valley Authority. An important factor in problem definition may be the professional training and experience of those who first confront a problem and seek to define it in operationally useful terms. It was not a sinister plot, but the state-of-the-art and professional orientation that led the Corps of Engineers to emphasize engineering works in their initial approaches to flood protection and control.

Public attitudes toward a problem, or perhaps better, the public philosophy, may be an important determinant of what is done about the problem and how it is approached. In a society that tends to accept floods as the will of God, defining the problem in terms of flood protection and control may not be understood. In a society which places high value on private ownership of real estate and independence in the use of that real estate, flood plain zoning and flood easements will be looked at with hostility.

More complex is the state of knowledge and technology both as it relates to the definition of problems and as it relates to their solution. A corollary factor is the accuracy and completeness of the knowledge and technology. Two illustrations: *First,* there seems to be a growing recognition that population growth poses some kind of a problem for society, although the parameters of the problem are often not carefully spelled out either in terms of living space or in terms of time. The Governor of Oregon announced early this Spring that his State did not want any more people. Articulate advocates of Zero Population Growth are uging that Boulder, Colorado limit its population to 100,000 and that Denver seek a limit of 1,500,000.

There is thus much loose talk about dispersal versus density with little or no attention being given to obvious complexities. One of these is that no matter what is done, the population of the United States will increase by about 100,000,000 in the next thirty years. These people will want to live somewhere and to maintain what in their time will be regarded as the American standard of living. Free movement within the nation is probably a constitutionally guaranteed right, but this issue aside, it is not at all clear that dispersal will result in a better environment and a higher quality of life than controlled density with planned green spaces and other amenities. Yet the simplistic solution of jurisdictional limitation may carry the day, partly because the state of knowledge does not permit a rational challenge. And in any case, there is much to suggest that population is a *world* problem and not simply an American or a Colorado problem.

The second illustration is the matter of phosphates in detergents. The basis for my comment is the careful review of this topic by Allen L. Hammond in the April 23, 1971 issue of *Science* (pp. 361-363). I came away from that article with a helpless feeling that what is virtually a national hysteria over the eutrophication of fresh water lakes, particularly Lake Erie, is leading to what will probably turn out to be unsound and costly policies. That article, in addition to pointing out the uncertainties about the role of phosphates in eutrophying lakes and raising questions about our abilities to control these processes no matter what we do about detergents, emphasizes that half the homes of the U.S. send their waste water directly to the oceans where the critical nutrient appears to be nitrate and not phosphate. Legal prohibition of phosphate—particularly since its elimination will result in lower quality and probably more costly detergents—represents a hidden tax on those users. One might add that the benefits of this hidden tax are likely to go primarily to the manufacturers of the phosphate-free product who are already becoming adept at touting their products in the imagery of saving the environment—at the same time probably porting to their stock holders the increased earnings that have resulted.[6]

What Is the Public Interest?

For several decades social scientists have been disparaging the concept of the "public interest" as simply a rationalization of individual interests. Only economic theory has been able to make a virtue out of greed, arguing (since Adam Smith) that if everyone sought his own interest, the sum of individual interests modified and adjusted in the give-and-take of the market would be the general interest. Group theorists in political science have suggested that just as individuals interact in market-place economics, so groups interact in the political market-place. In these theories of counterworking power, multiple group membership served to prevent any one group from destroying the others, for the larger the group, the more it moved toward a centrist position. Accommodation of diversity tends to characterize most large groups. In other words, the more extreme a group's position, the fewer its adherents. Walkouts and the formation of splinter groups is a characteristic of an open society. To those who pointed out the dilemmas resulting from apathy and non-participation, group theorists offered the concept of latent or potential groups, suggesting that when a need became intense enough, a group would form. But this hopeful view of how countervailing forces operate has been challenged by recent studies which have argued against the pervasiveness of group structure and questioned the extent to which a multiplicity of groups and the ease of their formation might be relied upon to balance unreasonable demands of any one group. The idea of countervailing power is an attractive one because like the unseen hand, it works automatically. But unfortunately it is not the whole story.

It seems to me then that we are left with three alternatives: (1) a return to the model of economic analysis which emphasizes the importance of rational calculation of individual utilities; (2) an existentialist or nihilist model (not far removed from the Hobbesian view of a "war of all against all") in which power is the significant goal and interaction but a game from which one seeks to get the best possible deal; or (3) a re-examination of the concept of the "public interest" not as an absolute and final measure of what is good and true and desirable, but as a goal which rational man seeks to achieve, using the best tools available for analysis and exploration of ends and means.

To be sure, decision-makers can only act on the basis of their own perceptions as to what is good or bad. But man is educable; his perceptions can be changed; he can by taking thought consider the interests of society. Perhaps those who have rejected the concept of the public interest as a viable principle have confused its measurement with its reality. Perhaps they do not recognize that personal perceptions need not be limited only to personal advantage, nor that they may not be broadened by education, analysis, study, and experience.

The reconciliation of facts, values, and interests is no easy task. And perhaps it can be accomplished more wisely if not more easily by the continued efforts to improve the rational basis for decision and to increase consequent and responsible behavior on the part of those involved—citizens, groups, bureaucrats, officials, and politicians. This is the continuing challenge to those of us engaged in research and in teaching.

What's the Problem?

[1] Garrett Hardin, "To Trouble a Star: The Cost of Intervention in Nature," *Bulletin of the Atomic Scientists,* XXVI, No. 1 (January 1970), 17.

Environmental Policy and Political Decisions: The Reconciliation of Facts, Values, and Interests

[1] W. R. Derrick Sewell and Harold D. Foster, "Environmental Revival," *Environment and Behavior,* III, No. 2 (June 1971), 125-126.

[2] W. R. Derrick Sewell, "Behavioral Responses to Changing Environmental Quality," *Environment and Behavior,* III, No. 2 (June 1971), 119.

[3] The political use of reorganization is reviewed by Harold Seidman, *Politics, Position, and Power* (New York: Oxford University Press, 1970).

[4] Robert A. Dahl, *Who Governs?* (New Haven, Conn.: Yale University Press, 1961).

[5] "Elite Mass Behavior and Interaction, *American Behavioral Scientist,* XIII, No. 2 (1969), 167. The entire issue is devoted to this subject.

[6] See Norman Wengert, "Public Participation in Water Planning: A Critique of Theory, Doctrine, and Practice," *Water Resources Bulletin,* VII, No. 1 (February 1971), 26-32.

3   The Effluent Society

The river Rhine, it is well known,
Doth wash your city of Cologne;
But tell me, nymphs! what power divine
Shall henceforth wash the river Rhine?

Samuel Taylor Coleridge, 1852

The United States has become an effluent (as well as an affluent) society. Major rivers have become open sewers and large lakes have become cesspools. In the words of Justus Fugate, Chairman of the Committee on Water Resources of the American Municipal Association, "the scientific borderline we have set up between sewage water and drinking water is a precarious one. We live on the edge of a human or mechanical failure in our water purification works that could bring pestilence upon us and the danger grows every year."

Not only are polluted waters a health hazard, but they destroy aquatic life and close off outdoor recreation opportunities. The Federal Water Pollution Control Administration reports pollution-caused fish kills with monotonous regularity, and at a time when outdoor recreation demands are vaulting upward, water-based recreation areas are being drastically reduced through pollution.

How Has All This Happened?

More people produce more effluent. An increasingly affluent society uses more water and creates more pollution *per person*. Industrial expansion and technological advancement generate both a greater quantity and a greater variety of pollutants. Relatively little effort has been expended on research in pollution control, so the science of water quality control is still in its infancy. There has been little or no incentive for industry, municipalities, or private individuals to clean up their water; streams and lakes have been in the public domain—nobody's problem. Until very recently water pollution was considered to be, in President Eisenhower's words, "a uniquely local blight."

Until recent years there was, in most areas of the country, sufficient "original water" so that the discharge of pollutants into rivers, lakes, and harbors did not create either a serious health hazard or a serious threat to recreational and other uses of water. As a consequence the science of waste treatment and disposal was neglected. It has a long way to go to catch up with industrial technology. There are, therefore, serious technical problems in waste disposal which need to be solved. The effects of many new, "exotic" industrial wastes on human and animal life are as yet unknown. Some pathogenes and so-called "nutrient" wastes are not removed by the usual sewage disposal processes.

Lack of uniformity in state antipollution laws has created problems, since weak pollution control laws may constitute a competitive industrial advantage. Actually a high degree of uniformity is essential, because water pollution is not a local problem. The movement of surface and ground waters does not respect local or state boundaries. Furthermore the increased mobility of people and the increasingly wide and rapid distribution of goods disperse the hazards of local polluted waters throughout the nation. Those who maintain that water pollution is a local problem are living in a day that has long since passed.

As the demand for water increases, it will become increasingly necessary to use more water more than once. Already, according to former Secretary of Health, Education, and Welfare Ribicoff, the total flow of the Ohio River is used 3.7 times before it enters the Mississippi.[1] As more water is used more times, more hazards to health, aquatic life and recreation will be created, and more funds must be expended on treating wastes or on purification plants or both. Within limits, the problem can be attacked at either end. That is, the emphasis may be placed on treating wastes before they enter a body of water or on purifying water before it is used. Neither approach can be altogether effective alone, but if the only consideration is potable water, the two approaches may be considered as interchangeable alternatives.

As the costs of maintaining water quality increase, there will be increasingly intensive attempts to shift these costs to "someone else." Thus those persons and firms who require pure water but who generate a minimum of pollutants can be expected to advocate greater emphasis on the treatment of wastes before they enter the water. On the other hand, those who are responsible for discharging large quantities of pollutants can be expected to emphasize purification before use. Furthermore, the latter group can be expected to place water quality in a medical frame of reference. In such a context, the only water in question becomes that which is to be consumed by humans, so the emphasis (and cost) automatically shifts from pollution abatement to water purification.

The controversy over treatment at entrance versus treatment at destination ignores recreational uses of the water between the two points. Recreationists and wildlife interests recognize that America's vanishing water-based recreation resources can only be protected by minimizing pollution at the point where it enters the water.

According to the President's Council on Recreation and Natural Beauty,

The problem is particularly acute in the major rivers that flow through the hearts of metropolitan areas. Waterborne wastes destroy beauty and make water-related recreation undesirable or impossible.

The Potomac, the Hudson, and the Mississippi illustrate the problem. The Potomac's most serious pollution is in precisely the reach of the river with greatest potential for enjoyment by the 2 1/2 million residents of the Washington, D.C., metropolitan area. As the Potomac slowly flows through the Nation's Capital, its load of silt, filth, and acid from farms, mills, and mines blends with discharge from overloaded sewers to nourish an algae bloom and a summer stink that rises from the river for miles below the metropolis. The Hudson, from Albany to Manhattan, is an open sewer. Scavenger eels, one of the few animals that can live in waters loaded each day with 200 million gallons of raw sewage and the effluent of dozens of factories, have been known to attack sanitary engineers taking water samples. The Mississippi, at St. Louis, is so polluted that test fish placed in a sample of river water diluted with 10 parts of clean water die in minutes.

In the future an expanding population will require more industry and agriculture. Each will produce more waste and at the same time require more clean water. In addition to the problem of coping with the increasing volumes involved, cleaning up water is becoming more complicated.

Today's wastes from homes, industry, and agriculture include new and complex chemical compounds which are more difficult to identify and treat; detergents are only one example. The rapid pace of urbanization at suburban fringes results in siltation of water caused by erosion from lands stripped of vegetative cover. Runoff from city streets carries increasing volumes of wastes that are difficult to handle in treatment plants. Following heavy rain or snow, municipal sewer systems that carry combined storm water and sewage deliver substantial amounts of many communities' sewage raw to the receiving stream, lake, bay, or ocean. Coastal oil pollution, such as from the tragic spill from the tanker *Torrey Canyon* which blighted the coast of England in 1967, is a newly recognized hazard.

Thermal pollution, caused by discharge of water at high temperatures from power plants, also is cause for increasing concern as the number of nuclear power plants along ocean and river shorelines increase.

Electric power generation has doubled every 10 years since 1945. The rate of increase continues to jump so that some analysts estimate that the doubling time for increase in demands may now be as short as five years. More moderate estimates give 10 years to double the power demands. Either are staggering increases.

About 70 percent of the industrial thermal pollution load in the United States today is caused by the steam electric power industry. Power plants are now discharging into United States waterways 50 trillion gallons of heated water a year, in some cases with devastating effects on the environment and aquatic life.

By 1980, the power industry will use one-fifth of the total fresh water runoff of the United States for cooling and is predicted to spew forth 100 trillion gallons of heated discharge.[2]

What Has Been Done?

Obviously not enough has been done, but the problem has not been ignored. The first attempt by the Federal government to control water pollution appears to have been Section 13 of the Rivers and Harbors Act of 1899. This legislation prohibited the discharge of certain wastes into the navigable waters of the United States. Violators are subject to criminal prosecution with possible fines and imprisonment. This old law has been largely dormant until recent times, but it has not been superseded by later legislation. During 1970 and 1971 several hundred cases were filed under this resurrected old statute. One of the interesting features of the law is that persons bringing information leading to conviction are entitled to half the fines. During 1970 Congressman Henry S. Reuss of Wisconsin filed information with U.S. attorneys against 270 companies for alleged pollution abuses. On June 4, 1971 Reuss was awarded $1750 as his share of the fines levied against two Wisconsin polluters.

President Nixon has also taken advantage of the old Refuse Act by establishing a permit system to be administered by the Corps of Engineers. On December 23, 1970 he reminded Congress that

> Last February I transmitted to the Congress a comprehensive water pollution program, as part of my 37-point program designed to protect our environment. My proposals included legislative measures to make the establishment and enforcement of water quality standards more effective and expeditious. Unfortunately, no congressional action has been taken on my water pollution control proposals. I will continue to seek enactment of these proposals during the next session of the Congress.
>
> In the meantime, I am directing the immediate initiation of a new, coordinated program of water quality enforcement under the Refuse Act of 1899, an act whose potential for water pollution control has only recently been recognized.

The first comprehensive attempt at water pollution control was the Water Pollution Control Act of 1948 (62 Stat. 1155). The stated purposes of the Act were ". . . to conserve such waters for public water supplies, propagation of fish and aquatic life, recreational purposes, and agricultural, industrial, and other legitimate uses."

The Federal Water Pollution Control Act of 1956 (70 Stat. 498) amended and replaced the Water Pollution Control Act of 1948 with the stated objective: "To extend and strengthen the Water Pollution Control Act."

On February 23, 1961 President Kennedy sent a "Special Message to Congress on Natural Resources." In his introductory remarks he said:

> Our Nation has been blessed with a bountiful supply of water; but it is not a blessing we can regard with complacency. We now use over 300 billion gallons of water a day, much of it wastefully. By 1980 we will need 600 billion gallons a day.
>
> Pollution of our country's rivers and streams has—as a result of our

rapid population and industrial growth and change—reached alarming proportions. To meet all needs—domestic, agricultural, industrial, recreational—we shall have to use and reuse the same water, maintaining quality as well as quantity. In many areas of the country we need new sources of supply—but in all areas we must protect the supplies we have.

President Kennedy then went on to outline his recommendations for Congressional action. Congress responded with the Federal Water Pollution Control Act Amendments to the Federal Water Pollution Control Act of 1956 (75 Stat. 204). These amendments raised research funds to $5 million per year; grant-in-aid funds to states were raised from $3 to $5 million per year; and an aggregate of $570 million was authorized for constuction grants through June 30, 1967. The Act strengthened and expanded Federal authority in pollution abatement enforcement by extending Federal juridsiction from "interstate" waters to "interstate or navigable" waters, including coastal waters.

Supporters of the Act included the National Association of County Officials, the United States Conference of Mayors, the AFL-CIO, the Izaak Walton League, the Wildlife Management Institute, the National Wildlife Federation, and the Sport Fishing Institute. The major provisions of the bill were generally objected to by the Farm Bureau Federation, the Chamber of Commerce of the United States, the National Association of Manufacturers, and the American Paper and Pulp Association.[3]

The Water Quality Act of 1965 (79 Stat. 903) continued and accelerated work on the pollution problem—which continued to grow worse. It created a Federal Water Pollution Control Administration, headed by an Assistant Secretary, in the Department of Health, Education, and Welfare. It provided for the establishment of water quality criteria, and once more, grants for sewage treatment plants were sharply increased.

The Clean Water Restoration Act of 1966 (80 Stat. 1246) continued the fight by greatly increasing appropriations for Federal grants to construct municipal waste-treatment facilities. It established a "clean rivers restoration" program, increased funds for research, and doubled the amount of Federal support available to state and interstate water pollution control agencies to strengthen their programs.

In the meantime, the Water Pollution Control Administration had been transferred from the Department of Health, Education, and Welfare to the Department of the Interior. This transfer was intended to facilitate coordination with such Department of the Interior agencies as the Bureau of Sport Fisheries and Wildlife, the Bureau of Commercial Fisheries, the Geological Survey, the Office of Water Resources Research, the Bureau of Reclamation, the Office of Saline Water, the Bureau of Mines, and the Bureau of Outdoor Recreation. Finally, in December 1970, the water pollution control activity was transferred to the newly formed Environmental Protection Agency.

A comprehensive water pollution measure was sidetracked in the last hours of the 1968 Congressional session. In 1969 Congress failed to act on a water pollution bill for the third year in a row. Finally the Water Quality Improvement Act of 1970 (PL 91-224) was approved on March 25, 1970 after five months of deadlock in a conference committee. The new law was aimed primarily at preventing oil spills by increasing the liability of petroleum companies up to $14 million for cleanup costs. The Act also strengthened restrictions on thermal pollution from nuclear power plants, provided for criteria covering the effects of pesticides in lakes and streams, and changed the name of the Water Pollution Control Administration to the Federal Water Quality Administration.

In addition to the Federal actions cited above, states, municipalities, and private industry have made a very substantial effort to maintain water quality—an effort which cannot be catalogued here. Since 1952 the United States has spent some $15 billion on municipal sewage treatment plants and other water treatment facilities. But it has not been enough! According to a General Accounting Office report issued in November, 1969, there has been no improvement in water quality. And David D. Dominick, Commissioner of the Federal Water Pollution Control Administration, says, "In the last 10 years, the quality of the nation's water has probably degenerated." Even in Honolulu, the "paradise of the Pacific,"surrounded by thousands of miles of open sea, surfers encounter brown, bubbly stains in the once clear azure water—the visible consequence of pumping 20 billion gallons of raw sewage into the ocean each year.

While Federal, state and local governments were spending billions to reduce water pollution, American industry was accused of dragging its feet and of responding to the water pollution crisis mainly with public relations campaigns. The Potlatch Forests Inc. recently ran a national advertising campaign showing a beautiful view of the Clearwater River carrying the caption, "It cost us a bundle but the Clearwater still runs clear." When it was found that the photograph was actually taken 50 miles upstream from the Potlatch paper plant (which dumps 40 tons of suspended wastes into the river each day), the president of the firm explained, "We tried our best. You just can't say anything right any more—so to hell with it." Similarly, Southern California Edison ran an ad depicting a healthy lobster over the caption, "He likes our nuclear plant." As it turned out, the lobster had been borrowed from the tanks of a local marine biologist. Such practices have caused a spate of citizen suits against industrial firms and intensified demands for tighter regulation and heavier penalties on polluters.

The Conservation Foundation has reported that during the period 1963-70 the voters of nine states approved bond issues for water treatment plants by an average affirmative vote of 65.9 percent. A 1970 Louis Harris Poll found that 54 percent of all Americans were willing to pay more taxes to finance pollution control programs. Perhaps in response to these changed views, President Nixon said in his 1970 State of the Union Address:

I Shall propose to this Congress a $10 billion nationwide clean waters program to put modern municipal waste treatment plants in every place in America where they are needed to make our waters clean again, and to do it now.

We have the industrial capacity, if we begin now, to build them all within 5 years. This program will get them built within 5 years.

. . . .

We no longer can afford to consider air and water common property, free to be abused by anyone without regard to the consequences. Instead, we should begin now to treat them as scarce resources, which we are no more free to contaminate than we are free to throw garbage in our neighbor's yard.

Senator Frank E. Moss of Utah has called water pollution a "galloping national disease which must be met on a massive basis if we are to control it." Our past attempts to control pollution appeared to be "massive" at the time, but they turned out to be too little and too late.

In this chapter Supreme Court Justice William O. Douglas describes the condition of our lakes and rivers today. Senator Frank E. Moss of Utah realistically analyzes the politics involved in water policy decisions. Murray Stein, who has for years been the principal Federal enforcement officer in water pollution abatement proceedings, describes the process and the problems involved in Federal attempts at control. Robert N. Rickles makes a convincing case for the role of industry in pollution control. Lastly, Leonard B. Dworsky reviews past efforts to improve water quality and sets forth an "Effective and Credible Program for Water Pollution Control."

An Inquest on Our Lakes and Rivers*
Justice William O. Douglas**

"IT'S TOO THICK TO DRINK and too thin to plow." The speaker was a tall, lean middle-aged man long identified with the University of Pennsylvania's crews who raced on the Schuylkill river in sculls. That day the water of the Schuylkill did, indeed, look like the viscous liquids of a cesspool as we peered at it from a Philadelphia bridge.

But the Schuylkill is pure, compared with some of our other waterways. Recently I revisited Houston, Texas, and the Buffalo Bayou, as fascinating a waterway as God ever made, which skirts the San Jacinto Battleground, famous in Texas history. Once it sparkled with myriads of life. The alligator was there and many species of fish. Birds without number frequented it, including great white pelicans and the water turkey that swims under water in pursuit of fish and has so little oil on its wings and body that it must spend long hours each day on the sunny side of a tree, drying its feathers. Then men dug out Buffalo Bayou, making it wider than a football field, deep enough for ocean liners and 50 miles long. As a result, Houston today is the nation's third largest port, supporting the largest industrial complex in the Southwest. But Buffalo Bayou today is a stinking open sewer and a disgrace to any area. It carries to the Gulf the sewage of about 2,000,000 people and 200 industries. One need not be an expert to detect both its chemical and its fecal order. Buffalo Bayou is now a dead river, supporting only the gar, a symbol of ugliness. A red-brown scum covers the surface and occasionally streaks of white detergent foam appear. Fascinating Buffalo Bayou is now a smelly corpse.

Almost every community faces a substantial pollution problem. Rock Creek, once a sparkling stream fed by a spring in Maryland, was for years one of

---

*Playboy, XV, No. 6 (June 1968), 95-98, 177-181. Copyright © 1968 by William O. Douglas. Reprinted by permission of Playboy and William Morris Agency, Inc.
**William O. Douglas is an Associate Justice of the Supreme Court of the United States.

Washington, D.C.'s main attractions. Today it is a serious health hazard. It receives discharges from District sewers that are combined to carry both storm waters and sewage at times of heavy rain; people use it as a dump; the zoo puts its wastes into Rock Creek. The famous creek that Teddy Roosevelt tried to preserve is so heavy with silt from upstream construction projects that an old water wheel that once ran a gristmill will not work. And one who talks to the experts in the nation's capital learns that it will take until 2000 A.D. to convert Rock Creek into sanitary swimming holes for children.

The entire Potomac is so heavily polluted that it taxes the ingenuity of public-health experts to make the water both safe to drink and palatable. Every city in the several states the Potomac drains has a sewage-disposal plant, but the population explosion has made most of those plants inadequate to handle the supply. The Army Corps of Engineers, instead of coming up with an over-all sewage-disposal system that would clean up the Potomac and Chesapeake Bay as well, proposes a huge dam at Seneca that would destroy 80 miles of the river, produce a fluctuating water level that would expose long, ugly banks of mud and that would, the engineers say, provide a head of water adequate to flush the Potomac of sewage—at least in the environs of Washington.

Lake Erie, the fourth largest of the Great Lakes, is almost a dead lake. In addition to sewage from many cities, it receives over a ton of chemicals a minute from plants in four states. Beaches along the lake shore have had to be closed. Boating has dropped off because of the filth that accumulates on the hulls. Sport fishing has declined. Commercial fishing is only a small fraction of what it was. Pickerel and cisco disappeared and trash fish took their place. Large areas of the lake were found to have zero oxygen; plant life and fish life disappeared and the anaerobic, or nonoxygen, species of aquatic life (such as worms) took over. "What should be taking place over eons of time," one Public Health Service officer said, "is now vastly speeded up"—due to the pollutants. This expert says that Lake Erie is very sick and will have a convalescence running into many years.

Lake Michigan is sick, according to Secretary of the Interior Stewart L. Udall; and unless corrective steps are taken, it, too, will be dead. Michigan is, indeed, in a more precarious position than Erie; for while the latter is the beneficiary of a cleansing flow from Superior and Huron, Lake Michigan is isolated.

Some parts of the Ohio river have zero oxygen and not even the hardy trash fish can live there. At a zero oxygen level, a river becomes septic. A healthy river, the experts say, must have five parts of oxygen per million parts of water. When it has two parts per million, it has "the minimum quality which can be tolerated" for fish life.

The pollution of the Willamette river in Oregon is one of the nation's most notorious examples. I believe it was in 1946 that Stanley Jewett of the Fish and Wildlife Service and I took fresh, healthy rainbow trout and put them in a steel-mesh cage and lowered them at the mouth of the Willamette. We estimated that the oxygen content of the water at that point was probably 0 mg. The fish were, indeed, fairly inert within five minutes. The river has not improved since that time. As a matter of fact, its summer flow marks such a low concentration of dissolved oxygen that a salmon probably could never get through alive, whether it was going upstream or coming down. While there is very little upstream migration at that time, there is considerable downstream migration.

Fish need a dissolved oxygen concentration of 5 mg. per liter to survive, and the Willamette studies indicate that the level in its lower reaches drops to somewhere between 0 mg. and 2 mg.

The problem of the Willamette is largely created by seven pulp mills. With two exceptions, these mills use a sulphite pulping process, rather than cooking chemicals by condensing and burning wastes as do plants with more modern processes. About 70 percent of the damaging pollutants in the Willamette comes from the pulp mills, and the pulp mills have pretty well controlled the state politics of Oregon when it comes to pollution control.

The St. Lawrence Seaway, which connects Duluth, Minnesota, with the ocean, is hailed as a great achievement. But there is already alarm over the pollution taking place (a) by vessels emptying their bilges in the Great Lakes, (b) by garbage disposal and (c) by the dumping of raw sewage.

The Merrimack in Massachusetts, to whose pollution Thoreau objected in 1839, has been getting progressively worse. It has turned a filthy brown and emits bubbles that carry nauseating gases.

In the lower Mississippi, millions of fish turn belly up and die. Near St. Louis, chicken feathers and viscera pile so high they stop a motorboat. In portions of the Hudson, only scavenger eels live.

The Presumpscot river near Portland, Maine, gives off malodorous hydrogen sulphide from paper-pulp sludge that has accumulated over the decades.

Beautiful Lake Tahoe—the sapphire that lies partly in Nevada and partly in California—seems doomed. I recently flew over it in a small plane; and the brown streaks of sewage had already possessed nearly half of the lake. The gambling casinos on the lake's edge attract tens of thousands, and it is largely their sewage that is doing the damage. Two hundred thousand gallons of sewage a day enters Lake Tahoe.

Progress seemed under way when a Federal abatement order in 1966 caused California and Nevada to sign an interstate agreement that would, among other things, export the sewage by pipeline out of the Tahoe drainage basin by 1970. But in 1967, Governor Reagan upset the settlement by turning over the problem "for study" during the next 18 months to two California and three Nevada counties.

The powerful forces that may turn the tide are the citizens' groups that are rallying public opinion. The case is, in a way, easy to plead, for the impending demise of Tahoe can be seen from almost any height.

The same story could be told about some stream or about some lake in every state of the Union, except possibly Alaska, where the total population is still only about 250,000. But where people pile up and industry takes hold, the problem of pollution multiplies.

A typical city of 100,000 produces every day of the year one ton of detergents, 17 tons of organic suspended solids, 16 tons of organic dissolved solids, 8 tons of inorganic dissolved solids and 60 cubic feet of grime.

While most cities have sewage-disposal plants, many communities do not; and the use of septic tanks and cesspools in congested areas has raised profound problems that affect the quality of the underground percolating waters. Indeed, the earth of an entire area may become so polluted that the natural processes of drainage purification and bacterial action are so overtaxed they are ineffective. Where the surface supply is also in jeopardy, the problem of a safe water supply then becomes almost insoluble. Some parts of the country, notably Suffolk County, New York, have approached this critical condition.

Of the cities and towns that have sewage-disposal plants, it is estimated that about 18 percent still discharge untreated waste into the country's waterways.

Some progress is being made. A compact of the six New England States plus New York has put all their waterways into various classes. Class A is uniformly excellent water. Class B is suitable for swimming, for fishing, for irrigation and for drinking after it is treated. Class C is suitable for boating, for fish life, for irrigation and for some industrial uses, while the other classes are largely available only for industrial uses. It is to the lower categories that the Merrimack, which I have already mentioned, has been relegated.

The Congress has been busy, and recent acts under the title of Federal Water Pollution Control have put into motion important machinery. Each state was given until June 30, 1967, to adopt water-quality criteria applicable "to interstate waters or portions thereof" within the state, and to submit a plan for the implementation and enforcement of those water-quality criteria. These standards are subject to Federal approval. In the absence of state action adopting water-quality criteria, the Federal Government can move and establish its own. After the standards are fixed, there are methods for policing and enforcing them. As this article is written, the hearings are going on across the country.

Why the program was put in the Department of the Interior is a mystery. For Interior harbors two of our worst polluters—the Bureau of Mines, which allows acid to despoil our waterways, and the Bureau of Reclamation, whose projects now fill our streams with salt.

Missouri recently held its hearings on standards for the Missouri river. Missouri has a water-pollution-control association that pointed out at the hearing that the Missouri river was an excellent water supply for half the people of the state and for a significant portion of its industries. The association, however, went on to say: "Use of the Missouri river for removal and ultimate disposal of the sewered wastes of cities and industries has economic value far greater than does use of the river as a source of municipal and industrial water supply. Without exception, cities and industries along the Missouri river could obtain adequate supplies of water of good quality from subsurface sources. Likewise, other means can be found for transportation, fish and wildlife propagation, livestock watering and recreation." In other words, this association proposes that everybody abandon the Missouri and, in the cause of economics, leave it to the polluters.

This association at the hearing predicted economic doom unless streams in Missouri are used for their capacity to assimilate wastes, saying that the failure to do so would "lower standards of living and the general economy and decrease employment."

In taking direct aim at those who like a clean river for its beauty, for its swimming holes, for its fishing, boating and canoeing, the association said at the hearing: "While the entire public will share in paying the cost of maintaining that water quality, only a fraction of the public will enjoy the benefits of those water uses for which water-quality requirements are most demanding."

The inertia of those who have a vested interest in pollution is one obstacle. These interests are powerful. They are represented by most of our vast industrial complex. They are made up of huge metropolitan areas like New York, and they have never made any attempt to treat their sewage. They are made up of many who still look upon a river as having no value except as a carrier of wastes.

In addition to the inertia is the cost of cleanup, and the cost is going to be staggering. For example, the city of St. Louis recently undertook a contract to build a sewage-disposal plant—not an up-to-date variety, but one of the most primitive nature. It will contain only a primary treatment process, which does little more than settle out the solids. This contract alone is estimated to cost at least $95,000,000. While the Federal share of these programs was promised for from 30 percent to 50 percent of the cost, the Federal budget has already been drastically cut, due to Vietnam expenditures; and the appropriation of the Federal Water Pollution Control Administration was cut by two thirds for the fiscal year ending June 30, 1968.

Industrial use frequently requires cool water for its processes, the water eventually returning to the river at a high degree of temperature. This process, if continued, may raise the temperature of the entire stream. A stream for trout must be a cool-water stream. Raising a stream's temperature may change its entire life, ruining not only its recreational potential but its commercial potential as well; e.g., its production of shellfish.

This has happened to several streams, notably the St. Croix in Minnesota and the lower Potomac in Virginia. The heating of the lower Potomac waters is apparently modifying vast populations of microscopic plants that start the food chain in the river. It has reduced the white perch and certain flatfish and caused the soft-shelled clams to disappear. It has killed tens of thousands of crabs.

The dangers of thermal pollution multiply fast; and with the oncoming use of nuclear power that demands great quantities of cooling water, the risks ahead are increasing.

Saving a stream from this fate means requiring industry to build cooling towers for its water and using the same water over and over again.

Strip mining for coal is another source of great infection. Strip mining uses massive machinery to remove coal near the surface. And it is a process notorious for desecrating wild land and poisoning pure water. There is sulphur in these Appalachian lands, and sulphur when wet produces sulphuric acid, which destroys all vegetation and all aquatic life in the streams and ponds that it reaches. At least 4000 miles of Appalachian streams are being poisoned in this way. TVA as well as private operators are the despoilers, TVA flying the Federal flag of conservation. It uses coal from strip mining to run its stand-by steam plants.

Why must we the people tolerate this ruination of our mountain waterways?

The problem has been neglected so long, the population has been increasing so fast, that the conditions across the country have reached an emergency status. So the crisis that has been developing around our waterways is one of the greatest we have had to face, at least since the Civil War.

And so the battle lines are being drawn in the late 1960's.

We in America have no monopoly on this pollution problem. Europe knows it intimately, and recently the conditions on the Rhine reached such desperate proportions that steps are under way to preserve the river.

The same awareness exists in the Soviet Union. We are told by the Soviet Academy of Science that in the heavily industrialized Ural Mountains area there is not "one single unpolluted river." Domestic and industrial water supplies have been greatly impaired. Fish have been deprived of spawning and feeding grounds and pollution has been so severe in spots that some Russian rivers have become impassable.

When I was in Siberia in 1965, I visited Lake Baikal. The lumber industry was getting under way and the cutting caused soil erosion that filled the river beds with mud and even brought it into the lake. Lake Baikal is unique in scientific circles. It has, it is said, the purest water in the world and it is the site of intense Russian scientific endeavors. When I was there, Russian pulp mills, newly constructed near Lake Baikal, were running their discharge pipes to the lake. The Russian scientists were up in arms and their power and prestige in the Soviet Union was so great they were able to get a change that might save the lake from pollution. The alternative they proposed was that there should be constructed a long pipeline that would carry the industrial wastes from the pulp mills through a small mountain range into a stream flowing north into the Arctic Ocean. By 1968, the Russian scientists had lost their battle and Lake Baikal was being polluted by the industrial waste from the new pulp mills.

The answer to the problem of pollution is no longer a mystery. Wherever and whenever it takes place, technology has most of the answers and the problem is to mobilize the people and the financial resources to clean up the lakes and rivers. Science is constantly putting these problems in new dimensions. Thus great progress made in desalting water from the ocean—an experiment headed up by Israel beginning about 20 years ago. While costs are still higher than those normally associated with the creation of municipal water supplies, they are within reach once the urgency is felt.

In 1964, when Fidel Castro decided to cut off all Cuban water on Guantánamo Bay, we decided to be independent of him and quietly installed a big desalting plant. Sea water is heated under pressure to 195 degrees F., when it flashes into steam. This process is repeated many times, the steam producing a condensate that is almost tasteless, since it contains no minerals. At Guantánamo we are producing one gallon of fresh water out of 16 gallons of sea water. Now, we produce at Guantánamo 2,250,000 gallons a day—more than enough to meet the needs of the base; and with the steam that is generated, we operate an electric power plant of 1500 kws.

The point of this is that not only is desalting useful to seacoast cities short of water but it is also useful to take the nutrients out of sewage, making it possible to return pure water to the river or the lake and to pipe the residue off to centers where it can be processed for industrial or agricultural use. The avenues leading to the solution of the pollution problem are numerous and science is constantly opening up new ones.

The problem of our rivers does not end with pollution. The erection of dams is probably our problem number two. Dams for hydroelectric power became a very popular political slogan about 30 years ago. Hydroelectric power is cheap power and it has become associated in the public mind in this country with *public* power. Whether a dam is built to generate public power on the one hand or private power on the other, it still ruins a river as a free-flowing stream. There is no turning back the clock by removing the dams that we already have built. But there is still opportunity to save what remains of our free-flowing rivers and seek our power from other sources. The remaining free-flowing rivers that we have are national treasures and should be cleaned up and preserved for their great recreational and spiritual values.

Sometimes these dams are proposed for flood control, sometimes for a water supply. There may be no alternative to one dam or a series of dams when it comes to flood control or for water supply. Yet even here, if the design is to save a free-flowing river, such dams as are needed can be put way upstream or on a tributary, saving the main waterway for fishermen, canoeists, swimmers, and the like.

A case in point is the Potomac river. As I have said, the Corps of Engineers has planned a dam to provide a head of water to flush the river of sewage. It has also proposed dams for a water supply, and there is no doubt but that the metropolitan area of the nation's capital needs prudent planning in that connection. But here again, alternatives are available. There is the estuary that runs for about 30 miles from Little Falls just above Chain Bridge down into Chesapeake Bay. This part of the estuary is not salt or brackish water. It is tidal water that stays fresh. The technicians will probably deny that the water is fresh, because the water in the estuary contains tracings of salt. But those small portions of salt still leave the water potable, and it is potable water that is needed for the city's domestic use.

So in making plans for the city's future water supply, a pumping plant could easily be installed below Little Falls to move into action when the water above Little Falls becomes dangerously low. The estuary contains 100 billion gallons of potable water and this, plus the flow of the river, is enough to keep the nation's capital supplied for the indefinite future, no matter how big it grows—*once the Potomac is cleaned up.*

Why does the Corps of Engineers therefore suggest dams instead of a pumping plant in the estuary plus complete sewage treatment and removal of all of the pollutants from the water? That remains a mystery. Many think it is because the Corps builds dams very well and does not do other things quite as well and, therefore, it imposes upon society its specialty, like the chef who imposes his own favorite dish on all the patrons! That has led some to say, "We pay the farmers not to plant crops. Why don't we pay the Corps of Engineers not to build dams?"

My point is that the free-flowing river usually can be saved by the use of alternatives and our search should be for those alternatives.

The reason for this is accentuated when one studies the history of the dams. In my state of Washington, there is a very fine dam on the Wenatchee that is now useless because it is sanded in. There have been suggestions that the dam be blown out so that the sand can escape. But the fish experts veto that proposal, because it would ruin spawning grounds for 20 or 30 miles downstream. So the dam stands as a white elephant.

Go to Texas and you will see dam after dam silted up and no longer useful, or fast becoming such, as at Lake Austin, Lake Kemp, Lake Corpus Christi, Lake Dallas, Lake Bridgeport, Eagle Lake, Lake Waco, Possum Kingdom Reservoir and Lake Brownwood.

The life of a dam there is shorter than the life of a dam in the Pacific Northwest, because rivers in Texas run heavy with silt.

Dams that ruin free-flowing rivers are temporary expedients for which we pay an awful price. The search, as I said, should be for other alternatives, whether the dam be used for power, public or private, water supply, flood control or irrigation.

I have mentioned the powerful Corps of Engineers as one of our despoilers. TVA is another. As this is written, TVA is promoting the building of a dam on the Little Tennessee—not for power, not for irrigation, not for flood control. The dam, it is said, will provide new industrial sites for industry. But TVA already has hundreds of industrial sites that go begging for purchasers or lessees. Why destroy the Little T? It is some 30 miles long and is the best trout stream in the Southeast. Its water is pure and cold. Its islands are wondrous campgrounds. Its valleys are rich and fertile, being some of the very best agricultural lands in the South. Here was the home of Sequoya, the great Cherokee chief. Here are the old Cherokee village sites never mined for their archaeological wonders. Here is the old Fort Loudoun, built by the British in 1756. All of these wonders will be destroyed forever and buried deep under water for all time. Why not save this recreational wonderland for our grandchildren? Why allow it to be destroyed in a real-estate promotion by TVA?

The truth is that our momentum is toward destroying our natural wonders, converting them into dollars. The modern Genghis Khans are not robber barons; they fly the "conservation" flag; they promote "employment" and "development" and "progress." They have many instruments at their command. Industrial waste and sewage is one; destruction of free-flowing rivers through the building of dams is another.

Yet in spite of this destructive trend, there are a few encouraging signs.

The cause of free-flowing rivers received new impetus in 1964 when Congress created the Ozark National Scenic Riverways, which will preserve in perpetuity portions of the Jack's Fork river in Missouri. By this law, Congress directed that the natural beauty of the landscape be preserved and enhanced, that the outdoor resources be conserved and that the Secretary of the Interior establish zones where hunting and fishing are permitted. A related idea is expressed in the Wild Rivers Bill that Senator Church of Idaho has been promoting. It passed the Senate in 1967 and is now pending in the House. This proposed National Wild River system would comprise large segments of the Salmon and Clearwater in Idaho, the Rogue in Oregon, the Eleven Point in Missouri, the Buffalo in Arkansas, the Cacapon and its tributary the Lost river in West Virginia, and the West Virginia portion of the Shenandoah. The Wild River area would be administered for water and wildlife conservation, and for outdoor-recreation values. Yet it would not interfere with other uses such as lumbering, livestock grazing, and the like, though it would bar industrial wastes and sewage. The idea is to hand down to the oncoming generation a few of our important free-flowing streams in a pleasing and relatively unaltered environment.

There is a growing interest among the states in the preservation of their free-flowing rivers. Maine has taken the lead in saving the Allagash, a famed canoe waterway even before Thoreau, which runs north through Telos Lake to the St. John. Most of this will now be preserved as a wilderness waterway, with a belt of land between 400 feet and 800 feet wide on each side that will be managed to maintain the wilderness character of the waterway. The electorate in November 1966 approved a bond issue to help finance the land- and water-rights acquisition. Federal funds will also help in the acquisition program. The state will control all campsites. Most motors will be barred, this being a canoe sanctuary for hunters, fishermen and those who like the thrill of white water.

In 1947, Congress approved a Water Pollution Control Compact between the New England States, and they have made considerable progress in providing water-quality standards and in classifying rivers. But sad to say, quite a number of the New England rivers, conspicuously the Merrimack and Nashua, are put in the lowest categories, which means they are little more than carriers of waste.

In 1961, Congress authorized the Delaware River Basin Compact between Delaware, New Jersey, New York and Pennsylvania. Some progress has been made in establishing water-quality standards for that river.

On September 26, 1966, the Hudson River Basin Compact became law, whereby Congress gave New York, New Jersey, Vermont, Massachusetts and Connecticut authority to preserve the natural, scenic, historical and recreational resources of the Hudson, to abate water pollution and develop water resources, to preserve and rehabilitate the scenic beauty of the river and to promote its fish and wildlife and other resources. Now the troublesome Hudson, saturated with raw sewage, can be surveyed in its entirety and over-all planning instituted that in time may make it safe, healthwise, even for swimming.

There is another interesting development—this one in the state of Washington. The Yakima river flows off the eastern slopes of the Cascades to form the Columbia near Pasco. In its upper reaches it is a clear, cold, free-flowing river filled with trout, excellent for swimming and a fine canoe waterway. Mrs. Douglas and I became disturbed at a creeping real-estate development. Real-estate operators are selling lots on the river front and it is plain that in time the riverbank will be packed with houses. Sewage from their cesspools and septic tanks will pollute the waters. Industry is moving in, and there are telltale signs that industrial wastes are beginning to poison the river. We helped form the Yakima River Conservancy to design state procedures for protecting this watercourse. Others in the state capital took up the cause; and now there is a bill pending that would set aside this part of the Yakima and parts of several other rivers in Washington as wild rivers, putting under special zoning control a sanctuary belt that is one quarter of a mile wide on each side of each of these rivers. In this way, the natural state of a river will be preserved, its free-flowing character maintained, its scenic values and its purity honored, while no inconsistent use will be banned. In other words, agricultural uses could go on unimpaired: even some residential sites and campgrounds could be sanctioned. But the essential character of the stream will be kept inviolate; and 100 years from now, there will be unspoiled waterway wonders for our great-great-grand-children.

Some ponds and swamps in national wildlife refuges and game ranges are under the jurisdiction of the U.S. Fish and Wildlife Service; and it is directed under the Wilderness Act of 1964 to make recommendations concerning their preservation as roadless wilderness areas. In 1967, numerous hearings of that character took place; one of the first concerned the Great Swamp in New Jersey, which harbors otter, beaver, and many other species of wildlife and many botanical wonders. Developers have had their eyes on it, especially for an airport. No decision has been reached by the agency of the Wilderness issue. The lands around the Great Swamp have been increasing in value and the speculators' appetites for the Great Swamp are keen. But for most of us, what Brooks Atkinson recently wrote is the essence of the cause: "In Great Swamp the property values are low because the land is good for nothing except life, knowledge, peace and hope."

The Forest Service and Park Service are also required by the Wilderness Act of 1964 to determine what roadless areas will be preserved in their respective domains. The hearings, now going on and to take place, will sometimes involve the fate of rivers. A notorious example is the Minam river in the Wallowa-Whitman National Forest of eastern Oregon, one of the very few rivers in the Pacific Northwest not paralleled by a road. Lumbermen are anxious to build such a road, not only to make money from timber sales but primarily to make a small fortune in building the road itself. The Minam—as crystal clear as any in the land—would be heavily silted by logging; the road would soon be clogged with cars; and the banks would be packed with people. The quiet and seclusion of the sanctuary would be lost forever and the natural character of the free-flowing Minam would disappear.

There will be a chance to save a number of waterways under the Wilderness Act from all pollution and all "development."

The same, of course, is true of many lakes in the high country. But as respects the lakes in our low country, we have made amazing progress. The Dust Bowl of the Twenties and Thirties taught us something of soil and water conservation. At that time, our natural ponds and marshes were fast being drained. The cycle has been reversed. Due largely to the Soil Conservation Service, about 1,500,000 new farm ponds have been formed. These have some recreational value, but their greatest impact probably has been on the duck population. Many are wonderful fish ponds. Over half of them have been a great boon to waterfowl. Those new ponds in the North Central States are in areas where several hundred million bushels of waste corn are commonly left in the fields. These are prized feeding grounds for waterfowl and probably have changed some of the ancient flyways.

In 1960, President Eisenhower vetoed the proposed Federal Water Pollution Control Act, which would have increased Federal grants for the construction of sewage-treatment works and such purposes. His veto was based on the fact that water pollution is "a uniquely local blight" that must be assumed by state and local governments.

That Federal attitude has changed under Presidents Kennedy and Johnson, so that today there is a pervasive program for Federal control, in case the states fail to act promptly. The diminishing Federal funds available for cleanup of the rivers and lakes of the nation is part of the tragedy. Another is that the Eisenhower attitude still obtains in critical agencies such as the Bureau of the Budget. And in the absence of a tremendous popular drive, the critical conditions promise to get worse and worse.

One expert in the field of preservation of our streams and lakes recently said, "We can hardly expect to be as smart in the future as we've been stupid in the past." But with the mounting public concern evident on every hand, it may be possible by 2000 A.D. to restore some of our watercourses and lakes to their pristine condition.

The Politics of Water*
Senator Frank E. Moss**

The longest oral argument made before the U.S. Supreme Court in this century did not come in any of the cases concerning the great social issues, or subversion, or the rights of accused persons. That distinction went to *Arizona* v. *California*—a water case.

In the average case, the court hears about an hour of oral argument. The

---

*Frank E. Moss, *The Water Crisis* (New York: Frederick A. Praeger, 1967), pp. 11-21, 27-28. Reprinted by permission.
**Frank E. Moss is a United States Senator from Utah.

offshore oil cases involving Texas and Louisiana were allotted more than sixteen hours. *Arizona* v. *California* was allotted twenty-two hours. Before the argument was heard, a Special Master (an officer of the court who is skilled as a trial examiner) was appointed. The first appointed master died, and a second was chosen. In total, their work took eight years. They heard 340 witnesses, reviewed 25,000 pages of testimony, and reported findings in a volume of 433 pages. The final decree of the court was handed down in 1964. Arizona won, and obtained the right to 2.8 million acre-feet* of water from the Colorado River.

Arizona v. *California* symbolizes the mounting struggle to get water for competing uses and rival regions. It is true that the West has always fought over water, while, to most of the nation, water has been—like air—there for the taking. But five years of drought in the Northeast and a rising tide of pollution have made the nation aware at last of the incalculable value of this resource.

Increasingly, the control of water becomes the key to prosperity, growth, and political and economic power in the United States.

To put water resources to use, the people of the United States have invested a tremendous $180 billion in facilities—dams, hydroelectric installations, treatment plants and sewers, irrigation works and reservoirs, dikes and levees. In 1961, the Senate Select Committee on National Water Resources estimated that by 1980 some $230 billion more would have to be spent.

Investments of this magnitude—plus the advantages that regions and industries gain from use of the water—have generated massive political pressures involving cities, states, big business, trade and service associations, farmers, conservationists, the many federal agencies concerned with water, and the Congress.

Enactment of the Water Quality Act of 1965 stirred a hornet's nest. Big industry, faced with the possibility of having to clean up the nation's waterways, registered strong opposition at the National Water Conference sponsored by the U.S. Chamber of Commerce in December of the same year. The federal government was pilloried by an array of executives who favored local standards and controls. Their speeches were part of the politics of water, intended to warn Congress and the new Water Pollution Control Administration to tread lightly lest industry's wrath be incurred.

The Washington *Evening Star,* often a spokesman for business enterprise, took issue with the philosophy emanating from the U.S. Chamber meeting. An editorial said:

> The National Water Quality Act was passed in October. By now, industries affected by the law—paper mills, oil refineries and chemical plants—should be aware of their responsibilities in cleaning up the nation's streams. But judging from remarks made at the national water conference . . . they have yet to get the message.

The message had been presented courteously but clearly by James M. Quigley, Assistant Secretary of Health, Education, and Welfare, who shortly thereafter was named Acting Commissioner of the new Water Pollution Control Administration. Mr. Quigley stated that the task of his agency was to prevent, as well as abate, pollution. He apparently parted company with his audience when

---

*An acre-foot is the measure of the volume of water sufficient to cover an acre of ground to a depth of one foot, or 325,851 gallons.

he told the business leaders: "You must accept and act on the principle that the cost of pollution control from now on is part of the cost of doing business."

But Governor Henry L. Bellmon of Oklahoma asserted that the object of pollution abatement programs must be the attainment and preservation of usable waters and "not the elimination of waste discharges." He proclaimed that one of the unavoidable multipurposes of our streams is to serve as a receptacle for waste. If what appears to be the Bellmon philosophy were to prevail, the nation's water could be polluted beyond redemption. It may be necessary to dump waste into rivers, but it is highly undesirable to do so. If dumping is to continue without destroying the waters, the waste must be purified to reduce as much as possible its deleterious effect downstream.

In favoring state and local—rather than national—standards, the U.S. Chamber and its audience had good self-serving reasons. Speaker after speaker called for local controls and self-regulation. John O. Loga, executive vice president of Olin-Mathieson Chemical Corporation, helped to set the stage for a new round in the politics of water. Mr. Logan called for federal tax concessions or other incentives to induce industry to clean up the nation's streams, saying:

> The chemical industry believes in a positive attitude and maximum self-regulation as the best means of providing solutions to its water resources problems. It does also support appropriate control programs and control agencies at the regional, state and local level, with emphasis on the lowest level *capable of doing the job.* Where Federal participation is desirable the chemical industry will cooperate. It will support research-oriented public programs.

Herbert S. Richey, president of the Valley Camp Coal Company of Cleveland, admitted that industrial water users have not been "fully responsive" to their obligations. Nonetheless, he equated the Water Quality Act with "the *threat* of dictatorial Federal control."

According to George Olmstead, president of S.D. Warren Company, a Boston-based paper manufacturer, any truly comprehensive pollution abatement program involved a "social cost" to be borne by the public regardless of the source. And, in Mr. Olmstead's view, need existed for "really realistic" time schedules to perform a task that he estimated would cost a billion dollars for his industry alone. Whether or not Mr. Olmstead feared federal control, he was quite ready to have the federal government pay "a substantial part of the capital expenditures for waste treatment facilities"—through fast tax write-offs, investment credits, other special subsidies from the taxpayer, or all three.

Dayton H. Clewell, senior vice president of Socony-Mobil Oil, told of efforts of his industry to end pollution from petrochemicals. He correctly stated that no single sector of the population was free of blame for the condition of our waters.

Industry's point of view—at least as represented by the Chamber—was summed up by Robert P. Gerholz, a Flint, Michigan, real estate developer and president of the Chamber, who warned the corporation executives to seek state regulation to head off federal "coercion." Mr. Gerholz said:

> I submit that there is no national problem. I do not believe that the problem can best be met in a national context . . .
> I submit that better results will emanate from voluntary and

cooperative efforts of industry, municipalities, and state governments to conserve and redeem water resources than from programs
handled by Washington's many agencies.

An opposite stand was taken by *The New York Times* in its editorial of
December 16, 1965, which stressed:

> There is no inherent right to pollute water. A businessman who
> pours untreated filth or acids or chemicals or chemical wastes into a
> river is, often without realizing it, an enemy of the public good.
>   The American people know that the day of the unrestrained
> polluter is fast drawing to a close, although not fast enough in our
> view. Recognizing this, some manufacturers hope merely to shift the
> burden of cleaning up their own operations from their stockholders
> to the general public. They ask either Government subsidies or fast
> tax write-offs to pay for pollution control facilities for their plants.
>   We see no justification for either direct or indirect subsidies. To
> grant additional subsidies to major polluters would, in effect, be to
> penalize unfairly the businessmen who have installed in the past or
> who now are in the process of installing the necessary equipment on
> their own initiative and at their own expense.

The nature of the Water Quality Act of 1965 was itself determined by the
politics of water—and these considerations, in turn, determine the usefulness of
the law. Commissioner Quigley has declared that its aim is "to encourage the
states to establish their own water quality standards for the parts of interstate
waterways which flow within their boundaries." The law gave the HEW
Secretary no authority until June 30, 1967. Then he could act only in the cases
of states that fail to submit satisfactory standards. If, at that time, the Secretary
could impose a minimum standard, the act might perform its hoped-for task. But,
said Mr. Quigley:

> The entire process of establishing and enforcing standards is
> surrounded by safeguards [for industry].
>   The Secretary's authority is not arbitrary. A conference of
> affected parties must be held before Federal standards are set. There
> is a provision for a hearing board, on which each affected state is
> represented, and on which there is to be a balance of interest. The
> board has authority to make findings as to whether the standards set
> by the Secretary shall be approved or modified. And in setting
> standards, the Secretary must be mindful that the standards must
> meet tests of "physical and economic feasibility" in the courts,
> should their violation trigger an enforcement action.

Much as water seeks its own level, it appeared that pollution control might
be the lowest standard that HEW would accept with the threat of prolonged
court action to face. Almost certainly, lobbying activities in state legislatures

could be expected to be intense. One hope was that a greater federal presence in water quality enforcement of itself would result in diminished pollution. At least, both industry and municipalities understood that federal intervention could expand if local log-rolling resulted in continued stalemate.

Pollution is but one sector of the battlefront. The politics of water extends far beyond questions of who will enforce quality and who will pay the bill for abatement. With a federal investment alone of $50 billion in water projects, it would be naive to expect otherwise. Flood control, hydroelectric power, regional economic growth and decay—all these depend upon Congressional authorizations and appropriations. So do payrolls and business profits; so do the operations of many federal agencies.

Conflict of Use

The genesis of the politics of water is *conflict of use*—the difficulty of making a fixed supply of water stretch to meet all demands. Before looking further at the pressures and power structures, it is necessary to examine briefly the uses of water.

Men require water for five basic needs: personal use, industrial use, agricultural use, transportation, and electric power generation.

Personal use means drinking, bathing, maintaining the home, and maintaining the city. It includes all uses of water for recreation—boating, swimming, fishing, and hunting waterfowl—and the care of lakes, streams, and fountains to maintain their beauty.

Industrial use means every use for processing, cooling, or the disposal of waterborne wastes of manufacturing and processing plants. In 1965, there were 150,000 such establishments in the United States using water in their operations.

Water for agriculture means all use for food and fiber production.

Transportation includes use of waterways to move goods or to move passengers for hire. Every year, more than a billion tons of shipping move on the inland waterways of the United States.

Water is used two different ways to generate electric power. One is the damming of streams to produce hydroelectric power. The other is production in steam plants. Tremendous quantities of cooling water are required for the latter.

To classify the uses of water is, of course, to oversimplify. For example, although commercial fishing is an industrial use, its water requirements are entirely different from those for manufacturing and processing. Recreation includes sport fishing and duck hunting; yet the need for water to support wildlife habitat is not limited to the sport it affords. Not being a "use" of water, floods cannot be put into one of the classifications; yet control of flooding is part of water management.

No one of the five uses can be said to be, singly, the most important. In theory, radical adjustments might be made in the amounts of water utilized for different purposes. Last to be given up would be water for drinking and for essential health needs. But for survival as the world's leading industrial nation, we must have ample water for all purposes.

A complicating factor in defining water uses is the differing degrees to which they are "consumptive." For consumptive use, in the definition generally accepted, water must be diverted from its natural channels. Thus, city water is taken from streams or lakes and channeled through a water system for consumption, and it is then returned to a water course in a degraded form and usually in a different place. Similarly, industrial uses and irrigation both require diversion; irrigation water not consumed by plants returns to water courses only some time later, mostly through the ground.

In contrast to these consumptive uses on the part of municipalities, industries, and agriculture, most other uses require quantities of water "in place." Any substantial alteration, either to the physical character of a water course or to its quality, affects its value to fish and wildlife and may change its suitability for recreation and its esthetic value. Power generation requires construction on river beds, but seldom alters water quality. (A storage reservoir may even improve quality by permitting silt to settle and the water to change in color from a dirty brown to a clear blue.) Dikes and levees for flood control may complicate the use of the water that flows in the channel.

The national interest requires water for all uses, but regions and economic groups seek to control water resources for their own—often conflicting— purposes. What is it they seek?

As already noted, industry wants to use rivers and lakes as cheap facilities for the disposal of wastes. Industry also wants large quantities of water for cooling and processing and for the inexpensive barge transportation that developed waterways afford. In addition, it is advantageous for industry to be close to markets, and large concentrations of population are found around major rivers.

Cities—many of them—also want to use waterways as inexpensive receptacles for human and industrial wastes. The citizens of the cities want low charges for water and for sewer service. At the same time, millions of citizens want extensive clean waters on which to sail and water ski, and in which to swim. They want large areas of rivers, lakes, and wetlands for fishing and waterfowl hunting.

Western farmers want large quantities of inexpensive irrigation water. They get much of it at 2 cents per 1,000 gallons. Water from federal reclamation projects is sold to irrigators according to the portions of dam construction costs allocated to irrigation, which are repaid in fifty years, but without interest.

The shipping industry wants well-regulated waterways and protected ocean harbors. It wants permission to use them to dispose of its human and machine wastes.

Both "investor-owned" and "consumer-owned" power companies want the right to dam streams to generate electricity, often with no thought of providing such other benefits as flood control, storage, recreation, and water supply.

A Man's Own Choices

Competition for water touches many Americans in a personal way—affecting their living conditions and pocketbooks.

In Kentucky, an employee of an automobile manufacturer works in a plant on the Ohio River. The plant was located there to take advantage of low-cost water transportation. The worker's wages are good, and he likes his job. But his plant and others upstream pollute the river. Its wastes are unpleasant and must be highly treated for use in his home.

In New Jersey, an executive builds a new country home in a fashionable section reclaimed from marshland. Formerly, the swamp was a stop for waterfowl migrating on the Eastern Flyway. But the migrants now pass over the area, and the homeowner must travel farther than he once did to enjoy duck hunting.

In Buffalo, a salesman of business systems enjoys good commissions from sales to industrial plants located along the Great Lakes. But the plants pollute the lakes; contamination of Lake Erie has closed his family's favorite beach. In Nashua, New Hampshire, a woman who owns real estate avoids a tax increase when a bond issue to build a sewage treatment plant is voted down. But on warm summer nights, she has to endure disagreeable odors from the Nashua River. In Idaho, a dairy operator must sell choice bottom land and move his plant because the location will be flooded when a federal reclamation project is completed. But the area will gain irrigation water and a population increase, and the demand for his dairy products will go up.

As such competition for water control affects more and more persons, the great conflicts between regions and economic groups are generated or exacerbated.

At the height of the 1965 water shortage in the Northeast, Mayor Robert F. Wagner of New York told a "crisis team" dispatched to the city by President Johnson that New York would not indefinitely release 200 million gallons daily from its watershed reservoirs to prevent salt-water intrusion in the Delaware River up to Philadelphia's intake pipes. This warning came despite a Supreme Court decision, handed down years ago, requiring New York to release at least that amount.

Calling a "war over water the ultimate absurdity," *The New York Times* asked settlement "across the conference table or in the courts." A compromise was reached satisfying the interests of both cities. It provided that New York would no longer release the 200 million gallons a day into the Delaware. Instead, the water would be "banked" in three reservoirs available alternately to New York and Philadelphia on an emergency basis. To keep salt out of Philadelphia's water supply, four temporary intake pipes were mounted on barges farther up the river.

Will Chicago take another 750,000 gallons of Lake Michigan water a day to flush waste down the Illinois River, or will the water continue to go over Niagara Falls, generating electric power?

Will a federal dam be built on the Nez Perce site on the Snake River, with a large reservoir to provide storage and recreation in addition to power generation, or will a private power company build a "run-of-the-river" dam at the High Mountain Sheep site to produce power and pay taxes?

Will Northern States Power Company build a steam generating plant on land it owns along the St. Croix River, or will a Wisconsin-Minnesota joint commission work out a solution satisfying advocates of a wild-rivers concept?

Questions like these come oftener and with more insistence as we press harder to divide up our waters for more uses.

Of all politico-economic pressures, none is more intense than the struggle "to bring in new industry." Every governor of every state works for industrial development, and every candidate for governor promises to try harder. Promoting new industry is a principal occupation of chambers of commerce. Most states have industrial commissions, which, financed by tax money, run advertisements and organize conferences to inform business leaders of the area's advantages. Business and political leaders alike relish announcing the establishment of a new business or the securing of a new government contract for an existing plant.

The productivity of labor in relation to cost is a powerful inducement to locating an enterprise. So are climate, a congenial atmosphere for employees, and, of course, water: water for use and water to carry off wastes. The community with a river to pollute has a powerful argument for the location of a big plant. The one with water restrictions is not "encouraging" industry.

The availability of water is a prime consideration in the location of virtually every industrial development.

* * *

The lobby and pressure groups concerned with water seem endless in number. They are not confined to organizations supporting or defending a particular federal agency. Just as the Chamber of Commerce helps industry define its position for Congressional purposes, so the National Association of Manufacturers battles the "federal presence" and legislation that might require responsibility for water quality by NAM members. The National Parks Association wants no tampering with water resources within the parks, and it wants more water-based parks. The Wilderness Society wants to keep virgin forests forever unspoiled. The Izaak Walton League seeks water pure enough for fishing; the Sports Fishing Institute wants to "shorten the time between bites." The Sierra Club wants to keep nature wild and untamed. The Trustees for Conservation, the National Audubon Society, and the Citizens Committee for Natural Resources have similar concerns.

If the private power companies are highly successful lobbyists, much the same must be said for public power groups. The National Rural Electric Cooperative Association has successfully defended the Rural Electrification Agency and the 2 per cent interest rate for REA projects. The American Public Power Association has won the respect of the private companies, if not their love. Both the NRECA and APPA endorse comprehensive multipurpose projects, particularly if a large public power component is included. Sometimes, however, they have supported public power projects without regard to maximum multipurpose use.

Organized labor, individual unions, the National Grange, and the Farmers Union have generally supported multipurpose development. The Auto Workers, in a move diametrically opposed to that of the U.S. Chamber of Commerce, held an antipollution conference in Detroit to emphasize union interest in cleaning up the Great Lakes. The Farm Bureau Federation, an outgrowth of the U.S. Chamber of Commerce, has usually followed industry's position on water clean-up, conservation, development, and power.

Some organizations—notably the League of Women Voters—have supported beneficial legislation from the standpoint of the national interest. *The Big Water Fight,* a book compiled by the league's Education Fund and published in 1966, contains case histories of citizen action campaigns. Many of these campaigns resulted in the solution of state and local water problems (for instance, in numerous localities, they forced construction of sewage treatment plants). In addition, this local action provided strong backing for federal water resources legislation.

Water lobbying will not, of course, be ended however beneficial may be the changes in the nation's water management methods. The views of individuals and organizations are necessary to the American legislative and political process, and these views will always be expressed on existing operations as well as proposed changes.

But the critical condition of the nation's water resources in the early 1960's reflected the activities of groups organized to promote limited interests, often in the context of the less intensive use of natural resources decades ago. Today, the need these groups have for a share of America's waters cannot be met unless our waters are restored and preserved.

**Regulatory Aspects of Federal
Water Pollution Control***
Murray Stein**

Consider the following quotation taken from a classic case dealing with the effects of industrial water pollution:

> The exigencies of the great industrial interests must be kept standing in view; the property of large and useful interests should not be hampered or hindered for frivolous or trifling causes. For slight inconveniences or occasional annoyances, they ought not to be held responsible. . . .
>
> It is certainly true that owing to the want, if not necessities, of the present age . . . some changes must be tolerated in the channels in which water naturally flows, and in its adaptation to beneficial uses. Reasonable diminution of its quantity, in gratifying and meeting customary wants, has always been permitted. So, its temporary detention for manufacturing purposes, followed by its release in increased volume, is a necessary consequence of its utilization as a propelling force. Nor must we shut our eyes to the tendency—the inevitable tendency—of these and other uses, in which water is an indispensable element, to detract somewhat from its normal purity. These modifications of individual right must be submitted to, in order that the greater good of the public be conserved and promoted. But there is a limit to this duty to yield, to this claim and right to expect and demand. *The water course must not be diverted from its channel, or so diminished in volume, or so corrupted and*

---

*Denver Law Journal, XLV, No. 2 (Spring, 1968), 267-278. Reprinted by permission.
**Mr. Stein is Assistant Commissioner, Federal Water Pollution Control Administration, United States Department of the Interior.

*polluted as practically to destroy or greatly impair its value to the
lower riparian proprietor.*[1]

This 1893 decision was one of the earliest of any significance in the history
of United States court action regarding water pollution. It has great relevance,
for better or worse, to attitudes widely held today, even though the riparian
rights doctrine it discusses does not prevail in the United States, and the
conditions of our waters have since vastly changed.

As might be expected, industries as they came into being and underwent
booming growth did not keep the judge's ideas on comparative injury in mind.
Even this relatively benign judicial restraint applied only to litigated cases, and
the paucity of reported water pollution cases attests to the negligible social
effect of private litigation in this area. In the development of this country,
industries were by no means the only offender. Towns and cities with their
burgeoning populations also indulged for decades in a profligate use of one of
the most valuable natural resources this richly endowed nation offered. The
combined indulgence was so widespread and so strong that the natural
assimilative process of many water courses could not keep up with the amount
of wastes being spewed into them. There was no public insistence that money
should be spent for proper waste treatment even though the costs generally
would have been much less than the cost of cleaning up an environment fouled
by pollution. Consequently, it did not take very long before the majority of our
major rivers and many smaller ones were seriously polluted.

The court in *Tennessee Coal* speaks of modification of the individual right
for the benefit of the common weal. Today this concept still guides us, but we
now realize that the promotion of the public interest has far wider implications
than were obvious to the author of that opinion, and that much more is at stake
now than when he set forth his guidelines. His words sound eminently
reasonable, but in the light of the status of the present environment and our
rising expectations they can be seen as somewhat deceptive. The time is long
overdue for taking a more rigid view than that taken by the judge on what to
accept and what not to accept in water quality. Because we are all too familiar
with the damaging consequences of pollution, we cannot afford to be as tolerant
as he was when he urged that degradation of water should be prevented only if it
is so pervasive as "practically to destroy or greatly to impair" the value of water.
It has been estimated that industry contributes equally as much biochemical
oxygen demand to the nation's streams as all municipalities combined and
generates and discharges even more of most other pollution materials.

Today our general awareness has shifted from mere appreciation of the
economic advantages a water-using industry brings to a particular area to a
broader realization that many more human and other factors are pertinent to an
area's quality of life and that they are more complex than the compartively
simple interests directly served by any one industry. This new awareness stems
from the realization of many important points, not the least of which is the
knowledge that the effects of pollution can far outweigh the advantages to
industries and municipalities and thus to the public of intemperate disposal of
unsatisfactorily treated wastes. We need to emphasize a reversal of the 19th
century approach and to give people a higher priority than property and profits.

I. Congressional Action

Perhaps the current water supply and pollution problems should be blamed on the fact that earlier water conditions were not overwhelming soon enough to prompt recognition of the trouble that was forthcoming. Until recently, not enough of a hue and cry was raised to translate into preventive action and, worse still, not enough anxiety was articulated to carry over into remedial action once the damage was done. Despite the general feebleness of the public voice, at the turn of the 19th century, Congress passed the first piece of legislation which bore on water quality.

The authority of Congress to legislate in matters of water pollution control and prevention derives from the commerce clause of the Constitution. In the exercise of its jurisdiction over the navigable waters of the United States in connection with the regulation of interstate and foreign commerce, Congress has asserted the federal interest and responsibility in protecting the quality of these waters.

The Rivers and Harbors Act of 1899, among other things, prohibited the discharge of deposit into any navigable waters of any refuse matter except that which flowed in a liquid state from streets and sewers. As the first specific federal water pollution control legislation, its primary purpose was to prevent impediments to navigation.

In the 20th century, legislation pertaining to water quality has come before every Congress except during the war years. However, prior to the end of World War II, Congress had enacted into law but two of these proposed bills. Health implications of water pollution received attention in the Public Health Service Act of 1912 which authorized investigations of water pollution related to disease. The Oil Pollution Act of 1924 was enacted to control oil discharges in coastal waters damaging to aquatic life, harbors and docks, and recreational facilities.

This measures described were only indicative and not representative in themselves of the many varied proposals introduced in Congress during the first half of this century. Many different approaches to the problem were put forth in these proposals. Some of them conceived the federal role in water pollution as being strongly regulatory with wide enforcement powers. Among the bills that found their way into the hoppers were those which provided for a federal permit system for the discharge of wastes and a prohibition against the purchase of paper by the federal government from any manufacturers who discharged wastes into a stream. On three separate occasions, in 1936, 1938, and 1940, comprehensive water pollution control legislation narrowly missed final enactment or approval. After World War II renewal of efforts resulted in the enactment by the 80th Congress of the Water Pollution Control Act of 1948. This law was admittedly experimental and initially limited in duration to a period of five years which was extended for an additional three years to June 30, 1956.

Comprehensive water pollution control legislation of a permanent nature was finally attained by the amendments enacted in 1956. The amended Act was administered by the Surgeon General of the Public Health Service under the supervision and direction of the Secretary of Health, Education, and Welfare.

Among other things, this act

(1) Reaffirmed the policy of Congress to recognize, preserve, and protect the primary responsibilities and rights of the states in preventing and controlling water pollution;

(2) Authorized increased technical assistance to states and broadened and intensified research by using non-governmental research potential; authorized collection and dissemination of basic data on water quality relating to water pollution prevention and control;

(3) Directed the Surgeon General to continue to encourage interstate compacts and uniform state laws;

(4) Authorized grants to states and interstate agencies for water pollution control activities, and to municipalities for the construction of waste treatment plants;

(5) Modified and simplified procedures governing federal abatement actions interstate pollution;

(6) Authorized the appointment of a Water Pollution Control Advisory Board; and

(7) Set up a program to control pollution from federal installations.

Proposals to amend the Federal Water Pollution Control Act to provide for a still more effective program of water pollution control were introduced early in the first session of the 87th Congress, and received the endorsement of President Kennedy in his February 1961 message on natural resources.

In July 1961, President Kennedy signed into law the Federal Water Pollution Control Act Amendments of 1961. These amendments improved and strengthened the Act by

(1) Extending federal authority to enforce abatement of intrastate as well as interstate pollution by making "navigable" waters subject to enforcement jurisdiction; and strengthening enforcement procedures;

(2) Increasing amounts authorized for financial assistance to municipalities in the construction of waste treatment works for each of the six following fiscal years; raising the single grant limitations; and providing for grants to communities combining in a joint project;

(3) Intensifying research toward more effective methods of pollution control; authorizing for this purpose annual appropriations and the establishment of regional and field laboratories;

(4) Authorizing the inclusion of storage to regulate stream flow for the purpose of water quality control in the planning of federal reservoirs and impoundments; and

(5) Designating the Secretary of Health, Education, and Welfare to administer the Act.

As in prior legislation and all succeeding legislation, the Act declared Congressional policy affirming the primary responsibilities and rights of the states in preventing and controlling water pollution. Consequently, the federal functions in the area were designed to be carried out in the fullest cooperation with state and interstate agencies and with local public and private interest.

It may be readily perceived that the programs authorized by the Federal Water Pollution Control Act grouped themselves into three major areas of effort—financial and technical assistance, research, and enforcement. All stimulated voluntary action. Where such voluntary action was not forthcoming, enforcement authority could make remedial action mandatory. The end product, abatement of pollution and its prevention and control, has always been the aim and purpose of all three of these coordinated program areas.

Extensive changes in the federal water pollution control program were made in 1965 by enactment of the Water Quality Act. The program was entirely removed from the Public Health Service and constituted as an independent agency, the Federal Water Pollution Control Administration. It is clear from the legislative history that Congress had been dissatisfied with the slow tempo of regulatory action and hoped, by upgrading the program, to emphasize the importance and urgency of pollution control. On May 10, 1966, the Federal Water Pollution Control Administration was transferred to the Department of the Interior, and shortly thereafter an Assistant Secretary of the Interior for Water Pollution Control was appointed. With most of the federal government's water programs under one roof, better coordination and elimination of duplicated effort has been effected, and the entire Department is united to fight the water problems of the country.

II. Establishing Water Quality Standards

The most important addition to water pollution legislation has been the establishment of national water quality standards for interstate waters. Section 10(c)(1) of the Water Quality Act of 1965 required all 50 states, the District of Columbia, the Territories of Guam and the Virgin Islands, and Puerto Rico to submit to the Department of the Interior proposed water quality criteria, or standards, for interstate or navigable water. These standards are, in the words of the legislation, to "protect the public health or welfare, enhance the quality of water . . . ." Those establishing the standards should consider "their use and value for public water supplies, propagation of fish and wildlife, recreational purposes, and agricultural, industrial, and other legitimate uses." With their proposals for standards, which were to be submitted by June 30, 1967, the states included plans for implementing and enforcing them. The Secretary of the Interior is required to review them and either pass them or institute procedures as outlined in the Act, to work with the states in devising acceptable standards. By now, he has judged that the standards of most of the states adequately serve the cause of water pollution control, and he has approved many as official federal water quality standards.

To aid the states in establishing these water quality standards, the Department of the Interior issued guidelines which explained their purpose and desired function. These guidelines pointed out that the water quality standards were designed to upgrade existing water quality, except in those few cases where rivers are still in a state of natural purity. The standards could not "lock in" existing low levels of water quality, or condemn rivers to serve as sewers. No standards could allow any treatable wastes to be discharged without treatment or without the best practicable treatment unless it could be proven that lesser degrees of treatment were enough to provide high water quality. The standards were to be designed with a view to future water quality, taking into consideration urban and industrial growth and increased demands for recreational opportunity.

The Interior Department also issued guidelines for the enforcement and implementation plans required by the legislation. The plans submitted by the states include time schedules for achieving the water quality objectives. These time schedules include target dates by which each waste discharger must provide adequate treatment. The degree of treatment required depends, of course, on the quality of water required by the standards. The time schedules provide, generally, for the abatement of all existing conventional municipal and industrial pollution within five years. Programs for more complicated problems, such as combined sanitary and storm water sewer overflows, have been scheduled over periods as long as ten years. The measures to be used by the state pollution control agencies to ensure compliance are specified in the enforcement plans.

The standards themselves were set by the states after public hearings. At these hearings public testimony concerning all the water uses which involved interstate or navigable streams was invited. All water users, large and small, were considered—from a few solitary fishermen to a large fishing fleet, from a farmer watering a few head of cattle to a giant steel plant. The water uses under consideration also included those not yet in existence. A small town's potential as a future tourist center could have been deemed a critical economic fact. The obsolescence of an industry, and its likelihood of folding within a few years, also could have been important in determining the best use of the region's waterways. Predicted population changes over a long period of time had to be considered, although they could not be allowed to obscure the desires of the present population.

Water quality standards could not be established generally and then applied to specific bodies of water as they had been in some states prior to the Act. Each river, stream and lake may have its own characteristics. The people of a region may prefer to swim in one river, to fish in another. On some rivers industries are already established; other rivers are still pristine. The wildlife in one stream may already have been destroyed by pollution. Some rivers are dredged frequently for navigational purposes. Some are naturally silty. Others have natural growths of algae. All kinds of facts, physical and human, were to be judged in deciding the best that could be done with each body of water.

The Department of the Interior fully respected the desires of the states to treat each stream as a separate case. Uniformity was not the goal of the legislation. In fact, the only generalization to be made about the water quality standards is that they are all to serve in overcoming pollution. None of them will be permitted to allow respite in the anti-pollution struggle.*

---

*Some States have taken advantage of the travail, hearings, and publicity accompanying the establishment of the standards and have either updated or expanded existing intrastate standards or established intrastate standards for the first time.

III. Federal Enforcement Authority

It is not intended that the water quality standards be mere promises of good intentions. They are to be powerful weapons in combatting pollution because they are to be effectively enforced. The authority of the new federal Water Pollution Control Administration was expanded by the 1965 amendments to cover enforcement of these standards so that the Secretary of the Interior is empowered to act when the quality of interstate waters or portions thereof has been reduced below the level set. Once a state's quality criteria and implementation plans are adopted as federal standards, any violation of these standards is subject to abatement by enforcement action. If the violation of the standards has interstate effects, the Secretary of the Interior may proceed immediately to a suit against the polluters.

This does not mean that preference for cooperative action has been discarded at all. In certain situations, the Secretary will continue to base enforcement action on the existing order of procedures. Such situations are pollution of intrastate waters when a state governor requests federal action, and interstate cases when a state water pollution agency requests action. Current enforcement procedures will still be employed in another matter of pollution which was placed under the jurisdiction of the Secretary of the Interior by the 1965 Water Quality Act. This new authorization, termed the "shellfish provision," directs the Secretary to initiate enforcement action on his own when he finds that substantial economic injury is resulting from the inability to market shellfish or shellfish products in interstate commerce because of pollution of interstate or navigable waters and the action of federal, state, or local authorities.

By the Clean Water Restoration Act of 1966, federal enforcement authority was extended to international pollution when the Secretary of State requests the Secretary of the Interior to initiate an action. The regular conference and public hearing technique also is retained in such a case. To date, this new authority has not been applied to pollution involving boundary waters or rivers which the United States shares with Mexico and Canada, but the existence of such pollution situations involving international waters persuaded Congress to provide for it.

As laid down by the Federal Water Pollution Control Act, the enforcement authority covers interstate or navigable waters where pollution causes damage to the health or welfare of any persons. According to the *Appalachian Coal* case and similar decisions, a stream is considered navigable when it either is navigable in fact or has once been navigable or by the reasonable expenditure of funds can be made navigable. Being navigable means carrying some kind of commercial traffic.

Where pollution emanating from sources in one state endangers the health or welfare of persons in another state, initiation of the enforcement process is mandatory upon the request of a state governor, or an official state water pollution control agency, or a municipality in whose request the governor and state agency concur. It is similarly mandatory in intrastate pollution situations upon the request of the governor of the state concerned, when the effect of such pollution on the legitimate uses of waters is judged sufficient by the Secretary of the Interior to warrant federal action. The exercise of federal jurisdiction to abate interstate pollution without state request is required when the Secretary of the Interior believes on the basis of reports, surveys, or studies that such interstate pollution is occurring.

The enforcement procedures give ample opportunity for cooperative federal-state action. The procedures specified to be taken are (1) a conference, (2) a public hearing, and (3) court action. Each successive step is taken only if the preceding step is unsuccessful in securing compliance.

A. Conference

The initial stage of the enforcement process brings together the federal government and the state and interstate water pollution control agencies concerned. An enforcement conference operates informally and is not an adversary, courtroom proceeding. There are no defendants and no prosecution, although in a few instances the non-federal conferees have conceived of themselves in such a relationship. No strict rules of evidence are applied, and all statements offered are accepted as relevant. The conference inquires into the occurrence of the pollution subject to federal abatement, the adequacy of the measures taken to abate it, and the delays, if any, that are being encountered. As the conferences are public, each of the conferees is permitted to bring as many people as he wishes to speak, and each conference continues as long as anyone has anything to contribute. There is a distinction between the conferees and other participants, of course, since under the statute the conferees alone must come to conclusions and recommendations. However, private citizens, representatives of conservation groups, managers of industrial plants, politicians, and professors attend these conferences and are heard.

After an opening by the chairman a conference normally begins with the presentation of a federal report on the condition of the waters in question and the requirements for their improvement. The strategy is to present a factual report, win agreement on the diagnosis of the situation, and let the recommendations for action follow unavoidably as the only means of correcting the situation. The federal report is offered first as a courtesy to the state representatives, giving them an opportunity for responding to it if they so desire. However, any other conferee may report first; the agenda is arranged in consultation with the state representatives. As each state makes its statement, the industries and towns within that state often make separate statements. In line with Congress' declared policy of respecting the primary rights and responsibilities of the states in pollution control, private industries and cities are dealt with only through the state agencies.

At the conclusion of all statements, the conference usually recesses for an "executive session" among the conferees for the purpose of working out an agreement. In our concern for openness in conducting these conferences, we have tried to dispense with these closed sessions whenever possible.

The entire purpose of the conference is to see how much progress can be made toward a free, mutual agreement on a program of corrective action, assuming a finding that the waters under discussion are polluted and that such pollution is subject to abatement under the Federal Water Pollution Control Act. However, in the absence of adequate scientific and technical data, the conferees may agree that further study is necessary before a schedule can be established.

The 1966 amendments added a new tool for acquiring information necessary to producing a remedial schedule. The new section provides that upon request of the majority of conferees in any enforcement conference (or during the next stage, the public hearing) the Secretary may ask an alleged polluter to file with him a report on the kind and quality of discharges he is putting into a river or other body of water.

It has been impressively experienced that it is possible for the conferees to arrive at unanimous conclusions and recommendations to place before the public, the press, and the Secretary of the Interior for approval.

After the conference, the Secretary issues formal recommendations for pollution abatement which are usually identical to the recommendations of the conferees. If the conferees have reached no agreement, the Secretary must issue his own recommendations. Upon establishment of a remedial schedule, the states are encouraged to obtain compliance under their own authorities and are allowed at least 6 months to take the necessary actions.

At the enforcement conference, the public is the chief ally. Progress in pollution control depends almost entirely on the formation of community understanding of the problem and support for strong and vigorous action. Experience has demonstrated the importance of elucidating the future as well as the immediate consequences of water pollution; the urgency of the problem and the disastrous effects of procrastination; the widespread implications of water pollution, not only for commercial fishermen, conservationists, and other special interest groups but for the entire public and the entire economy of a region. Above all, it is important to project the water pollution problem on a canvas of future population growth and economic expansion.

Once these points are made clearly to a broad audience, half the battle is won. The best weapon against resistance to the requirements of pollution abatement is a widespread public knowledge of the problem and the efforts being made to combat pollution. Few industries want to incur a reputation of disregard for a community's water resources, particularly those which market directly their own finished product as compared to those which manufacture an intermediate product which is then turned into a finished product elsewhere. Few cities can refuse to provide adequate sewage treatment if their citizens really understand the penalties of water pollution, and are willing to vote the necessary funds to take care of remedial facilities.

Since the conference step of the enforcement procedures is held to be the method of choice in securing compliance, in my opening statement as chairman of an enforcement conference, I frequently quote from a United States Supreme Court opinion of 1921. In a suit against the State of New Jersey by the State of New York, the Court at that time pointed out the unsuitability of court action for settling disputes involving large concentrations of population and industry, the solutions to which require complicated technical judgment, mutual concessions, and detailed plans of action. Even though the conference is only the first step, it is most frequently the only step necessary. Of the 43 enforcement actions to date, only four have gone to the hearing stage, and of these only one went to the final stage of court action. Cooperative action taken in agreement with state and local authorities is therefore a method likely to be more earnest, more effective, and easier and less expensive for all concerned than action enforced as a result of moving to the next step or beyond.

B. Public Hearing

When remedial action within the period allowed is not taken, the Act provides that a public hearing shall ensue. The alleged polluters are made direct participants before a hearing board of five or more persons appointed by the Secretary. Testimony is sworn and statements of witnesses are subject to cross-examination. The hearing board makes findings on the evidence presented and recommends to the Secretary the measures which must be taken to secure abatement. The board's findings and recommendations are sent by the Secretary to the polluters and to the state agencies, together with a notice specifying a reasonable time, which may not be less that 6 months, to secure the abatement of the pollution.

C. Court Action

The last stage may be requested by the Secretary to be brought by the Attorney General when remedial action is not taken by the polluters within the time specified in the notice. In an intrastate pollution matter, the written consent of the governor is necessary to proceed with the court action.

In the operation of the water quality standards, when they are adopted and acquire federal stature, enforcement successes will continue to be measured by the number of cases that do *not* require court action. The assumption that the vast majority of cases can be solved through negotiation shall remain as a guidepost. When state, federal, and local authorities combine with private organizations and industries to pool technical know-how, financial resources, and their commitment to restoring the waters of our country, the stage is usually set for meaningful effective action.

Industry's Role in Pollution Abatement*
Robert N. Rickles**

One of my learned friends tells me that I am a most fortunate individual because I am doing the Lord's work and being paid for it. To support this contention he quotes the following passage from the revised litany of a small English parish:

> From all destroyers of natural beauty in this parish
>   and everywhere;
> From all Polluters of earth, air and water;
> From all makers of visable abominations;
> From ferry builders, disfiguring advertisers,
>   road hogs and spreaders of litter;
> From the villanies of the rapacious and
>   incompetence of the stupid;
> From the carelessness of individuals and
>   somnolence of local authorities;
> From all foul smell, noises and sights—
>   GOOD LORD DELIVER US!

Unfortunately, the Lord will *not* deliver us; only a concerted effort by industry, science, technology, government, and people can deliver us.

Industry stands ready to do its part. This is *not* a new posture. Industrial participation in pollution abatement dates to the earliest days of concern about environmental health and control. Almost all of the important developments in control equipment and processes for solid, liquid, and air pollutant control were developed by industrial concerns or university-industry teams. Such developments as fluidized sludge burners, polyelectrolyte flocculants, high efficiency biologic aeration processes and sulfur from gas extraction processes are all recent developments in this vein. There continue to be, as Congressman Daddario's committee has so ably pointed out, many unsolved problems in the field of environmental control. Much research and development is still needed and only industry can prove the commercial orientation so vital to obtaining a proper balance between economic costs and social values. What possible interferences exist to the orderly solution of these problems by industrial development teams? Two major ones stand out to my mind.

A. The first is that the pollution abatement field has been, from an industrial point of view, stagnant and unprofitable. It is important to understand that pollution abatement, industrial and municipal, exists only by

---

*Rice University Studies, LIII, Special Number (Spring 1967), 11-14. Reprinted by permission.
**Mr. Rickles is Director of Pollution Abatement, Celanese Corporation.

government fiat. Government must encourage rather than discourage the use of new equipment, techniques, and processes. Government must encourage the growth of the industry and the development of new techniques by making the use of such techniques profitable. This can be done by proper use of government fiscal, tax, and regulatory authority. If these were the case, the need for massive government research and development efforts would be greatly lessened and the rapid development of commercially realistic solutions would ensue.

I had the honor of organizing a workshop on pollution control for the AIChE last week in New York and heard two excellent suggestions made by Mr. Benn Jesser of M. W. Kellogg which, if adopted, would greatly increase the amount of industrial research and development in the environmental field. I personally endorse both suggestions. The first is that all environmental control research and development performed by industrial concerns receive credit against profit before taxes to the extent of 20% of those profits similar to the investment credit presently available (7%) and those increases suggested by Senators Cooper (14%) and Smathers (20%).

The second suggestion centers around the establishment of an AEC-like independent agency run by a combine of major process and process engineering concerns to manage the government research and development program in the environmental sciences field. I propose that Congress authorize the President to establish such a commission to be called the Environmental Sciences Commission.

I would like to pass onto three other aspects of the industrial problem. In the future we shall see increased water reuse. In many areas of the country the available water supply is already stretched thin. By 1980, the forecast is for the problem to be widespread. At the same time, effluent requirements will be sufficiently high that industry will want to and have to reuse such effluents on a large scale. Industry should begin to conduct research into this possibility and its effect upon plant operations.

Related to water reuse is the problem of product recovery. In the case of many industrial plants much of the effluent pollutants are valuable food or other products. An examination of waste streams and the consideration of effluent costs should lead to effluent minimization through product recovery. The order of questions to consider when investigating a problem of contamination are:

1. Does the unit have to produce pollutants?
2. If so, is the process being used one which will minimize the pollution?
3. Is the pollutant valuable?
4. Can the pollutant be detoxified?
5. Can the pollutant be dispersed?

The design of new production facilities should also follow these principles.

Of even more significance is the impact of environmental control upon product lines. We have already seen the conversion of the detergent industry nationwide and the coatings and solvents industries in the Los Angeles and San Francisco Bay areas due to the impact of environmental control regulations. Others under pressure include the automobile, gasoline, fuel oil, coal, and gasoline additive industries. This impact will be considerably greater than the expense of control devices.

All of these impacts upon industry indicate that industry must take a deep and continuing interest in environmental matters on all levels and in all forms.

B. The second problem relates to policy with regard to federally sponsored research and development. The entire policy of the federal government in this area—most especially related to patent policy, the grant program (limited until the last Congress to nonprofit institutions), and the internalization of funds—has been directed towards the freezing out of industrial concerns. This in turn has resulted in a substantial amount of study unrelated to reality. We trust that the results of the hearings in the last Congress will be a change in this attitude.

Industry has a second role in pollution control, that of a polluter. For me to say industry does not pollute would be nonsense, for every human activity pollutes the environment. Nor will I hide behind the subterfuge of quoting the amount of money which industry has spent to solve the pollution problem. Many companies have made substantial efforts; clearly these are not enough. We will not dwell on the past because every facet of our society—industrial, municipal, and individual—contributed to the deterioration of our environment. Industry did not respond fully nor did any other part of society because the ground rules were different, the problem unrecognized, and the requirements unstated. The point is that industry has recognized the demands and requirements of today and is taking action. We have said that we will correct those deficiencies as measured by today's standards and most importantly we are doing so! We are expending time, effort, and money. The problems will not be solved overnight; even those well defined with obvious solutions require engineering and construction. Many problems are not defined nor are solutions available to all defined problems. But, we are committed to an action course. This involves careful evaluations of our existing plants, and their effluents and environments, and changes in processes and operational procedures. It involves site surveys, directives to process engineering concerns that industry wants processes and plants with lower emissions. It involves dislocations in feedstocks and product lines. Most of all, it involves people—the training of operating and management personnel to "think clean," and it involves a substantial increase in the academic world's output of trained environmental engineers and scientists.

Most important, we must convince the bulk of American people that the upgrading of the quality of our life is a significant national goal. After all, most of the ugliness in our lives is a result of individual desires or actions. No industry creates the demand for slapstick subdivisions. No industry is backing up the Colorado River into the Grand Canyon. No industry litters Yellowstone and Yosemite with garbage and turns some of our most beautiful scenic locations into mirror images of our dirty cities and suburbs.

In short—industry and technology are ready to take up the "Lord's work" but the American people must understand that it will require *their* time, effort, money, and devotion.

Toward an Effective and Credible Program for Water Pollution Control[*]
Leonard B. Dworsky[**]

While the public demand for water pollution control remains loud, the political response has become deafening. The responsible political leadership in both parties has avoided the temptation to engage in competitive promises. But those seeking instant solutions and those whose political response has been guided by the pressure of Earth Day have created an image about the pollution problem that is difficult for the public to understand. This is a serious matter and unless the problem is clarified and the achievements that are likely to take place during the next five to ten years are clearly explained, the American people will be disappointed and their faith in government and technology will continue to diminish. The addition of unneeded further strains on an overburdened society need not happen if we share with the public a realistic appraisal of what is possible during the 70's.

Progress has been made during the last fifteen years but it has been offset by the rising tide of public expectations. We must help the public to adjust their expectations to real world solutions; help public leaders to understand what is promisable; and work hard to help them deliver on the promises. A large part of water pollution is controllable now at an acceptable price. We can achieve control over water pollution in the not too distant future (1980+) to meet high public expectations, also at an acceptable price.

But water clean enough to meet current public expectations will not be achieved within the next five years. During the last half of the 1970's we should be able to count a number of specific gains if we make some needed changes in our approach to water pollution control. Gains can include, for example:

> The removal of gross pollution from all municipal and industrial waste outlets, resulting from the installation of secondary waste treatment facilities or its equivalent.
>
> Demonstrating the use of advanced waste treatment technologies in 15-20 percent of municipal waste systems.
>
> Demonstrating control of total pollution on a regional-systems basis in 20 percent of the Nation's 225 sub-basin areas.
>
> The gradual reduction of DDT and other hard pesticides, and of detergents to acceptable limits if strong measures are instituted to ban their use or provide non-polluting substitutes.
>
> A recognizable reduction in the rate of deterioration of inland water bodies like the Great Lakes.

[*]A paper presented at the Fifty-first Annual Meeting of the American Geophysical Union, Washington, D.C., April 22, 1970. Reprinted by permission.
[**]Mr. Dworsky is the Director of the Cornell University Water Resources and Marine Sciences Center.

Substantially increased effectiveness in managing waste heat from electric power and industrial sources.

Improvement in the control over oil exploration, production, transportation and use.

In order to achieve these and other gains, marked changes are needed in the national water pollution control program. The following ten points represent some of these needed changes. The subsequent discussion includes a recommendation supported by a brief background statement.

Federal Jurisdiction Over All Navigable Waters.

A National Sewage and Waste Treatment Policy.

The Allocation of Federal Financial Aid and the Determination of Project Priorities.

Regional Water Quality Management Programs.

Planning an Effective National Pollution Control Program.

Facilitating the Use of Advanced Waste Treatment Technology.

Improved Enforcement of Pollution Control Laws.

Consolidation of Water Supply and Waste Water Service Functions in Local Government.

Water Pollution and Public Health Research.

Technology Assessment.

Federal Jurisdiction Over All Navigable Waters.[1]

The Congress should enact legislation in 1970 to allow the Federal Government to enforce pollution control in all navigable waters of the United States, either in cooperation with the States or by itself.

Background

The Congress has delayed too long in assuming jurisdiction over all the navigable waters of the United States for pollution control purposes. For thirty-six years from 1912 to 1948 the Congress refused to change national policy and accept any responsibility for Federal enforcement of water pollution control (except for the Oil Pollution Act of 1924). The shift from total state enforcement was initiated in the Water Pollution Control Act of 1948. By amendments in 1956, 1961, 1965, 1966 and 1970 the Congress has very gradually assumed a greater share of pollution control authority.

It has taken twenty-two years to bring Federal enforcement authority to its present posture. During the same period State authority has improved substantially and the concurrent authority that now prevails has strengthened water pollution control enforcement considerably. It is clear, however, that the full force of government will be required to bring water pollution under control, and it is imperative that no further delay be countenanced in developing a strong State-Federal enforcement team to bring this about.

Federal enforcement authority over all the Nation's navigable waters was proposed by President Johnson in 1966. The Clean Water Restoration Act of 1966 (The Water Pollution Control Act amendments of 1966) as passed by the Congress did not include this additional authority. President Nixon is again proposing this action in the current amendments now being considered by the Congress. This proposal should be acted upon favorably without delay.

A National Sewage and Waste Treatment Policy.[2]

Congress should adopt a national sewage and waste treatment policy which would require, as a national minimum, the installation of secondary municipal sewage treatment facilities everywhere and comparable waste treatment by industry.

In adopting such a policy Congress would:

Allow exclusions as necessary for the achievement of water pollution control goals (e.g., added phosphate removal on the Great Lakes and in comparable situations; require other higher treatment requirements where needed; or by-pass conventional secondary treatment with new technologies which would produce equal or better results);

Establish a short range target of bringing gross pollution under control and which, upon completion, would provide an accomplishment benchmark for the American people;

Simplify the process of achieving a necessary advance in controlling gross pollution by adopting a relatively uncomplicated procedure; and reduce delaying tactics at the local and state level by recalcitrants;

Use the prestige of the Congress in enunciating a clear and unambiguous policy;

Eliminate to a large degree the great obstacle of competition among the states to protect its industries;

Bring to completion an action that is already well underway and which is an accepted policy in most states and by the Federal Government for municipal waste treatment.

Background

The waters of the United States contribute greatly to the economic and cultural strength of the nation. In earlier days rivers bound the Nation together as transportation routes. Later they were used to water vast acreages of land and to support industry, cities and produce power. Today, in addition to all these, we are respecting the Nation's waters more and more for their cultural and natural values. Water pollution contributes to the destruction of all these purposes and the Congress by virtue of its control over navigable waters must establish clear and unambiguous policies for protection against water pollution.

Most of the Nation's waterways are interstate in character and this fact has been one of the major obstacles to pollution control. During the 1920's, state health departments tried to reach agreement on pollution control requirements on waters flowing from one state to another but failed. Interstate compacts formed during the 1930's and 1940's were helpful but were not sufficient by themselves. A major purpose of the 1948 Federal Water Pollution Control Act was to overcome the obstacle of having the quality of the Nation's waters controlled by 48 independent state programs.

A principal thesis in designing the national pollution control program has been that each river basin is different hydrologically and economically, and in other ways from other river basins. Therefore, it was thought that the development of water quality criteria, standards, treatment requirements and related control matters should be designed separately for each basin or regional unit and for each city and industry in order to achieve the best economy. This has resulted in the development of a complex national system difficult to administer.

What progress the Nation has made in water pollution control has been by incremental steps and it will not be achieved instantly, notwithstanding the loud voices that have been raised by those who, having lately perceived the problem, seek to do so. In very broad terms, primary waste treatment was initiated on a substantial basis during the 1920's and the beginning of the 1930's. From the mid 1930's through the 1960's older and obsolete plants have been renovated and new plants have been constructed, aiming toward the goal of secondary waste treatment. Increasingly industry, too, has followed this general path of development.

During this thirty-five year period much progress was made during the public works programs of the 1930's (roughly, a six year period); essentially no progress was made during the next twelve years as a result of World War II and the Korean War; and small progress was made between 1952 and 1956.

Between 1956 and 1970 annual construction levels have increased from about $200 million to over $800 million. An important part of this increase must be discounted because of inflation and increases in construction and material costs. By 1970, however, about two-thirds of the population in urban communities and about two-thirds of the community sewer systems of the Nation have been provided with secondary waste treatment facilities.

Unfortunately, the progress that has been made by industry is not known. I believe it to be substantial but in the absence of reliable information about such progress and the extent of the industrial component of the water pollution program, there is no good way to evaluate this part of the national water pollution control program.

It is evident, therefore, that progress has been painfully slow. Even though a speedup in constructing municipal waste treatment works through higher appropriations is being attempted, continued delays in reaching agreement on water quality standards; court action and other enforcement time-tables, development of regional systems; inter-local and industry-municipal cooperation are likely to result.

Another difficult problem, and one which is at the heart of the delays in abating industrial pollution, is the fear on the part of every state that a strong effort to control industrial pollution will place its industries at a competitive disadvantage with industries in other states. The United States Advisory Commission on Intergovernmental Relations pointed out this obstacle in a 1962 report and this basic question has not yet been met head-on by the Congress.

The design of a control program based on a detailed consideration of the problems and characteristics of each watershed has been supported for many years by proponents of a go-slow program to abate industrial water pollution. However, in recent years, under the pressure of a growing public concern and more stringent State and Federal action industrial leaders increasingly are calling for a national standard to minimize the competitive advantage that a plant in one state may have over a comparable plant in another state. These leaders are attempting to meet the public demands for an effective pollution control program and their views should be given high priority.

The President has recognized this philosophy for the national Air Pollution Control Program and has called for comparable effluent control at all point sources contributing waste to the atmosphere.

A similar policy should be established immediately by the Congress for the national Water Pollution Control Program.

The Allocation of Federal Financial Aid and the Determination of Project Priorities.[3]

The Congress should extensively revise its construction grant allocation procedure. A recommended revised allocation would provide, considering the $800 million F.Y. 1970 appropriation:

An allocation of 25 percent ($200 million) by the Congress to the states on a formula basis for use by them on projects determined to be consistent with an effective comprehensive program;

Authorization to the Secretary of the Interior to expend about 37 percent ($300 million) for an attack on major water pollution problems in the Nation;

Authorization to the Secretary of the Interior to expend about 37 percent ($300 million) to be applied to regional clean-up programs;

In addition, the Congress should:

Direct that such funds are to support and encourage the use of advanced waste treatment technology;

Develop procedures to involve itself much more directly in the process of project selection, insure a greatly improved program of reporting by the Executive Branch (Federal Water Quality Administration) on project planning and project completion. Congress, through its Public Works Committees, has a long experience in this procedure. A comparable arrangement, carefully developed to avoid criticism over "log-rolling" tactics, should be established for water pollution control processes.

Background

The history of water pollution control in the United States is characterized by "piecemeal" control procedures. In very few, if any, places in the Nation can it be claimed that water pollution in a significant water body has been effectively controlled even though substantial investments have been made in pollution control facilities. An analogous situation would be the construction of only half dams on river systems by dam builders.

For twenty-two years (1948 to 1970) the Congress has supported in principle this system of piecemeal development of pollution control works and for fourteen years (1956 to 1970) appropriations have been spent under this system. In providing financial aid to communities to construct pollution control works the Congress established a formula under which the monies were allocated to the states. The formula has been based upon population (50 percent) and per capita income (50 percent). Monies allocated to the states are then further allocated by the states to projects within each state, the priority of projects determined by a procedure developed individually by each state.

In theory, the Congress established a requirement to insure that the funds expended would be used in a planned manner to achieve effective pollution control. Section 8 (b) (1) of the Federal Water Pollution Control Act provides "No grant shall be made for any project pursuant to this section unless such project shall have been approved by the appropriate state water pollution control agency or agencies and by the Secretary and unless such project is included in a comprehensive program developed pursuant to this Act." (Section 3 of the Federal Water Pollution Control Act relates to the development of comprehensive programs).

In practice the requirement of approving a project within a comprehensive program has never been effectively utilized even though resources in excess of $100 million have been spent in search of comprehensive programs since the inception of the Act. In addition state approval of projects have more usually been granted on the basis of when a project is ready to go to construction rather as part of a logical plan to bring pollution under control in a specific region in a specific time period.

It is time to redesign this system. It has not produced the results desired and the report of the Government Accounting Office, Congress's own watchdog over expenditures, has indicated this in a report to the Congress.

The basis for a redesigned system should be to (1) effectively reduce major water pollution problems in the nation; (2) reduce the public stress over water pollution as an environmental concern by showing that success over pollution can be achieved; (3) seek the clean up of total river or sub-basin systems in an effective way; and (4) to advance the acceptance of new waste treatment technology resulting from the Federal Research and Development program.

Congress and the Administration has proposed modest changes in practice. Special recognition is being given to the problem of the Great Lakes and H.R. 16029 proposes to grant to the Secretary of the Interior authority to allocate 20 percent of the construction grant authorizations to problem areas. These changes do not go far enough and the principles they reflect should be broadened to allow the Secretary of the Interior much greater flexibility.

**Regional Water Quality
Management Programs.**[4]

Congress should initiate a series of regional water quality management studies as demonstration projects.

Background

Many river systems, sub-river systems, large metropolitan areas, estuaries and the like can perhaps best be managed as a single entity to control pollution. Political boundaries and the difficulty of achieving cooperation among large numbers of governmental bodies have been major obstacles to the development of such management arrangements. In addition, such obstacles have kept us from applying our full knowledge in science, technology and management skills to control water pollution.

An initial step in developing this process is to move toward a new type of client-engineer (planning/construction agency) relationship that can provide for the development of a model regional water quality plan by a planning agency (public, private or a combination thereof) under the authority of an appropriate client that has or can assume responsibility for the entire region.

Laws presently available in New York, Ohio and Maryland (and in Ontario in Canada and proposed in Pennsylvania) provide for the State to act as a client for a region, and to employ a planning agency for the development of a regional plan. The Federal Government, under the usual planning authorization process employed by the Public Works Committees of the Congress, can also authorize a planning program for a selected region using a Federal construction agency in cooperation with the Federal Water Quality Administration. An analogous arrangement in part already has been initiated by the Congress under the North-east Water Supply Study through the Corps of Engineers. In addition, River Basin Commissions under the Water Resources Planning Act of 1965 or organizations like the Delaware River Basin Commission can be useful instruments for planning model regional water quality control agencies.

Five such demonstration programs might be authorized in various sections of the Nation during the first year, to be followed by others as experience dictates.

It must be understood that the development of a regional management plan for quality control does not by itself insure the acceptance or adoption of the plan. Appropriate negotiations will be required among the Federal Government, the affected states and the local communities concerned to reach agreement on the implementation of such a plan. Federal Government leverage can consist of the use of its construction grant funds, its technical assistance program and other powers, including enforcement. States and localities, too, will have certain leverages available for negotiation. Out of the experience of the first regional planning and development programs, appropriate devices will emerge to allow the Nation to improve its ability to establish regional water quality management schemes.

Planning an Effective National Pollution Control Program.[5]

The Congress should authorize the Secretary of the Interior to collect information concerned with industries' contribution to the national water pollution problem and data related thereto in order to effectively plan a national water pollution control program.

Background

Planning a national water pollution control program requires that information be available about the problem in such terms as sources of pollution, location, name, number, characteristics, amounts and effects. Reasonably good information is available about municiapl sewage and waste water contributions. Unfortunately, and nearly incredibly, in 1970 the national water pollution control program has no effective procedure to gather data on the industrial component of the national pollution problem. In the absence of such data, it is apparent that we do not now have or can we effectively plan for a well designed national program.

The fault does not lie with the Department of the Interior's Water Quality Administration. The operating program as well as its predecessor agency in the Public Health Service has sought, for nearly a decade, authority to establish a procedure to gather such data. The Congress and the Executive Office of the President has full knowledge about the problem. The case for action has been extensively explored by a Committee on Government Operations Subcommittee headed by Congressman Robert Jones (Alabama). A report by the Jones Subcommittee pointed out nearly two years ago that if effective voluntary action was not taken to gather such data, the Congress should enact necessary legislation. A voluntary program is not what is called for today and the time is overdue for the Congress to act on this matter.

Facilitating the Use of Advanced Waste Treatment Technology.

The Congress should purposefully facilitate as a very high priority program the early use of improved waste treatment technology by cities, industries and by State and Federal governments.

Background

The ultimate goal of water pollution control in the United States should be the separation of water from contaminants with the view of approaching natural water conditions. A previous discussion in this paper noted the incremental nature of progress to date in treating waste waters. We are, however, approaching the time when the goal of separation of water from contaminants becomes not only desirable but possible. This is due to the developments that have taken place during the past half-dozen years involving the development of new waste treatment technologies.

Up to about 1965 substantially less than one million dollars a year was available for application to improving waste treatment technology. (From 1948 to 1956 less than $300,000 a year was available for *all* water pollution research within the Federal program. From 1956 until 1965 increased amounts became available, largely for Federally supported extramural research and demonstrations. Congress, in the Water Quality Act of 1965, finally established a substantially improved Federal research program, part of which was aimed at seeking the development of new waste treatment technologies.

The objective of this program can be aided by:

Making it more advantageous for that part of American industry that produces or would like to produce waste treatment hardware to more fully participate in the advanced waste treatment research and development program. The experience of the Departments of Defense and Transportation and of NASA in hardware development might provide a guide about how this could be accomplished;

Arranging for the wide demonstration of advanced waste technologies through a planned program so that public officials can readily see and become familiar with new developments;

Marketing techniques used to induce the use of other types of public works equipment (e.g., earth moving equipment, trucks, refuse collection and snow removal equipment etc.) by public works and other local officials should be utilized to create early acceptance of improved waste treatment technologies;

The Secretary establishing appropriate requirements and the Congress special subsidies to promote the use of new waste treatment technologies. The program goal in this effort for the next five years should be to construct a pollution control plant that includes some form of advanced waste treatment technology at convenient intervals throughout the Nation as illustrations to citizens and officials of what can be achieved with the new technologies.

Improved Enforcement of Pollution Control Laws.

The Federal Water Quality Administration should establish a largely expanded national enforcement staff, taking advantage of young law school graduates trained in environmental law.

Background

The Enforcement Program under the Federal Water Pollution Control Act has been of great value. The chief enforcement officer of the Federal Water Quality Administration has shown great dedication and courage in carrying out his responsibilities under the Act. The program, however, has had a limited effectiveness, due partly to the limitations of professional staff and due partly to the limited way in which the Federal enforcement effort has been utilized.

An expanded Federal Staff should:

Support the chief enforcement officer through continuous day in and day out efforts in the several regional offices of the Water Quality Administration;

Provide technical assistance to State pollution control enforcement authorities including the loan of trained legal personnel; provision of training of state legal personnel; the provision of specialized legal services; and other related aid;

Develop an effective enforcement program comprising a Federal-State enforcement team that will work in conjunction with scientific and technical personnel to bring about the early abatement of pollution through legal procedures.

The President and the Congress should assign great weight to the enforcement aspects of the national program to make most productive the relatively large amounts of Federal monies scheduled for the pollution control effort.

Consolidation of Water Supply and Waste Water Service Functions in Local Government.

The water supply and waste water utility services of local government should undergo a program of consolidation and reorientation.

Background

There are approximately 35,000 local water and waste water organizations in local government in the United States. In many places, primarily where a number of communities exist side by side, such organizations should be consolidated and their services reoriented to operate an essentially self-sufficient utility service comparable to the private electric, gas and telephone utility services.

State government should play a major role in this effort by:

Establishing a state regulatory agency (or strengthening an existing agency) whose responsibilities would include (1) the establishment of appropriate water and waste water service areas without regard to political boundaries; (2) the review and ultimate control over a rate structure that would provide for the maintenance of service to meet public needs, established standards of quality and other objectives including that of meeting future growth sufficiently in advance of needs.

Obligating such utility services to be legally liable to provide the services and to meet the objectives for which they are established.

The Federal Government should explore the way in which it can best contribute to these ends.

Water Pollution and Public Health Research.[6]

The National Institute of Environmental Health Sciences, Department of Health, Education and Welfare, should be given a specific and strong mandate by the Congress to bring about a better understanding of the relationship between water pollution and public health.

Specifically, the National Institute of Environmental Health Sciences should:

Determine the short and long term hazards to health of the contaminants now introduced into the Nation's water resources by society (e.g., industry, cities, agriculture); and

Play a major role in the assessment of new or exotic formulations from industrial research or operations that find or may find their way into the environment.

Background

The mission of the Institute is to concern itself with fundamental bio-medical research on the health effects of a wide range of constituents in the environment of man. The National Institute of Environmental Health Sciences is particularly concerned with the deleterious effects on health resulting from long-term exposures to low levels of chemical, physical, and biological substances, alone or in combination, in the environment.

The Institute is primarily related to the health effects of environmental agents upon man and is detached from immediate responsibility for the effect of man on the environment, interrelated as these often are. It has been freed from the immediate burden of regulation and control although it is held responsible for supplying the underlying knowledge required to make control possible and regulation realistic and defensible.

Among the regulatory agencies which will be the users of this underlying information are the Environmental Health Services of the Department of Health,

Education and Welfare, Water Quality Administration of the Department of the Interior, and many other Federal departments including Labor, Transportation, Housing and Urban Development, Commerce, Agriculture and the Department of Defense.

Technology Assessment.[7]

The Congress should establish a program of technology assessment to insure, to the degree currently feasible, the minimization of consequences harmful to man, plants, animals and other natural bodies as a result of the introduction of materials, machines or practices by science, industry, technology or other activities of man.

Background

This is a problem that is receiving considerable attention by the Congress and by the Executive Branch. In relation to the national water pollution control program it is essential that a vigorous attempt be made to assess the consequences of man's actions on the water resource in order to eliminate problems such as those resulting from the use of DDT, detergents and mercury.

Unless a program of assessment is initiated it can be stated with a high degree of assurance that more situations having very grave consequences on man and the natural ecology of earth will occur. It can be accepted that a satisfactory and effective program will not be developed easily or soon to carry out such an assessment program. It is important, however, that a start be made immediately in order to provide an operating base and to initiate a program of improvement.

The Effluent Society

[1] Remarks of Secretary Abraham Ribicoff, U.S. Congress, Committee on Public Works, House, *Hearings on H.R. 4036*, 87th Cong., 1st Sess., 1961, p. 323.

[2] The President's Council on Recreation and Natural Beauty, *From Sea to Shining Sea* (Washington, D.C.: U.S. Government Printing Office, 1968), pp. 94-96.

[3] See the testimony of these organizations in U.S. Congress, House, Committee on Public Works, *Hearings on H.R. 4036*, 87th Cong., 1st Sess., 1961, and Senate, Committee on Public Works, *Hearings on S. 45, S. 120, S. 325, S. 571, S. 861, S. 1475, and H.R. 6441* 87th Cong., 1st Sess., 1961.

Regulatory Aspects of Federal Water Pollution Control

[1] Tennessee Coal, Iron & R. R. Co. v. Hamilton, 100 Ala. 252, 260, 14 So. 167, 170 (1893) (emphasis added).

**Toward an Effective and Credible Program
for Water Pollution Control**

[1] Hearings on the Clean Water Restoration Act of 1966; U.S. Senate. Subcommittee on Air and Water Pollution, Committee on Public Works, 89th Congress, 2nd Session.
President Johnson's message, "To Preserve America's Heritage," dated February 23, 1966. Public Papers of the President's: Lyndon B. Johnson, No. 82. "I recommend that the Secretary be given the right to initiate enforcement proceedings when pollution occurs in navigable waters, intra-state or interstate".
Clean Water Restoration Act of 1966; Conference Report (House Report No. 2289) on S 2947, A Bill to Amend the Federal Water Pollution Control Act; 89th Congress.

H.R. 16028 embodying the Administrations proposals for 1970 legislation, 91st Congress, 2nd Session, February 18, 1970.

[2]White House Conference on Natural Beauty, May 24-25, 1965, Washington, D. C.; Statement by Leonard B. Dworsky, on Panel, Water and Waterfronts. Pages 144-147.

[3]Hearings on S 418, Committee on Public Works, U.S. Senate, 80th Congress, 1st Session, April, May 1947, pages 19-24, which became the Federal Water Pollution Control Act of 1948.

In an exchange with Senators Chavez, McClelland and Cooper about how the construction loan (at that time) monies would be allocated, Senator Robert A. Taft noted that there was no provision for a formula allocation; that the Surgeon General "shall set forth the order and sequence and priority for individual projects in accordance with their estimated importance and value in the elimination or reduction of water pollution" and "that in a thing like this you would take one river at a time".

[4]Leonard B. Dworsky, *The Management of Earth-Water,* Cornell Alumni Convocation, Boston, Mass., March 1969, 10 pages.

Leonard B. Dworsky, *Goals and Perspectives in Water Resources Planning,* Given at the Water Resources Planning Conference, Boston, Mass., May 16-17, 1968, 25 pages.

[5]The Federal Water Pollution Control Act of 1956 (P.L. 84-660) establishing a water pollution control basic data collection program.

Public Health Service Publications 69, 82, 86, 87, 88, 92, 110, 111, 119, 136, 143, 150, 153, 160, 317, between 1952-1954 which *identified, located,* and *named* each of the 22,000 cities and industries contributing to water pollution at that time.

The Critical Need for a National Inventory of Industrial Waste. 30th report by the Committee on Government Operations. Subcommittee on Natural Resources. Congressman Robert Jones of Alabama, June 24, 1968, H.R. 1579, 90th Congress, 2nd Session.

[6]*Report on a Research Program for the National Institute of Environmental Health Sciences.* Department of Health, Education and Welfare. National Institute of Environmental Health Sciences Task Force on Research Planning in Environmental Health Science.

[7]Hearings on Technology Assessment: Subcommittee on Science, Research and Development; Committee on Science and Astronautics; U.S. House of Representatives, 91st Congress, 1st Session, November 18, 1969.

Also see reference to technology assessment in (6) above.

See in addition

Leonard B. Dworsky, "Analysis of Federal Water Pollution Control Legislation, 1948-1966," *Journal American Water Works Association,* LIX, No. 6 (June, 1967).

Leonard B. Dworsky, *Documentary History of Conservation-Water and Air Pollution in the United States* (New York: Chelsea House, 1971), 900 pp.

4

The Garbage in the Sky

Thank God, men cannot as yet fly,
and lay waste the sky as well as the earth!

Henry David Thoreau

I will build a motor car for the great multitude ... so low in price
that no man ... will be unable to own one—and enjoy with his
family the blessing of hours of pleasure in God's great open spaces.

Henry Ford

There is only a fixed amount of air surrounding the earth. The supply is not infinite. We cannot expect to dump garbage in the sky indefinitely and hope that the wind will blow it away. The canopy of atmosphere is about 10 miles high over the tropics and about six miles high over the temperate zone. Most of the atmosphere we use is in the first two thousand feet. That's all there is.

The Atmosphere

The atmosphere is made up of roughly 80 percent nitrogen and 20 percent oxygen, with small amounts of other gases, water vapor, and man-made pollutants. Air, like water, does not respect political boundaries, so pollutants generated in one political jurisdiction may affect other areas. There are, of course, prevailing patterns of air movement, but the routes and speed of change in both velocity and direction are not as definite and predictable as they are in the case of water movements. The Mississippi River, for example, flows to the Gulf in a well defined channel and with a predictable volume and rate of flow. Air movements are not that predictable.

Air Pollutants

Air pollutants are mainly the result of burning—either in internal combustion engines or in "external" fires such as incinerators, heating plants, power plants, and various industrial mills, foundries and refineries. Cars, trucks, and buses produce about 90 million tons of pollutants each year and account for roughly 60 percent of the air pollution in the nation. The remainder is produced mainly by stationary sources. The major industrial air polluters are petroleum refineries, smelters, and iron foundries. Power plants are second (most electric power is produced by burning coal or oil), and heating buildings is third. Incineration of solid wastes ranks fourth in production of emissions from stationary sources.

Air pollutants fall into two general categories: particulates (ashes, soot, lead) and gases (sulphur dioxide, hydro-carbons, carbon monoxide). Ordinarily when we see air pollution we see particulates. More dangerous are the less visible gases.

Sulphur dioxide is a product of burning coal or oil which contains sulphur. Some 30 million tons are dumped into the air annually. When sulphur dioxide is combined with water it can form sulphuric acid. Coal and oil power plants are responsible for about half of the total sulphur oxide emissions. In 1965 Consolidated Edison alone burned 10 billion pounds of coal and 800 million gallons of fuel oil within the city limits of New York.

Hydrocarbons, as the name suggests, are compounds of hydrogen and carbon. Smog is caused by the interaction of hydrocarbons with nitrogen dioxide and the sun's rays. One product of this process is ozone, which can cause eye irritations and respiratory difficulties.

Carbon monoxide, produced mainly by gasoline combustion, is a toxic gas that cannot be seen or smelled. In small amounts this invisible killer will cause headaches, reduce perception and coordination, and presumably cause auto accidents. In larger amounts it has become a popular method of suicide. Los Angeles cars emit 20 million pounds of carbon monoxide every day.

In the major air pollution disasters of this century (the Meuse Valley of Belgium in 1930; Donora, Pennsylvania in 1948; and London in 1952), sulphur dioxide was the major cause of illness and death. More difficult to isolate and evaluate are the low level, long term effects of more or less continuous exposure to various pollutants. It is known, however, that emphysema is the fastest growing cause of death in the United States. The death rate from emphysema and bronchitis is nine times higher than it was 20 years ago. The incidence of lung cancer is about twice as high in cities as it is in the country. These trends do not constitute proof of the health hazards of air pollution, but if we wait for conclusive proof we may needlessly sacrifice many lives.

Solid Wastes, Air and Water Pollution

Air pollution, water pollution, and solid waste disposal are closely related. Within limits these methods of handling wastes are interchangeable. Solid wastes (garbage, paper, containers) can be ground up and dumped in the sewage system (increasing water pollution), or they can be incinerated (increasing air pollution). To most of us the disposal of solid wastes simply means that occasionally we see or hear a garbage truck. But the problem of what to do with the mountains of trash produced by our high consuming society is rapidly approaching crisis proportions in all large cities.

Governmental Action in Pollution Control

For many years air pollution was considered to be purely a local problem confined mainly to cities like Los Angeles, Pittsburg, or New York. By 1972, however, every city over 50,000 (and many smaller towns) had air pollution problems of varying intensity. Furthermore, pollutants from one locality frequently degraded the atmosphere of adjacent areas. Lastly, it finally came to be recognized that the imposition of strict control measures in one locality could place that city at a comparative economic disadvantage with other areas. In recognition of these factors, the Federal government eventually was forced to become involved in pollution control measures. Here we should notice that air pollution is more visible to more people than any other kind of environmental problem. Not only is it highly visible, but its causes are easy to understand. Therefore it became "public enemy number one" among the voters in urban areas where most of the population is concentrated.

The first Federal involvement occurred with the passage of a bill in 1955 (P.L. 84-159) which authorized a modest five million dollars a year for research on air pollution. The Clean Air Act of 1963 (P.L. 88-206) increased air pollution funding authorizations and provided legal remedies for governments at various levels. In 1965 a second section was added to the Clean Air Act directing the Secretary of Health, Education, and Welfare to formulate emission standards for motor vehicles. The first set of standards applied to new cars, beginning with the 1968 models. The Air Quality Act of 1967 (P.L. 90-148) strengthened previous control legislation. Among other things it authorized the Secretary of Health, Education, and Welfare to establish air quality regions throughout the country and empowered him to enforce air quality standards in the control regions if the states failed to act.

An amendment to the Clean Air Act in 1969 (P.L. 91-137) extended for one year research funds totaling $45 million for studies on fuel combustion.

The Clean Air Amendments of 1970

On December 31, 1970 President Nixon signed the breakthrough Clean Air Amendments Act of 1970 (P.L. 91-604), calling it a cooperative effort of both political parties. Conspicuous by his absence at the signing ceremony, and presumably not invited, was Senator Edmund Muskie, principal architect of the bill and at that time a potential candidate for the Presidency in 1972.

The House of Representative had passed an air pollution control bill on June 10, and the Senate passed the so-called Muskie bill on September 22. A major difference between the two bills was that the Senate bill specified definite time deadlines for the reduction of hazardous auto emissions, but the House bill did not. The automobile manufacturing companies and the Nixon administration had pressed for a provision which would authorize the Administrator of the Environmental Protection Agency (EPA) to set time deadlines for conformance to emissions standards. In the Conference Committee the Senate version of deadlines by law prevailed, and the bill was reported out with those provisions substantially unchanged.

The most significant section of the Act required that 1975 model automobiles must reduce carbon monoxide and hydrocarbon emissions by 90 percent as compared with 1970 models, and that 1976 automobiles must reduce nitrogen oxide emissions by 90 percent as compared with 1971 models. Furthermore, emission control devices must be effective for five years or 50,000 miles, whichever occurred first. The only apparent exception to these requirements was that the EPA Administrator was authorized to extend the deadlines for one year.

Some other provisions of this long and complex Act were:

1. authorization of $300 million for research over a three-year period;
2. provision for assistance to states in establishing air pollution control programs;
3. provision for controls on emissions from new stationary sources of pollution;
4. authorization of new regulations for auto fuels and for aircraft fuels and engines;
5. authorization for citizen groups to bring suits in Federal courts against alleged violators or against government agencies, including the EPA.

As Senator Muskie said, it was "a tough bill."

Whether the deadlines set out in this "tough bill" can be enforced seems questionable—even with the one year extension. If the auto industry does not meet the prescribed standards by the specified deadlines, will the EPA close down the industry and all its subcontractors and suppliers? Or will Congress amend the Act to extend the deadlines or reduce the emission standards?

Efforts of State and Local Governments

California, Michigan, and Wisconsin had anti-pollution laws before the Federal government became involved in the problem, and some other states and a few cities with severe air pollution problems are generally ahead of the field in their control measures. Los Angeles has done more to reduce air pollutants than any other city, but obviously it has not solved the problem. Perhaps the best that one can say of Los Angeles is that it would have been a lot worse, perhaps intolerable, if effective control measures had not been put into effect.

Prospects for the Future

We may conclude that much has been done to reduce air pollution, but that much more needs to be done, or pollution will increase in the years ahead. This is so because the number of mills, factories, and electric power plants is expected to continue to increase. Americans are expected, for example, to triple their use of electricity within the next 20 years. So even if anti-pollutant devices can cut emissions per unit in half, we will still have more pollution from power plants than we have now.

More efficient anti-smog devices on automobiles are not likely to substantially reduce total auto pollution. Such devices become less effective as cars become older, and—most important—the number of cars on the road is expected to continue to increase. In 1969 there were three million more registered motor vehicles than in 1968—and the rate of increase is expected to accelerate.

* * *

The first article in this chapter, "Why the Birds Cough" by William Steif, examines the pollution problems caused by automobiles. Next is an essay by Charles Zurhorst, "Who Pollutes the Air," which attempts to fix responsibility for the continuing degradation of the atmosphere. In the third article Charles F. Luce, Chairman of the Board of Consolidated Edison Company (probably the largest single air polluter in the world), speaks of "Utility Responsibility for Protection of the Environment." Finally, in "The Politics of Air Pollution," Gladwin Hill considers the problems inherent in governmental efforts to combat pollution.

Why the Birds Cough*
William Steif**

On the hot, muggy evening of August 28 last year, 30,000 people, mostly young, crowded onto the Boston Common, the big center city park, to hear a rock group named the Chamber Brothers. Many came in automobiles, which they parked beneath the Common in a three-tier, 1,500-car municipal garage built a few years ago.

In all, 1,300 cars were in the garage when the show was over. Much of the audience descended into the garage and, almost simultaneously, drivers turned on their motors and headed for the three toll-booth exists.

Within minutes youngsters began staggering out of the garage on foot, gasping and choking. Others passed out in their cars. Police carried at least twenty unconscious persons out of the garage. Ambulances took twenty-five persons to two hospitals, while oxygen was given to many other young people on the grounds of the Common. Fortunately, a quick-witted city official saw what was happening and ordered the toll-takers to stop taking tolls so that the garage could be cleared swiftly. Everyone recovered soon and went home. Twenty-four hours later the incident was nearly forgotten.

Yet the near-disaster at the Boston Common is an index to how air pollution from the auto has created a crisis in the nation.

There are other indices, some almost unnoticed.

Los Angeles—"where the birds cough"—is notorious for its auto-produced

---

*The Progressive, April 1970, pp. 47-54. Reprinted by permission.
**William Steif is a Washington staff writer for the Scripps-Howard News Alliance who specializes in coverage of environmental problems.

smog. Indeed, wealthy Angelenos used to drive down to Palm Springs, a desert resort 110 miles away, to escape the Los Angeles smog. But last summer, for the first time, long fingers of tear-producing, yellow-gray smog appeared over Palm Springs.

Or consider the experience of the twenty-two men working the toll booths at either end of the Brooklyn Battery Tunnel—all but one in their twenties and thirties. More than half were found to have dizzy spells from a higher-than average concentration of carbon monoxide in their lungs. Over the one-month period in which the twenty-two were studied, five of the men had blackouts.

The death rate from bronchitis and emphysema in the United States today is nine times as high as it was twenty years ago. At the present rate of increase, 180,000 Americans will die of these lung ailments in 1983.

The extent to which the nation's automobiles can be blamed for its polluted air has been known for years, but only in recent months have American political leaders, from President Nixon on down, been willing to listen to their scientific advisers and point the finger directly at the manufacturers in Detroit. In his State of the Union message at the end of January, the President said: "The automobile is our worst polluter of the air. Adequate control requires further advances in engine design and fuel composition. We shall intensify our research, set increasingly strict standards, and strengthen enforcement procedures—and we shall do it now."

Senator Edmund S. Muskie, Maine Democrat, welcomed this "rhetoric of concern" and promptly offered a detailed $975 million air pollution program which he hoped Mr. Nixon would support. Another leading environmentalist, Senator Gaylord Nelson, Wisconsin Democrat, went even further and suggested that the auto's internal combustion engine should be phased out starting this year unless the auto manufacturers develop pollution-free exhausts. The Democratic leadership in both House and Senate challenged the President to increase funding greatly for clean air programs.

In California, which pioneered in smog control legislation, and in some other states, politicians are vying with one another to produce tougher proposals aimed at the internal combustion engine. And in mid-February, as part of a thirty-seven-point program to rescue the environment, President Nixon issued strict new regulations for auto exhausts in the mid-1970s, proposed encouraging development of a "virtually pollution-free" car by spending $9 million a year on research, and asked for power to phase out the lead in gasoline.

The implications of the increasing clamor have not been lost on Detroit, where a $100 billion-a-year business is at stake.

Henry Ford II, chairman of the Ford Motor Company, in December called environmental pollution "by far the most important problem" facing the auto industry in the 1970s and pledged $31 million for vehicle pollution control in 1970. Only a few weeks later, General Motors President Edward N. Cole told the Society of Automotive Engineers' convention in Detroit that an essentially pollution-free auto could be built by 1980, and added: "We must be highly aggressive in taking action and, equally important, in getting credit for our accomplishments." GM, Ford, and Chrysler each put on major anti-pollution displays for the automotive engineers.

The companies' top executives, who a few years ago scoffed publicly at California's problems (with such wisecracks as, "What Los Angeles needs is filter-tipped people"), are quite circumspect today. GM's Cole even was willing to kick an old ally, the oil business, so as to make the point that lead in gasoline is dangerous and should be removed. Once President Nixon had spoken out against leaded gasoline, GM (followed closely by Ford) swiftly passed the word that it was redesigning the engines on most of its 1971 models so that they would operate on lead-free gasoline.

To understand why Detroit is on the defensive, it is necessary to understand the automobile's role in polluting the air.

The air is ambient—that is, all encompassing. It forms an envelope around the earth to a height of nineteen or twenty miles. Four-fifths of it is in the first seven miles above earth. Man used to consider the air infinite, but it actually is finite, amounting to between five and six quadrillion tons. That amount would seem to suffice for eternity, but many scientists now worry that we are expelling so many poisons into the air so quickly that we are in danger of changing its nature—in which case, "filter-tipped people" may become a necessity.

The draft of a national emissions standards study made for Congress by the National Air Pollution Control Administration (NAPCA) last year said:

"It has been suggested by eminent scientists that the net increase of pollutants such as particulate matter and carbon dioxide in the atmosphere since the beginning of the industrial revolution has affected the weather. Since 1860, fossil fuel burning has increased the atmospheric content of carbon dioxide about fourteen percent.

"Some scientists fear that increases in carbon dioxide will prevent the earth's heat from escaping into space, melt the polar ice caps, raise oceans as much as 400 feet, and drown many cities. Other scientists predict a cooler earth as the sunlight is blocked by increases in particulates. The results could be more rain and hail and even a possible decrease in the food supply."

Almost four-fifths of the air is nitrogen, almost one-fifth oxygen, the rest other gases and water vapor.

About thirty per cent of the oxygen inhaled by a person goes to the brain. Without it, the brain is fatally damaged within six minutes. The highly specialized tissue of human lungs—an evolution of millions of years—acts as a one-way screen, holding back the blood on one side but permitting the air's oxygen to make its way to the blood, where millions of red cells transport it to other body tissues and exchange the fresh oxygen for carbon dioxide, a waste which is conveyed back to the lungs and exhaled.

Almost everyone knows not to shut his garage doors when his auto's motor is running, but not many people know why.

The reason is that the auto's internal combustion engine emits great quantities of carbon monoxide, a poison which has an affinity for the blood's hemogloblin—the red cells transporting oxygen—about 210 times greater than oxygen. Thus, relatively small concentrations of carbon monoxide can deprive vital body functions of an oxygen supply. The result, as recent studies have confirmed, can be headaches, loss of visual acuity, decreased muscular coordination, loss of energy, blackouts, damage to the central nervous system, and reduced chance of survival from heart attacks.

Fresh air contains less than one-tenth of one part carbon monoxide for each million parts of air. The air in large American cities contains 100 times that amount of carbon monoxide. The bulk of it comes from the internal combustion engines of automobiles.

The best estimates available are that the United States puts about 188.8

million tons of pollutants into the air yearly. The "big five" in pollutants are:

CARBON MONOXIDE, tasteless, colorless, odorless, and lethal. About ninety-four million tons a year go into U.S. air, three-quarters of that from motor vehicles.

SULFUR OXIDES, which in combination with the moist membranes of the lungs form sulfuric acid, a poison. Some 30.4 million tons are expelled into the air yearly, two-thirds from burning coal.

HYDROCARBONS, organic compounds which are vital to the photo-chemical process by which smog is produced. Some 25.9 million tons go into the air annually, more than half from motor vehicles.

PARTICULATES, tiny bits of matter which become deadly irritants when combined with other pollutants. Some 21.5 million tons go into U.S. air, mostly from smokestacks.

NITROGEN OXIDES, another vital ingredient of smog. About seventeen million tons are expelled into the air each year, slightly less than half from vehicles.

Obviously, automobiles are the chief villains when it comes to carbon monoxide, hydrocarbons, and nitrogen oxides, though they are not wholly blameless in the other two categories. (For instance, autos spew out 200,000 tons of lead particulates annually, as a result of the almost universal practice of selling leaded gasolines to reduce engine knock.)

Even relatively low concentrations of carbon monoxide affect drivers, and peak-hour traffic jams in Los Angeles and Detroit have built up concentrations as high as 150 parts per million or even higher.

Hydrocarbons, on the other hand, seem to have little direct effect on health by themselves. High concentrations of nitrogen oxides may produce lung damage, but this is still only a tentative conclusion.

What is not tentative is the effect of "marrying" hydrocarbons and nitrogen oxides in sunlight: A whole new family of secondary products called oxidants results—irritating eyes, ears, nose, throat, and respiratory system, reducing visibility, damaging plants and materials, impairing lung function in victims of emphysema, even interfering with athletic performance of teenagers. There is also growing suspicion that oxidants have carcinogenic effects.

In Los Angeles, the smog is so bad that doctors advise 10,000 persons a year to leave the area. Eighty per cent of all metropolitan Los Angeles's air pollution is caused by automobiles. The same is true of Washington, D.C., where the number of cars per square mile is one and a half times as great as in Los Angeles.

The internal combustion engine is responsible for the smog, the carbon monoxide, and Detroit's vast business enterprises. The trouble with the internal combustion engine is that it is so popular. In the United States alone, there are ninety million autos and fifteen million trucks and buses on the highways. All but a handful use the internal combustion engine.

The engine burns its fuel within itself. Its carburetor mixes air with gasoline. The mixture is forced into combustion chambers (cylinders), where sparks explode the mixture intermittently, driving pistons. The power produced is transmitted to the wheels.

The problem is the intermittent explosion of the fuel—a process in which the fuel is never completely burned. A briefing paper prepared last August for Dr. Lee DuBridge, head of the White House Office of Science and Technology, reported: "There is strong evidence that the use of Federal standards geared to controlling the internal combustion engine will not result in the drastic inroads on the problem needed to safeguard public health. At best, the effect of present Federal standards will be to postpone in time the upward growth of pollution levels rather than to reverse the trend. . . . These controls [are] far less than adequate to cope with a problem already well out of hand. . . . There is no guarantee that the degree of control that is possible with the internal combustion engine will be adequate. . . . The problem is already beyond reasonable bounds."

Despite such warnings, it appears that the Nixon Administration, under benevolent guidance from the auto makers, is still placing its bets on modification of the internal combustion engine and its fuel. This, at least, was the gist of testimony from Assistant Secretary of Health, Education and Welfare Creed Black to the Senate Commerce Committee last winter during a hearing on a bill introduced by Muskie and the two Democratic Senators from Washington, Warren G. Magnuson and Henry Jackson, to encourage development of a low-emission auto by permitting the Government to pay up to twenty-five per cent above normal prices if the auto proved pollution-free.

GM and Ford, with Chrysler and American Motors trailing far behind, seem to have convinced the White House, HEW, and NAPCA that the internal combustion engine can and should be salvaged. The companies are now willing to invest $80 million to $100 million a year in research, and they are now taking this research seriously.

The odd thing is that the industry has been on notice since the mid 1950s that it would have to do something. By that time Los Angeles County, plagued with smog since World War II, had forced the shutdown of 1.5 million backyard incinerators and, when that failed to clear up the smog, had prosecuted oil refineries, steel mills, and 40,000 other industrial offenders. Nothing worked, the smog got worse, and the automobile was pinpointed as the culprit.

In the late 1950s the auto industry fought California state legislation, but in 1960 the first state law finally passed, requiring only a few simple adjustments in the auto's crankcase. Gradually the state tightened up its requirements and by 1965 the industry could no longer hold off Federal legislation; the 1968 models were the first affected, and all that was required, again, was a fairly simple cutback on carbon monoxide and hydrocarbon emissions.

More stringent Federal controls have been placed on 1970 and 1971 models, and as a result carbon monoxide and hydrocarbon emissions in the 1971 models will be reduced about three quarters from the emissions of those two gases in the pre-1968 models. But the new standards laid down in mid-February 1969 for nitrogen oxides do not go into effect until the 1973 model year, though California—with its stricter controls—is demanding reductions in nitrogen oxides in the 1972 models.

Farther away, in the 1975 model year, the Nixon Administration is demanding its first reduction in emissions of particulates (to a third of the present emissions); further reduction in nitrogen oxides (to a seventh of the present emissions); further reduction in carbon monoxide (to less than half the present standard); and further reduction in hydrocarbons (to less than a quarter of the present standard). The Administration's goal reportedly call for another fifty per cent reduction of the 1975 emissions levels in all categories by 1980.

Achievement of those goals would solve the problem, but there is strong reason to doubt that the goals can be achieved with the internal combustion engine. So far, the chief anti-pollution improvements on the internal combustion engine have taken two forms: Injecting air into the still-hot mixture going out the exhaust system, thus creating more thorough combustion, or regulating the carburetor jet or nozzle that mixes gasoline with air more precisely, so that less fuel goes into the mixture.

The latter method is used on about eighty per cent of new American cars because the former method requires an air pump and is more expensive. Using these two methods—and including the 1971 model year—total air pollution from automobiles will diminish somewhat in the 1970s, but by 1980, NAPCA says, it will be on the increase again because of the growing number of autos on the highways.

The auto makers have dragged their feet for fifteen years. For example, Chrysler has done a considerable amount of research on a turbine engine but maintains a total commitment to internal combustion. One of the big companies developed a catalytic converter in 1964—a device which would go a long way toward more complete combustion of gasoline if gasoline were unleaded—but simply laid it on the shelf; no one wanted to upset a symbiotic relationship with the oil industry. As late as May 1968, Henry Ford II was telling a magazine interviewer that he preferred a cooperative "research and development" program with several oil companies in the fight against pollution.

As for tests with such non-polluting vehicles as the electric car, Ford said: "We have tremendous investments in facilities for engines, transmissions, and axles, and I can't see throwing these away just because the electric car doesn't emit fumes." And when asked what his company's greatest problem was, Ford replied, "That's easy, making more money."

Only eighteen months later, Ford's attitude seemed to have changed radically. What may have helped him along was the Federal anti-trust suit filed ten days before President Nixon took office. The suit accused four big auto companies of conspiring to retard development and use of devices to control auto-produced air pollution. Under a consent agreement, the auto makers—without admitting their guilt—said they would not obstruct development of anti-smog devices and would make available, without fees, licenses of anti-pollution inventions to firms desiring them.

Detroit's new sincerity is verbalized this way by Chrysler's research director, George J. Huebner, Jr.: "There are no holds barred [on the anti-pollution effort]. This is an all-out effort. Maybe people are waiting to see if we will fall on our face. But we are not going to. . . ."

To cut pollution Detroit can install catalytic converters, which it has ruled out because of the gasoline problem, or get a replacement for the internal combustion engine, which it refuses to do for economic reasons, or develop an exhaust manifold reactor, in which exhaust gases are mixed with air and "after-burned" in large, insulated, stainless steel manifolds at high temperatures. Such manifolds will require large amounts of fairly exotic metals, cost $200 to $300 (to be passed on to the car buyer), and require more maintenance than most drivers give their cars. But the afterburners also could represent a huge new market for the auto makers.

There are alternatives to afterburners on the internal combustion engine. One is to reform the engine by direct injection of the fuel into each cylinder, metering the gasoline precisely, eliminating the carburetor, increasing horsepower and economy—and reducing emissions. Volkswagen, Mercedes-Benz,

Porsche, and Alfa-Romeo already have begun to build their engines in Europe this way, and there are hints that American manufacturers are working on the same principle.

A more radical alternative is to do away with the internal combustion engine entirely. A number of experimenters and small companies are working to perfect an external combustion or "steam" engine; others are pushing hard to make a practical and economical electric car.

The external combustion engine converts fuel energy into thermal energy of a working fluid. The engine has the singular advantage of burning its fuel much more completely than the internal combustion engine (since the burning is continuous) under lower temperatures and pressures. The quantity of carbon monoxide and hydrocarbons emitted from the steam engine is about one-twentieth of the amount emitted from an uncontrolled internal combustion engine. Steam turbines produced so far have shown variable nitrogen oxide emission rates, but most engineers believe there is no inherent barrier to the development of turbines with low nitrogen oxide emissions.

The silent steam engine does not need as much horsepower as the internal combustion engine because it does not lose as much power. Technically it is further advanced than the electric-powered car. But the steam engine has its drawbacks, too. More expensive metals and more precise tooling (for a closed system) are needed. Some believe the external combustion engine is overweight and accelerates too slowly. But possibly the biggest drawback has nothing to do with the engine itself; it is simply that the auto makers, who have the expertise and large amounts of necessary capital needed to solve the steam engine's remaining problems, also have the greatest vested interest in perpetuating the internal combustion engine.

Nevertheless, the steam engine appears to be the best of the far-out candidates to replace the internal combustion engine, and companies in California, Massachusetts, and Nevada—the last headed by retired millionaire William Lear, who made the business jet a great success—have experimental models in various stages of testing.

Another alternative—even farther out, most experts think—is the electric engine.

Development of a practical battery is still highly problematical, but there is another difficulty: If the nation's automobiles converted to electricity on anything like the present scale of use, demand for power to charge the batteries would soar. That, in turn, would mean building many more coal and oil-fired utility plants—and these are among the worst American industrial polluters.

Both GM and Ford have experimented with, and are continuing to work with, electric engines, the only sure way of getting zero emissions of pollutants from autos. General Dynamics, Gulton Industries, Allis-Chalmers, and Westing-house have all done work in this specialty, and some smaller firms actually have marketed a few dozen electric cars. But no one is especially sanguine about ending air pollution with electric cars.

A final alternative that is beginning to look much more feasible is use of a different fuel in the internal combustion engine. Either compressed natural gas or liquefied petroleum gas can be burned easily in present motors with relatively simple and inexpensive ($200 to $300) modifications. Mileage is better; so is economy. But again, there are problems.

Though such fuels cut pollution greatly (because the fuels burn much more completely), they must be used under pressure. That means a sealed system which, if ruptured in a mere fender-bender accident, could leak, catch fire, or explode.

The vendors of natural gas and petroleum gas deny that their wares are any less safe than gasoline, and they may be right. The Federal General Services Administration is testing a dozen vehicles on natural gas in Los Angeles and several dozen more in Houston and Mississippi, and has had encouraging experiences so far. Petroleum gas has been used in the municipal fleet of Tampa, Florida, for several years and in Chicago's bus system for more than a decade with success. Indeed, more than 200,000 vehicles, mostly trucks and specialized vehicles such as fork-lifts, have operated for some years on petroleum gas.

But problems of supply and distribution make it likely that these two fuels will be confined to fleets of trucks, buses, taxis, and possibly short-run rental cars.

All of which puts the problem of our fouled ambient air on the Nixon Administration's back again. Within NAPCA only a couple of million dollars yearly have gone to research—most of the agency's $60 million-a-year budget has been spent for establishing a bureaucracy that could set up air quality standards for fifty-seven metropolitan areas and promulgate those standards. Within the Department of Transportation, less than $1 million a year has gone to research, mostly to run a couple of smog-free bus experiments.

GM says it has been spending about $45 million a year on anti-pollution research and development, and Ford has been spending $28 million.

The man most angry about the record is Senator Muskie, who pioneered the early Federal legislation. He believes the Nixon Administration's approach—setting goals for industry which seem fairly distant in time—is exactly wrong. He believes that the only way to achieve results is through "a steady tightening of standards, on a regular and frequent basis, until an emission-free vehicle comes off the assembly line." He predicts that the short-changing of research, both by the Federal executive branch and by industry, will haunt the nation in future years.

Oddly enough, the Republican Governor of California, Ronald Reagan, seems to agree with Muskie. But then, he has heard the birds cough.

Who Pollutes the Air*
Charles Zurhorst**

In the year 79 A.D., a Roman scholar named Pliny the Elder breathed in a fatal overdose of sulfur oxide fumes from erupting Mount Vesuvius and became the first recorded human victim of air pollution. However, it was not until shortly after the discovery of coal in the twelfth century in England that air pollution began to create a recognizable problem which, as serious as it was, thwarted all legal efforts, even then, to combat it.

Over the years and through the Industrial Revolution of the eighteenth and nineteenth centuries, the degree of hazard steadily increased until, on October 26, 1948, in the small, hilly town of Donora, Pennsylvania, man was served an unmistakable warning that he was poisoning his air beyond human endurance.

For four days a heavy smog of waste gases, coal smoke, zinc fumes, and sulfur fumes blanketed the town. Visibility became so bad that workers had trouble finding their way to their homes. Black grime settled on and in everything, including the lungs of the town's inhabitants, and Donora's doctors were besieged by coughing, wheezing, nauseous patients. Of the town's 14,000 residents, 5,910 became ill, and 20 died.

Next, Los Angeles developed a persistent smog that increased proportionately with its population growth. Then air pollution forcefully attacked Pittsburgh, Detroit, St. Louis, Chicago, Houston, Birmingham, Washington, and other concentrated population areas. Today, according to the U.S. Public Health Service, over seventy-three hundred communities in the United States are afflicted with serious air pollution problems.

"Unless gas masks are to become a habitual part of our dress," says an official publication of the Department of Health, Education, and Welfare, "we must breathe the air as it comes to us, polluted or not.

"For most of us, more often than not the air is polluted with a host of gases and particles which we pump into our lungs and swallow into our stomachs. Some pollutants sting our eyes and throats, and others affront our noses. Still others find their way into our bloodstream, where they travel up and down the body, working their toxic ways as they go.

"It is in our respiratory system, and particularly in our lungs, that we are most vulnerable to air pollution. Life depends on the steady supply of oxygen from the lungs to the blood, and the steady removal of carbon dioxide from the blood by the lungs.

"These gases are transferred through hundreds of tiny balloons whose skins are one-ten-thousandth of an inch thick. This delicate tissue, if spread flat, would cover a tennis court, and when we are born we have many more balloons than we need for breathing.

*Charles Zurhorst, The Conservation Fraud (New York: Cowles Book Company, Inc., 1970), pp. 45-53. Reprinted by permission.
**Mr. Zurhorst has been a free-lance writer for 18 years.

"But one of the cumulative effects of air pollution is the progressive destruction of these balloons, and as we grow older, we lose some of our lung reserve. Unfortunately for many of us, we are not aware of the loss until much of our reserve is gone. And the damage is irreparable."

Damage comes from many sources, both at the same time and at different times. Air pollution can differ from place to place, and from time to time in the same place.

Carbon monoxide, which produces headaches, loss of visual acuity, and decreased muscular coordination, is found in heavy automobile traffic areas and in varying amounts, dependent on both traffic and weather conditions.

Sulfur oxides, which contribute to the incidence of respiratory diseases and premature death, are found wherever coal or oil is burned as fuel.

Nitrogen oxides, which are responsible for most of the haze that blankets cities, and contribute to respiratory diseases, are formed by the combustion of all types of fuels.

Hydrocarbons, which have produced cancer in laboratory animals, are discharged chiefly by automobiles.

Photochemical smog, which causes eyes to smart and throats to sting, is a complex mixture of gases and particles manufactured by sunlight from a combination of nitrogen oxides and hydrocarbons.

But where smog is indicative of pollution, 85 percent of all air pollution is invisible. This is one of its most dangerous characteristics. The most dangerous, naturally, is its threat to human health.

In 1963, air pollution killed 400 residents of New York City, and, during Thanksgiving week of 1966, was blamed for a total of 168 deaths in that city.

An Egyptian stone obelisk, exposed to Manhattan's contaminated air, deteriorated more during eighty-six years in its location in Central Park than it had during the entire preceding thirty-five hundred years it had spent in Egypt.

A ten-year-old child who has spent his or her entire life in New York City will have suffered the effects of smoking half a pack of cigarettes a day—without ever having touched one.

Barbed wire, which usually lasts about twenty years in farm use, rots away in four when exposed to the contaminated air of an average American city.

Nor is such pollution limited to big cities. Air over the grasslands of western North Dakota has, on occasion, been found to be tainted with poisonous pollution.

In Yellowstone National Park, the particles that comprise smog have increased, over a five-year period, from one hundred per cubic centimeter of air to one thousand.

And never be fooled by believing that the inside of an air-conditioned home or office can offer more than scant protection. Pollution can come right through the filters.

This is the air that Americans inhale at the rate of fifteen thousand quarts per person per day. It contains filth, dirt, and poison gases. And, if it were subject to the nation's pure food and drug laws, it would be illegal to ship it from state to state because, the U.S. Public Health Service says, "It is unfit for human consumption."

Who is responsible for all this pollution? Many conservationists and politicians would have it believed that it is solely the result of uncontrolled emissions from the smokestacks of industrial manufacturers. This is far from the truth.

According to the U.S. Department of Health, Education, and Welfare, of the 142 million tons of pollutants being dumped into the nation's atmosphere each year, manufacturing accounts for but 23 million tons.

Electric power generation, space heating, and municipal refuse burning outdo this figure by 10 million tons, with a total of 33 million. The major culprit is the combined need and desire of the American people to be mobile.

Transportation is responsible for putting 86 million tons of pollutants each year into the nation's atmosphere and into the public's lungs. As the population grows, so will this figure.

And, while a federal law does rule that all new cars must be equipped with devices that reduce the exhaust of carbon monoxide, nitrogen oxides, and hydrocarbons, there is no requirement in this law that the efficiency of these devices be maintained. Possible benefits could well be shortlived, making this a typical ineffective control measure. The Department of Health, Education, and Welfare admits that "the current standards will only improve the situation in the short run."

It also should be noted that automobiles are not the only transportation form responsible for air pollution. Congressman Henry Reuss charges, "In a single day, aircraft using Washington National Airport deposit thirty-five tons of smoke particles and other pollutants over the national capital area." Any other city with an airport would suffer comparably to its air traffic.

And, according to the National Academy of Sciences, the coming age of supersonic jet transports could also be an age of global gloom—unless jet fuel can be altered in some way. A single particle of jet exhaust introduced into a stratospheric cloud can grow into smog at a rate comparable to a golf ball swelling to the size of the Empire State Building in thirty seconds.

So far, all the halfhearted efforts by federal, state, and local governments have failed even to check air pollution, much less reduce it. And, although the technological means of controlling most sources of contamination does exist, the amount of pollutants being dumped into the nation's atmosphere is currently rising at a rate of three million tons per year—by the U.S. Department of Health, Education, and Welfare's own figures.

Yet, in the face of this acknowledged but unpublicized fact, the federal government continues to sidestep the responsibility of control enforcement. The Air Quality Act of 1967, for instance, does little more than boost the spending of taxpayers' dollars provided for in the weak and cumbersome Clean Air Act of 1963.

Federal responsibility in the area of air pollution rests with the Department of Health, Education, and Welfare—although this responsibility is limited to "assuming leadership." In practice, HEW designates air quality control regions, develops and publishes air quality criteria, and prepares and publishes information on available control techniques. The various states then set their own air quality standards within each air quality control region and, theoretically, establish plans for implementation of these standards.

But with nature's winds making air an interstate commodity having no regard for political or established boundaries, standardization of all state and municipal criteria and enforcement would be necessary for even a potentially effective program. This is not about to happen.

In sixty-one American cities that do have air pollution control programs, twenty cities administer the program through their health departments, thirteen through separate agencies, eight through their building departments, nine through their safety departments, and eleven through a variety of other departments. Standardization of enforcement laws for all these cities would be virtually impossible to achieve, and the mere cooperation of these agencies with each other would be awkward.

In addition, before enforcement could be carried out there would have to be much internal municipal house-cleaning in practically all American cities and towns. Few, if any, local governments are as yet willing to undertake this task, as it would mean increased local taxes. The house-cleaning need is explained by the Department of Health, Education, and Welfare in its statement, "Town dumps and incinerators are the most obvious sources of air pollution."

In the entire United States, there are only three hundred municipal incinerators—and 75 percent of these are inadequate. And, of the twelve thousand "land disposal sites" (dumps), 94 percent have been criticized by the U.S. Public Health Service because they "represent disease potential, threat of pollution, and land blight."

It would be difficult for a mayor to condemn contamination discharged from an industrial process while staunchly defending the necessity for an open-burning municipal dump. And he might find it politically embarrassing to complain of a smoking public utility plant while protesting that funds were not available to make his city's incinerator operate efficiently.

Examining the records closely, it would seem difficult for the federal government to have any state or municipality take its pollution control recommendations seriously.

For the fiscal year 1970, Congress authorized $134.3 million for air pollution control programs. The Department of Health, Education, and Welfare said it needed only $95.8 million.

If progress were being made by HEW, this would be a noteworthy gesture. With no progress being made, it is difficult to decide how to react—other than that something is wrong somewhere.

The House Subcommittee on Conservation and Natural Resources learned that for thirteen years HEW had been spending taxpayers' dollars on sulfur oxides research, both without plan and without knowledge of similar research being done by other government agencies. It also learned that HEW's research efforts were concentrated on everything except the root of the problem— chemical treatment of coal to make it a usable, pollution-free fuel.

And, unfortunately, the U.S. Department of Health, Education, and Welfare was found to be contributing to air pollution by using inefficient incinerators. Other federal agencies that contribute to the problem through poor incineration, open burning, or use of low-grade fuel include: the Army, the Navy, the Air Force, the Corps of Engineers, the Atomic Energy Commission, the Department of Commerce, General Services Administration, the Department of the Interior, the Department of Justice, the National Aeronautics and Space Administration, the Post Office Department, the Smithsonian Institution, the Tennessee Valley Authority, the Department of Transportation, and the Veterans Administration.

Ron Linton, former chairman of an HEW task force, stated at a congressional hearing that "lack of interagency coordination is the program's most serious present deficiency."

Unfortunately, no federal installation, no factory, no automobile, no municipal incinerator is "an island." An atmospheric lid, caused by nature and called an inversion, can trap air close to ground level and spread it over wide areas.

On November 27, 1962, one such atmospheric lid spread polluted air over a twenty-two-state area inhabited by 87 million men, women, and children, causing untold illness and premature death. No single state was responsible. No single municipality could have prevented it—with any amount of federal funds.

As a result, until federal air pollution control action becomes realistic, and subsequently effective, no state, no city, no town, no farm can afford to be complacent about contamination of the atmosphere—particularly the following metropolitan areas, which are listed in order of the severity of their air pollution danger to the health of their residents.

New York, New York; Chicago, Illinois; Philadelphia, Pennsylvania; Los Angeles/Long Beach, California; Cleveland, Ohio; Pittsburgh, Pennsylvania; Boston, Massachusetts; Newark, New Jersey; Detroit, Michigan; St. Louis, Missouri; Gary/Hammond/East Chicago, Indiana; Akron, Ohio; Baltimore, Maryland; Indianapolis, Indiana; Wilmington, Delaware; Louisville, Kentucky; Jersey City, New Jersey; Washington, D.C.; Cincinnati, Ohio; Milwaukee, Wisconsin; Paterson/Clifton/Passaic, New Jersey; Canton, Ohio; Youngstown/Warren, Ohio; Toledo, Ohio; Kansas City, Missouri; Dayton, Ohio; Denver, Colorado; Bridgeport, Connecticut; Providence/Pawtucket, Rhode Island; Buffalo, New York; Birmingham, Alabama; Minneapolis/St. Paul, Minnesota; Hartford, Connecticut; Nashville, Tennessee; San Francisco/Oakland, California; Seattle, Washington; Lawrence/Haverhill, Massachusetts; New Haven, Connecticut; York, Pennsylvania; Springfield/Chicopee/Holyoke, Massachusetts; Allentown/Bethlehem/Easton, Pennsylvania; Worcester, Massachusetts; Houston, Texas; Chattanooga, Tennessee; Memphis, Tennessee; Columbus, Ohio; Richmond, Virginia; San Jose, California; Portland, Oregon; Syracuse, New York; Atlanta, Georgia; Grand Rapids, Michigan; Rochester, New York; Reading, Pennsylvania; Albany/Schenectady/Troy, New York; Lancaster, Pennsylvania; Dallas, Texas; Flint, Michigan; New Orleans, Louisiana; Fort Worth, Texas; San Diego, California; Utica/Rome, New York; Miami, Florida; Wichita, Kansas; High Point/Greensboro, North Carolina.

If you live in or near one of these metropolitan areas, your life literally is in danger. You are daily being poisoned through the apathy and political fears of the officials you elected to serve you.

Utility Responsibility for Protection
of the Environment*
Charles F. Luce**

About a year ago when I spoke as Under Secretary of the Department of the Interior, I observed that

> The electric industry in my judgment will be measured as much by its effect upon the quality of our environment as by its ability to provide economical and reliable energy. I am optimistic enough to believe that, whichever yardstick is applied, will measure up.

A year ago my viewpoint was that of an official in a federal department which has important legal responsibilities to protect the natural environment of America. Today I bring a somewhat different view-point to the problem of utility responsibility for protection of the environment, that of a chief executive of an electric utility which serves a large city. Happily, I don't have to eat last year's declaration of optimism. Working within the electric industry as I have for the past nine months, I find its leaders are keenly aware of their responsibility to build and operate facilities that, insofar as practicable, will protect and even improve the natural environment. I find, also, a growing awareness of responsibility to protect and improve not just the natural environment but the social and economic environment of the communities served by the utilities. This latter concern, in the end, may prove to be the more significant to our industry's—and our nation's—future.

The classic statement of public utility responsibility is that a public utility has the duty to provide adequate service to all applicants at reasonable prices and without discrimination. For public utilities which supply electric energy this is an enormous responsibility. Not only must the utility supply today's needs of its customers for electric energy, it must forecast what those needs will be decades into the future, and make investment commitments of large sums of capital based upon the forecasts. If construction costs or interest rates are high, the utility cannot wait for more favorable conditions before it makes these investment commitments. Nor, perforce, can any utility decide, as some industrial corporations have decided, to move its operation to another part of the country where investment opportunity seems better. A public utility is joined in perpetual wedlock, for better and for worse, to the community it serves.

As large as this traditional responsibility may be, today a new and even larger concept of utility responsibility is emerging. It is not a substitute for, but

---

*Arizona Law Review, X, No. 1 (Summer 1968), 68-73. Reprinted by permission.

**Mr. Luce is Chairman of the Board, Consolidated Edison Company of New York, Inc. This article is based on his remarks before the Federal Bar Association, Bureau of National Affairs Briefing Conference, Washington, D.C., March 15, 1968.

a logical extension of the traditional responsibility. It says that, as public utilities, we must not only provide good service to all upon just terms, but we must do so *with due regard for protecting—even improving—the environment.* And it extends not only to concern for the natural enviroment—clean air, pure water, the natural landscape, quietude—but also for the social and economic environment of the communities we serve. It has become very important to utilities whether Negroes and Puerto Ricans have decent jobs and housing and education and recreation. It has become important not just because it is morally right but because as public utilities we have an interest in the social and economic well-being of all the people we serve. They are our customers. If the social and economic vitality of our cities wanes, our investors, employees, and consumers are directly and adversely affected.

The new concept of public utility responsibility is not easily applied. For example, should a utility spend $140 million to put 25 miles of transmission lines underground when they can be placed overhead for $12 million? If so, who should pay the added costs: the people who live in the areas where the lines are to be buried and thus benefit directly? All the customers, through rates? Taxpayers? Which taxpayers: local, state or federal? Suppose a utility operates in a market with an adequate supply of skilled labor. Should it nevertheless expend money to train members of underprivileged groups to raise their levels of opportunity? Should ratepayers or taxpayers bear the cost of the training program? Should a utility spend $2 million extra to make a generating station better looking, and perhaps build a playground next door to it? How deeply should it get into public recreation? Is not its primary duty to provide plentiful low-cost energy?

There is a natural temptation, I think, to go overboard for protection of the environment. To be for natural beauty or social justice is like being for motherhood and the flag. But we must remember, as electric public utilities, that the basic job entrusted to us by society is the provision of plentiful, reliable, economic electric energy. We cannot perform that job without some impact on the environment. It is not our option to decline to serve new electric loads, which is the only way that we could altogether preserve what remains of the nation's natural environment. If we build a nuclear plant we will discharge unnatural heat into the waters or into the air. If we build a pumped storage project, we will create an unnatural reservoir in the hills. If we install jet engines in the cities to meet peak electric loads we will creat unnatural noise and air pollution.

But as electric utilities we are not alone in changing nature. Does a well designed electric transmission line damage the natural landscape any more than a bridge or a superhighway? Can society afford to place all transmission lines underground any more than to replace all bridges and superhighways with tunnels? Are the architectural achievements of man always and necessarily inferior to the natural landscape? These broad questions, I think, can be answered quite easily. But in particular cases, there are very hard questions which can be resolved only by exercising that elusive quality we call good judgment.

Engineers, who comprise most of the technical competence of a modern electric utility, are not specially trained to make this type of decision. Engineering discipline measures function, economy, strength, and safety—but not aesthetics or social utility. What disciplines, then, do train a utility executive to apply the new concept of public utility responsibility?

Surely, engineering is the starting point, and the teachings of economics and accounting also are important. But architects and doctors and chemists and ecologists must be consulted, too; and when utilities address themselves to social and community problems, they must consult educators, political scientists, sociologists and psychologists. There is another discipline I must not neglect to mention: the law. Perhaps the lawyer, who is trained to assemble and organize relevant facts, to apply logic, and to deal with contentious situations, is as well equipped as any professional man to grapple with the management decisions that face a modern utility executive.

I do not mean to suggest that courts, which are staffed by lawyers, will have an easy time enforcing the new concept of utility responsibility. In general, I doubt that its enforcement will lie in the courts, nor even primarily in administrative bodies. It involves daily questions of judgment and of taste that the principles of *stare decisis* and the procedural delays of due process are ill-equipped to deal with. But there is a tribunal in which the new concept will be enforced. It is, indeed, the ultimate judge of the worth of all economic and social institutions. I refer, of course, to public opinion. If our industry is to keep the public respect and esteem it has earned—upon which our privilege to serve the public ultimately rests—we have no choice but to apply a broad concept of public utility responsibility.

How to finance the new concept of utility responsibility is another hard question. Utilities are not eleemosynary institutions. All costs of service must be reflected in our rates, or charged to the Company's stockholders as corporate gifts. Investors are entitled to earn a fair return on the investment of their savings. If a particular utility does not offer investors a reasonable return, they will place their savings with another company which does. This is consideration that every utility manager, confronted by the tremendous need for new capital to finance expansion, is constantly aware of.

Thus far I have spoken only in general terms of the new concept of utility responsibility. Specifically, what does it mean? Let me illustrate, for a few minutes, by examples of how we are seeking to apply it in New York City and Westchester County. I hasten to say that we make no claims at the Edison Company to greater accomplishment in this area than many other electric utilities which serve large cities.

Looking first at concern for protecting the natural environment, the biggest concern in New York City is clean air. Consolidated Edison is by no means the worst air polluter. Motor vehicles, which emit more than 50 percent of the total load of air pollutants, must be awarded that dubious distinction. Incinerators of apartment houses, office buildings, industries, and the city itself put more than twice as much particulate matter into New York's air as the Edison Company. The furnaces of New York buildings which burn high sulfur residual oil put as much sulfur dioxide in the air as all of our plants. In 1967 our plants contributed less than half of the sulfur dioxide in New York City's air and about 15 percent of the particulates. Over-all, we were responsible for not more than 12 percent of the *total* air pollution in the city. But our customers, who daily see our tall, gaily painted smokestacks, quite naturally give us credit for causing a much bigger share of the problem.

Our ultimate goal is to eliminate every Con Edison smokestack in town, and to reduce to zero our contribution of air pollution. Our long-range solution to the problem is nuclear energy and, hopefully, pumped storage. By 1980 we expect to generate 75 percent of our electricity in nuclear plants, compared to only 4 percent today.

We also have shorter-range solutions to our part of New York City's air pollution problem. Soon we will have spent $150 million on air pollution control devices, including precipitators that remove 99 percent of the ash from the stacks of our coal burning plants. Since last November all the fuel oil we burn has contained only 1 percent sulfur, and starting next month all the coal we burn will have 1 percent or less sulfur. In 1968 we will reduce our stack emissions of sulfur dioxide and particulate matter by roughly one-third. We also are seeking a change in oil import regulations comparable to that in effect on the West Coast, which would enable us to buy, economically, oil with as little as 5/10ths, or even 3/10ths, of one percent sulfur content. We have offered to assist the City to build efficient, central incinerators which would burn refuse without air pollution, and produce by-product steam we would purchase to supply steam customers.

As we attempt to solve the air pollution problem through nuclear power plants, we must face up to another kind of pollution—thermal discharges—which may prove even harder and more expensive to control than air pollution. The most efficient nuclear plants discharge about two-thirds of their total energy as low grade heat. Even the most efficient coal-burning electric plants discharge about 50 percent of their energy in this manner. This waste heat must be dissipated either into the atmosphere by cooling towers, or into a natural body of cool water. Cooling towers are typically tall and ugly, and frequently emit a plume of steam. They are also expensive. If the waste heat is dissipated into a natural body of water, it may adversely affect the aquatic fish and plant life. The best solution would be to find a use for the waste heat, but since it is low grade this is not easy. The next best solution, we think, is to build the nuclear plants on large bodies of water capable of absorbing the heat discharge without damage to the ecology. In our case, tidewater locations are the best possibilities. All of the British commercial nuclear plants, I understand, have been located on tidewater.

By no means does the foregoing constitute a complete catalogue of the Edison Company's concerns for the natural environment. To improve the city's appearance, we are removing all of our old gas storage tanks, renovating the exteriors of generating stations, placing all distribution lines in new subdivisions underground. To make the city less noisy, we are procuring new and quieter equipment to break the city pavement, and installing transformers which produce a minimum hum. In suburban Westchester County, we have announced that we will not seek new rights of way for transmissions lines. After we have used existing rights of way to the maximum extent, additional high voltage lines will be placed underground.

Our concern for the social and economic environment of our service area thus far has been expressed mainly in employment policies. Thirty percent of our new employees last year were Negroes and Puerto Ricans. Some 12 percent of our total work force now come from these minority groups. About 10.5 percent of our skilled craftsmen come from these groups, as do 8.5 percent of our white collar employees. In cooperation with Local 1-2, Utility Workers of America, we have a new job training program for high school dropouts, and a new part-time employment program for high school juniors and seniors in danger of dropping out because of economic pressures. Both programs can lead to permanent employment with us.

In addition to these employment and training programs designed to get at the root cause of urban and racial problems, we participate in short-range programs designed to ease the more immediate pressures. We have developed a vacant lot near a generating plant into two baseball diamonds and a football field. This year, perhaps through the Urban Coalition, we will make a financial contribution to support summer programs devised by the City of New York. These include youth councils, play streets, sprinkler caps, street movies, bookmobiles, bus trips to out-lying recreation areas, and the like.

There is much more that we can do, and hope to do, to help solve our city's problems. I hope we can cooperate more closely with the public schools to make their vocational educational programs more effective. I hope, too, that we can take an active role in housing programs, especially the remodeling and upgrading of older housing within the city. I cannot forbear mentioning, either, another way in which we contribute to the city's social and economic betterment: we pay 8 percent of all the real estate taxes collected by New York City.

The title for these remarks limited me to *utility* responsibility for protecting the environment. In closing, however, I should point out that throughout the business community, of which electric utilities are only a part, there is being articulated a new sense of environmental responsibility. Business must, of course, not lose sight of the need for profits. They are the savings which, when reinvested, enable our economy to expand. The most efficient economies in the world, and those which distribute their benefits among the people most widely and equitably, are organized on the profit principle. But within the framework of this profit system there is unquestionably a quickening of concern for the impact of business decisions on the environment that can only augur well for the future of our land, and our form of society.

**The Politics of Air Pollution: Public
Interest and Pressure Groups***
Gladwin Hill**

Many people have expressed dismay that the problem of air pollution should have become "embroiled in politics." It could not be any other way.

Because it is a collective problem of society, air pollution has to be dealt with at the governmental level, and government and politics go hand and hand.

The alleviation of air pollution is, in the first instance, a political problem. The choking public turns automatically to its elected representatives for relief. It is only after corrective policies have been conceived in the political arena that such other major elements of the problem as scientific data, technology and economics generally can be tackled.

As a political problem, air pollution is extraordinarily difficult. The essential function of politics is to reconcile conflicting interests of groups of citizens. In

*Arizona Law Review, X, No. 1 (Summer 1968), 37-47. Reprinted by permission.
**Mr. Hill is Chief of the Los Angeles Bureau of the New York Times.

the simplest form, it's a matter of one specialized group (*e.g.,* steel manufacturers) versus another specialized group (such as steel importers). One degree more difficult, for the politician-mediators, is when the problem involves a special group (such as the cotton industry) vis-à-vis the public at large (cotton consumers). The ultimate degree of difficulty is when the conflicting groups are identical people, and government is forced into the psychiatric role of refereeing mass ambivalence. That is the extraordinary problem posed by air pollution.

Everybody wants clean air; it is virtually impossible to find anyone who will argue that dirty air is preferable. Yet when we inquire into who it is that is contaminating the air, it turns out to be the same "everybody"—people, with their trash burning, their factories, their power plants, their automobiles, their very breathing. If there were no people, there would be no air pollution problem.

The crux of the problem, at this juncture, is that while everybody wants cleaner air, people are not entirely ready to make the readjustments, social and economic, necessary to achieve the results they want.

Clean air, yes—but don't deprive me of my backyard incinerator. Clean air, yes—but don't ask me to pay more taxes to support a pollution control agency. Clean air, yes—but don't make the corporation I own stock in spend a lot of money on fume-suppressing equipment.

Those are the contradictions with which government and politics have to grapple, and which underlie the often inadequate and unsatisfying results of their efforts to date.

The typical case is City *C* in State *S,* which suddenly finds its atmosphere intolerable. (Federal experts say that any community with 50,000 or more people, and the average amount of industry, automobiles, waste disposal and spells of atmospheric torpor, is subject to disagreeable air.) The citizens of City *C* turn in desperation to the law—and find only the rudimentary "smoke ordinances" stemming literally from medieval times. These are inadequate because what they say in effect is that if an individual polluter upwind is afflicting you with noxious vapors, you can invoke the law on him. They don't apply to the situation where thousands of polluters' small contributions of fumes combine to create a nasty community-wide situation. If the local lawmakers try to draft a more comprehensive ordinance, they find themselves in a legal area that probably has been pre-empted by the state, in some such form as "health and safety" laws.

This brings the choking citizens of City *C* to the state legislature seeking relief—and smack into the arena of politics. The legislators, under sufficient pressure, schedule hearings. The public pressure groups, from labor unions to conservation associations, rally around and testify plaintively. The special-interest groups—those whose oxes are about to be gored by any regulatory legislation—rally around too.

The legislators' heads spin. They're up to their eyebrows in strange things they've never heard of before—Ringelmann readings, sulphur dioxide emissions, hydrocarbon measurements. Giving them the benefit of the doubt, in our hypothetical State *S* the legislators screw up their courage and, under expert guidance, frame noble corrective legislation. Then an odd thing happens. The air-breathing citizenry that was in the spectators' gallery, cheering the legislators on, suddenly fades away—and filters back into the legislature through side doors, wearing the other hats, as home-incinerator operators, automobile drivers, and corporation stockholders, resistant to regulation. As the corrective laws reach the point of enactment, it transpires that myriad bits of dentistry have pulled their teeth. The sonorous preamble extolling clean air is still there, the enabling clauses, perhaps even an imposing appropriation of money. Under the measures, control agencies can be set up and experts hired to run them. But soon it may become evident that they don't really have the authority to do much but sit there writing recommendations and reports.

That, or less than that, has been the pattern more often than not in cities and states across the country. For evidence, simply take, on the one hand, the cities and states that purport to have meaningful air pollution legislation; and, on the other hand, the cities or states that, after a reasonable period of adjustment, have indeed remedied air pollution even from stationary sources alone, leaving out the special problem of automobiles. Such places are hard to find.

The focal problem is that politics is traditionally the art of compromise. And air pollution, in the severity in which it is developing in many localities now, is something that is no more subject to compromise than pregnancy. A bucket either contains what is poured into it, or it overflows. The atmosphere either can absorb, dilute and dispel the wastes projected into it, or it becomes saturated and regurgitates the excess back into people's faces. Once the saturation point has been passed, the area of possible compromise—a workable diminution of the loads of waste imposed on the atmosphere—is difficult to arrive at. The legislators, harrassed, preoccupied and technically unqualified, can't do this. At best they can set up governmental mechanisms under which experts can tackle the job. And the experts can't do the job unless they have the public support—which, as noted, at this point is equivocal.

Is, then, the extraordinary problem of air pollution too severe a test for the adversary system under which government generally deals with public questions?

On the contrary, even though the nation's skies are not spectacularly clearer than a few years back when the public first realized the problem, remedial progress is impressive. Overloading the atmosphere with contaminants was a feat that took mankind hundreds of years. It is hardly expectable that the damage can be undone overnight. Nationwide efforts against air pollution have been under way less than a decade. Yet already the structure, and many of the operations, of reform are approaching those in the field of water pollution, in which corrective efforts date back to the 1880's.

How much is the amelioration of air pollution being impeded—or, possibly, expedited—by the fact that it is a problem so inexorably committed to the political arena? It may surprise some that there is evidence in both directions. Because air pollution regulation tramples on so many toes, impinges so much on accustomed, if not exactly God-given, freedom of action, it automatically evokes a great deal of opposition. This ranges from the disinclination of citizens to give up their backyard incinerators or deodorize their automobiles, to organized, methodical resistance from segments of industry. But conversely, because air pollution is such an ubiquitous and pressing problem, it has shown itself in many instances to be much *more* sensitive than most problems to public pressures for reforms.

Air pollution intrinsically is the most non-partisan of public problems. Smog chokes alike the Democrat and the Republican. So remedial efforts seldom assume conventional partisan colorations. The hurdle that air pollution regulation has to surmount, particularly at the local level, is less likely to be labelled Republican or Democrat than Establishment—the entrenched interests, the status quo—which in a particular case may be predominantly either Democratic or Republican. In either case, the entrenchment is likely to have some partisan orientation, which means that the cause of air pollution reform may not be dealt with purely on its merits, but as part of a bundle of Establishment affairs. It can become one of the logs in the great game of political log-rolling.

There is little question, for instance, that in Los Angeles, where more has been done about pollution abatement than in any other city, the process has been facilitated by the fact that city and county government (as throughout California) are by law non-partisan. When pollution control administrators—operating as a function of county government—have to go to the politicians for money or muscle, they don't have to worry about partisan cleavages among the politicians, or about whose badge a certain politician is wearing. The reign of non-partisan government for more than half a century has moderated the entrenchment of special interests, at least to the extent of not giving them the shelter of a partisan structure.

The situation contrasts sharply with New York City, the classic spawning-ground of partisan machine politics. New York, by federal definition, has a worse air pollution problem than Los Angeles.[1] New York engaged a top pollution expert, Austin Heller, to help solve its problems. The city has projected ambitious abatement programs. But when Los Angeles pollution officials were called back to New York as consultants, they were appalled by the political obstructions with which abatement officials had to contend.[2] Despite the ambitious programs, as recently as a few months ago diners in outdoor restaurants were still plagued with gross chunks of fly ash in their food—the most elementary and easily corrected sort of air pollution.

This is not to imply that the Establishment in any community is *per se* opposed to pollution reform. There are always progressive and regressive elements in any Establishment, or local power structure—even within the usually dominant industrial-commercial element in an Establishment. Indeed, it can be argued that Los Angeles' considerable success in dealing with smog from stationary sources (now reduced to twenty percent of total air pollution)[3] was made possible only by the fact that the Establishment—thoroughly scared, as of 1946, by the implications of air pollution—took the lead in mobilizing public opinion against it.

Nor can machine politics be put down categorically as an obstruction to pollution abatement. Sometimes it works the other way. A notable example is Chicago, where more is being done about cleaning up the air than in many cities. It is an axiom of current American politics that in Chicago an important ingredient in any big public project is the personal imprimatur of Mayor Richard J. Daley. He has put his weight on the side of a pollution cleanup.

In looking at the political dynamics of air pollution, attention inevitably centers on industry. Of the nation's total burden of air pollution—estimated by the U.S. Public Health Service at some 133 million tons of contaminants a year—industrial *operations* are responsible for less than half: twenty-two million tons from manufacturing and fifteen million tons from electric power generation. Space heating and refuse burning account for 11 million tons. The rest—eighty-five million tons—comes almost entirely from motor vehicles.[4] The extent to which the responsibility, if there is any such thing, for this automotive portion of the pollution load rests upon the automobile industry, the petroleum industry, or motorists, could be argued in many ways. But in terms of political realities, rather than moral responsibility, growing public awareness of the automobile's big part in smog has tended to put the auto industry in the same uncomfortable position as if the car effluvia were coming out of the smokestacks in Detroit. Along with it, in the air pollution picture, are such economic giants as the steel industry, the power industry, the petroleum industry, the chemical industry, the pulp and paper industry, and many lesser enterprises.

Generalizing broadly, it may be said that industry has shared the public's ambivalence about air pollution reform. On the one hand, industry has laid out millions of dollars for pollution control equipment and for research. On the other hand, it is rather consistently found in negative postures in regard to control legislation. This should surprise no one. If industry had not been inherently opposed to all sorts of regulation, it might long since have been regulated to death by well-meaning people. Corporate management's major concern is its responsibility to shareholders; and shareholders—even when as citizens they complain about foul air—are notoriously disapproving of corporate outlays for "non-productive" facilities. To be sure, all business enterprises have an implicit responsibility of good citizenship. But just what constitutes good citizenship is not always easily defined in respect to as complex a problem as air pollution, especially when the community itself may be divided on courses of corrective action.

Industry exerts pressures at all the political levels. In Washington, air pollution is one of many concerns on which industrial representatives testify at hearings, lobbyists buttonhole legislators, and public relations men grind out propaganda. Corresponding activity goes on at state capitals, with a particular industry or even a particular corporation having special leverage. On the local level, industry's role has ranged from taking the lead in civic cleanup campaigns to threatening to pull out of town if regulation is imposed (a familiar threat that is seldom if ever carried out).

The courts figure along with the legislative chambers as pressure-points. In Los Angeles, the basic authority of the county's air pollution control agency has been vainly challenged by oil, steel, utility and plywood companies in a series of suits that have gone as high as the United States Supreme Court.[5] The Western Oil and Gas Association has just dropped, after a four-year legal battle, an effort to nullify the agency's regulation that during seven especially smog-prone months of the year, industry must burn natural gas instead of oil.[6]

On the other hand, industry can be very cooperative. In 1967, the Los Angeles County Air Pollution Control District promulgated perhaps the most far-reaching piece of quasi-legislation ever to come from local government in this country. The agency's technical experts calculated that an appreciable if small part of air pollution was fumes from the large amount of building painting constantly going on in a metropolis of seven million inhabitants—fumes that could be minimized by modification of paint formulas. Accordingly the agency drew up a new regulation that in effect dictated to the nation's paint industry what ingredients it could use in its products—if it wanted to sell them in Los Angeles.[7] The requirements were arrived at through months of collaboration with paint industry trade groups, who sent representatives to endorse the measure when it was approved by the county board of supervisors without a moment's debate.

Nationally, industry has tended to react to smog's volume more as a public relations problem than as a chemical problem. This is natural and not necessarily undesirable, although it has been a perplexing relationship to many logically-minded executives who could see no correlation between chemical compounds and the public relations heat they were generating.

With some degree of regulation a foregone conclusion, industry has been torn two ways in its strategy of accommodation. One way is to try to keep regulation as much as possible at the state level, where industry may be more influential than in Washington. But there is a point—and it is being approached throughout much of our economy and particularly in the realm of pollution—where this strategy runs into diminishing returns. That is where the matter of regulation extends to many or all of the fifty states. Then an industry may find itself whipsawed vertiginously among conflicting requirements of different states, resulting in not only complexity and confusion but uncomfortable competitive disadvantages. Then pressures develop for uniform, federally-ordained standards—although as liberal ones as can be obtained. In both the fields of water and air pollution, at this point in history, there is often a babel of expressions in both directions at the same time, varying with particular interests.

The politician's problem is to separate fact from fiction, sincerity from expediency, in representations from various quarters of industry. This calls for scientific, technological and economic data. The difficulty of assembling and collating this data into a form intelligible to nonprofessionals, and disseminating it to the people who need it, accounts to a great degree for the mixed results to date in politics' attack on air pollution.

Viewed through long-range glasses, the national effort against air pollution so far has been a somewhat disjointed scramble consonant with the sudden onset of the affliction—a sort of land rush, with different parties dashing in different directions, and with many of the ground-rules of logical political and administrative procedure temporarily inoperative.

As with water pollution, the states proved very laggard in taking appropriate action, so the federal government stepped into the vacuum. It moved in, anomalously, through the back-door of health, via the Department of Health, Education and Welfare—even though, from the public's current viewpoint, the health implications of smog are quite secondary to the aesthetic and economic considerations.

Congress, almost unwittingly, was persuaded to delegate to the Public Health Service jurisdiction over the state of the nation's air, even over conditions which do not demonstrably affect health. At first this looked like a rather token grant. The emphasis was on research and the funds allocated were minuscule. But this proved the stepping stone to sweeping regulatory powers.

Following the pattern set with water pollution, the Public Health Service obtained explicit authority to deal with "interstate" air pollution situations, to the point of putting recalcitrant offenders in jail. Initially this sounded like a matter of dealing with a factory near the Vermont boundary that was spewing fumes across the line into New York. It quickly transpired, however, that the problems of no fewer than seventy-five of the nation's principal metropolitan areas had interstate ramifications. One by one, the Public Health Service, through its division now entitled the National Center for Air Pollution Control, has been tackling these metropolitan areas, instituting formal abatement proceedings, and framing corrective programs which if not executed on a reasonable schedule could bring federal injunctive action and contempt of court penalties.

Early in 1967 the Public Health Service promulgated the most comprehensive air pollution control action in history: the requirement that all 1968 model cars should have special smog control equipment[8]—a measure implicitly affecting every habitant of the country.

The point is that, while Congress has conducted extensive hearings and deliberations on all these steps, they were effected with a minimum of the tohu-bohu that normally surrounds far-reaching, controversial political actions. This was possible because the lawmakers had the tacit support of public opinion—a large if latent nationwide pressure group—that was strong and was impelled by the intricacies of the problem to give government virtually a blank check.

The next phase in the abatement effort will have special political interest. Federal regulation of automobiles stops, in effect, at the factories. For the mechanical requirements to be effective, there will have to be supporting state legislation covering maintenance and inspection of the equipment. This is not so urgent at the moment, because over 90 percent of the vehicles operating are pre-1968 models without fume-control equipment. It will become increasingly urgent as about 10 percent of the automobile population is replaced annually with new cars. On the one hand, there will inevitably be pressures to "go slow" on such legislation. On the other hand, if the states are sluggish about adopting enforcement legislation, federal officials are in a position to penalize them through reductions in various subsidies related to motoring.*

The fluidity of smog politics cuts two ways. It makes the progress of nation-wide remedial measures erratic and not necessarily logical. But it also makes the problem extraordinarily sensitive to citizen pressures.

An example occurred in the final stages of enactment of the 1967 Air Quality Act. Ardent reform forces collided with "go slower" opinion over two proposed features of the act. One, an amendment introduced by Senator George Murphy at the behest of California air pollution officials, said that notwithstanding federal pre-emption of jurisdiction over new-car fume controls, individual states could impose stricter standards after a simple showing of need to the Secretary of Health, Education and Welfare. An amendment introduced by Rep. John Dingell of Michigan, and supported by the automobile industry, sanctioned state variances only at the Secretary's discretion after prolonged administrative procedures. The auto industry's argument was that it did not want to get into a tangle of differing state standards. It was nip and tuck which amendment would prevail. An avalanche of a half million letters from California at the last minute, among other representations, helped swing the decision in favor of the Murphy amendment.[9]

On citizen group that had a big hand in this pressure was a California organization entitled Stamp Out Smog ("S.O.S."). S.O.S. consists of some 200 women, only about thirty-five of whom, according to the organization's

*[See R 208(a) of the early draft of S. 780 which would have authorized the Secretary of Transportation to require emission control device inspection procedures as a condition to granting funds for highway safety programs, and after 1969, for all federal aid highway funds, under 23 U.S.C. R 402 (1966). Hearings on S. 780 Before the Subcomm. on Air and Water Pollution of the Comm. on Public Works, 90th Cong., 1st Sess., pt. 2, at 748 (1967). Ed.]

founder, Mrs. Michel Levee of Beverly Hills, could be called real activists. S.O.S., when it was founded in 1957, deliberately avoided the mass-membership approach usually favored by citizen pressure groups. Instead, it sought the written authorization of other organizations, from garden clubs to labor unions, to speak for them in the field of air pollution, which S.O.S.'s key members spent months studying until they knew far more than most legislators. S.O.S. got the proxies of some 450 organizations with an aggregate membership of over 450,000. This leverage, along with the women's expertise, has made them an influence respected alike by legislators in Washington and Sacramento, and by California air pollution officials.

Even less elaborate citizen efforts can generate important pressures. Early in 1967, several hundred boat and home owners in the Los Angeles suburb of Redondo Beach united to fight periodic showers of sulphuric acid compounds emitted by the smokestack of a Southern California Edison Company generating plant on the waterfront. Like power plants across the country it burned ordinary fuel oil with a high residue of sulphur dioxide gas, which in combination with moisture can form actual sulphuric acid. Like other power companies, the Edison Company had been smarting for years from citizens' complaints, and had spent millions on huge experimental "bag house" facilities to filter out the objectionable chemicals. But a power plant of that sort will discharge as much as 500,000 cubic feet of gases per minute, which is almost an impossible volume to treat in any way. The "bag house" facility did not work well. The plant's discharges were legally in violation of regulations of the Los Angeles County Air Pollution Control District. But, the protesting citizens found, the power company had gone over the control agency's head to a county appeals board and had obtained a succession of variance permits on the argument that the plant's air pollution was unavoidable in the absence of alternative fuel. The protesters went to the next variance hearing and argued that Edison could burn high-grade, low-sulphur oil. Edison rejoined that an assured supply of low-sulphur oil was unobtainable under existing federal oil import regulations. The protesters argued that Edison should bring more pressure on the government for revision of the import restrictions. Other concerns across the country also were pressing for a change. The focus of the battle shifted to Washington hearings on revision of the import regulations. And, almost miraculously, before the year was out tankers began arriving at Los Angeles with the necessary low-sulphur oil.

Similar pressures arose from citizens of New York City, where the Consolidated Edison Company's oil-burning power plants are responsible for an important portion of the smog. In this case the alternative fuel proposed was natural gas. But the Federal Power Commission had long maintained the policy that natural gas reserves were too limited for it to be used as boiler fuel, and had turned down previous applications for enlargement of the cross-country flow to New York City for use in power plants.

Argument on the policy was reopened in 1967. Witnesses at Federal Power Commission hearings, in addition to representatives of a score of utility companies, included spokesmen for the Department of Health, Education and Welfare, and for the New York City organization Citizens For Clean Air, Inc. On November 6 the commission, while trying to avoid a troublesome precedent by stipulating that the factor of air pollution was *not* a critical consideration in its decision, authorized an increased natural gas flow to New York for Edison boiler fuel. One commissioner, Charles R. Ross, in his concurrence, diverged from the majority to state particularly: "In my opinion, the severity of the air pollution problem in New York City and the relationship of gas supplies towards relieving that problem was a relevant and necessary consideration in my decision to grant this certificate."[10]

Politics is, at its best, a projection of public opinion with all its cross-currents, and the interaction between these two elements, changing from day to day, is the crux of air pollution abatement progress.

In Los Angeles, where public opinion is most firmly consolidated in favor of stiff anti-smog measures, over a period of two decades there has not been a discernible murmur of objection against the cost of supporting the nation's largest abatement agency outside of Washington. It is the Los Angeles County Air Pollution Control District, which has over 300 full-time employees and a budget of nearly $4 million a year, which works out to more than 50 cents per capita for the population covered. Although this cost is trivial in the age of affluence and effluents, citizens elsewhere in the nation generally have either been unwilling to spend anything like this, or they are uninformed as to the desirability of spending it.

The agency's record of 36,565 citations for air pollution violations since 1955, with a conviction rate of 96 percent and some $880,000 in fines imposed, signifies strong moral support in the community.* The record, when mentioned to civic leaders elsewhere, often evokes astonishment and incredulity—along with some obvious apprehension that they may be confronted with imposing such rigorous enforcement.

Los Angeles' control district director is Louis J. Fuller, a former high-ranking police department officer. He is an urbane and astute man, far above the oft-derided "cop mentality." But he brought to the job the conviction that in ameliorating air pollution, anything less than iron-clad enforcement of his agency's regulations would negate the whole effort.

But his success has hinged more on his keen political sense. He derives his authority from the five-member board of supervisors that is the county's governmental apex. The supervisors, preoccupied with many other community problems, often have no more than a layman's familiarity with some aspect of the pollution situation. Fuller, before seeking ratification of some important new step—such as amplification of the agency's code of one hundred-odd abatement rules—tactfully makes sure that the supervisors are thoroughly familiarized with the pros and cons of the move. By the time the matter is broached publicly, his support is "wired in." This is a diametric contrast with the familiar picture of the "smog czar," who, overestimating his mandate, acts with unilateral flamboyance that may embarrass and antagonize the surrounding political establishment. On such points of political finesse pivot success, failure, or frustration in smog abatement.

These are some of the dimensions of the politics of air pollution today. What they may be tomorrow, it should be evident from the foregoing, is fairly unpredictable.

But since the alternative would seem to be eventual mass suffocation, presumably the nation in due course will overcome its air pollution problem. When it does, politics, with all its imponderables, will have been the main avenue to achievement.

---

*Statement by Louis J. Fuller, director, Los Angeles County Air Pollution Control District, Feb. 15, 1968. The statistics quoted cover the period from 1955 through 1967.

The Politics of Air Pollution:
Public Interest and Pressure Groups

[1] United States Public Health Service Press Release (August 4, 1967) reprinted in *Hearings on H.R. 9509 and S. 780 Before the House Comm. on Interstate and Foreign Commerce*, 90th Cong., 1st Sess., Ser. 90-10, at 193 (1967).

[2] Taken from the author's confidential interviews with participants.

[3] Statement by Louis J. Fuller, director, Los Angeles County Air Pollution Control District, Feb. 23, 1968.

[4] Report by Dr. John Middleton, director, National Center for Air Pollution Control (U.S. Public Health Service), Washington, D.C., March 1967.

[5] *See* Union Oil Co. v. California, 351 U.S. 929 (1956).

[6] Los Angeles County Air Pollution Control District Rule 62.

[7] Los Angeles County Air Pollution Control District Rule 66.

[8] 33 Fed. Reg. 112 (1968).

[9] Air Quality Act of 1967 § 208(b), 42 U.S.C.A. § 1857d—1 (Supp. Feb. 1968).

[10] Transcontinental Pipeline Corp., Opinion No. 532 (1967), Federal Power Commission Docket No. CP65-181, Phase II.

5 The Politics of Poison

This is the way the world ends,
Not with a bang but a whimper.

                                    T. S. Eliot

In dedicating the Patuxent Wildlife Research Center in 1963, Secretary of the Interior Stewart Udall said:

> This laboratory is dedicated to Man—to his search for knowledge about the natural world around him—to his wise use of the tools for controlling that world. The work done here may prevent or halt the threat of the "silent springs" that stalk the earth—for this laboratory marks the beginnings of a new national awareness of the present and potential danger we have almost thoughtlessly brought to the world in which we live.

Rachel Carson's controversial book *Silent Spring,* published in 1962, alerted Americans to the dangers "that stalk the earth" from the indiscriminate use of chemical pesticides. We should notice at the outset that pesticides are poisons and that their purpose is to kill. Common sense and casual observation indicate that they kill more than the "target population." The Bureau of Sport Fisheries and Wildlife publishes with monotonous regularity its morbid annual report on pollution-caused fish kills. Very likely the indirect effects of pesticides are more significant than the obviously lethal direct effects. When persistent pesticides are ingested, they are stored in body tissues and are passed from animal to animal through the food chain. Fish and Wildlife Service studies have documented a three thousand-fold increase in concentrations in the chain from invertebrates to fish to fish-eating birds.

Pesticides are carried far from the site of their original application by birds, winds, and water. By 1971 pesticide residues had been found in literally every corner of the world—including Antarctica, where they showed up in the penguins. Still another danger is that pesticides may combine with other chemicals in the environment to produce a more toxic poison than the original compound. Most important is the unknown effect on man of small and more or less continuous dosages. Every person in the United States now carries in his body measurable amounts of DDT residue, dieldrin, and other chlorinated hydrocarbons.

Over time, some insects can develop an immunity to given pesticides. In the summer of 1971 the California Department of Public Health reported a "population explosion" of the Culex tarsalis mosquito, which had apparently developed an immunity to all known pesticides. This mosquito can carry Venezuelan equine encephalomyelitis (VEE) and another variety of sleeping sickness which is often fatal to humans. When such incidents occur, the usual reaction is to develop new and more deadly compounds which, in turn, tend to escalate the hazards to man and to the eco-system generally.

Added to all of this is the frightening paucity of knowledge about the effects of pesticides on the eco-system and on man himself. More than 60,000 pesticide compounds have been registered for sale in the United States alone. The development and sale of this large number of formulations within a relatively short time would appear to make adequate testing an impossibility. The continued large scale, indiscriminate use of pesticides could very well be the gravest threat to the survival of mankind on this earth.

Over against the dangers summarized above is the undeniable fact that pesticides have reduced or virtually eliminated some diseases, and that their use has immeasurably stepped up world food production and lowered the price of food. According to the U.S. Department of Agriculture,

Our high standard of living in the United States, including freedom from insect-borne diseases, is directly related to effective pest control. Many of our major food crops would be in the luxury class and available only to the wealthy if it became necessary to rely only on means other than chemicals to protect such crops from pests. The "balance of nature," as a panacea for the pest control ills of man, is a fallacy. Nature never has been in balance. With the advance of civilization, man has worked continually to tip the balance in his favor and it will become more important to do this as the populations of the earth continue to increase.

Pesticides are required in this country for the production and protection of food, feed, and fiber, and for protecting plants, animals, and man from serious diseases. No one questions this. The question is, how can this be accomplished with safety, economy, and efficiency.

Chemicals are used against pests by the American public today as weapons of choice because they are more effective and economical than any other methods of control yet developed. In only a few instances are there other available effective methods. Pesticides registered with the U.S. Department of Agriculture are safe to use if directions are followed. In relation to total volume, instances of misuse are few.[1]

The pesticide problem could very well be the most difficult of all ecological problems. There is no doubt that pesticides have already caused severe dislocations in many eco-systems and that they constitute a serious threat to the survival of mankind. At the same time, there is no doubt that they have saved the lives of thousands of people and have helped to increase agricultural production substantially, with a consequent lowering of food costs and a better diet for millions of people. Part of the phenomenal increase in agricultural production has come about as the result of crop specialization. Such specialization simplifies the ecology of the region (puts it out of balance), which necessitates artificial methods for controlling insect pests. It is not likely that we shall return to the diversified family farm; the trend throughout the world is in the opposite direction. That means a greater need for chemical pesticides.

Some problems appear to be insoluble; perhaps this is one of them.

Governmental Action to Reduce Pesticide Hazards

What has the government done to reduce pesticide hazards? The basic law is the Federal Insecticide, Fungicide, and Rodenticide Act (61 Stat. 163), passed in 1947. Under this law "economic poisons" must be registered with the U.S. Department of Agriculture before they can be marketed in interstate commerce. Registration applications are processed by the Agricultural Research Service of the Department of Agriculture. Applications are also reviewed by the Food and Drug Administration, the Public Health Service, and the Department of the Interior.

The coverage of the 1947 law was extended by the Nematocide, Plant Regulator, Defoliant, and Desiccant Amendment of 1959 (73 Stat. 286). Most important was the passage of an amendment in 1964 to prohibit "protest registration" (78 Stat. 190). Prior to that time a manufacturer could continue to market a poison which did not comply with the 1947 law until such time as the Department of Agriculture could develop evidence to prove it unsafe and take legal action to remove it from the market.

The Department of Agriculture was criticized by the House Government Operations Committee in its November 1969 report for laxity in enforcement procedures. Congressman L. H. Fountain called enforcement of the 1947 Act "an almost incredible failure." Earlier the General Accounting Office had reported that, in 1966, 2751 pesticides had been tested: 750 were found to be in violation, and 562 of these were considered to be major violations. However, only 106 enforcement actions were taken to remove violating products from the market. Furthermore, the GAO stated that no violations had been reported to the Justice Department for prosecution in 13 years.

The pesticide registration functions of the Department of Agriculture were transferred to the new Environmental Protection Agency in December 1970 under the President's Reorganization Plan No. 3.

The Federal Food, Drug, and Cosmetic Act of 1938 required that tolerances be established for pesticide residues in food. A 1954 amendment strengthened the basic Act by providing that any raw agricultural commodity could be condemned if it contained a pesticide residue which had not been "exempted" or was present in excessive amounts.

It may be significant that despite numerous hearings and investigations, and the introduction of dozens of bills, Congress took no action on pesticide control measures from 1964 through 1970.

Most of the states have laws modeled after the Federal Pesticide Act.

Liability suits involving pesticides are ordinarily decided on common law principles. Perhaps the Environmental Defense Fund, headquartered in New York, has been most active in bringing suits on grounds of ecological damage.

DDT

Much of the opposition to pesticides has concentrated on DDT. This poison has been used longer than most of the other chemicals, so more data are available on its effects. The great advantage of DDT as a killer is that it is "persistent"—it breaks down slowly. This persistency also makes it most hazardous to fishes, wildlife, and man. As Robert Rienow has pointed out, in any discussion of food chains we should recognize that man is at the end of the chain. Paul Ehrlich has warned of an even greater hazard—the possibility that ocean phytoplankton could be destroyed by DDT. Such destruction would not only cause the death of most marine animals by starvation, but would also sharply reduce the amount of oxygen in the air we breathe.

Conservation organizations have opposed the use of DDT almost from the time it was first commercially marketed in 1945. Congressmen who have generally opposed tighter restrictions on pesticides commonly represent agricultural constituencies. Prominent in this group have been Senators Roman Hruska (Nebraska) and B. Everett Jordan (North Carolina) and Representatives Jamie Whitten (Mississippi) and House Republican Leader Gerald R. Ford (Michigan).

Despite the efforts of DDT manufacturers and their agricultural supporters, the use of this compound has been substantially restricted. In March 1969 the Food and Drug Administration seized 28,150 pounds of Coho salmon with high DDT residues. The next month Secretary of the Department of Health, Education, and Welfare Robert H. Finch named a commission to study persistent pesticides and their relationship to environmental health. In their November 12 report this group recommended a virtual ban on the use of DDT. On November 20, 1969 Agriculture Secretary Clifford Hardin issued a 30-day ban on chlorinated hydrocarbon pesticides in Department programs. In March 1970 the Department of Agriculture cancelled registrations on DDT and other persistent pesticides around water environments, including marshes and wetlands, except where deemed essential for control of disease. In August 1970 registrations on DDT were cancelled for many classes of livestock, lumber, buildings, forest trees, and more than 50 fruit and vegetable crops. By 1970 six states (Arizona, Michigan, Wisconsin, California, Florida, and Washington) had restricted use of DDT at the state level. Finally, in January 1971, the new Environmental Protection Agency banned the sale of DDT in interstate commerce.

While domestic use of DDT is being reduced, an increasing quantity is being purchased by AID and UNICEF for foreign malaria control programs. Of the 125 million pounds of DDT produced in the United States in 1968, over 90 million pounds was sold for foreign use.

* * *

This chapter begins with biologist Rachel Carson's now famous "Fable for Tomorrow" and goes on to her essay on "The Obligation to Endure," which requires, she says, "the right to know." Congressman Jamie L. Whitten of Mississippi follows with a convincing case for the continued use of pesticides for both disease control and increased agricultural production. T. J. White, Manager of the Pesticides Department of American Cyanamid Company, defends the use of pesticides in a scholarly, low-key article and speaks of the "benefit-risk principle." Political scientists Robert and Leona Train Rienow have the last word with their article "Our Rising Standard of Poisons." These selections bring into sharp focus the central issues of the "Politics of Poison."

A Fable for Tomorrow*
Rachel Carson**

There was once a town in the heart of America where all life seemed to live in harmony with its surroundings. The town lay in the midst of a checkerboard of prosperous farms, with fields of grain and hillsides of orchards where, in spring, white clouds of bloom drifted above the green fields. In autumn, oak and maple and birch set up a blaze of color that flamed and flickered across a backdrop of pines. Then foxes barked in the hills and deer silently crossed the fields, half hidden in the mists of the fall mornings.

Along the roads, laurel, viburnum and alder, great ferns and wildflowers delighted the traveler's eye through much of the year. Even in winter the roadsides were places of beauty, where countless birds came to feed on the berries and on the seed heads of the dried weeds rising above the snow. The countryside was, in fact, famous for the abundance and variety of its bird life, and when the flood of migrants was pouring through in spring and fall people traveled from great distances to observe them. Others came to fish the streams, which flowed clear and cold out of the hills and contained shady pools where trout lay. So it had been from the days many years ago when the first settlers raised their houses, sank their wells, and built their barns.

Then a strange blight crept over the area and everything began to change. Some evil spell had settled on the community: mysterious maladies swept the flocks of chickens; the cattle and sheep sickened and died. Everywhere was a shadow of death. The farmers spoke of much illness among their families. In the town the doctors had become more and more puzzled by new kinds of sickness appearing among their patients. There had been several sudden and unexplained deaths, not only among adults but even among children, who would be stricken suddenly while at play and die within a few hours.

There was a strange stillness. The birds, for example—where had they gone? Many people spoke of them, puzzled and disturbed. The feeding stations in the backyards were deserted. The few birds seen anywhere were moribund; they trembled violently and could not fly. It was a spring without voices. On the

---

*Rachel Carson, *Silent Spring* (Boston: Houghton Mifflin Company, 1962), pp. 1-3. Copyright © by Rachel L. Carson. Reprinted by permission of the publisher, Houghton Mifflin Company.
**Rachel Carson was a biologist and writer.

mornings that had once throbbed with the dawn chorus of robins, catbirds, doves, jays, wrens, and scores of other bird voices there was now no sound; only silence lay over the fields and woods and marsh.

On the farms the hens brooded, but no chicks hatched. The farmers complained that they were unable to raise any pigs—the litters were small and the young survived only a few days. The apple trees were coming into bloom but no bees droned among the blossoms, so there was no pollination and there would be no fruit.

The roadsides, once so attractive, were now lined with browned and withered vegetation as though swept by fire. These, too, were silent, deserted by all living things. Even the streams were now lifeless. Anglers no longer visited them, for all the fish had died.

In the gutters under the eaves and between the shingles of the roofs, a white granular powder still showed a few patches; some weeks before it had fallen like snow upon the roofs and the lawns, the fields and streams.

No witchcraft, no enemy action had silenced the rebirth of new life in this stricken world. The people had done it themselves.

The Obligation to Endure*
Rachel Carson

The history of life on earth has been a history of interaction between living things and their surroundings. To a large extent, the physical form and the habits of the earth's vegetation and its animal life have been molded by the environment. Considering the whole span of earthly time, the opposite effect, in which life actually modifies its surroundings, has been relatively slight. Only within the moment of time represented by the present century has one species—man—acquired significant power to alter the nature of his world.

During the past quarter century this power has not only increased to one of disturbing magnitude but it has changed in character. The most alarming of all man's assaults upon the environment is the contamination of air, earth, rivers, and sea with dangerous and even lethal materials. This pollution is for the most part irrecoverable; the chain of evil it initiates not only in the world that must support life but in living tissues is for the most part irreversible. In this now universal contamination of the environment, chemicals are the sinister and little-recognized partners of radiation in changing the very nature of the world—the very nature of its life. Strontium 90, released through nuclear explosions into the air, comes to earth in rain or drifts down as fallout, lodges in soil, enters into the grass or corn or wheat grown there, and in time takes up its abode in the bones of a human being, there to remain until his death. Similarly, chemicals sprayed on croplands or forests or gardens lie long in soil, entering

---

into living organisms, passing from one to another in a chain of poisoning and death. Or they pass mysteriously by underground streams until they emerge and, through the alchemy of air and sunlight, combine into new forms that kill vegetation, sicken cattle, and work unknown harm on those who drink from once pure wells. As Albert Schweitzer has said, "Man can hardly even recognize the devils of his own creation."

It took hundreds of millions of years to produce the life that now inhabits the earth—eons of time in which that developing and evolving and diversifying life reached a state of adjustment and balance with its surroundings. The environment, rigorously shaping and directing the life it supported, contained elements that were hostile as well as supporting. Certain rocks gave out dangerous radiation; even within the light of the sun, from which all life draws its energy, there were short-wave radiations with power to injure. Given time—time not in years but in millennia—life adjusts, and a balance has been reached. For time is the essential ingredient; but in the modern world there is no time.

The rapidity of change and the speed with which new situations are created follow the impetuous and heedless pace of man rather than the deliberate pace of nature. Radiation is no longer merely the background radiation of rocks, the bombardment of cosmic rays, the ultraviolet of the sun that have existed before there was any life on earth; radiation is now the *unnatural* creation of man's tampering with the atom. The chemicals to which life is asked to make its adjustment are no longer merely the calcium and silica and copper and all the rest of the minerals washed out of the rocks and carried in rivers to the sea; they are the synthetic creations of man's inventive mind, brewed in his laboratories, and having no counterparts in nature.

To adjust to these chemicals would require time on the scale that is nature's; it would require not merely the years of a man's life but the life of generations. And even this, were it by some miracle possible, would be futile, for the new chemicals come from our laboratories in an endless stream; almost five hundred annually find their way into actual use in the United States alone. The figure is staggering and its implications are not easily grasped—500 new chemicals to which the bodies of men and animals are required somehow to adapt each year, chemicals totally outside the limits of biologic experience.

Among them are many that are used in man's war against nature. Since the mid-1940's over 200 basic chemicals have been created for use in killing insects, weeds, rodents, and other organisms described in the modern vernacular as "pests"; and they are sold under several thousand different brand names.

These sprays, dusts, and aerosols are now applied almost universally to farms, gardens, forests, and homes—nonselective chemicals that have the power to kill every insect, the "good" and the "bad," to still the song of birds and the leaping of fish in the streams, to coat the leaves with a deadly film, and to linger on in soil—all this though the intended target may be only a few weeds or insects. Can anyone believe it is possible to lay down such a barrage of poisons on the surface of the earth without making it unfit for all life? They should not be called "insecticides," but "biocides."

The whole process of spraying seems caught up in an endless spiral. Since DDT was released for civilian use, a process of escalation has been going on in which ever more toxic materials must be found. This has happened because insects, in a triumphant vindication of Darwin's principle of the survival of the fittest, have evolved super races immune to the particular insecticide used, hence a deadlier one has always to be developed—and then a deadlier one than that. It has happened also because, for reasons to be described later, destructive insects often undergo a "flareback," or resurgence, after spraying, in numbers greater than before. Thus the chemical war is never won, and all life is caught in its violent crossfire.

Along with the possibility of the extinction of mankind by nuclear war, the central problem of our age has therefore become the contamination of man's total environment with such substances of incredible potential for harm— substances that accumulate in the tissues of plants and animals and even penetrate the germ cells to shatter or alter the very material of heredity upon which shape of the future depends.

Some would-be architects of our future look toward a time when it will be possible to alter the human germ plasm by design. But we may easily be doing so now by inadvertence, for many chemicals, like radiation, bring about gene mutations. It is ironic to think that man might determine his own future by something so seemingly trivial as the choice of an insect spray.

All this has been risked—for what? Future historians may well be amazed by our distorted sense of proportion. How could intelligent beings seek to control a few unwanted species by a method that contaminated the entire environment and brought the threat of disease and death even to their own kind? Yet this is precisely what we have done. We have done it, moreover, for reasons that collapse the moment we examine them. We are told that the enormous and expanding use of pesticides is necessary to maintain farm production. Yet is our real problem not one of *overproduction?* Our farms, despite measures to remove acreages from production and to pay farmers *not* to produce, have yielded such a staggering excess of crops that the American taxpayer in 1962 is paying out more than one billion dollars a year as the total carrying cost of the surplus-food storage program. And is the situation helped when one branch of the Agriculture Department tries to reduce production while another states, as it did in 1958, "It is believed generally that reduction of crop acreages under provisions of the Soil Bank will stimulate interest in use of chemicals to obtain maximum production on the land retained in crops."

All this is not to say there is no insect problem and no need of control. I am saying, rather, that control must be geared to realities, not to mythical situations, and that the methods employed must be such that they do not destroy us along with the insects.

The problem whose attempted solution has brought such a train of disaster in its wake is an accompaniment of our modern way of life. Long before the age of man, insects inhabited the earth—a group of extraordinarily varied and adaptable beings. Over the course of time since man's advent, a small percentage of the more than half a million species of insects have come into conflict with human welfare in two principal ways: as competitors for the food supply and as carriers of human disease.

Disease-carrying insects become important where human beings are crowded together, especially under conditions where sanitation is poor, as in time of natural disaster or war or in situations of extreme poverty and deprivation. Then control of some sort becomes necessary. It is a sobering fact, however, as we shall presently see, that the method of massive chemical control has had only limited success, and also threatens to worsen the very conditions it is intended to curb.

Under primitive agricultural conditions the farmer had few insect problems. These arose with the intensification of agriculture—the devotion of immense acreages to a single crop. Such a system set the stage for explosive increases in specific insect populations. Single-crop farming does not take advantage of the principles by which nature works; it is agriculture as an engineer might conceive it to be. Nature has introduced great variety into the landscape, but man has displayed a passion for simplifying it. Thus he undoes the built-in checks and balances by which nature holds the species within bounds. One important natural check is a limit on the amount of suitable habitat for each species. Obviously then, an insect that lives on wheat can build up its population to much higher levels on a farm devoted to wheat than on one in which wheat is intermingled with other crops to which the insect is not adapted.

The same thing happens in other situations. A generation or more ago, the towns of large areas of the United States lined their streets with the noble elm tree. Now the beauty they hopefully created is threatened with complete destruction as disease sweeps through the elms, carried by a beetle that would have only limited chance to build up large populations and to spread from tree to tree if the elms were only occasional trees in a richly diversified planting.

Another factor in the modern insect problem is one that must be viewed against a background of geologic and human history: the spreading of thousands of different kinds of organisms from their native homes to invade new territories. This worldwide migration has been studied and graphically described by the British ecologist Charles Elton in his recent book *The Ecology of Invasions*. During the Cretaceous Period, some hundred million years ago, flooding seas cut many land bridges between continents and living things found themselves confined in what Elton calls "colossal separate nature reserves." There, isolated from others of their kind, they developed many new species. When some of the land masses were joined again, about 15 million years ago, these species began to move out into new territories—a movement that is not only still in progress but is now receiving considerable assistance from man.

The importation of plants is the primary agent in the modern spread of species, for animals have almost invariably gone along with the plants, quarantine being a comparatively recent and not completely effective innovation. The United States Office of Plant Introduction alone has introduced almost 200,000 species and varieties of plants from all over the world. Nearly half of the 180 or so major insect enemies of plants in the United States are accidental imports from abroad, and most of them have come as hitchhikers on plants.

In new territory, out of reach of the restraining hand of the natural enemies that kept down its numbers in its native land, an invading plant or animal is able to become enormously abundant. Thus it is no accident that our most troublesome insects are introduced species.

These invasions, both the naturally occurring and those dependent on human assistance, are likely to continue indefinitely. Quarantine and massive chemical campaigns are only extremely expensive ways of buying time. We are faced, according to Dr. Elton, "with a life-and-death need not just to find new technological means of suppressing this plant or that animal"; instead we need the basic knowledge of animal populations and their relations to their surroundings that will "promote and even balance and damp down the explosive power of outbreaks and new invasions."

Much of the necessary knowledge is now available but we do not use it. We train ecologists in our universities and even employ them in our governmental agencies but we seldom take their advice. We allow the chemical death rain to fall as though there were no alternative, whereas in fact there are many, and our ingenuity could soon discover many more if given opportunity.

Have we fallen into a mesmerized state that makes us accept as inevitable that which is inferior or detrimental, as though having lost the will or the vision to demand that which is good? Such thinking, in the words of the ecologist Paul Shepard, "idealizes life with only its head out of water, inches above the limits of toleration of the corruption of its own environment . . . Why should we tolerate a diet of weak poisons, a home in insipid surroundings, a circle of acquaintances who are not quite our enemies, the noise of motors with just enough relief to prevent insanity? Who would want to live in a world which is just not quite fatal?"

Yet such a world is pressed upon us. The crusade to create a chemically sterile, insect-free world seems to have engendered a fanatic zeal on the part of many specialists and most of the so-called control agencies. On every hand there is evidence that those engaged in spraying operations exercise a ruthless power. "The regulatory entomologists . . . function as prosecutor, judge and jury, tax assessor and collector and sheriff to enforce their own orders," said Connecticut entomologist Neely Turner. The most flagrant abuses go unchecked in both state and federal agencies.

It is not my contention that chemical insecticides must never be used. I do contend that we have put poisonous and biologically potent chemicals indiscriminately into the hands of persons largely or wholly ignorant of their potentials for harm. We have subjected enormous numbers of people to contact with these poisons, without their consent and often without their knowledge. If the Bill of Rights contains no guarantee that a citizen shall be secure against lethal poisons distributed either by private individuals or by public officials, it is surely only because our forefathers, despite their considerable wisdom and foresight, could conceive of no such problem.

I contend, furthermore, that we have allowed these chemicals to be used with little or no advance investigation of their effect on soil, water, wildlife, and man himself. Future generations are unlikely to condone our lack of prudent concern for the integrity of the natural world that supports all life.

There is still very limited awareness of the nature of the threat. This is an era of specialists, each of whom sees his own problem and is unaware of or intolerant of the larger frame into which it fits. It is also an era dominated by industry, in which the right to make a dollar at whatever cost is seldom challenged. When the public protests, confronted with some obvious evidence of damaging results of pesticide applications, it is fed little tranquilizing pills of half truth. We urgently need an end to these false assurances, to the sugar coating of unpalatable facts. It is the public that is being asked to assume the risks that the insect controllers calculate. The public must decide whether it wishes to continue on the present road, and it can do so only when in full possession of the facts. In the words of Jean Rostand, "The obligation to endure gives us the right to know."

Good Health and a Full Larder*
Jamie L. Whitten**

In the summer of 1943, soon after Allied forces had swept into Italy, a case of typhus was confirmed in the dirty, crowded southern port of Naples. Neapolitans and Allied forces *alike* prepared for the worst. Since the Middle Ages, epidemic typhus has been the companion of war. Napoleon's retreat from Moscow can probably be ascribed to typhus as much as to freezing winter weather. The disease is caused by a microorganism borne by the body louse, which is little known where people bathe and wash their clothes regularly. But in war, soldiers must spend days and weeks without taking a bath or changing their clothing. In war, homes are destroyed, people live crowded and dirty in any hole they can find, sanitation breaks down. The louse follows as naturally as darkness follows sunset.

By the middle of December, 1943, 83 cases of typhus had been reported in Naples. By the end of the month the number had risen to 371. The dreaded epidemic had arrived. The stage had also been set for the debut of DDT in the protection of public health.

DDT had been shown in laboratory tests to be effective against the body louse and a 10 per cent powder in pyrophyllite, a talc-like material, had been developed. One of its advantages was that it retained its effectiveness for weeks, killing any lice that might hatch after treatment as well as those caught when the dust was applied. It had checked a typhus epidemic in a test in a Mexican village and it had controlled lice in the people of North Africa. Naples was to be its first test in a full-scale epidemic in a war-ravaged city.

Dusting stations were set up all over Naples. Teams with hand and power dusters worked from house to house, dosing people, beds, clothing. Institutions received the same treatment, and in some of the larger hospitals and prisons dusting was a routine measure every two weeks. Corpses of typhus victims were dusted as well as mourning survivors. If a quick survey showed that less than 70 per cent of the people in a block had been treated, the whole block was dusted again.

By early February, 1944, the epidemic was broken. The number of cases in and near Naples was held to 1914. For the first time in history, a wartime typhus epidemic had been halted before it had run its normal course.

Thereafter, little 2-ounce cans of DDT powder went wherever the GI's and their allies did. No one seems to have worried about what effect possible residues in their tissues might have; it had been proved safe from toxic effect for use on the body and there were more serious threats to worry about. As the war in Europe sped on to its blazing end the use of DDT became routine, checking epidemics in liberated concentration camps and in protection of groups of wandering refugees and doubtless preventing much more. Later, in the Korean

*From *That We May Live* by Jamie L. Whitten. Copyright © 1966 by Litton Educational Publishing, Inc., by permission of Van Nostrand Reinhold Company, pp. 43-49, 51-56.
**Mr. Whitten is a Member of Congress from Mississippi.

conflict, lice were found to have developed resistance to DDT and a new control material using pyrethrum and lindane was adopted. But if every other achievement of DDT is forgotten it will still be remembered for its control of typhus in World War II.

As this historical example dramatically shows, the benefits of pesticides are not limited to one field. Public health workers the world over have used them to fight the most dreaded scourges of mankind. Farmers find them essential to assure high yields and outstanding quality in their crops. They are invaluable for protecting our forests and ranges from destructive outbreaks of pests. And they have a valuable place in the home, lawn, and garden, where most people gain their acquaintance with them. This chapter tells the story of pesticides in these four fields.

Public Health

Epidemic typhus is only one of the diseases borne by lice—relapsing fever and trench fever are others—and the louse is only one of 10,000 kinds of little creatures, including insects, ticks, and mites, that infect man directly or indirectly with disease. Most of these do so only occasionally and incidentally, but many species of mosquitoes, flies, fleas, and mites stand out as more menacing disease carriers. At least 27 diseases, including some of the world's deadliest, can be controlled partly or completely by DDT and its allies.

Malaria, for instance, was once a serious problem in the United States, but today it is practically nonexistent, largely because of antimosquito campaigns soon after World War II.

People commonly think of diseases as being caused by bacteria, which are a plant form of life, or viruses, which seem to be little more than protein molecules. Malaria, however, is caused by a tiny protozoan parasite, an animal form of life. Rampant in a man's bloodstream, it causes successive attacks of chills and fever. It may kill a person or it may debilitate him so that he can devote only a fraction of his normal energy to his work. It can subside only to return months later, even though no new infection has occurred.

The parasite has a complex life cycle that requires both human and Anopheles mosquito hosts. Though this mode of transmission is what made the disease so tenacious, it is also its weakness, for if a link in its life chain can be broken it is as good as wiped out. Thus if the number of people carrying the organism falls below a certain point, the disease is no longer endemic in the population and not enough mosquitoes will find enough infected people for the parasite to multiply. And, if the insect vector can be eliminated, malaria will die out of the blood of the people, for it can never complete an essential phase of its life nor be transmitted to another person.

By the eve of World War II, malaria, once widespread in this country, had been confined to the Southeast. But there it was a costly and enervating disease, striking 900,000 people and killing 4000 in one year as recently as 1935.

When I was a boy, in the hill section of Mississippi on the edge of the Delta, it was known that the Anopheles mosquito carried malaria, but the people generally had not accepted the fact. Older people still thought that malaria was contracted from "miasma," the mist or fog that lies late in the afternoon over the sloughs and bayous of the Delta. They knew there was some connection between such places and the disease.

When I was about ten years old I contracted malaria and was unconscious, near death I am told, for several days. I carry scars now from quinine inoculations. Following the illness, I took quinine in chocolate syrup for a period that seemed like years, though perhaps it was only a matter of months. I suffered no recurrence of the disease, but my sister contracted another type of malaria and was subject to severe recurrent attacks for nine or ten years.

In the final attack on malaria, a federal-state eradication program was launched in 1947, aimed at both the parasites in human beings, which were vulnerable to war-developed drugs, and the vectors. The campaign made use of DDT's unusual residual powers, discovered and developed at the Department of Agriculture laboratory at Orlando, Florida, in World War II. Sprayed on a wall where mosquitoes rest, DDT kills the insects for weeks. The peak of the mosquito-control phase was reached in 1948, when the inside walls of more than 1.3 million homes in 360 counties were sprayed. By 1950 reported malaria cases were down to 2184. Eight years before there had been 58,781 cases—and 861 deaths.

Interestingly, one of the few flare-ups of malaria in the country since then occurred in 1952, when a Korean veteran on a camping trip suffered a relapse. Mosquitoes picked up parasites from him and transmitted them to a nearby girls' camp. The outbreak was quickly controlled, but such experiences indicate that there may be revivals of malaria introduced by returning veterans from Vietnam.

Malaria has been wiped out in other large regions of the world. One of these is Italy, which had been so identified with the disease that she gave it its name (literally, "bad air"). Under a strong public-health campaign, malaria had been on the decline since the beginning of the twentieth century, but had staged a comeback during the war, from 55,000 cases in 1939 to 411,600 in 1945. Residual DDT spraying of human dwellings began in mosquito-infested areas in 1944. The decrease in malaria mosquitoes was spectacular. In one test carried out with a control area, a square yard of a wall in an untreated area harbored 185 mosquitoes and the average per square yard in a treated section was 0.06. The incidence of swollen spleens in people, a sign of malarial infection, also dropped. The Pontine Marshes, a deadly malarial region for thousands of years, soon was the home of 100,000 healthy people, and areas that had been regarded as submarginal became highly productive farmland. Malaria deaths have been practically unknown since 1948. Similar stories could be told for many other countries.

Mosquitoes also carry yellow fever, or yellow jack, which used to strike terror in many parts of America. A deadly virus disease, now largely eradicated in our country, it still lurks in the jungles of South America and Africa, and since 1950 it has flared up in Panama and Costa Rica.

Dengue, or breakbone fever, a painful and debilitating virus disease, is also carried by the yellow fever mosquito. In 1922, Texas had more than half a million cases of dengue. At times in World War II this illness incapacitated large numbers of American troops on Guam and other Pacific islands.

Encephalitis, caused by several different viruses that attack the central nervous system, is transmitted by several species of mosquito. In the tropics mosquitoes also carry elephantiasis, a disfiguring malady in which the victim's extremities and genitals become grotesquely swollen because of small round-worms that hatch in the bloodstream and establish themselves in the lymph glands.

The housefly has shared man's food and bred in his waste for ages. Its filthy habits, its range of 13 miles or more, and its huge appetite make it one of the great carriers of disease. It has been known to carry typhoid fever and to contaminate food and utensils with organisms causing dysentery and diarrhea. Flies are believed to have a part in spreading the germs of cholera, yaws, trachoma, and tuberculosis. A cousin, the tsetse fly, carries the African sleeping sickness that affects vast areas of that continent. Rat fleas carry bubonic plague and murine typhus. Ticks and mites—technically not insects at all but a class of arthropod called the acarids, kin to the spider—transmit scrub typhus, relapsing fever, forms of typhus and encephalitis, and other diseases.

* * *

Agriculture

Today the American housewife can enter a supermarket and buy food for her family's dinner that is higher in quality than could have been imagined thirty years ago. At the fresh-fruit counter she can buy unblemished apples and grapes; at the vegetable section she can find potatoes without insects or blight or even sprouts; at the frozen food case she can pick up peas that taste better than if she had picked them in her own garden yesterday; at the meat section she can select the best government-graded beef. Sometimes she may grumble that the best cuts of steak are well over a dollar a pound, but if she stops to think she will realize that the cost of food has risen much more slowly in the last decade than her family's income.

Such bounty is the envy of the world. As we have seen, not all the credit for such abundance goes to pesticides. Nevertheless, they can claim a major and indispensable share. The economic benefits of pesticides to farmers and consumers alike are simply incalculable. Here too, there is hardly anyone in the world, let alone the United States, who has not received tangible benefit from the agricultural use of pesticides. Even the hungry of underdeveloped areas of the world are a little less hungry for this reason, for America has been able to share her own surplus with other people as well as help them make better use of their own agricultural resources.

Chemical insecticides are used to combat more than 10,000 species of insects that are always waiting to steal man's food wherever they have the chance—in the field, in the grain elevator, on the pantry shelf. Altogether they cost us at least $4 billion a year. Though the chemicals have given man an advantage in the conflict, the advantage is tenuous, for many insects have a capacity to develop resistance to a given insecticide. So far, man has maintained his advantage by developing new insecticides to use whenever older ones have faltered in effectiveness. In the 48 states, excluding Alaska and Hawaii, agriculture uses some 225 million pounds of control materials a year. About 14 million pounds of fumigants are also used for stored materials.

Practically every crop has its own insect pests. Take apples, for instance. The United States produces more dessert and cooking apples than any other country: 2.8 million tons a year. Apples have the codling moth, which as a larva causes the unappetizing holes that once marred practically every apple. The moth's ravages have been so great in some areas that many orchards have been abandoned or destroyed. The Grand Junction, Colorado, section and north-western Arkansas are examples. In one of the most recent tests of the value of insecticides on fruit, apple trees in West Virginia that had no sprays after the petals of the apple blossoms dropped showed 87 worms per 100 apples. On trees sprayed with Guthion, 100 apples turned up only three or four worms. And of course many other pests like apples as well as people do—for instance, the apple maggot, the plum curculio, orchard mites, and the San Jose scale. Many pests require control with different materials applied at different times, and the methods have to be changed from year to year and from region to region.

Or look at corn. Of the world's annual production of 190 million tons, the United States produces half, about 95 million tons. American production has risen despite a shrinking acreage; though many other factors are involved, the use of modern insecticides is a major reason. On sweet corn, the kind one buys for "corn on the cob," the most serious pest is the corn earworm, a little green caterpillar that later turns into a drab little moth. Consumers, naturally, demand corn without worms. In a test in Florida in 1957 and 1958, an untreated field produced an average of only 1.6 worm-free ears of corn per 100. The rate in a field treated with Sevin, a carbamate type of insecticide, was 86.2 per 100.

The alfalfa weevil, a native of Europe, has been a pest in the West since 1904 and has spread rapidly in the East since 1951, apparently from another introduction. In many areas the growing season's first cutting of alfalfa would now be a total loss without insecticides. In a 1964 test in Maryland, malathion and methoxychlor applied 18 days before cutting increased the yield of the first and second cuttings from 1.6 to 2 tons per acre and the protein content from 16.9 to 20 per cent. An investment of $5 per acre yielded an increase of $20 in the value of the hay.

Insects have a direct effect on farm animals, too. Anyone who has ever seen the misery that insects can cause to a cow might well advocate insect control for the same humane motives that concern him about accidental poisoning of wildlife. Perhaps they will welcome the fact that economic motives as well as humanitarian ones have led farmers to seek ways to reduce these kinds of insect pests.

One cattle tormentor is the horn fly, a bloodsucker about half as large as a housefly. Horn flies usually cluster on the back and shoulders of an animal and leave only to lay eggs in fresh cow droppings. In warm weather a new generation can appear as frequently as every two weeks, and if unchecked as many as 4000 may infest a single cow. The only way to control the horn fly is with such insecticides as toxaphene, methoxychlor, and malathion in the form of sprays, dips, and back-rubbers. In one test in Kansas, an insecticide caused beef cattle to gain as much as 15 pounds more a month than untreated animals.

Similar benefits in terms of increased milk production have been proved for dairy cattle, which are pestered by a variety of biting flies by day and mosquitoes by night. An experiment in treating dairy herds in Illinois resulted in an increase in butterfat production of as much as 29.8 per cent.

The crop that has long been the staple of much of the South and West, cotton, is the target of a wide assortment of insect pests, including lygus bugs, boll weevils, bollworms, and cotton fleahoppers. Long-range studies in three different states show not only the long-range benefit of insect control with cotton but document the marked improvement in control that occurred when DDT arrived on the scene. In Waco, Texas, treated plots yielded an average of 34 per cent more cotton than untreated plots from 1939 to 1945. From 1945 to 1958 the increase was 53 per cent. In Tallulah, Louisiana, where the test program began in 1920, the increase was 26.4 per cent before 1945, 41.3 per cent after. In Florence, South Carolina, the postwar increase was the greatest of all—from 23.6 per cent to 53.9 per cent.

Small wonder that the cotton-growing Mississippi Delta region has one of the highest rates of pesticide application in the country. The Delta, an extremely fertile region on both sides of the Mississippi River, begins just below Memphis and extends 200 miles or more to the south. In the growing season hundreds of motor vehicles and aircraft apply tons of insecticides to the cotton fields, and other crops, such as wheat, oats, soybeans, and cover crops, receive less regular applications. The roar of spraying and dusting aircraft is as common as the noise of tractors. Such treatments are absolutely essential, for the warm, humid climate of the Delta produces an unbelievable number of destructive insects. Yet the Delta nourishes a flourishing wildlife population, and the Department of the Interior is spending large sums in an attempt to get rid of the swarms of blackbirds that blanket the area.

The harvest of a crop by no means marks the end of the insect problem. In cereal grains, for instance, insects destroy at least 5 per cent of the world's production and degrade the quality of what remains. Various weevils and beetles can cause the loss of as much as 10 per cent of stored grain in one season in the Great Plains region, and in the deep South losses can run as high as 9 per cent a month. The chief foes have such names as the saw-toothed grain beetle, the flat grain beetle, the red flour beetle, and the Angoumois grain moth.

The Department of Agriculture is fighting to keep one of the world's worst pests of stored grain, the khapra beetle, from gaining a foothold in this country. The khapra beetle resists ordinary treatments. When it is found, the storage area must be covered tightly with tarpaulins and fumigated with deadly methyl bromide gas. By 1962 a total of 671 establishments in the West and Southwest had been treated. Interceptions at ports of shipments of infested grain products also reached a peak of 249 that year, from a level of 36 only five years before.

Pesticides, Pollution, Politics, and Public Relations*
T. J. White**

Pesticides

Pesticides are means—chemical, mechanical, biological—that kill pests such as insects, plant diseases, weeds and vertebrate pests such as trash fish, unwanted birds or rodents. Pesticides are wide ranging in number, kind, efficiency, cost and good and bad side effects. They are hard, persistent, soft, intermediate in action, low hazard or toxic depending on the choice of definition you prefer.

Pesticides are regulated at the federal and state levels. Chemical pesticides, in spite of much clamor, are probably more highly regulated than any other items entering interstate commerce. There are laws and regulations relating to labeling, packaging, transporting, applying, using, disposing and residues on food. We think they should be regulated because of their nature. We argue for uniform legislation, which is a must, and this means federal legislation rather than state or local. Regulation by state or local agencies could provide inadequate protection for the concerned public. Pests and pesticides do not limit their effects to state or local boundaries.

The 1970 interagency agreement among the Departments of Agriculture, Health, Education and Welfare, and Interior is a positive step in improved regulation of pesticides. Agriculture has an interest from the standpoint of needs and uses, Health, Education and Welfare from the standpoint of health, and Interior from the standpoint of conservation. Thus the three really interested federal departments have a say-so in what pesticides will or will not be offered for sale in interstate commerce. This agreement, by the way, is going to make our business more complicated, but Cyanamid favors it.

Pollution

We are all concerned about the effects of pollution on environmental quality. Pesticides are pollutants in some degree or another. But what isn't a pollutant, including you and me? You may have read of Goodwyn Goodwill whose only desire was to leave this world a better place for his having passed through it. He was a happy man until he took up the study of ecology. Goodwyn Goodwill became so concerned he was harming the ecology of our planet that his only solution was to drop dead. He did, was cremated, and his ashes were scattered. Alas, most of his remains became smog and the 10 parts

---

*Remarks prepared for delivery at the Outdoor Writers Association of America Annual Conference, Coeur D'Alene, Idaho, June 22, 1970.

**Mr. White is the Manager of the Pesticides Department, Agricultural Division, American Cyanamid Company. Reprinted by permission.

per million of DDT in his ashes floated back down to earth. Arthur Hoppe of the *San Francisco Chronicle,* who wrote Goodwyn Goodwill, tells us the moral of the story is, "As you go through life, don't worry about doing the most possible good. Just worry about doing the least possible harm."

Concentrating a moment on the idea of doing the least possible harm to the quality of our environment while doing the most possible good for mankind, brings me to the point of benefit versus risk of pesticides. The idea of benefit-risk is accepted in principle by most everyone. However, principle to practice is a difficult road because our self interests and values tend to lead us in different directions at the same time.

The recent Department of Health, Education and Welfare Commission on Pesticides and their "Relationship to Environmental Health" (which was the basis for action by the White House to announce the phasing out of certain chlorinated hydrocarbon insecticides) reported:

> Our society has gained tremendous benefits from the usage of pesticides to prevent disease and to increase the production of foods and fibers. Our need to use pesticides and other pest control chemicals will continue to increase for the foreseeable future. However, recent evidence indicates our need to be concerned about the unintentional effects of pesticides on various life forms within the environment and on human health. It is becoming increasingly apparent that the benefits of using pesticides must be considered in the context of the present and potential risks of pesticide usage. Sound judgments must be made.

I repeat the last sentence, "Sound judgments must be made."

A biased conservationist and an equally biased pesticide manufacturer have great difficulty in making a sound judgment in the area of pesticides and environmental quality. The judgment must be based on evidence, not environmental emotion or increased profit potential. Hopefully, the evidence will be objective in establishing the degree of benefit or risk to mankind. This is a *call for reason* over emotion on both sides of the issue.

Nothing in life is free. To receive something, we must give something. There are some in industry and in agriculture who say, "We can't get along without certain pesticides." This is nonsense. We got along without them before and we could again, though perhaps not forever and certainly not in anything like the manner to which we have become accustomed.

However, the real question is do we want to change the basic standards regarding food and health in this country? Pesticides are necessary to produce the quantity and quality of food required for our growing population. Pesticides are necessary to provide for the protection of health including those pesticides that make hunting and fishing more enjoyable by reducing mosquito and fly populations and repelling black flies.

We, as citizens, have to evaluate the alternatives and determine how far we want to go. We can go from a no-pesticide situation to a selection of only one, two, three or more. It is a case of measuring the benefits against the risks. It is a case of making judgments relating to what we determine are acceptable standards.

At present and in the next several years, the amount of pesticides contributing to overall pollution will be reduced by restricting sale and use. Many pesticides are currently sold on a permit basis and many more states will enact similar legislation. These pesticides so regulated include the so-called hard pesticides and those that are highly toxic. The permit holder will be responsible for the application in a manner that minimizes pollution and hazard. More uses for pesticides will be cancelled as has happened already for certain pesticides. Pesticides that contribute less pollution, less hazard, frequently less effective control and cost more will be more widely used. This change will be continuous, not static.

What I just said relating to less effective control of pests has an interesting ramification. Many of the accomplishments of our society are based on technology. The technologist is always striving for improvement—perfection—100%. In the world of pesticides, we're saying less effective control is perfection. It is like telling the football team not to score a touchdown, just go to the twenty-yard line. We face a tremendous task in making that point with the technologists in our industry, in government and with users.

The current U.S. Department of Agriculture policy stipulates that pesticides will be used where the needs are essential but used in such a way as to minimize their hazard to the environment and their danger to human health. This is being accomplished through use-by-use, chemical-by-chemical examination of each pesticide now being used or those to be introduced. Decisions are being made on that basis.

Politics

Politics will play a major role in the future of pesticides and environmental quality. Each and every one in this room can influence the decisions affecting pesticides and environmental quality. Earlier I mentioned the interdepartmental agreement among the federal Departments of Agriculture, Health, Education and Welfare, and Interior. This agreement is politically motivated. It was influenced by interests in conservation, in public health, and in agriculture.

The pesticide industry has been portrayed in the press as a "bad guy" because it makes use of the recourses available in the laws regulating pesticides. In our system, we believe in checks and balances. Should an administrative agency have dictatorial power over any industry? Hardly, unless 1984 is here!

Frequently a bureaucracy is fantastically slow moving. In following administrative procedures, it appears to be dragging its feet and has been accused of being in bed with the industry it regulates. That isn't our experience. At times the politicians get carried away and start promulgating regulation by press release. Many of you have been exposed to and I dare say influenced by such actions. Regulation by press release has no legal standing but can ruin a product or an industry such as occurred with the cranberry industry in 1959. We don't think regulation by press release is good or responsible government.

Politics are now centered on foreign, urban and consumer problems. Agriculture is no longer a factor in determining legislation. This is an interesting paradox. Man needs food to survive but the food producers have no real voice.

They, as a group, are a political nonperson. Will the public become so concerned about pesticides that the politicians react in an unrealistic and oppressive way that results in less and poorer quality food at higher prices? Will anxiety prevail over reason?

Public Relations

The pesticide industry is based on technology. The technologist has, through error, thought that public relations were relations with the users of his products. The pesticide industry has not realized that public relations are just that—relations with the general public. The result is a gigantic credibility gap with the public.

The average consumer believes that food comes from the supermarket. The farmer is nothing more than a subsidized, far-off person who requires tax money to live. Some conservationists are concerned that pesticides are the prime cause of poor fishing, poor hunting, poor bird watching, or that pesticides are the only cause of endangerment to fish and wildlife. These conclusions are easy to draw because of DDT residues in the fish in Lake Michigan, or the delayed reproductivity or thin-shelled eggs of many birds. These are facts that have been highly publicized. Pesticides versus fish and wildlife is a problem—there is no question.

But let's look at some benefits of pesticides.

1. The Bureau of National Affairs reports that U.S. food production would fall 25 to 30% without pesticides.

2. A reduction in food production of this magnitude means that about one third more land would have to be utilized. The availability of this land is suspect. Of course, its use would involve destroying the habitat of wildlife.

3. Food costs would rise 50 to 100%. Currently food costs 16.5% of our income. It would cost 33% of our income without pesticides.

4. Much of the food so produced would be considered inedible by today's standards.

5. Farm prices are lower by 9% than they were 20 years ago.

6. Malaria is controlled in the United States.

7. Florida and other areas are habitable resort areas because of chemical control of mosquitoes.

Not many people realize these facts. They think that they just happen. These are important facts that are meaningful to the public. Please tell them.

Cyanamid and other companies are looking for the technological breakthroughs that will make pesticides less and less environmental contaminants. Our research dollars are being directed toward discovery of products that are selective in action, low in hazard, and exhibit minimum side affects. We currently are developing a product called ABATE® Mosquito Larvicide and

Insecticide that is quite specific in action—it kills only mosquito larvae—not adults, not eggs. It is very low in hazard to fish and wildlife and is nonpersistent. We've been working on this project for over five years and have not made a profit yet but hope to sometime in the future. We are gambling millions of dollars in this and similar projects.

As you are all well aware, the written and spoken words are most interesting to study. Words are concrete, abstract, dramatic, and speculative. It "sells" to use speculative words like "may," "could," "might," or dramatic words like "insidious" and "biocide." These words allow the writer to conjecture on the unproven. What editor wants dull copy? This manipulation of words is also a public relations problem the pesticide industry faces.

In conclusion, pesticides aren't all right, neither are they all wrong. Careful use of pesticides will materially benefit man and they will contribute some to environmental contamination. We, like you, want maximum pest control with minimum environmental contamination.

Abuse and misuse of drugs, automobiles, alcohol, guns and regrettably, pesticides are problems in our world. Prohibition is not the answer. Regulation, education, technology and reason are the solution.

I have already indicated that the subject of pesticides has given rise to numerous questions in the minds of the public. Here is a sampling of other questions you may have had from your readers and listeners, along with what we believe are objective answers.

When We Speak of "Pesticides," Just What Does This Term Cover? Pesticides, in the modern sense, include insecticides, fungicides, herbicides (weed killers), rodenticides, plant growth regulants, defoliants, nematocides, miticides, desiccants, and related chemicals.

How Long Have Pesticides Been Used? Contrary to popular belief, pesticides are not entirely new inventions. An Egyptian scroll dating back to 1500 B.C. gives formulas for preparing pesticides. Nearly 3000 years ago, Homer, the Greek poet, wrote about "pest-averting sulphur." This was one of the first chemicals used to kill pests.

What Are the Economic Facts Attributed to Pests and Disease in the Agricultural Area? Insects and plant diseases have caused serious economic loss in the past. For example, potato blight in the mid-1800s destroyed the potato crop in Ireland and caused mass famine. Millions of people died. In 1850, in Illinois, chinch bugs destroyed grain worth the equivalent of $12 million in food. In 1864, grasshoppers swept through the Great Plains and caused crop losses worth the equivalent of $200 million in food and fiber. In the 1890s, the boll weevil from Mexico devastated the cotton crop in Texas. By 1910, insects were estimated to be taking 20 percent of our annual vegetable production and 22 percent of the wheat crop. Today, without the controls of modern pesticides, crop and livestock authorities estimate that insects and disease would reduce food and fiber production by as much as 40%.

How Many Companies Are Involved in the Manufacture of Pesticides? More than 50 companies in the United States manufacture basic pesticide chemicals. These are formulated into brand-name products by more than 2500 other companies. They are marketed to farmers, public health agencies, foresters, conservationists, wildlife agencies and homeowners.

How Many Chemicals or Products Are Involved?   There are about 900 basic pesticide chemicals formulated into approximately 45,000 brand-name products. All are registered with the Pesticides Regulation Division of the U.S. Department of Agriculture's Agricultural Research Service. Of the total some 250 basic chemicals are registered for use in food and feed production, all of these having been on the basis of careful tests by the Federal Food and Drug Administration for specific uses, on specific crops, and at specific times, and tolerances established for such uses. These tolerances are safely within the amounts of pesticides which scientists have determined may remain on the food crop without injury to the consumer. Tolerances are specific for each pesticide and each crop and are set by regulation.

What Is the Target for This Large Array of Chemicals?   There are on record 850,000 species of insects, 80,000 species of fungi, 1,500 parasitic plant diseases, 12,000 species of nematodes of which 1,500 are parasitic, and 2,600 weed species of which 600 are known to cause economic loss. While not all are found in the United States, there are some 10,000 insect species that are presently classified as public enemies. Increasing international travel is causing problems. We live in constant danger that more destructive pests may hitch-hike their way into our rich farmlands.

Where Does the Chemical That Will Eventually Become a Pesticide Product Originate?   In chemical manufacturing, researchers plan the synthesis of new chemical structures and numerous intermediates as a part of basic research. These chemicals are screened on a routine basis to determine pesticidal activity on plants, insects, fish, birds, and some mammals. Out of every 4,000 chemicals put through the testing screen, only 40, on the average, merit further study. These select few are given a more thorough examination in the laboratory, the greenhouse and field tests to reduce the number to the one or two showing the most promise.

Who Controls the Registration of a Pesticide Product?   Registration of a pesticide is, itself, a long and thorough process. Involved are the Pesticide Regulation Division of the U.S. Department of Agriculture; the Fish and Wildlife Service pesticide evaluation staff of the Department of Interior; the Public Health Service pesticide evaluation staff of the Department of Health, Education and Welfare; and the Food and Drug Administration of HEW. The Federal Insecticide and Rodenticide Act and Federal Food, Drug and Cosmetic Act are the primary Federal laws involved. These Federal agencies are staffed by scientists, specializing in 14 different fields, who evaluate the pesticide as it concerns everybody involved from the consumer to the man pulling a lever in the plant manufacturing the product. Unless general agreement is reached by these scientists, the product cannot be marketed.

What Are the Benefits to Mankind from the Use of Pesticides?   Pesticides contribute directly toward achieving man's goals of better health and longer life.

They have enabled us to increase our food supply, expand medical knowledge, improve sanitation, eradicate or control disease-carrying pests, and obtain adequate exercise and recreation. Pesticides contribute to better health by helping farmers and growers produce an abundance of safe, nutritious foods at reasonable prices. Pesticides help by improving sanitation, eradicating or controlling disease-carrying insects, flies, and rodents on the farm, in processing and storage, in the market place, and in the home. Pesticides help protect humans against such pest-carried diseases as malaria, typhus, sleeping sickness, and yellow fever.

Is Overuse of Pesticides a Common Practice? Pesticides are not cheap and farmers do not normally use more than they should. Farmers recognize that extra applications of a pesticide will increase production costs and reduce profits. If anything, farmers are more likely to skimp on pesticide use to save money.

Do Pesticides Upset the "Balance of Nature"? Pesticides are but one tool man uses to preserve his environment. They no more upset the so-called "balance of nature" than too many mosquitoes or too many weeds. Change and competition are inevitable in nature. Intensive production of food and fiber, a necessity in promoting man's well being, has in itself upset nature's balance. Insects and diseases increase in proportion to available hosts. In ecological terms, any situation is temporary.

Are Chemicals Incompatible with Nature? Chemical pest control is neither foreign nor incompatible with nature. Animals and plants are chemical factories. They regulate their growth, reproduction, and relations within their environment by chemical signals and exchanges.

What Consideration Is Given to Wildlife Protection When a Pesticide Is Developed? When a company applies for federal registration of a new pesticide, it must furnish information about possible hazards to mammals, birds, and fish at recommended field treatment level. Acceptance depends on the degree of safety to wildlife. Federal study of pre-marketing research determines this—NOT the manufacturer. Hazards to wildlife are further reduced by off-season application when birds are not using the area; reduction of insect food causing birds to feed in other areas; and the fact that only a small portion to total U.S. acreage is treated in any one year. Registrations can also be changed if unforeseen hazards develop.

How Has Wildlife Fared since Introduction of Synthetic Organic Pesticides? Big game populations have at least doubled since 1948. Total harvests of deer, elk, moose, and antelope have increased from less than one million to over two million animals since 1948. Black bear numbers from North Carolina up to New England have held their own or steadily increased. Upland game birds have done astonishingly well. Grouse populations have been maintained despite increased hunting pressure. Wild turkey, so few in the 1930s, yielded hunters a harvest in 1967 of over 118,000 birds. The most unusual record is of the mourning dove, faring so well that hunters were permitted a harvest of 41.9 million in 1967. The breeding bird census, sponsored by the Bureau of Sport

Fisheries and Wildlife since 1966, now encompasses the whole country and covers more than 350 species. Too early for reliable trends, it does show that some bird species have very large populations. For example, robins are on the increase, as are eastern meadowlarks. Cardinals and mockingbirds have extended their range as far north as Canada. "Pest" birds, the ring-winged blackbird, starling , and English sparrow, have enjoyed a virtual population explosion.

What about Reports That Certain Species Are Being Endangered by Pesticides? The osprey decline on the east coast started in the 1880s and the peregrine falcon in the east was in trouble before pesticides ever came on the scene. Man's persecution of the bald eagle is a matter of record. Even today, it is reported that 70 percent of eagles found dead died from gunshot. If "drastic" changes" in wildlife patterns could be laid at pesticides' door, it would have become evident long before now, because modern pesticides have been in widespread use for well over 25 years, an unusually long observation period. In any 50 year period in the world's history, some species have been unable to meet changing times and have become extinct. Happily, most species find our biosphere habitable and their increased numbers attest to this.

What is The "Benefit-Risk" Principle We Hear about Regarding Pesticides? This simply means you weigh the risk of using a product against the benefits derived from its use. If we are willing to change our standards we could go from no pesticides to the use of only one, or two or three, or whatever number you might choose. However, this would mean that we might not eat as well as we do in both quantity and quality. Our patios might not be as comfortable on a summer evening, and we might have to go fishing without the benefits of a mosquito repellant, which incidentally, are pesticides. The "Benefit-Risk" principle applies to all forms of pollution. Recently the U.S. Forest Service and the Ely, Minnesota Outfitters' Association proposed that non-burnable containers be banned from the Boundary Canoe Area. From now on, only dehydrated, freeze-dry or other foods and beverages packed in burnable containers will be allowed. They acknowledge that burning the containers adds to air pollution but that risk is far over shadowed by the benefits of eliminating litter pollution!

Our Rising Standard of Poisons*
Robert Rienow and
Leona Train Rienow**

Biologist Rachel Carson has been accused, because of her *Silent Spring,* of "pushing the panic button" in regard to the progressive poisoning of our total environment by man-made toxicants. It was not Rachel Carson who pushed the panic button. It was the production experts who have been leaning on this button ever since the baby boom with the cry, "We cannot possibly feed the growing nation or produce the raw materials for their needs without a mammoth program of chemical control." Miss Carson merely exposed our predicament.

We are told that our varied diet—indeed, the ability of our producers to feed our growing multitudes at all—depends upon our willingness to accept an ever-increasing dose of poison not only in all that we eat, drink, touch, or wear, but in our muscles, tissues, and even in our brains. If this is so, it would seem that our standard of living has slipped a big notch somewhere.

When we discover (July, 1966) that since the commercial introduction of DDT in 1946, the use of synthetic pesticides has increased from a million pounds annually to the "massive dispersal" in 1965 of nearly *one billion* pounds, we can be confident that we are "living dangerously" at last. When we learn that we are at present ingesting eight times as much poison as we did in 1940 and that by 1975 we will be absorbing four times as much as we are absorbing today, it is evident that the notches are still slipping at an accelerated rate. Again, quantitatively, as in other things, we are at the apex of production; qualitatively, we are starting downhill at a trot.

It is with great emotion that the chemical buffs reiterate that the more than 900 million pounds of unselective pesticides which drench the earth and air each year are *indispensable* to outwit the swarming pest population. How could we conquer the twenty kinds of mites and insects and eight species of diseases of apples, for example, without fifteen or twenty sprays a year? And what foolishness to bend the back to hack out the crab grass around the patio, when 40 million pounds of herbicides soaked into the soil (and possibly thence into the water supply) will do it for all our lawns and patios so neatly?

When grandfather reminds them that fine apples were produced not too many years ago by relying on the "natural enemies" of the pests and then for decades thereafter by relying on only one or two sprays per season, the chemical buffs have an answer for that, too. They respond that the protective species of insects, nature's answer to the pests, have long ago been eliminated by the sprays. Birds, lizards, toads, wasps, and other helpful animals such as skunks

---

*Robert Rienow and Leona Train Rienow, *Moment in the Sun: A Report on the Deteriorating Quality of the American Environment* (New York: The Dial Press, 1967), pp. 153-163. Copyright © 1967 by Robert Rienow and Leona Train Rienow. Used by permission of the publisher, The Dial Press.

**Robert Rienow is a Professor of Political Science at the State University of New York, Albany. Leona Train Rienow is a journalist whose most recent publication is *The Year of the Last Eagle* (New York: Ballantine Books, Inc., 1970).

have also been killed off around agricultural lands and there is no longer any recourse but to spray more energetically each year. Worse: we are told that as fast as they invent some virulent knock-out drops for a species of insect pests, that species becomes immune to the poison, and the chemists must produce another poison with still more kill-potential. "We not only need [pesticides]," declares a Cornell College of Agriculture bulletin, "we are highly dependent on them."

Apparently the Department of Agriculture and the chemical buffs are right; we are caught in a relentless vise. We are pursuing a path from which there is no longer any retreat and that hourly grows more fraught with danger. If so, we have come to a rather dismal pass. The *Insecta,* some 1,000,000 species of them (possibly 600,000 classified), have endured and flourished on this planet since the Silurian age some 250 million years ago, and it is an excellent bet that they will outlive upstart (1 million-year-old) man. They are "the most successful animal on earth." Unless man comes to terms with creatures or can enlist some weighty help from nature herself, he is fighting a losing war. Yet undoubtedly he will remain in there slugging it out alone until he is too weak to lift another test tube.

In the meantime, regardless of how "indispensable" the chemicals in our food are, the fantastic amounts of food additives, both "intentional" (661 million pounds in 1965, a 58 per cent rise in ten years) and "incidental" foster a serious and foolhardy situation. As Dr. David B. Hand of the Department of Food Science and Technology at Geneva, New York, and other specialists insist, a volume of incidental additives—pesticides, herbicides, fungicides—although "not intended," may well be "unavoidable," given our present and especially our prospective population demands and our philosophy of expediency.

However, the intentional additives—some 2,600 chemicals used in food production by 80,000 or more manufacturers, processors, and packers—which are used to preserve, embalm, flavor, color, emulsify, thicken, bleach, leaven, clarify, acidify, brighten, or change the consistency of foods may well be another story. Dr. Frank Bicknell notes: "Food which cannot go bad is bad food;" i.e., if it won't support weevils or even bacteria, it won't healthfully support you (just another living creature) either.

Many of these strange, unpronounceable chemicals are found on labels; many more (as in the cases of bread and ice cream) are not listed at all. How many housewives realize that we are buying and consuming 8 million pounds of coal tar products in food and cosmetics every year?

When you read a label listing chickle, butadienestyrene, isopropene, saturated aliphatic hydrocarbons, polyvinyl acetate synthetic resins, butylated hydroxyanisole, butylated hydroxytoluene, propyl gallate, would you know you were reading a chewing gum label?

Who can keep up with 45,000 or more chemical formulations used in food processing? And when a cow is fed a formulation containing "prednisone acetate, procaine penicillin, dihydrosteptomycin sulfate, methylparaben and propylparaben in peanut oil-aluminum monostearate-polyoxyethylene sorbitan-tristearate vehicle," who among the chemical wizards who dreamed up this monstrosity of artificial nutrition is competent to swear that what comes out of the cow and goes into the baby is either wholesome or safe?

When Professor of Civil Engineering Daniel F. Jackson of the University of Syracuse breakfasted with delegates to New York State's annual health conference at the capital in June of 1965, he waited until the last gulp of coffee had been consumed before he analyzed what additives—both incidental and intentional—they had just eaten. In the fruit juice: benzoic acid, dimethyl polysiloxane (antifoaming agent), DDT, parathion (possibly), saccharin. In the bacon and ham: DDT, chlordane, toxaphene or other pesticides, especially in the fatty parts; also stilbestrol (artificial female sex hormone), aureomycin, mineral oil residue from the wax paper. In the eggs: decomposition products from fatty acids, mono- and diglycerides, isopropyl citrate, mono-isopropyl citrate, DDT, various antibiotics. In the rolls: ammonium chloride (conditioner), mono- and diglycerides and polyoxyethylene (softeners), ditertiary-butyl-para-cresol, coal tar dyes, vitamin fortifiers. In the butter: nordihydroguaiaretic acid, oxidation products from interaction with hydrogen peroxide (decomposition), magnesium oxide, AB and OB Yellows (coal tar) diacetyl, DDT or other insecticides. In the coffee, in addition to possible cereals, traces of insecticides.

"You can see," concluded the Professor, "you are really getting more for the money than appeared on the menu."

The Interior Department reveals that one part of DDT in one *billion* parts of water kills blue crabs in eight days; one part per *billion* in more understandable phraseology is the relationship one ounce of chocolate syrup would bear to 10 million gallons of milk! The chemical people make a great deal of the "safety" of the various death potions "when used as directed." Yet an analysis of dead wild pheasants in California on lands on which "accepted and normal" sprays had been used showed them to be so saturated that one biologist remarked, "these birds are sizzling hot."

Millions of fish have died in the Mississippi River, reportedly from endrin. While 95 per cent of the fish that die in Missouri streams die from toxaphene poisoning, the swarms and phalanxes of spraying planes dive, whirr, and perform aerial acrobatics, flying from dawn to dusk over the wheat fields in an orgy of soil and water poisoning, says Dr. James Whitley of the Missouri Conservation Commission. In New York State spraying is eliminating the trout in Lake George, Blue Mountain Lake, Paradox, and Schroon; the Finger Lakes are losing thousands of fish from the spraying done at campsites and parks. Few realize that such spray often drifts for many miles. The effects of Sevin, a new organic carbamate substituted for the chlorinated hydrocarbons, are unknown; although its residual life is much shorter, one of its breakdown products is said to be l-naphthol, listed as "very toxic."

While fish slaughter presents the most dramatic and observable spectacle as the victims float glass-eyed and odorous on rivers and lakes, the bird and wildlife kill is even more serious: pheasants, quail, and mallards at Patuxent, Maryland; ducks, bald eagles, geese, pelicans on the Tule Lake Wildlife Refuge in California; mule deer in Montana and Colorado and New Mexico; shrimps, crabs, and mollusks along the coasts, especially in Louisiana; doves, pigeons, foxes, badgers in the prairie states; salmon hawks, gulls, golden eagles in Washington and Oregon; the myrtle warblers and red-eyed vireos at Hawk Mountain, Pennsylvania; all the ospreys in the Connecticut River basin; the peregrine falcon utterly vanished from the entire Northeastern states as a breeding bird.

Pesticides are especially concentrated in game animals that roam and feed. "For instance, approximately 70 per cent of the woodcock examined recently contained heptachlor epoxide (average 1.6 ppm) for which there is a 'zero tolerance' " in domestic meats. Deer collected from an area sprayed with one pound per acre of DDT for spruce budworm control, contained DDT residues, some in excess of legal tolerance for domestic meats, says Dr. John L. Buckley, Director of Patuxent Wildlife Research Center of the Bureau of Sport Fisheries and Wildlife.

The New York State Joint Legislative Committee report continues that in California game birds are so "hot" they have all but closed the hunting season. In Louisiana 186 woodcock contained heptachlor. Both DDT and heptachlor are now present in woodcock in the northern states. "Are we paying too high a price in biological damage for the unquestioned benefits of pest control? I think we are," says Dr. Buckley, "and sometimes, as in use of DDT for Dutch elm disease, we don't even get the benefits we pay for." He adds, "one may well question whether it is rational to eat game meats containing residues that would be unacceptable in domestic foods." Add this to the perils of hunting.

Said Mr. Udall, speaking before the Audubon Society's annual convention in 1963, "The unnerving fact is that pesticide residues have been found in virtually every type of warm-blooded animal across the land. . . . Man himself is slowly building up in his body small, but relentlessly cumulative, traces of chemicals." And the chlorinated hydrocarbons possess such "movement" (carried by winds, birds, animals, waters) over the globe that they are now found not only in the flesh of isolated savage tribes (who did nothing to deserve them), but even in arctic penguins, seals, and in the flesh of fish that live 100 miles out in the sea!

A report of the Department of the Interior listed endrin as "about 50 times more toxic than DDT. The other pesticides—dieldrin, aldrin, chlordane, and toxaphene—fell in between." In other words, although we have mountains of evidence of the killing properties of DDT because we have been using it the longest, it is nonetheless far less toxic than the newer poisons of which we as yet know almost nothing. Comments a British Ministry of Health pamphlet for medical practitioners: *"no* specific chemical tests for endrin poisoning exist."

But in addition to "movement" and toxicity the chlorinated hydrocarbons also possess great longevity. Dr. Robert L. Rudd, Associate Professor of Zoology at the University of California, Davis, tells of plots treated experimentally with 100 pounds of DDT in 1947, which still had a residue of 28.2 pounds per acre in 1951. Chlordane, dieldrin, heptachlor, and benzine hexachloride also last for a long time in the soil.

"Most concern," says Dr. Rudd, "has been directed toward the surviving toxic fraction of the parent chemical. A new phenomenon has shaken dependence on this simple measure. Breakdown or conversion products have been found to be more toxic than, or to complement the toxicity of, the parent residue."

Thus, when heptachlor "breaks down" it converts into epoxide, which is even more lethal; aldrin, said to "disappear rapidly," merely converts into the more poisonous dieldrin. Is the folly of such prolonged poisoning of the earth, from which we gain all our sustenance, comprehensible?

Then there are the systemic poisons. A thorough analysis of Cygon 267, a typical systemic, describes how this poison not only keeps killing for two weeks after spraying but also invades the stems and foliage and is circulated to other parts of the plan to kill insects through the plant's juices. (What is the difference, a spokesman for the FDA asks, whether the agricultural poison is *on* the fruit, or *in* the fruit, so long as the "tolerance" rating is the same?) This would seem to knock the last props right out from under all the millions of Americans who have been sedulously scrubbing and peeling their fruits and vegetables in the hope of avoiding the pesticide. They can, however, now save themselves a lot of time and trouble.

Query: Why do Department of Agriculture authorities assure us that systemics are very "short-lived" in their effects, when the ads for farmers stress their "long-lasting" qualities? Doubtless there are comforting answers to all these bewildering questions somewhere.

Because, as mentioned, DDT has been in use far longer than most toxicants, we know much more about it, and none of what we have learned is good. We have long known that it builds up in the fatty tissues of warm-blooded animals (including man), seemingly harmless until the host suffers some illness or stress. It has been proved beyond a doubt by many experiments that when something occurs to use up the body fat of an animal or bird, the insecticide accumulation is suddenly released into the blood stream where it often ends the animal's career in a very unpleasant manner.

We are not going to be unscientific enough to extrapolate the results of animals' reactions over to humans. The House Appropriations Committee's *Report on Pesticides,* which came out on April 19, 1965, castigates Rachel Carson for inferring that mammals who breathe, move, eat, drink, and have blood, nerves, cells, and organs alarmingly like man's, might also react like man to unselective poisons.

The Committee agrees with her that certain pesticides do cause cancer, sterility, and other distressing conditions in both man and beast. But it continues, "However, [the book] is unscientific in drawing incorrect conclusions from unrelated facts, and making implications that are based on possibilities as yet unproved to be actual facts." We do not here wish to be guilty of such irrational reasoning.

Nor are we taken in when Dr. Clarence Cottam suggests that "metabolic and physiological processes in man are not greatly different from those found in other vertebrate animals." We stand safely by the House Committee *Report.* Dr. Cottam is Director of the Welder Wildlife Foundation of Texas (and former member of the committee on pesticides of the Ecological Society of America), so he is probably not as unbiased in his observations as, say, some of the medical authorities interviewed by the House subcommittee and subsidized by the national chemical companies.

Yet when we amiably accept the report's repeated statement that it is unscientific to infer that animal bodies react similarly to man's when faced with concentrated poisons, stress, and the like, we find ourselves in the arms of a strange dilemma. What, then, are all the laboratories doing with their millions of experimental animals? What is the excuse, then, for these gigantic outlays of billions of dollars and millions of small (and unimportant, of course) lives? (However, all this is but an irrelevant digression.)

* * *

But let the biologists carry on their quarrel with the poisoners of life and earth. They are beginning to make an impression. We are concerned here more with the implications of the poison policy to the American way of life.

We have considered the increasing degradation of our standards of wholesomeness in food and environment. But there is more. What is happening to the integrity and trust that should exist between a government and its people? What does it signify that we are willing to accept every year greater compromise with a known evil rather than expend the effort to combat it? What of the bombardment of untruths to which we are submitted by our officials to maintain public complacency? When it becomes more important to sustain the serene upward progress of the economy than to safeguard public health, what happens to a nation's well-being? When it becomes more important not to rock the economic boat than to be honest, what happens to a people's faith in its leaders?

First, there is the "tolerance" fallacy. Pesticides undergo at least two years' testing by their manufacturers, whereupon the FDA usually takes 1/100 of the amount that was found in the two years' tests to have visibly harmed or killed animal subjects and establishes a permissive dose which is then legally acceptable for swallowing *in unlimited doses* by the citizenry over seventy-five years. This little stinger, we are reminded with passionate earnestness, is an absolute essential to "our standard of living."

Very well. But instead of the repeated and highly unscientific avowals that the tolerances set are harmless, we should be frankly told: *This tolerance is a wild guess based on insufficient research. We cannot assure you that it is "harmless" over a period of time. But since our pesticides have far outrun our research and we are moreover under great pressure to approve tolerances for these new poisons, you will have to make the best of it—that is, if you wish to maintain your supermarkets in their present bursting splendor.*

* * *

What do all the thousands of "minute, insignificant" tolerance-doses of chlorinated hydrocarbons, the antibiotics, organic phosphates, herbicides, hormones, systemic insecticides, rodenticides, fungicides, preservatives, arsenic additives, the omnipresent sodium nitrates and sodium nitrites, tranquilizer residues, coal tar colors, the emulsifiers, propionates, and possible carcinogens add up to in an average American's six-month diet, for instance? What, exactly, are the biochemical properties of the fifteen additives in a cake mix? Perhaps it is scientific to declare that all these additives add up to nothing—because one small tolerance-dose of parathion, for instance, may add up to nothing?

Although the courage of the federal Food and Drug Administration's banning of certain dramatic killers is to be commended, it is disturbing that biocides are often permitted to enjoy extensive sales, Department of Agriculture backing, and the opportunity widely to poison soil and human bodies over a period of many years before they are banned. Especially irritating (and dangerous) are the pontifical, positive assurances of minor local officials, who couldn't be more ignorant on the subject, that the man-made guesses called "tolerances" are dependable and not to be questioned. In every crisis, on every challenge, the tolerance is cited as though its guarantee was inscribed on a tablet of God instead of being what it is—an expedient compromise of truth with economic interest. *No official is competent to assert honestly that the tolerances permitted by regulation are without harm now or in the future.* We are getting a double dose of poison: literal and verbal.

* * *

When a proscribed poison becomes too prevalent in a product, we simply legalize it. It is a convenient system for our purposes. Thus, the tendency when "safe" tolerances are exceeded is toward a "creep-up" of the permitted minimum to conform with reality. But not only are the limits on established poisons creeping up; each day finds new and more virulent ones glutting the markets—and each of these boasts its own tiny contribution of venom to the American smörgasbord, a contribution that may be added to all the others for a poison total that has never been computed and to which there is no limit.

Considering offhand the thirty-seven poisons permitted to be present in minute tolerances on cherries (not to mention a considerable number of other contaminants, such as the copper compounds, that are also permitted in the field and for which there are no tolerances), the great amount of press attention given to the minor fracas over the addition of more mineral oil and glycerine to the children's peanut butter appears grotesque. All our standards of reasonableness seem to have collapsed. It is not without significance that an FDA release stressing the need for pesticides mentions their importance to "the nation's economics, health and recreational activities," in that order.

Once in a while an unfortunate incident breaks out into print; an adult man spills a little of a 25 per cent solution of an insecticide on his skin and dies in forty minutes; a carload of carrots is seized containing large amounts of a lethal spray; a few shipments of milk are dumped into the river; a plane pilot spraying a small Minnesota town for mosquitoes gets his cans mixed and accidentally uses parathion intended for crops, and the town has to be evacuated. (Parathion is described as so deadly that if a child rolled in sprayed grass it would probably die, yet there is a one part per million tolerance established for parathion in all our food.)

But in each such report, however, some impressive authority is quoted in the second to the last paragraph, assuring the people that all is well; everything is in hand; the threat of pesticides is "insignificant from a health standpoint." Although DDT has been found "in every complete meal analyzed in this country," testified Dr. Wayland J. Hayes, Jr., Public Health Service toxicologist, before the Committee chaired by Senator Abraham Ribicoff, its concentration is "small and harmless."

We were told that heptachlor was harmless when used as directed and that none of it was appearing in our foods. Then, considerably later, it was revealed that "ten times improved analytical procedures" enabled discovery of minute amounts of this killer in cows' milk, and it was withdrawn from dairy production. Aldrin and dieldrin were registered by our government as safe for years; then on February 2, 1966, after a closed-door conference of U.S. Department of Agriculture officials and the manufacturers' representatives, the registration of these pesticides for use on vegetables, grain, and forage crops was suddenly canceled.

How many other tolerances have been established and the public assured they were "safe" before the scientists even possessed the analytical procedures to detect them on marketed foods? We have no quarrel with the valor that it takes to admit an error and to redress it; but we sometimes wonder wistfully if it is necessary to be decieved with such conviction when the authorities are fully conscious of their own ignorance and are aware that they are responding to organized pressures of interest groups?

In answer to our query a letter from Senator Everett M. Dirksen, fervent defender of pesticides, assures us that "pesticides we have today have been in use for over twenty years and science has observed no manifestations in man." Let us examine this statement.

First, the avalanche of the most deadly poisons we now use has been conceived in recent years—many of them are but two to ten years out of the test tubes. Second, science has "observed no manifestations in man" probably because it hasn't been looking for them.

The Fish and Wildlife Service found that a number of dead eagles picked up had accumulations of DDT not only in the body fat but also *in the brain*. Zoologist Douglas James at the University of Arkansas found that the same insecticide apparently affected the central nervous system of quail and caused a decline in learning ability. *Query:* How many human brains have been opened after death to investigate whether or not they were so damaged?

Men die from such "natural causes" as liver, heart, or kidney trouble—or so read, in the medical phraseology, the death certificates. *Query:* How extensive has been the research in such unspectacular deaths to determine the victim's poison burden as a contributor to the disease?

We all know the answers. Time and the chemical tide wait for no man, nor for his autopsy either (unless his death presented acute or suspicious poisoning symptoms).

The Politics of Poison

[1]U.S. Congress, Senate, Committee on Government Operation, *Interagency Coordination in Environmental Hazards,* Appendix I to Part I, 1965. 88th Cong., Second Sess.

6 Governing the Ocean Environment

> Ruin is the destination towards which all men rush, each pursuing his own best interest in a society that believes in the freedom of the commons.
>
> Garrett Hardin

One of the boldest and most difficult adventures in international cooperation will culminate in the United Nations Conference on the Human Environment in Stockholm, Sweden on June 5-16, 1972. One hundred and thirty countries will be represented, along with several international organizations. One of the principal items on the agenda will be the governance of the oceans; this may be the top priority item for the United States delegation.

Control of the ocean environment may be the key to international cooperation for preservation of the planet. Needless to say, effective measures for governing the oceans will be extremely difficult to accomplish. Nevertheless, the United States cannot afford to rest on its continental island and allow the oceans to be destroyed. Saving the oceans may indeed be the most crucial of the environmental problems discussed in this book.

The Ocean Commons

The oceans, which cover 70 percent of the earth's surface, have long been looked upon as a commons belonging to everyone and to no one. The term "commons" originally referred to a common pasture for livestock. The use of such a commons by competing herdsmen inevitably produced both conflict and the destruction of the commons. This process of conflict and destruction of grazing land has occurred repeatedly throughout history: in China and all the way across the continent of Asia, through Northern Africa, parts of Southern Europe, and finally in American West.[1] Livestock grazing on the commons could proceed without conflict or destruction of the resource only so long as there was sufficient room for everyone. Initially there *was* plenty of room in each case, but the concept of an infinity of resources and space remained prevalent long after the commons became overcrowded. In this sense the ocean has always been looked upon as an infinite commons, described by such words as "boundless," "endless," and the like. Even when nations have claimed portions of the ocean as their exclusive property, such properties have been thought of as a commons by people of the state making the claim.

Allied with the infinite commons concept has been the idea of new frontiers just beyond the horizon. Throughout history men have sought to conquer frontiers partly because they were there to be conquered. Stated differently, frontiers exist to be conquered just as mountains exist to be climbed.

The oceans have always been a commons; they are now described in a House of Representatives report as "A Challenging New Frontier."[2] This challenge of conquering the frontiers of the ocean commons bodes ill for the peace of the world and the viability of the oceans.

The Haunted Dump

We have always used the oceans as a garbage dump with an assumed infinite capacity to absorb refuse. In an essay entitled "The Haunted Dump," Wesley Marx puts it this way:

> In grade B crime movies members of the vice syndicate invariably outfit an upstart competitor with cement "shoes," row him out to sea, and gleefully push him overboard. This cinematic cliche is another testimonial to man's ageless belief in the ocean as the perfect haven for castoffs. We have been tossing, shoveling, squirting, leaking, spilling, sinking, draining, and dumping unwanted things into the ocean for centuries.
>
> This carefree disposal—which supports an entire branch of knowledge, underwater archaeology—today nears floodtide proportions. An industrial society's most prominent product is wastes, wastes that grow in volume, variety, and toxicity and continually threaten to engulf us in gross ugliness and pestilence. As a solution to this pernicious productivity, the ocean is not only considered a handy dump but an economical one, fully capable of delousing—or at least concealing—mankind's tailings, with little or no assistance from man himself.[3]

This dumping commons is not infinite, as we once believed; we have now successfully polluted portions of the continental shelf, and we are making inroads on the ocean itself. Thor Heyerdahl's navigator had this to say of his papyrus raft voyage across the Atlantic: "For weeks at a stretch we saw no sign of man—except his garbage, and we saw that all the time." The floating garbage seen by Heyerdahl and his crew was an indication of the damage that industrial civilizations are inflicting upon the fragile oceans.

The list of marine pollutants is long and growing rapidly. Domestic wastes from cities, heat from power plants, chemical wastes from factories, atmospheric fallout from gasoline vapors, fertilizers, and insecticides, radioactive wastes, and an increasing number of oil spills are being dumped faster than the ocean can dilute, disperse, or degrade them. An estimated 48 million tons of solid waste was dumped in the oceans by the United States alone in 1968. In addition, new chemicals are being produced at the rate of 400 to 500 annually and dumped in the ocean—before we know the effects of existing pollutants on ocean ecology.

Black Death for Life in the Blue

Continuing oil spills create what Cyrus Adler has called "black death for life in the blue." Most of the accidents will continue and very likely increase in frequency and volume. Consider this partial listing of major oil spills since 1967. On March 18, 1967 the supertanker *Torrey Canyon* ran aground on a well-marked granite reef in broad daylight and dumped 118,000 tons of crude oil into the sea. Within a month British and French beaches were covered with oil, and millions of birds and fishes were dead. One year later the Liberian tanker *Ocean Eagle* stranded and broke up at the entrance to San Juan Harbor. In the spring of 1968 the *Esso Essen* sprang a leak off the Cape of Good Hope and lost 30,000 barrels of crude oil. Another casualty was the tanker *Andron,* which sank off the coast of Southwest Africa with 117,000 barrels of oil aboard. In November 1968 a hose ruptured and let 60,000 gallons of diesel fuel pour into Humboldt Bay near Eureka, California. In December 1968 a 365-foot tanker broke in two in the Panama Canal. One year later the supertanker *Marpeesa* (nearly twice the size of the *Torrey Canyon*) blew up and sank off the west coast of Africa. On February 6, 1970 the tanker *Arrow* ran aground in Chedabucto Bay off Nova Scotia and broke in half. A week later the Greek tanker *Delian Appolon* ran aground in Tampa Bay. In January 1971 two Standard Oil tankers collided near San Francisco's Golden Gate Bridge and dumped 840,000 gallons of oil into the sea. A few days later a Humble Oil Company tanker ran aground in heavy fog at New Haven, Connecticut, sending 386,000 gallons of diesel fuel into the harbor. During March 1971 the tanker *Texaco Oklahoma* broke in two and sank off Cape Hatteras, North Carolina with 220,000 barrels of sulphur fuel oil aboard.

In January 1969 a Union Oil Company well blew out in the Santa Barbara channel. Although this was a small spill compared to the *Torrey Canyon* disaster (one to three million gallons), it triggered a massive public reaction and, more than any other single incident, was responsible for the nation-wide movement to save the environment.

The danger of marine pollution from oil spills is increasing rapidly for several reasons. The number of tankers is increasing (from 2,500 in 1955 to 3,600 in 1966). Tankers twice as large as the *Torrey Canyon* are being constructed in Japan and West Germany. And rapid progress in the technology of offshore drilling has increased the number of wells now in operation and projected for the near future. (About 16,000 wells have already been drilled off the coasts of the United States alone. Within 10 years drilling at four to six thousand feet will be possible.) All these factors combine to vastly increase the possibility of major oil spills.

Ocean ecology is highly complex and sensitive to disturbance. The basic source of marine life is a community of microscopic, seagoing plants called phytoplankton. These tiny plants grow through a photosynthesis process combining energy from the sun with water and carbon dioxide. In addition, there is a vast array of animals, ranging from minute zooplankton to whales, who live by devouring phytoplankton and smaller animals. Other microorganisms break down waste materials and dead marine life. Any disturbance in this food chain can have serious consequences, especially if it affects the basic plants and animals.

In recognition of some of the problems outlined above, Congress passed the Marine Resources and Engineering Development Act (P.L. 89-454) in 1966. This landmark Act created a National Council on Marine Resources and Engineering Development in the Executive Office of the President and directed the President to appoint a 15-member commission to undertake a study of ocean programs and recommend a new organizational structure for managing Federal marine activities. The Commission, under the chairmanship of Julius A. Stratton, issued its report, *Our Nation and the Sea,* in January 1969. The report recommended the creation of a separate and independent agency to coordinate marine programs, which were scattered throughout 22 different departments and agencies. Acting on this recommendation, the President submitted Reorganization Plan No. 4, which was accepted by Congress and which resulted in the creation of a new National Oceanic and Atmospheric Administration within the Department of Commerce. It is likely that the new agency will be able to carry on existing programs more efficiently, and the presence of a separate agency may help to focus attention on marine problems. But doing the same things better is not enough. We need a massive national commitment backed up with substantial funds to prevent the oceans from becoming wet deserts. In the words of Senator Ernest F. Hollings, "Shall we spend a fortune to explore the Sea of Tranquility and, at the same time, deny the pennies necessary to discover and preserve the seven seas here on earth?"

One result of the Santa Barbara blow-out was the issuance on August 22, 1969 of a new set of regulations governing offshore oil leases. These regulations tightened safety rules in an effort to prevent future blowouts, gave the U.S. Geological Survey access to drilling logs and other data, and made leaseholders responsible for cleanup costs of oil pollution from offshore rigs, regardless of spills resulting from willful negligence.

The Water Quality Improvement Act of 1970 (P.L. 91-224) was aimed primarily at oil spills. The House and Senate had passed separate bills providing for damages in oil spills, but the Conference Committee remained deadlocked for five months on a disagreement as to the amounts and conditions of liability. During the time the bills were in the Conference Committee, several oil spills occurred. Whether these spills influenced the Committee is conjectural, but the bill finally reported out, and signed by the President, was closest to the "tough" Senate bill. The major provision of the Act established a liability to the United States for oil spills of up to $100 per ton of oil or $14 million for a vessel, whichever was lower, and up to $8 million for a spill from either an onshore or an offshore stationary facility. The Act also established unlimited liability for spills resulting from willful negligence.

Everybody for Himself

A second major problem with respect to the ocean commons is the tendency for each individual exploiter of marine life to get all he can while the getting is good. There is no incentive for him to conserve fishes or other ocean resources, because if he doesn't make the catch, someone else will. And we are becoming increasingly efficient in "harvesting" the sea. Such unrestricted exploitative competition will inevitably reduce the amount of available food from the sea. Paul R. Ehrlich warns us that "far from being a food panacea, the sea may not even be able to continue to support the limited yield we now extract from it." Such depradations may not only eliminate particular species (certain species of seals and whales, sea turtles, Atlantic salmon, and Pacific sardines are near extinction), but in the process they may disturb the ecological system—sometimes with disastrous and unforeseen consequences.

Finally, the presence of the ocean commons, "laden with untold riches," will inevitably provoke intense international competition and strife, especially since the technology is now available, or close at hand, to profitably exploit previously unattainable ocean resources.

The United Nations has attempted to resolve some of the problems outlined above but with minimal success. The U.N. International Maritime Consultative Organization (IMCO) administers the 1954 Convention for the Prevention of Pollution of the Seas by Oil, but with limited success. The 1972 Stockholm conference on Problems of the Human Environment will consider marine problems among other matters. Management of the world's fishery resources is carried out through a multitude of intergovernmental organizations operating under a series of multilateral and bilateral treaties. The United States is party to six multilateral fishing treaties and also has bilateral fishing agreements with Japan, Canada, and the Soviet Union. The United States is also a member of the 1958 Geneva Convention on Fishing and Conservation of the Living Resources of the High Seas. Forty nations (including the United States and the Soviet Union) have ratified the 1958 Geneva Convention on the Continental Shelf, which declares that a coastal nation has exclusive jurisdiction over the inanimate resources of the continental shelf adjacent to its shores out to a depth of 200 meters or as far as exploitation permits. In effect, this means that a nation can claim jurisdiction as far out as it can go, limited only by the vague requirement of "adjacency."

A 42-member U.N. Committee on Peaceful Uses of the Sea was formed in 1968 to study and make recommendations to govern exploitation of the oceans. In December, 1969 the U.N. General Assembly passed a resolution calling for a moratorium on further exploitation of the deep seabed until an international regime could be established. While one cannot say that these efforts have been failures, they generally suffer from lack of funds and enforcement authority. In very general terms, the strong, rich nations tend to favor a continuation of unrestricted competition for the ocean's wealth, while the weaker, less developed nations favor international control of the oceans and the seabed. So far, the concept of the ocean commons has prevailed, and as Senator Claiborne Pell puts it, "You really have complete anarchy reigning."

* * *

In the selections that follow, Cyrus Adler analyzes the biological effects of pollutants on ocean eco-systems; Senator Gaylord Nelson considers the problems of large scale ocean dumping and proposes a "tough environmental management" program; Senator Claiborne Pell discusses the international implications of unrestricted, exploitative competition for the "wealth of the seas"; and in a wide-ranging article, Robert Rienow reviews both domestic and international policies and proposes an "international regime of oceanic stewardship" based upon the ecological realities of a sick sea.

Ocean Pollution Problems*
Cyrus Adler**

The seashore has always been a favored place to live. In the U.S., 45% of the population resides in counties adjacent to the ocean areas. And despite the 19th Century's westward tide, this percentage has been increasing since 1850.

Among the methods man uses to dispose of his waste is the dumping of that waste into nearby waters. Since the oceans are handy to our large cities, it is inviting—and apparently economical—to use them as giant trash dumps. Thus the oceans have become the world's natural pollution sinks. A former chairman of the California State Water Pollution Control Board speaks glowingly of the ocean as such a sink: "The great economy inherent in the discharge of urban sewage and industrial wastes into near shore water for final disposal is apparent to all who will investigate. It is doubly apparent to those charged with the responsibility of disposing of such wastes without excessive cost to the public or menace to public health. If the ocean, or one of its arms, can be reached with a sewer outfall, within the bounds of the economy, the specter of an expensive, complete treatment plant grows dimmer and dimmer and dimmer until it fades entirely and, to the great satisfaction of those who have to gather funds for the public budget, (as well as you and I who have to pay the bill) the good old ocean does the job for free.

"And, small wonder that we look to the sea for this assist. Its vast area and volume, its oxygen-laden waters, its lack of potability or usefulness for domestic and industrial purposes, present an unlimited and most attractive reservoir for waste assimilation."

Treating the Mess

Admittedly, the oceans can absorb huge quantities of waste. There are allegedly 12 billion cubic feet of ocean available for the disposal of the wastes from each individual on earth—without harming the ecological balance. This hypothetical figure is based on sanitary engineering estimates that normal sewage can be mixed with sea water in the ratio of 1 part sewage to 200 parts water and

---

*Science and Technology, No. 93 (October 1969), 18-21, 24-25. Copyright 1970 by International Communications, Inc. Reprinted by permission.
**Cyrus Adler is currently President of the Offshore Sea Development Corporation. He was formerly Chairman of the New York section of the Marine Technological Society. He is a Professor of Marine Science in New York University's graduate school.

still allow biochemical processes in the water to naturally purify the waste to a harmless state.

At least nine U.S. counties with populations of over 50,000 empty their sewage, sans treatment, directly into the ocean. Most of the cities in this group—please note—border on the Pacific, where a relatively narrow continental shelf and good water movement give rapid access to the deeper parts of the ocean.

It is another story along much of the Atlantic coast. There, the continental shelf juts out more than 70 miles; refuse deposited into the shallow sea, and the problems it raises, can accumulate unless some special "cleaning" mechanism exists.

Pollution dispersal can occur through a combination of mechanisms: These are diffusion and convection—the dominant factor being convection. The Gulf Stream, for example, races along the lower Atlantic coast line at about 5 knots and then sweeps across the Atlantic to British shores. At the opposite end of the scale are such as the Black Sea, which are almost totally stagnant. On an average, most of the oceans move at about 5 cm. per second.

While also important to pollution dispersal, relatively little attention has been devoted to diffusion—not just the phenomenon of molecular transfer, but motion due to the translation of suspended matter—more properly, eddy diffusion. Both molecular and eddy diffusions are expressible by Fick's Law, although the constants for each differ by orders of magnitude.

Where broad coverage ocean sweeps do not exist, variable currents and diffusion parameters can create widely ranging conditions in a relatively narrow region. Therefore, within a radius of only a few miles in the vicinity of New York, extremely polluted and relatively contamination-free conditions may exist in proximity. It is not unusual for the phosphate content in these regions to range from 1 to 2 micromolar to extremely undesirable conditions of 10 to 20 micromolar within a mile or two.

The problem, then, is that man tends to concentrate waste products in rather restricted areas. Thus, for many Atlantic shore areas—with huge industrial waste and population concentrations—the treatment of the sewage may be necessary.

Man as a Polluter

Since all rivers lead to the sea, even those wastes not directly dumped into the oceans may ultimately end up there. For example, air pollutants from chimney stacks precipitate back (or are carried back) in rainfall to earth, and eventually find their way, in the form of runoff, to the sea. More than one billion gallons of non-industrial waste effluent is discharged daily into the waters of the Hudson River and Long Island Sound. All the waste eventually goes to sea.

Fatty scums, plastic debris, rubber goods and wood products that float on the surface are readily visible results. But present also are the settling sludges from toilets, pesticides and other pollutants. Naturally, this whole mess is loaded with bacteria lusting for oxygen, depriving all other life of this required gas.

Because of such pollution, 1.2×10^6 acres of estuarial U.S. shellfishing grounds have presently been declared health hazards by the Public Health Service.

Meanwhile, industrial pollution is increasing at approximately 4.5% per year. Contributing to the effluents of industry are: atomic and chemical wastes, oil spills, spoil (dug-up earth sludge combination from river bottoms), insecticides and thermal effluents.

The seas have become huge septic tanks for atomic wastes. The majority of radioactive particles from atmospheric nuclear bomb testing settle out of the atmosphere, into the sea. During the past few years, of course, atomic waste from atmospheric explosions has decreased because of the limited test ban agreed to by the world powers. But while this problem has receded, another one has bloomed.

The growing number of nuclear power plants causes concern about what to do with expended—but still hot—fuels. Hot wastes have been sunk in sealed containers to the furthest depths of the Atlantic, hopefully to remain there innocuously for long periods. Unfortunately, some of the metal capsules containing this radioactive material have imploded under the 30-ton pressure. And because the water surrounding the burial site water has more motion (perhaps as much as 5 cm. per sec.) than might be desirable, the situation has been compounded. Moreover, the bottom of the Atlantic is not the barren wasteland originally imagined. In any event, the AEC is actively studying the effects of radioactive waste dumped into the oceans.

Another potential source of nuclear contamination rides with nuclear submarines and merchant vessels. To date, at least two American nuclear submarines, incorporating fast and relatively potent nuclear reactors, have been lost at sea. Fortunately, their reactors remained intact.

The occasional Strategic Air Force bomber that crashes into the ocean also represents a possible source of contamination. The memorable mishaps off Spain and on Iceland a few years ago produced a measurable (but insignificant) release of radioactivity from uranium bomb detonators.

Chemical Cauldron

Chemical wastes are another rapidly increasing problem. The chemical industry is growing at such a rate that present abatement programs are having little, if any, noticeable effect. The types of chemical-waste pollution are variegated.

Sodium chloride and sodium sulphide are dumped from syrup and sugar refining plants. Inks and dyes are spilled by printing ink companies. Chlorides, sulphates and plating wastes are emptied from metal foundries, typesetting machines and aircraft part companies. Oil wastes are added by refineries. Cyanides and hydroxides are dispensed by electroplating plants. In addition, the extensive use of insecticides, herbicides, fertilizers and other agricultural chemicals are believed to cause serious kills of particularly sensitive marine animals.

Other chemical items that pollute the ocean are heavy metal ions of copper, chromium, nickel—all particularly hazardous to many forms of sea life—and organic chemicals such as phenols and amines, detergents, and wastes from slaughter houses. To make matters worse, heavy metal ions and phenols interfere with the efficient operation of municipal waste treatment plants, complicating the treatment problem.

Many chemical wastes occur in the form of heavy sludges that are extremely difficult to eliminate by treatment. Thus, petrochemicals and metal refinishing products (almost of necessity) are dumped untreated into the oceans. To minimize the shore line effects, companies sometimes barge their sludge out to sea. But most often, industrial wastes are simply dumped into municipal sewers.

Incidentally, by "sludge" I refer to the solid matter separated from waste water during treatment. There are two types: primary and digested. Primary sludge is the solid waste material that accumulates during the initial stages of sewage processing—usually by sedimentation, floatation or screening. It is putrescible and difficult to handle. After secondary sedimentation, an excess of recycled floc (clumped material) is generated in an aeration basin. This material (activated sludge) can be collected in sedimentation basins.

If the sludge is passed through a biological digester—now befittingly called digested sludge—it loses some of its foul odor. But digestion is an expensive process and accounts for as much as 40% of total treatment cost.

When properly diluted, sludge, and raw sewerage for that matter, can contribute to the nourishment of sea plants and animals. In East Asia, carp are placed to fatten in cages fed by sewer pipes. Fish are commercially grown in sludge ponds in Munich. Human waste ("night soil") has been used directly for centuries as fertilizer.

Several possible pollutants that have made headlines recently are military chemicals and mined petrochemicals. The Army planned to dump several hundred thousand tons of outdated, World War II nerve and mustard gas canisters into the Atlantic. Only after public outcry, because the gas was slated to be shipped by rail through populated areas, did the Army ask the National Academy of Science to determine possible dangers, including such facts as: How much gas would dissolve and what percentage would be liberated to the atmosphere; what the diffusion rate would be; and what effects various concentrations would have on sea life.

Blackened Waters

Oil spills are haphazard occurrences thought to cause considerable damage to wildlife and recreational areas. Their effects are, however, largely unknown. Three major sources of oil-on-water pollution exist:

1. Catastrophic destruction of tankers. The *Torrey Canyon* spilled 30 million gallons of oil when it ran aground off the southwest coast of England in 1967. And, as large as the *Torry Canyon* was, it was only about a third to a fifth the size of the newer tankers.

2. Offshore oil drilling. The Union Oil Company's accident off the Santa Barbara coast earlier this year is a prime example of such pollution. Before the

leak could be plugged, enough oil pressured out to form a drifting ocean swath 10 miles long and 200 feet wide.

3. Deliberate cleaning of tanks by ship operators in local waters. There are about 100 oil handling terminals, 100 commercial and naval shipyards and over 60 oil tank cleaning firms in the U.S., where oil is liberally disposed to the sea during cleaning operations.

Most oil spills, therefore, occur near land in estuaries and coastal waters—areas of prime importance to the existence of plant life such as shellfish, shore birds and dermesol fish. Oil contamination of the seas represents a hazard to many species of sea birds. The oil grounds them, they can't forage and they fall easy prey to predators. The decline of the British auk over the past thirty years is attributed to oil spills. The British have estimated that 20,000 guillemots and 5000 zargells died as a result of the Torrey Canyon disaster alone.

However, when spilled on the sea, or washed up on beaches, oil quickly loses its more toxic, volatile components and therefore has no measurable, deleterious effect on plankton or larger organisms. While there is some concern that sea-going mammals may be affected (whales may die from an oil dousing), there is little evidence that fish are affected, although the oil may taint fish and bivalves, making them disagreeable to the palate.

Crude oil spills are relatively shortlived; the ugly spreads will—without any help from man—virtually disappear in a few weeks. Oil that has spread will then evaporate, be decomposed by bacteria into water and CO_2, dissolve in the sea water, and gradually wane away. The actual remnant time depends on the type of crude oil, the temperature of the water and the nature of the sea. For example, Lybian oils with a low content of residuals (that is, substances boiling below $400°$ C) will evaporate more rapidly than constituents from the sulfate oil of Kuwait. Certain oils, such as Venezuelan oils with high values of asphaltenes, spread and are emulsified more readily than others.

When desirable to disperse the oils more rapidly, emulsifiers and solvents can be used. These chemicals can be sprayed onto the surface. Agitating the surface, either with a screw or a powerful jet of water, will usually disperse the oil into extremely small droplets. Each drop, covered with emulsifier, cannot coalesce with the others and eventually disperses into the sea. This sort of treatment is valuable for minimizing damage to beaches. But while oil has little effect on ocean life, the emulsifiers commonly used to disperse oil can be dangerous to marine life. For example, shellfish succumb to detergent concentrations between 10 and 300 parts per million of sea water. Smaller marine invertebrates die at concentrations as low as 1 ppm.

Because many harbors and estuarial basins might eventually fill from the waste dumped or naturally settling into them, the Corps of Engineers, as well as private dredgers, constantly clear channels and slips. In the process, they create another form of pollution. The Corps has assigned certain offshore areas as dumping grounds for this dredged material (spoil), and all life on the bottom of the ocean at these dump sites has ceased to exist. In the U.S.A., agricultural chemicals totaling more than 1 billion lbs. are used each year. These include about 150 million lbs. of insecticides and fungicides, and 35 million lbs. of arsenic salts.

Insecticides are a form of industrial pollution particularly destructive to marine life. Persistent pesticides, such as chlorinated hydrocarbon, DDT, dieldrin, endrin and others, have harmful effects on marine organisms. There is great variation of the toxic effects of pesticides (and chemicals) ranging from a 90% mortality for oysters, eggs and larvae for 0.05 parts per million of DDT, to an actual enhancement of growth. This latter effect may be due to a kill-off of parasitic bacteria.

Chlordane, heptachor and rotenone inhibit growth within 24 hours of application in concentrations as low as 0.01 parts per million. One part per million of DDT causes the death of oyster larvae; 0.025 parts per million interfere with growth. In 1964, the U.S. Public Health Service established endrin, which had been used by sugar cane growers to kill cane borers, as the probable cause of 10 million fish killed in the Mississippi River Basin and the brackish waters of the Gulf of Mexico. The fish blood showed a 1000-fold increase in concentration of the chlorinated hydrocarbon.

The consequences of pollution are not always direct. Eight percent of the available shellfishing grounds off the U.S. have been declared unsafe because of a hepatitis hazard. (However, contracting hepatitis from bivalves is more a possibility from shellfish that ingested naturally growing dinoflagellates.)

Other pollutants may promote conditions that unbalance the ecology. Naturally, all marine life requires oxygen in order to survive. When chemical or biological wastes are dumped into the water, they compete with the marine life for the available oxygen—and often win the battle.

**Marine Environment and Pollution
Control: The Future of the Sea***
Senator Gaylord Nelson**

Mr. President, I am introducing legislation today which, in its broadest terms, is a human survival act. Its concern is with the pollution of the Great Lakes, and now, of the sea, a situation that poses dangers to the future of the human race that rank with those posed by the threat of nuclear war.

The legislation is entitled the Marine Environment and Pollution Control Act of 1970. One portion of the bill would establish a tough new national policy to halt the reckless exploitation and the destruction of our vital marine environment, and would substitute an environmental management plan beyond State waters that would be aimed at achieving a harmonious relationship between man and the source of all life, the sea.

Another part of the legislation would deal specifically with the disposal of tens of millions of tons of wastes into the sea from New York and other major cities on the ocean coastlines, in the Gulf of Mexico, and in the Great Lakes. I will explain in detail the provisions of this legislation later in the statement.

*Speech delivered in the United States Senate, Washington, D.C., February 19, 1970

**Gaylord Nelson is a United States Senator from Wisconsin. Before his election to the U.S. Senate, he served two terms as Governor of Wisconsin. He originated and was co-chairman of the nationwide Earth Day in 1970.

For the past year, the tragic story about the destruction of the sea has been unfolding at an accelerating pace. For people the world over, it is a shocking, surprising story, which they may first receive in disbelief. Throughout history, we have believed the sea was a limitless resource, as indestructible as the earth itself. And, as with all our other resources, we have acted accordingly, abusing it in the name of "Progress," somehow never realizing until very, very late that, like all other systems of the planet, the sea is a fragile environment, sensitive and vulnerable to the debris of civilization.

Our persistent refusal to accept these facts about all environments on earth is, in the view of many scientists, hurling us headlong to unprecedented worldwide disaster.

The sea is a fragile environment because, among other things, its only really productive areas are extremely limited. They are the Continental Shelves, the narrow bands of relatively shallow, highly fertile areas that extend from our coastlines, the same areas on which our myriad and dramatically increasing ocean activities are focused. Our shipping, mineral extraction, fishing, recreation, and waste disposal all are concentrated in these relatively small, fragile areas.

Destroy life on the Continental Shelves—which is what we are doing now—and, for practical purposes, the oceans are rendered a desert. Fertile coastal waters are 20 times as productive as the open ocean.

Destroy the richness of the sea, and you eliminate one of the greatest potential resources for feeding an exploding world population. Even today, there are nations, such as Japan, that depend almost entirely on the sea for their food and for many other critical resources.

Upset the intricate ecological systems of the oceans, and you run the grave risk of throwing all natural systems so seriously out of balance that the planet will no longer sustain any life.

The evidence is pouring in that we are already well on the way to causing drastic and lasting damage to the ocean environment.

Citing the steady buildup of toxic, persistant pesticides in the oceans, many scientists now believe that another 25 to 50 years of pesticide use will wipe out the oceanic fisheries.

Scientists investigating a massive die-off of seabirds last year off Britain found in the dead birds unusually high concentrations of another deadly pollutant, toxic industrial chemicals used in making paints and plastics, and in other industrial processes. Concentrations of toxic mercury and lead have also been reported in instances at alarming ocean levels.

Scientists now see new dangers to marine life and human beings as well from the potential buildup through the food chain of long-term poisons from the crude oil that is now being spilled, dumped, or leaked into the oceans by man's activities at a rate of 1 million tons a year.

The oil is showing up far from its original sources. Scientists towing a net recently in the Sargasso Sea hauled in oil tar lumps as much as 2 inches thick. The Sargasso Sea is 500 miles south of Bermuda in the Atlantic Ocean.

In addition to oil, author-explorer Thor Heyerdahl sighted plastic bottles, squeeze tubes and other debris in the mid-Atlantic during his papyrus raft trip last year. At one point, the ocean water was so filthy the raft crew could not use it to wash the dirty dishes.

In the Pacific Ocean, some still undetermined ecological change has caused a population explosion among a species of starfish. It might be just another fascinating incident if it were not for the fact that the starfish, which feeds on living coral, can, in great enough quantities, cause serious erosion on islands protected by coral reefs and lead to the destruction of food-fish populations that inhabit the reefs.

Closer to home, the oil well blowout in the Santa Barbara Channel last year stunned our Nation. Anyone who still believes the sea is invulnerable to the same devastation we now see in rivers across the land should talk to the citizens of Santa Barbara.

Or they should ask the residents of Cleveland, Detroit, Toledo, Chicago, Milwaukee, Green Bay, or Duluth-Superior. For the past several decades, we have been methodically destroying the Great Lakes, among the largest bodies of fresh water on earth. Lake Erie is degraded almost to the point of a cesspool. Lake Michigan is seriously polluted, and is about to be ringed with nuclear powerplants discharging massive heat wastes. Lake Superior, the largest, cleanest Great Lake, is now threatened. On the Minnesota north shore, a mining company is dumping 60,000 tons of iron ore process wastes into the lake each day.

One need only to have glanced over the newspapers for the past few days to get a sense of the pattern that is developing off our coastlines. Off the gulf coast, an intense fire has been burning out of control for several days on an oil well platform. If the situation is not brought under proper control, raw oil from the well could seep over vast areas of the gulf, spreading to wildlife and bird preserves, stretches of coastal marshland, and recreation beaches. Off Nova Scotia, oil spreading from a wrecked tanker has contaminated nearby shores and is killing seabirds, and the same thing is happening off Florida as oil spreads from another wrecked tanker.

The situation in a few years will be much worse. If present trends continue, according to a recent report by the President's Panel on Oil Spills, we can expect a Santa Barbara-scale disaster every year by 1980.

The report also confirmed that we do not have the technology to contain the oil from massive blowouts and spills. In fact, scientists are pointing out that current control techniques, such as massive use of detergents to break up oil slicks, can be even more damaging than the spills themselves.

Yet, in blunt testimony to our sorry history of exploiting our resources at any risk to the environment, 3,000 to 5,000 new oil wells will be drilled annually by 1980 in the marine environment. The pressure is on even in polluted Lake Erie, where only widespread public resistance has prevented drilling there to date.

By ironic coincidence, Federal plans for new oil lease sales in U.S. offshore areas were announced only a few days before the Presidential panel's 1969 oil spill report.

Because of the dramatic and sudden nature of its occurrences and damages, oil pollution has been the most visible of the marine environment problems. A second, less visible, but just as significant threat is from the wastes that are overrunning the industrialized, crowded metropolitan areas along our coastlines.

Progress—American style—is adding up each year to 200 million tons of smoke and fumes, 7 million junked cars, 20 million tons of paper, 76 billion "disposable" containers, and tens of millions of tons of sewage and industrial wastes.

It is estimated that every man, woman, and child in this country is now generating 5 pounds of refuse a day from household, commercial, and industrial wastes. To quote Balladeer Pete Seeger, Americans now find themselves "standing knee deep in garbage, throwing rockets at the moon."

The rational way out of this dilemma would be using the country's technology and massive resources to develop systems to recycle our wastes, making them valuable "resources out of place," or treating wastes to the highest degree that technology will permit.

Instead, in the classic American style, we have been taking the easy way out. Rather than planning ahead to handle the byproducts of our affluent society, we have invariably taken the cheapest, most convenient route to their disposal, regardless of the environmental consequences. Until fairly recently, the easy way has been to dump our debris outside the city limits, or into the nearest river or lake.

But now, the end of one city means the beginning of another, especially in our sprawling metropolitan areas. And either the river or lake is already grossly polluted with other wastes, or water quality standards are demanding that the polluters install decent treatment facilities.

With this tightening situation, one might think that we would finally begin a national effort to establish effective and environmentally safe waste management plans.

Instead, we have found another way to avoid the costs of environmental controls: Dump the debris into that supposedly bottomless receptacle, the sea. The attractions are many. The fact is that environmental regulations in our coastal waters are so loose it is like frontier days on the high seas, a field day for laissez faire polluters. One recent private report points out the gross inadequacies in offshore environmental regulations:

Few applications for offshore waste dumping permits are even denied, even when environmental agencies strongly oppose the dumping. In fact, the report could find no instance where the U.S. Army Corps of Engineers—in most cases, the lead agency for regulating the dumping—had ever rescinded a disposal permit, even when the polluter had clearly violated it. The reason, according to the report, is that authorities and responsibilities in the marine environment are so uncertain that public agencies may be reluctant to take action that might lead to court tests;

Furthermore, most dumping is carried out so far offshore that no present regulations of any Federal, State or local agency explicitly apply;

Although many public agencies are concerned in various ways with ocean dumping, rarely do any of them have a comprehensive picture of the total offshore waste disposal activities in the area;

Regular monitoring of ocean dumping is almost nonexistent, leaving the way wide open for abuse of already inadequate permit terms;

Finally, guidelines to determine how dumping will affect fragile ocean ecology and the marine food chain do not exist. Thus, decisions on the dumping permits are made with a tragic lack of vital information as to the consequences.

In this situation, it is often cheaper for a city to send its municipal wastes out to the ocean depths via a barge; or for an industry to relocate to the coastline from an inland area with tough water quality standards, so it can discharge its wastes directly into coastal waters without having to install costly pollution control equipment.

Because the effects of the ocean dumping are slow to appear, it is a problem that only now is breaking into public view. But when all the facts are in, I am convinced that continued unrestrained dumping clearly will spell a tragedy that will make Santa Barbara pale by comparison.

In the United States, cities, industries, and other polluters are now disposing 37 million tons of wastes into the marine environment every year, and this does not include Great Lakes figures.

Predictably, our mass consumption, mass disposal society is responsible for one-third to one-half of the world's pollution input to the sea.

The cities and metropolitan areas involved include San Francisco, Los Angeles, San Diego, Boston, New York, Philadelphia, Baltimore, Charleston, St. Petersburg, Miami, Port Arthur, Galveston, Texas City, and Houston.

The wastes—dumped at sea from barges and ships—run the gamut of by-products from the "affluent" society. They include garbage and trash; waste oil; dredging spoils; industrial acids, caustics, cleaners, sludges, and waste liquor; airplane parts; junked automobiles and spoiled food. Radioactive wastes, poison gas, and obsolete ordnance have also been dumped in the sea by atomic energy and defense agencies.

Along our Pacific coast, 8.8 million tons of these wastes were dumped in 1968 alone.

Along the heavily populated east coast, 23.7 million tons were dumped that year.

And along the gulf coast in 1968, 14.6 million tons of wastes were dumped.

A leader for the whole country in the dumping of wastes into the sea is metropolitan New York. In a recent year, dumping for this area off the New Jersey and Lond Island coasts came to 6.6 million tons of dilute industrial waste acids, and 573,000 tons of cellar dirt.

The sewage sludge, dumped 11 miles offshore, has spread over a 10- to 20-square-mile area of the ocean bed, killing bottom life, cutting oxygen levels, poisoning the sea waters. A wide area outside the dumping grounds is also contaminated, possibly by the sewage sludge. Dumping of other wastes is being carried out in five other undersea areas off New York.

The results of several decades of ocean waste disposal off this vast metropolis are grim portents for the future of much of the U.S. marine environment if the practice is allowed to continue.

Off New York, outbreaks of a strange fish disease, where fins and tails rot away, have been reported since 1967.

Recreation-destroying red tides have recently closed local beaches, particularly during the summer of 1968.

Massive growths of nuisance organisms, such as seaweeds and jellyfish, are now prevalent.

Once huge oysterbeds in New York Harbor have been all but eliminated.

Nearly all local clamming areas have been closed because of contamination.

Many swimming beaches are now closed every summer for the same reason, and there are indications that the sewage sludge dumped far offshore may now be creeping back in on the currents.

Now, in the face of this marine disaster, suggestions are being made that the New York dumping grounds be moved anywhere up to 100 miles offshore. Whether this is feasible on even an interim basis, it is highly doubtful it offers any permanent solution. New Yorkers 40 years ago thought they had escaped much of their waste problem when the present offshore dumping grounds were selected. Past history gives little cause for confidence that dumping even 100 miles into the sea will prevent grave consequences 40 years from now.

In fact, the evidence from the present New York situation, and from the effects of other United States and worldwide marine activities, indicates firmly that if we are to avoid setting off further disaster in our vital offshore areas, the dumping should be phased out entirely along our coastlines and the Great Lakes. The legislation I am proposing would require such a phase-out in 5 years, a deadline which respected authorities have indicated would be reasonable, if a concerted effort is started now to find alternative, safe means of waste disposal or recycling.

The only exception would be when the Secretary of the Interior determined that an alternative was not yet technically available. Then, a temporary permit could be issued until an alternative was developed.

The legislation will also deal with the wastes pouring directly into the ocean and the Great Lakes from numerous outfalls of municipal and industrial waste disposal systems. As I pointed out earlier, the alternative of piping our wastes directly into the sea is becoming increasingly attractive from an economic point of view, as water quality standards are tightened inland. Yet from an environmental point of view, moving to the edge of the sea for cheap waste disposal and cheap water supplies will only accelerate the pollution of the sensitive offshore areas. It is a trend that must be halted now, and the legislation I am introducing will allow only liquid, nontoxic wastes, treated at levels equal to the natural quality of the receiving waters, to be disposed of at sea, with the exception noted above, where an alternative was not technically available.

Now, on one 30-mile stretch of the New Jersey coast alone, there are 14 sewer outfalls discharging directly into the ocean, with more planned. In New York harbor, 20 New Jersey companies are either in court or under orders to halt pollution. According to Federal figures several years ago, the estuarine waters of the United States received 8.3 billion gallons of municipal waste discharges per day.

Clearly, wholesale waste disposal and dumping into the ocean environment is a practice that is rapidly becoming a national scandal. It reflects another near total failure of our institutions to come to grips with a grave new challenge of this modern, complex age. And it is one more tragic instance of polluters and Government, with the consent of a lethargic public, avoiding rational environmental planning now, and letting future generations pay the price.

To date, we have been spending only a pittance in this country on new, more effective ways of handling our wastes, while we spend tens of billions of dollars to put man on the moon, or to fight the Vietnam war. Legislation now pending before the Senate, the Resource Recovery Act, would be an important step forward in the urgently needed effort to manage this country's mounting solid wastes.

Ironically, while we continue to accelerate the gruesome process of polluting the sea, industry, our crowded cities, commercial ventures of all kinds, and even public agencies are making big new plans to carve up this rich, little regulated frontier for profit or for the tax dollar.

Already, the Defense Department holds one of the biggest chunks of marine environment—a total of approximately 300,000 square miles used for missile testing grounds and military operations.

But jurisdictions are so confused in the increasingly busy offshore waters that one mining operator had to turn back his sea bed phosphate lease when he found it was in an old Defense Department ordnance dump.

Crowded metropolitan areas are looking to the sea as the answer not only to their waste disposal problems, but for their space shortages as well. In the next few years, it is possible that construction of floating airports will begin for New York City, Los Angeles, and Cleveland. Floating seaports and floating cities may not be far behind.

And population and use pressures on our coastal areas will continue to escalate. Already, more than 75 per cent of the Nation's population, more than 150 million people, now lives in coastal States, and more than 45 per cent of our urban population lives in coastal countries.

Now, the coasts provide recreation for tens of millions of citizens. And the demand for outdoor recreation is increasing twice as fast as our burgeoning population. Yet in the face of these growing needs and expectations, the coasts are in danger of being crowded and polluted out of the market as recreation resources. In effect, Americans are slamming the door on their last escape route to a livable world. Our choice now is to either clean up our environment, or survive in surroundings we never thought we would have to accept.

Again, we look to the sea for distant answers. Within 33 years, we can expect permanent inhabited undersea installations and perhaps even colonies, according to the commission on the year 2000, a group established by the American Academy of Arts and Sciences.

In another activity, oil tankers, a more frequent source of pollution than oil wells, are being built to huge scales, cutting transportation costs but increasing environmental danger. The *Torrey Canyon* tanker was carrying 118,000 tons of crude oil when it broke up off England in 1967, a disaster that soaked miles of beaches with oil and killed more than 25,000 birds. Today, there are tankers being designed with a 500,000 ton capacity.

In addition to bringing new pollution dangers, the tankers will probably help create a new industrial seascape off our coasts. Since our ports are not big enough to handle these super ships, offshore docking facilities will have to be built.

In the Gulf of Alaska, heavy tankers could soon be operating to ship oil from the southern end of the proposed Trans-Alaska pipeline. Meanwhile, other oil and gas interests are proposing leases for drilling in the gulf. Leasing could put the tankers and oil rigs on a collision course, with massive oil spills as a result.

In another area of resource use, a company will soon begin an experimental mining operation off the southeast Atlantic coast in which a vacuum device will draw materials off the sea bed, and half way up, separate out fine wastes and spew them into the undersea in a broad fan. An almost certain result will be the smothering of bottom life over a wide area.

On Georges Bank, a rich international fishery off the New England coast, studies have identified areas with tremendous oil and gas potential, posing possible conflicts.

The evidence is clear. If tough environmental management steps are not taken now, the outcome of this bustle of new activity is certain. We will ultimately make as much a wreckage of the oceans as we have of the land. There will be constant conflicts between users, more reckless exploitation, perhaps the total destruction of marine life, and through the whole process, public agencies will be relegated to their all too frequent ineffective role of referees between competing resource users.

The Oceans: Man's Last
Great Resource*
Senator Claiborne Pell**

After millenniums of exploiting and often destroying the riches of the land, man is now hovering acquisitively over the wealth of the oceans that cover three-quarters of the Earth. In the no man's land of the seabed, a scramble for minerals and oil, for new underwater empires secured by advancing armies of technology, could well set a new and wider stage of world conflict.

Even the most conservative estimates of resources in the seabed stagger the imagination of a world grown used to dire predictions of incipient famine and exhausted mineral resources. In the millions of miles of ocean that touch a hundred nations live four out of five living things on Earth. In the seabed, minerals and oil have been proved to exist in lavish supply. The oceans are a source of pure water and food protein; of drugs and building materials; even possibly a habitat for man himself and a key to survival for the doubling population on the land.

Man may yet learn to use a tiny fraction of this wealth. Unless international law soon determines how it shall be shared, that fraction alone could set off a new age of colonial war. Is the deep seabed, like the high seas, common to all, or is it, like the once wilderness areas on land, open to national claim by use and occupation by the first or the strongest pioneer? The question of what is to be done to regulate and control exploitation of the seabeds is no longer an exercise for academics and global thinkers. At stake is not just the prize of great wealth; pollution or geologic accident in the ocean deeps is no respecter of national boundaries.

A few years ago, "practical" men dismissed speculations about wealth in the sea as economic foolishness. It would never, they said, be economically profitable to exploit the seabeds no matter how great the riches to be found there. They underestimated the lure of gold as the mother of invention. Yet, such pessimists may well be proved right in a fashion they did not anticipate. In these pioneer years of the ocean age, the damage done sometimes seems to exceed the benefit reaped. Beaches from England to Puerto Rico to California have been soaked in oily slime. Fish and wildlife have been destroyed. Insecticides, dispersed in the Rhine River, killed fish and revived fears of other lethal legacies that may emerge from our casual use of waterways as garbage dumps. The U.S. Army, until deterred recently by a few alert legislators, was disposing containers of chemical agents in the Atlantic despite some predictions that severe damage to the marine environment could not be ruled out, because of either deterioration of the containers or unforeseen underwater accidents. The future disposal of increasing amounts of atomic waste is an unresolved problem. Millions of acres of offshore seabed have been leased for drilling. Largely in ignorance, we are tinkering with our greatest source of life.

*Saturday Review, LII, No. 41 (October 11, 1969), 19-21, 62-63. Copyright 1969 Saturday Review, Inc. Reprinted by permission.

**Claiborne Pell is a United States Senator from Rhode Island and Chairman of the Senate Foreign Relations Subcommittee on Ocean Space.

The incredible magnitude of the oceans' resources can be measured by just one isolated example: the metal content of manganese nodules, for years a curiosity with no realizable value. One study of reserves in the Pacific Ocean alone came up with an estimate that the nodules contained 358 billion tons of manganese, equivalent, at present rates of consumption, to reserves for 400,000 years, compared to known land reserves of only 100 years. The nodules contain equally staggering amounts of aluminum, nickel, cobalt, and other metals. Most of these resources exist at great depths of 5,000 to more than 15,000 feet, yet within five to ten years the technology will exist for commercial mining operations, a development that will open to exploitation virtually unlimited metal reserves. Closer to home, the University of Wisconsin discovered a deposit of manganese worth an estimated $15-million in the shallow waters of Green Bay in Lake Michigan.

More familiar to most of us is the accelerated pace of offshore oil drilling that now extends more than fifty miles out to sea and accounts for 15 per cent of U.S. oil production. In the twelve years between 1955 and 1967, offshore production of crude oil increased from seven million to 222 million barrels. Estimates of known reserves of natural gas have more than tripled in the past fifteen years, and each advance of scientific exploration of the ocean beds brings to light new finds that would gladden the eye of the most hardened veteran of the California gold rush.

Perhaps the least developed resource, and one of critical importance to spiraling population figures, is the use of the seas for farming techniques or "aquaculture." Present methods of fishing can only be compared with primitive hunting with a bow and arrow; if fish were cultivated like livestock, the present world fish catch could easily be multiplied by five- or as much as tenfold. The production of protein concentrate and the distillation of fresh water are still experimental in an economic sense; there is no reason to believe that they too cannot become both useful and profitable. Aquaculture could also be applied to a variety of marine plant life.

Nor is the potential confined to what we can extract from the seas or the seabed. In crowded England, serious plans have been developed to build entire cities just off the coast. Offshore airports may solve the demand for large tracts of jet-age space near such large coastal cities as New York and Los Angeles. Some Americans, quick to take advantage of the legal confusion that reigns beyond coastal waters, have planned to build independent islands atop seamounts and reefs outside the three-mile limit. Indeed, a romantic notion, but one with, it is suspected, the more prosaic aim of avoiding the constrictions of domestic law concerning gambling and taxes. One such venture has been restrained by the courts on the grounds that the reefs and seamounts attach to the seabed on the continental shelf, and are, therefore, under U.S. jurisdiction. In another case, a year or so ago, the United Nations was presented with an application for permission to extract minerals from the bed of the Red Sea in an area fifty miles from the coastal states. The Secretariat dodged this thorny question, citing lack of authority to act. Such claims are no longer isolated or frivolous. Much of the wealth of the oceans is now both proved and exploitable beyond that part of the continental shelf once considered to mark the practical limit of exploitation and national claims. This Pandora's box is as full of political hazards as it is of manganese. Parts of the Gulf of Mexico became such a forest of drilling rigs that an agreement was necessary to clear shipping lanes. This spring, the Dominican Republic granted a single oil concession covering some three-quarters of a million acres of offshore seabed, and many other small coastal nations are looking for an economic bonanza in the leasing of drilling rights. Under what safety and pollution regulations will such developments take place? How far out may any nation grant such leases or undertake such exploitation?

In short, diplomats and politicians who five years ago looked backward to the slow evolution of mining the sea and found nothing to engage their immediate concern have been overtaken, as is frequently the case in this day, by the less stately pace of technological change. If the know-how of ocean exploitation has gathered momentum of its own, the same cannot be said for any reasoned approach to orderly development under a regime of law.

Two years ago, faced with the prospect of orbiting weapons in the legal void of space, nations did agree on a treaty to limit the uses of outer space. Similar concern has not been so evident in the realm of ocean space, perhaps because people are so used to taking marine environment for granted.

A less charitable view might suggest that one of the inhibiting factors is the prospect of making a good deal of money, an incentive not present at the moment in space, except for the manufacturers of hardware here on Earth.

Yet, the oceans offer no less a fearsome stage for escalation of the arms race. The seabed already abounds with a multiplicity of sounding devices and other defensive technology. High "mountain" ridges in the ocean bed offer tempting sites for the deployment of nuclear weapons, and there is no reason why the Soviet Union and the U.S. might not seen be planting ABMs eyeball to eyeball on the Atlantic ridge. Thanks in large part to initiatives in the United Nations, the question of arms control in the seabed is under discussion at the Conference of the Committee on Disarmament in Geneva. Last spring both the Soviet Union and the U.S. offered differing proposals to ban the emplacement of weapons of mass destruction on the seabed—proposals that hopefully could forestall this new escalation of the nuclear race.

If the prospect of a new arms race on the ocean floor precipitated efforts to focus world attention on the problem, there is no lack of other and equally explosive possibilities for conflict. How far may the claims and undertakings of coastal states extend seaward? By whose permission, if any, is exploitation of the ocean deeps undertaken? Who is entitled to the proceeds, and who is to establish and enforce rules governing the safety of such exploitation? There have not been, as yet, any murders or muggings on the ocean floor. If there were, what law would apply? No one knows. The laws of the high seas, which have evolved over so many centuries of our casual passage across their surface, are not wholly applicable by extension to the ocean floor.

In a study of the full range of our national interests in marine resources, made public early this year, a special Presidential Commission on Marine Science, Engineering, and Resources noted, rather matter-of-factly, that the threat of "unbridled international competition for the seas' resources may provoke conflict," and recommended a series of international agreements that would create new legal political frameworks for the exploitation of the mineral resources underlying the deep seas. There is no lack of proposals for such a regime; their specifics are as various as the magnitude of the interests involved.

As could be expected, the differences among nations reflect political power and geographic accident. In a letter to the Spanish ambassador in 1580, the first

Queen Elizabeth of England wrote that "the use of the sea and air is common to all, neither can a title to the ocean belong to any people or private persons, forasmuch as neither nature nor public use and custom permit any possession thereof." The Queen may have had in mind the Treaty of Tordesillas, signed a little more than a century earlier by Spain and Portugal, dividing all the world's oceans between them. That treaty did not survive the emergence of a superior naval power, and the Queen's views of freedom of the seas prevailed.

Four centuries later, the same dispute has been revived beneath the seas. There are those who would carve up the shelf and the seabed among the major maritime powers, and there are others who would insure freedom of the ocean beds beyond a narrow claim of national jurisdiction equivalent to the customary three-mile or twelve-mile claim of jurisdiction over territorial waters on the surface.

The three-mile limit claimed by the U.S. is the measure of a cannon shot in the eighteenth century. It may be regrettable that nothing so simple as a cannon shot was used to determine an equivalent measure on the seabed, since efforts to date—with more sophisticated standards—have only compounded the confusion that began in 1945 when the U.S., largely at the behest of the oil industry, unilaterally extended its sovereignty to include the bed of the continental shelf (that portion of the submerged land mass that extends at relatively shallow depths seaward, in some places for more than a hundred miles). Other nations followed, and in 1958 an international Convention on the Continental Shelf declared that a nation's jurisdiction over the shelf extends to a depth of 200 meters (about 650 feet) or "beyond that limit to where the depth of the superjacent waters admits of the exploitation of the natural resources." For coastal nations with extensive shelves, it was the most painless territorial conquest in history. Few then suspected that effective exploitation of resources would soon take place far deeper than 200 meters, or that the "exploitability" clause of the convention—as interpreted by the oil industry and others—would, in effect, grant a license to move in the ocean beds to the limits of a nation's power to defend its claims.

Strategic interest in what goes on in the seabeds off our shores further complicated efforts to decide whether our national interests would be best served by limited claims—as in the waters above—or by a more expansive goal. Yet the same rationale of maximum maneuverability, which is the basis of the jealously guarded right of freedom of the seas, argues equally strongly for a narrow claim of jurisdiction on the seabed. Beyond that narrow band, our own military, like their opposite numbers in the Kremlin, would prefer to trust to luck and muscle in making the best of all possibilities. The oil industry has no such dual interest; it wants to carry the flag as far as effective exploration permits.

And what of the small nations who believe, not unreasonably, that the riches of the seas should not be left up for grabs by the already rich and powerful?

It was this prospect, as well as the looming threat of a new weapons race, that two years ago brought forth two different proposals for an international regime for the seabed. In the United Nations, the government of Malta introduced a resolution that would place the riches of the sea under international administration to be used for the benefit of mankind. In the U.S. Senate, I introduced a treaty, based in part upon the Treaty on Outer Space, and one that would, in my judgment, deal more realistically than does the Maltese proposal with the competing economic and political interests in ocean space.

Other detailed proposals have been made—by the National Petroleum Council at one end of the spectrum, and by the Commission to study the Organization of Peace, the World Peace through Law group, and the Center for the Study of Democratic Institutions in Santa Barbara at the other. Neither of these opposing views, whether favoring unilateral action by the U.S. or advocating extensive internationalization of the seabed, is entirely practicable.

The oil industry advises a clubby agreement among the major maritime powers extending their jurisdiction by their own actions to the limits of their technological capacity for exploitation at least to that point where the continental slope meets the abyssal ocean floor. Such a claim would encompass most of the known wealth and would, they argue, neatly delimit the lines of jurisdiction and so insure maximum stability. What might happen in the event of the emergence of a powerful nonmember of the club is not clear, but history provides some clues. In advocating such an approach, the National Petroleum Council piously noted that it "is in the best interest of the United States whether or not it is in the best interests of the American oil and gas industries." So pleased is the industry with this act of statesmanship that the publisher of the *Oil Daily* felt impelled to comment editorially that "we rather doubt there is a record of a more high-minded, patriotic, and statesman-like position involving comparable interests in the whole range of the industrial economy."

Those proposals that advocate international administration of the resources of the sea, or of the profits from their exploitation, also suffer from practical defects, however useful their purpose may appear in theory. Only a few nations, most particularly the U.S., possess both the technology and the financial capability to proceed with the exploitation of the oceans. The financial risks and investments are enormous, and it is unlikely—and unreasonable—to expect that they would be assumed for altruistic purposes. It is clearly essential that any exploiting company be assured of security of tenure and the right to profits.

Adequate protection of economic incentive and investment security is not, however, irreconcilable with the thought that these resources should also provide some revenues for the common benefit of mankind. Ambassador Arvid Pardo of Malta once estimated that at the present rate of development, annual revenues could reach $6-billion by 1975, if a regime such as he proposed were established by 1970. His figures assume that the fees paid would be the equivalent of those now paid to national governments for offshore drilling leases, and that they would cover all exploitation beyond the relatively narrow confines of a 200-meter depth or a lateral distance from the shore of twelve miles. Such a sweeping concept of internationalization is not likely to prove acceptable, but his estimate paints a tantalizing picture of the measure of funds that could be generated by licensing fees even on a much more limited scale.

Another practical defect in some of the proposals for international administration of the ocean beds, and one even closer to the bedrock of practicality in the present political climate of the world, is that it is simply not realistic to expect any great power to surrender to an international body control of a resource in which its national security interests are so substantially involved unless those interests are fully recognized and protected. Any international regime must be responsive to the realities of power or be doomed to failure.

Despite substantial and specific differences, most advocates of some international regime share a common purpose: to avoid an underseas land grab; to forestall a new nuclear arms race; to control marine pollution and, by extension, other actions that might upset the ecology of the oceans; and to insure some equitable distribution of the wealth for the common benefit of mankind. The same philosophy was stated earlier by President Johnson when he said, "Under no circumstances, we believe, must we ever allow the prospects of a rich harvest in mineral wealth to create a new form of colonial competition among the maritime nations. We must be careful to avoid a race to grab and to hold the lands under the high seas. We must ensure that the deep seas and the ocean bottoms are, and remain, the legacy of all human beings."

As a result of the initiative of Malta, the United Nations created a temporary, and now permanent, forty-two nation subcommittee of the General Assembly to deal with the seabed. Meetings of the subcommittee and its working groups have focused attention on the need to know more about our marine environment; gradually there has been a distillation of basic principles that seem essential to the orderly evolution of a body of law, however minimal. But it is evident that the sea that divides has yet to unite mankind, to paraphrase Longfellow. Except for occasional propaganda forays among the developing nations, the Soviet Union has taken the view that the least done, the better. Some Latin American states have made claims of jurisdiction extending out 200 miles on the seabed as they have also claimed a 200-mile territorial sea in the water above. Other small coastal nations, once in favor of internationalization, are now hoping to get richer quicker by leasing drilling rights off their coasts.

Technology, however, does not await the resolution of political differences, and we are fast approaching a point where the pace of exploitation may govern, rather than be governed by, sound political judgments. If there are, as seems likely, fewer risks in supporting at least a minimal international regime than in a wide-open scramble for control of the seas, it is necessary that we soon agree on some basic principles to serve as guidelines until a treaty can be negotiated.

First among these principles, and one that is embodied in the treaty I have proposed, is the recognition that the seas shall remain the heritage of mankind, open to all nations for peaceful purposes, and not subject to national appropriation by any.

To resolve the boundary problem, the treaty would set the limits of national jurisdiction at a depth of 550 meters or a lateral distance from the shoreline of fifty miles, whichever is greater. The depth measure encompasses most of the geographic shelf. The lateral measure assures those nations with little or no shelf, the security of determining what goes on in the ocean depths within that distance of their shores.

The treaty further proposes that exploitation of the seabeds beyond this limit be licensed by an independent international body to be established by the United Nations. Such a body would be constituted to reflect the realities of power and interest of the major nations. The World Bank is one example of an international body not directly under the aegis of the U.N. and in which both political power and technical expertise are adequately represented so decisions may be both informed and enforceable in terms of practical support. Licenses would be granted for extensive periods to insure security of tenure; the fees paid for the licenses would be used for an agreed international purpose.

Provision is also made in this treaty for the settlement of disputes by a panel appointed by the International Court of Justice, and the treaty draft also envisions an international sea guard, the equivalent of our Coast Guard, to which nations might contribute or lend research and scientific vessels for exploration and to supervise the observance of established standards of safety and pollution controls. Finally, the treaty proposes international regulation of the disposal of atomic waste.

In sum, the treaty provides a sensible and practical means of regulating a resource that is no respecter of national boundaries any more than are the air waves; it ensures a limit on national territorial claims as we have already done in Antarctica; it limits the nature of activities in an area of common danger as we have done in outer space; and it should, someday, become as unremarkable as all the many international agreements that now govern air traffic, maritime lanes, radio frequencies, international mails, and all the incidents of everyday living now taken for granted.

Perhaps most important, it assures incentive for development by technologically advanced nations, while making available a source of funds to benefit poor nations. If there is any single critical issue on this planet, it is not nuclear bombs or ABMs; it is the vastly greater explosive force of billions of men living ever closer to the edge of famine.

It is inconceivable that this last great resource of our planet should not ease the grip of poverty and hunger on much of the Earth. And how tragic it will be if a few centuries hence, these vast oceans that nourish life should become the instrument of our death, a not impossible end. Could those of our early settlers who first viewed the Great Lakes possibly imagine a day—a few short years in the sweep of history—when Lake Erie would become a lifeless testament to the unbridled depredations of men and machines? And, if they had foreseen such consequences, would they then have sought a rule of law to control the license of man? As we view the now abundant oceans around us, it is something to think about. The answers, one way or the other, may not be long in coming.

Manifesto for the Sea*
Robert Rienow**

Jeremiah, as he wailed "There is sorrow on the sea; it cannot be quiet," was seemingly but drawing a literary backdrop for his lamentations. Even he could not have anticipated that one day the mighty oceans would be literally the subject of despair.

The myth of great and unfathomable seas—a limitless frontier of exploitation—lies at the base of the legal and political regime that marks man's historic

*American Behavioral Scientist, Vol. II, No. 6 (July-August, 1968), 34-37. Reprinted by permission.

**Robert Rienow is a professor of political science at the State University of New York, Albany. He is co-author of Moment in the Sun and has written extensively on environmental problems.

relationship to those seas. We still intone with Byron:

> Roll on, thou deep and dark blue ocean, roll!
> Ten thousand fleets sweep over thee in vain;
> Man marks the earth with ruin—his control
> Stoops with the shore.
>
> —Childe Harold

And because we are mesmerized by the endless beating of the eternal waves into agreeing with the poet that the seas are invincible, we admit, long after it is thoroughly outmoded, the doctrine of *res nullius.* Even as we maul and poison the oceans, destroying the delicate chains of life so intricately assembled, we stubbornly cling to the doctrine that the sea is big enough to absorb the assorted blows of man, individually and collectively.

We have not yet adjusted our thinking to the mastery of technology. Because the seas could gulp a schooner and all hands aboard without a belch, we forget that a loaded 200,000-ton oil tanker is an indigestible item. Because a liner or two could spew their slops overboard with impunity, we have come to believe that we need put no limits on the filth that we pipe to the depths. Because the once-pure oceans are seemingly illimitable, we make them the dumping grounds for the hottest by-products of our atomic age, a deadly assortment of long-lasting radioactive wastes.

Yet because these premises are false, a critical urgency has arisen. Hundreds of conglomerate nations, pressed by burgeoning, hungry populations, are now attacking the seas with the full vigor of unrestrained technological prowess. If we would save them and their resources from death, we must soon cease the abuse and establish a new protective regime of law not yet imagined by man—a law able to combat the massive destructive powers which humanity has come to possess.

Our entire philosophy is contrary to our need. It is the ancient, worn-out credo of "inexhaustible" resources, the myth which has so grossly impoverished our once rich resource base. But in the case of the seas, the myth has been multiplied a thousand times.

Indeed, we use the seas not only as a soporific against the reckoning that our fecundity and industrial productivity must surely impose upon us, but as a glittering promise beyond anything we have yet known. Predicts Dr. William A. Nierenberg, Director of Scripps Institution of Oceanography, in an outburst of optimism: "We're learning more and more about food chains and we know the oceans could yield enough protein on a sustained basis to feed 30 *billion* people."[1]

Not only unlimited food, such as it may be, will be seined from the ocean's depths, but minerals will be mined, oil trapped on its floor, and great underseas cities glimmer through its watery aisles, cloistered havens for our unwanted millions. Dr. Donald F. Hronig, Science Adviser to the President, summarized these bullish prophecies by concluding that "The ocean is big business right now, and the rate it's going, it's reasonable to expect it will become an even bigger business in the years ahead."

This frontier legend of the seas paints a pristine, limitless, and romantic cornucopia of the deep. With oceanographers chafing in the lead to generate the enthusiasm, we are regaled with fabulous statistics. There are 1.5 trillion tons of manganese nodules pimpling the ocean floor, enough minable phosphate material off the coast of Mexico to last, at present rates of consumption, for 4000 years, and enough oil to fill 25% of the entire oil production of the world.

This, then, is our image of the sea—a prodigally bounteous, untamed frontier bursting with potential riches for all. The myth is founded on public ignorance of a type foreboding of tragedy. It is abetted by a less than honest assessment by the sea's fervent exploiters. Minerals and oil may be there in untold quantities, but the dangers to men, and the pollutive destruction of the waters in obtaining them, are never stressed. As for the sea harvest of food which is depended upon to stave off the famines to come, the fatuity of such predictions is that they ignore completely the nature and delicacy of the sea's life chains. And there is no note taken of the fact that the productive part of the sea is largely on its fringes—the continental shelves, the bays and estuaries. The wide expanse of the sea is ecologically a watery desert.

"Preserving habitat for salt-water fish requires controlling the development of tidelands, tidal bottoms, and all the fringing brackish water habitat. This is the part of the sea called the *estuarine zone*. The word estuary as used here describes any of the protected coastal areas where there is a mixing of salt and fresh waters, including all the tidal rivers, marshes, tideflats, lagoons, bays, and shallow sounds," explains John Clark, writing for the American Littoral Society.[2] "Two out of every three species of useful Atlantic fish," he adds, "depend in some way upon tidal lands and the shallowest of our bays for their survival. Even oceanic fish often have complex life cycles which bring them into coastal bays, lagoons, and tidal rivers at tiny young stages of their lives."

It has been estimated that 90% of the salt-water fish are taken in shallow coastal waters. More importantly, the parts of the ocean bordering the land are the fertile environment in which flourishes the plant growth on which bait fish, shellfish, shrimp, and plankton all thrive. "The richest coastal marshes produce ten tons of plant stuff per acre per year—more than six times the amount (one and one-half tons) of wheat produced per acre, on a world average."

Even the undersea farming that excites the imagination of some scientists is planned to take place in the estuaries, coastal swamps, and shoreline areas. Dr. John H. Ryther of Woods Hole Oceanographic Institution points out that the productivity of the one and one-fourth million acres of mangrove swamps in the Philippines, if applied to the raising of milkfish in ponds, would in itself produce a tonnage of protein food equal to the present fish harvest of the entire United States. Aquaculture is designed to be practiced near the shores.

Yet it has been made evident that the seas are most shockingly vulnerable to the insults that stem from the activities of man in the very place where man and ocean meet. The traditional "accepted" use of coastal waters for the outfalls of municipal and industrial sewage systems is now seriously questioned, as the wastes mount geometrically. "In recent years," says a team of scholars, "many have realized that, although the oceans contain an almost limitless supply of diluting water, other beneficial and economically important uses of the nearshore ocean waters must be considered when an ocean outfall is designed for the disposal of sewage."[3]

Up to now the pollution of harbors, bays, and estuaries has been carried to the point of hazard or nuisance on the basic assumption that the tidal scrubbing would be effective. We are, indeed, with our overburden of wastes and our identification of coastal waters with the vast expanse of the oceans, destroying an environment which is at the same time both separate from the seas and yet highly interdependent. The multiplication of people and their industries is fast rendering barren the most fruitful part of the seas. "Coastal and estuarine regions of the sea which receive large amounts of organic wastes often produce sulfides from the bottom sediments in concentrations so high that animals and plants inhabitating these environments are damaged seriously."[4]

Direct outfalls may make of a bay or harbor a disease-ridden and noisome thing, as in the town of Winthrop Harbor in the Boston vicinity. There, the fascinating and profitable array of life forms that marks a seacoast was suffocated by an overwhelming growth of sea lettuce, feeding on the ingredients of the raw sewage that was being dumped in ever greater quantities from the North Metropolitan Sewer near Deer Island.

As we continue to pollute each of our 22 watersheds, all the vast quantities of inland wastes are added to the coastal burden of pollution. All up and down the coasts, each river spills its accumulated filth and contaminants at its mouth, in volumes that even the indefatigable tide cannot overcome. With river valleys the choice habitation of man, it follows that the rivers provide the plumbing system for most of mankind, and the coastal waters of the seas become an elongated septic tank. The Thames estuary is today a notorious sewer. The domestic industrial effluents of a million people pour down the estuary of the once-lovely River Tyne. Should you consult the engineering manuals rather than the travel folders, you will find, instead of a lyric description of the sunrise over Hawaii's famed Kailua Bay, the less savory discussion of the sewage daily discharged into it. You will be enlightened by the figures of sewage burden from Nanaimo and the sulfate discharge of the 700-ton-a-day mill into the Northumberland Channel of the North Pacific.[5] Yet the time is close at hand when the very odor alone of such waters will force the tourist agencies (albeit for a different reason) to join the ecologists and engineers in their mounting concern for the debauchment of the world's bays.

Added to the befoulment by sewage and industrial effluents, we now face the swelling floods of thousands of concoctions of pesticides and herbicides which drain constantly down into the rivers' mouths. It was the late Lloyd Berkner, eminent scientist and dean of the Dallas Graduate Research Center, who first called attention to the lethal effects of these pesticidal compounds on the floating diatoms of the sea, manufacturers of 70% of the oxygen in the air we daily breathe.[6]

Long-lasting DDT is particularly deadly to fish life. "The Interior Department reveals that one part of DDT in one billion parts of water kills blue crabs in eight days."[7] Yet this vicious and discredited pesticide, which has proved to be all but eternal in its toxicity and is peculiarly lethal to aquatic life, is flushed off the watersheds of every major farming country without restraint into the most productive areas of the world's oceans. Pomeroy et al mention the depredation visited upon mullet *(mugil cephalus)*, menhaden *(brevoortia tyrannus)*, and the commercial shrimps *(penaeus spp)* which enter the marsh creeks in spring and spend most of the summer feeding there.[8]

Many of the pesticides, indeed, were particularly "formulated to combat terrestrial arthropods—spiders, insects, etc., distinguished by their jointed feet and limbs, segmented bodies, and horny skeletons. In other words, what selective toxicity is built into these pesticides is directed to the arthropods. Unfortunately, it happens that a number of our most valuable marine food species, including lobsters, crabs, and shrimp, are also hapless arthropods."[9] It has also been found that some varieties of plankton important in the diet of oysters and clams are especially vulnerable to minute concentrations of herbicides, much smaller concentrations than are employed for the extensive weed control programs upstream.

As if sewage industrial effluents, and pesticidal-herbicidal compounds were not enough, our civilization makes still another death-dealing assault upon the nurseries of the seas. The fallout from nuclear explosions that spreads itself about the earth in the falling rain also gathers in the watersheds' drainage, collecting finally in the estuaries along with the wastes that spill out of uranium mills,[10] dribble from atomic installations, and find their way from industrial and medical applications to the outfalls on the banks. Thus, the Severn, the Blackwater, Britain's Solway Firth,[11] as well as the seas off the Irish and Netherland coast, are causing increasing concern because of their growing concentrations of radioactive wastes. Over the short period of six years there has been a progressive and measurable increase of Strontium 90 and Cesium 137 in the coastal water, fish, mussels, and shrimps in the North Sea.[12]

These are but examples; the threat is universal. A careful evaluation by a team of scientists repeats that "Future additions of *significant amounts* of radionuclides to the estuarine and marine environment, whether accidental or intentional, will almost certainly occur in a variety of climatic, geographic, and geologic areas."[13]

As if this steadily advancing radiation of our seafood nurseries were not fast enough, we are still (after more than twenty years of waste disposal research) directly dumping our radioactive poisons into our coastal seas. "A Canadian report states that more than 16,000 drums, each containing 55 gallons of low-level waste, were dumped off the coast of California from 1946 to 1957. At Harwell (U.K.) contaminated solid waste, consisting of building material, protective clothing, laboratory equipment, animal remains, etc., is first reduced in volume as much as possible, and subsequently either stored or discharged into the sea. The total volume of this waste amounts to approximately 3200 cubic feet per week, weighing about 29 tons."[14]

The pressure for this kind of sea disposal of radioactive wastes becomes intense as one ponders the fantastic estimates for the future. "In the United States, it is estimated that the nuclear power industry will have produced three thousand million curies of radioactivity in 27 million litres of solution by 1970, and 60 thousand million curies in 1.1 billion litres of solution by the year 2000."[15] The safety of these disposal arrangements, which has the support of a body of scientists, has been founded on a pair of assumptions: that there are "deeps" where the lethal debris will remain isolated, and that what escapes will be greatly diluted.

Both assumptions are currently challenged. Many experts hotly argue that our research as to the circulation, mixing, and sedimentation in the deep sea is pitifully inadequate. Russian scholars are most doubtful about the current practices. Nicolas Gorsky, a member of the U.S.S.R. Geographical Society, notes the vertical mixing or circulation described by Professor Zubov which "ventilates the deep layers of the ocean and also raises to the surface a layer rich in nutrient phosphates and nitrates, forming a basis for abundant life. But this process will bring death if pernicious radioactive solutions from the waste products of the atomic industry accumulate in the ocean depths."[16]

More important, Professor Gorsky describes another similar phenomenon known as "upwelling:" Because of winds, currents, or the relief of the ocean bed, deep, cold layers of water, laden with nutrients, come to the surface and lap the continental slope or the submerged banks. This phenomenon is especially marked on the Atlantic coast of North America, the California coast, and the western coast of both South America and Africa.

"The regions where upwelling occurs are exceptionally rich in plant and animal life, including fish. If the water rising to the surface should be contaminated with substances dissolved out of radioactive wastes it will mean the end of the highly productive fisheries in these regions."[17]

Indeed the Russian conclusion is that it is impossible to isolate or localize the poisoning of the seas. Even if the currents and movement of the water did not focus on the shores, the concentrating factor in the oceanic food chains is itself a competent countervail to dilution. Thus, in the central Pacific Ocean, "plankton were found to contain on the average nearly 500 times the general water concentration of fallout activity. An examination of the fish of the German bight coastal area shows that the radioactivity level remains constant even when nuclear tests decrease."[18]

We cannot register all the land-based insults to the ecosystems of the seas. But there is one more we must note: the threat from off-shore and shore-based oil drilling operations as well as by the still very inadequately policed regulation of oil spillages, accidental and deliberate, from ocean-going vessels.[19] Thus there exists an insensate and unremitting strangulation of the world's bays and estuaries wherever demographic and economic growth press the shores. Against all this assorted mindless aggressiveness of man, smugly ensconced behind the legal embattlements of the nation-state, the seas are wholly defenseless, open to their ultimate death. The sole item of concern over Earth's oceans has, to date, centered on the traditional, barnacle-encrusted, primitive doctrine of the freedom of the high seas. This outworn manifesto is comprised of: "(1) freedom of navigation; (2) freedom of fishing; (3) freedom to lay submarine cables and pipelines; and (4) freedom to fly over the high seas."[20]

All of these are exploitive rights; they do not pretend to tackle the preservation of the common seas or the ecological realities concerning their survival as living elements in a world suddenly drenched in an outpouring of pollution, poisons, and petroleum. At our breakneck and improvident pace, we now face the eventual destruction of our most productive asset of the future for lack of laws to protect it. "The catchy phrase 'Freedom of the Sea,' " remarks Edward W. Allen, "bespeaks a noble concept, that is, if applied with noble aspirations, but it can be a deceptive cliché if utilized to conceal ignoble motivations."[21] The day when a tide could scrub the estuaries clean and there still existed interminable miles of lonesome beaches, when the seas could absorb our ecological insults, is long past.

When will we come to grips with the exploding issue of marine pollution? We have grappled tentatively with the question of the rights of co-riparians in an international drainage basin to a proper share of whatever water is of acceptable quality. It is asserted that "there are principles limiting the power of states to use such waters without regard to injurious effects on co-riparians."[22]

Hopefully, there are few defenders today of the Schooner Exchange doctrine—the principle invoked by Attorney General Harmon in the Rio Grande dispute of 1895—that the jurisdiction of a state within its territory is exclusive and absolute and susceptible only of self-imposed limitations. In contradiction, what a nation does with its rivers, states Griffin, is subject to the legal rights of each co-riparian state in the drainage basin. "No international decision supporting any purported principle of absolute sovereignty has been found."[23]

It is some advance to formally recognize that the seas are an international drainage basin of which all littoral states are "co-riparians." For on ecological principle alone (however the legal precedents direct) the well-being of the seas as a living, productive ecosystem for the benefit of the community of nations is wholly dependent on what happens to the margins and the land masses.

However, at present we concede jurisdiction over marginal seas on grounds of defense to littoral states because we still assume their stake is superior to that of the community of nations. The international approval of the continental shelf doctrine and the adoption of the convention of Fishing and Conservation of the Living Resources of the Sea give an authority to coastal states also on the basis that they have a primary interest.

Thus the primary legal interest continues to be exploitive; it is a matter of staking out national claims under the misleading guise of "conservation." The direction of American concern is evident from this budget extract: Out of an annual total of $462.3 million for United States federal marine science spending, $191.6 is for national security, $49.2 for fisheries development and seafood technology, and but $9.5 million for pollution abatement and control.[24]

The present flabby attitude of the nation-states, that condones the destruction of coastal waters by the drainage of poisons and pollutants, is a malignant threat to the welfare of the seas and therefore to the welfare of mankind. It is imperative that we develop a modernized legal regime that affords protection to the maritime interests of the community of states as a whole. This objective calls for the international regulation of watersheds with the family of nations viewed as co-riparians.

A. P. Lester, British barrister, while assessing the rights of riparians to clean water, noted that "state responsibility for extraterritorial damage to the territory of another state has been based upon the concepts of neighborship, abuse of rights, and international servitudes."[25] None of these principles in its traditional garb is adequate to the preservation of the physical integrity of the sea against the destructive forces and wastes of twentieth-century industrialism.

If Grotius in his day could find a common stake of all the riparians to the water of a river, certainly we today must recognize the valid claim of the family of nations to productive coastal waters and estuaries. Having identified the fringes of the seas as the vital element in the seas' well-being, and the growing dependency of all mankind on the future harvest of the oceans, one must readily conclude the superior claim of the international community to the ecological health of coastal waters.

Unless we want to be faced with the globe-enveloping spectre of a dead and stinking ocean, we are faced with the task of somehow evolving an international regime of oceanic stewardship. Besides international controls of pollutants and of the use of rivers and estuaries, such a regime would embody a creative application of the legal principle of servitudes, under which sovereign jurisdiction over rivers would yield to the prescriptive rights of the family of nations to a viable system of seas.

There is little time left to debate the juridical niceties. Already the chlorinated hydrocarbons (DDT, its cousins and derivatives) have traveled the biological waterways and concentrated in the complex oceanic food chains, so that not only is every species of fish used by man contaminated, but the carnivorous birds who feed on seafood are in real trouble. Biologists report that the last twenty remaining pairs of Bermuda petrels are dying out for want of fertility of eggs because of DDT; their extinction is forecast within ten years. The peregrine falcon is now extinct as a breeding bird along the east coast of the United States. Ducks, geese, and gulls are often so loaded that their eggs are "hot."

The irony is that man, who is the source of all this poisoning, is himself the end of these many varied food chains; he eats the choice large fish who have concentrated the poisons from algae all the way up, and he thus becomes the final residuary of the very lethal concoctions he has created to use on other life. Indeed, it should be evident that he cannot long continue in such folly without jeopardizing his own existence.

What we need now is an entirely new manifesto of the sea built not, as in the past, on legal limitations alone, but constucted primarily on the ecological realities of a sick sea in what may be fatal crisis.

Governing the Ocean Environment

[1]See Phillip O. Foss, *Politics and Grass* (Seattle: University of Washington Press, 1960).

[2]U.S. Congress, House, Committee on Foreign Affairs, *The Oceans: A Challenging New Frontier*, House Report 1957, 90th Cong., 2d Sess. (Washington, D.C.: U.S. Government Printing Office, 1968).

[3]Wesley Marx, *The Frail Ocean* (New York: Ballantine Books, Inc., 1967), p. 59.

Manifesto for the Sea

[1]*Christian Science Monitor*, Jan. 13, 1958, p. B-7. Italics added to quote.

[2]John Clark, *Fish and Man, Conflict in the Atlantic Estuaries* (Highlands, N.J.: Am. Littoral Society, 1967), p. 1.

[3]H. H. Carter, J. H. Carpenter, and R. C. Whaley, "The Bacterial Effect of Seawater under Natural Conditions," *J. Water Pollution Control Federation*, XXXIX, 7 (July, 1967), 1184.

[4]See Y. Hata, H. Miyoshi, H. Kodota, and M. Kimata, "Microbial Production of Sulfides in Coastal and Estuarine Regions," Second International Conference on Water Pollution Research, Section III. Marine Disposal; Tokyo, Japan, Aug. 24-28, 1964, abstracted in *J. Water Pollution Control Federation*, XXXVI, 3 (March, 1964), 327.

[5]"Estuarine and Marine Pollution, Biological and Chemical Features of Tidal Estuaries," a review of the literature by Werner N. Grune. *J. Water Pollution Control Federation*, XXXVII, 7 (July, 1965), 973ff.

[6]Lloyd Berkner, "Man Versus Technology," *Social Education*, XXXI (April, 1967), 281.

[7]Robert and Leona Train Rienow, *Moment in the Sun* (New York: Dial, 1967), p. 156, citing Fish & Wildlife Service news release, Sept. 7, 1965.

[8]L. R. Pomeroy, E. P. Odum, R. D. Johannes, and B. Roffman, "Flux of ^{32}p and ^{65}Zn through a Salt-Marsh Ecosystem," *Proceedings of Symposium, International Atomic Energy Agency*, Vienna, May 16-20, 1966, p. 186.

[9]Rienow and Rienow, *op. cit.*, p. 195.

[10]C. S. Taigvoglon and R. L. O'Connell, *Waste Guide for the Uranium Milling Industry*, HEW Technical Report, W62-12, 1962, pp. 45-56.

[11]R. J. Lowton, J. H. Martin, and J. W. Talbot, "Dilution, Dispersion, and Sedimentation in some British Estuaries," in International Atomic Energy Agency, *Disposal of Radioactive Wastes into Seas, Oceans, and Surface Waters*, Vienna, 1966, pp. 189ff.

[12]W. Feldt, "Radioactive Contamination of North Sea Fish," *ibid.*, p. 739.

[13]F. G. Lowman, D. K. Phelps, R. McClin, V. Roman de Vega, I. Oliver De Padovani, and R. J. Garcia, "Interactions of the Environmental and Biological Factors on the Distribution of Trace Elements in the Marine Environment," *ibid.*, p. 251.

[14] "Disposal of Radioactive Waste," *IAEA Bull.*, II, 1 (Jan., 1960), 4.

[15] *Ibid.*, p. 4.

[16] "Is the Ocean in Danger?" UNESCO *Courier* (English ed.), July-Aug. 1959, p. 30.

[17] *Ibid.*, p. 30.

[18] W. Feldt, "Radioactive Contamination of North Sea Fish," *IAEA, op. cit.* note 11, p. 752.

[19] See Robert and Leona Train Rienow, "The Oil around Us," *New York Times Magazine*, June 4, 1967.

[20] See Henry Reiff, *The United States and the Treaty Law of the Sea* (Minneapolis: Univ. of Minnesota Press, 1959), p. 322.

[21] Edward W. Allen, "Freedom of the Sea," *Am. J. Intnatl. Law,* XL (1966), 814.

[22] William L. Griffin, "The Use of Waters of International Drainage Basins under Customary International Law," *Am. J. Intnatl. Law,* LII (1959), 50.

[23] *Ibid.*, p. 59.

[24] P. Eleson, "Underwater Ordnance," *Ordnance,* May-June, 1967, p. 548. See also Jan.-Feb., 1967, issue, p. 418, for the program of the National Council on Marine Resources; and the March-April, 1967, issue, pp. 454-455, for a budgetary analysis of oceanography programs.

[25] A. P. Lester, "River Pollution in International Law," *Am. J. Intnatl. Law,* LVII (Oct., 1963), 833ff.

7   The Population Bomb

> Now, here, you see, it takes all the running you can do to keep in the same place. If you want to get somewhere else, you must run at least twice as fast as that.
>
> Lewis Carroll

There will be twice as many people in the world by the year 2000. The earth will still be the same size.

By 2000 we will have to run at least twice as fast to stay in the same place. We will need not only twice as much oxygen, water, food, clothing, and shelter but twice as many schools, hospitals, highways, and factories as we do now—and we will produce at least twice as much pollution and garbage. In the United States, if present trends continue, we will triple or quadruple our use of resources, even though our population will not increase as rapidly as that of the world as a whole.

Population Trends and Projections

Demographer Philip M. Hauser has estimated that by the Neolithic Period, some 10,000 years ago, world population had reached a level of about 10 million persons. At the beginning of the Christian era there were an estimated 250 to 300 million people, and by 1650 the number had risen to about 500 million. Stated differently, it took some two million years for mankind to reach a population of half a billion persons. Then the pace quickened.

> But to add a second half billion took only two centuries (before 1850); a third half billion less than half a century (before 1900); a fourth half billion little more than a quarter of a century (shortly after 1925); a fifth half billion less than a quarter of a century (by 1950). The sixth half billion added to world population required only ten years (by 1960), and the seventh addition of half a billion took only eight years (by 1968).[1]

All animals tend to produce more offspring than are needed to perpetuate the species. Ordinarily their numbers are kept in some kind of balance by predators, disease, and famine. The human animal has generally been subjected to these same kinds of control, except that in recent times he has vastly increased his ability to overcome the control mechanisms. Predators, except for other humans, no longer threaten him. Food supplies have become more abundant and more stable through specialized agriculture, so that men no longer need depend on the uncertainties of hunting. Lastly, control of disease has been vastly improved—especially during this century. The old mass killers—malaria, typhoid, smallpox, cholera, yellow fever, and typhus—have been eliminated in some parts of the world and sharply reduced in others. There has not been a major epidemic since 1919, when influenza caused an estimated 25 million deaths.[2] These factors have combined to reduce the death rate drastically. In the mid-seventeenth century the death rate in Europe was about 40 persons per thousand per year; today, it is fewer than 10. At that time life expectancy was 35 years or less; today it is 70 or more. While the death rate throughout the world has been dropping dramatically, the birth rate has remained essentially stable. The result has been the so-called "population explosion," which is *adding* more than a million people every week to an already overburdened planet.

The present birth rate in the United States is probably lower than it ever has been; along with those of some Northern European countries, it is among the lowest in the world. This low birth rate produces a growth of about 1 percent per year, which means that it will take about 70 years for the population of the United States to double. If this rate continues, we will have 400 million people before 2040. While this growth rate is low compared to those of most Asian, African, and Latin American countries, it may in fact be more disastrous, because Americans use up resources at a much faster rate. Wayne H. Davis considers this aspect of the problem in his article "Overpopulated America."

Population Concentrations

Throughout the history of the United States we have become increasingly urbanized—that is, an increasingly higher proportion of the population lives in urban centers. This trend toward movement to the city has been generally common throughout the world. The act of concentrating large numbers of people in a restricted geographical area in itself *creates* problems of pollution, sanitation, health, transportation, and crime—to mention a few. As an example, if the people of California were distributed evenly throughout the state, there would be no smog problem. So the basic population problem of the United States, and the rest of the world, is compounded by the tendency of populations to congregate in massive metropolitan centers.

Starvation and World Peace

Some 10,000 people die of starvation every day. Millions more are undernourished or malnourished. During the past two and a half decades the United States has given away more food and more food-producing technical assistance than all the rest of the world put together for all previous time. But it has not been enough, and it will never be enough as long as "Every time your heart beats three more new hearts start to beat and—contrary to all of man's previous history—most of them survive to cut down by just so much your share in the world's products."[3]

In spite of all our foreign assistance, the gap between the "have" and the "have not" nations is rapidly widening. And, what is perhaps of greater political significance, the "have nots" know it. Partly because of their release from colonial status, partly because of improved world-wide communications, and partly because of economic assistance programs, there has occurred since World War II a "revolution of rising expectations." Most of these expectations are doomed to disappointment, because population growth will cancel out any possible economic gains. When people expect nothing, when they have no hope, they may quietly starve without thinking of aggressive action. It is when they have expectations that are frustrated or violated that they revolt.

When the expectations of the "have not" nations are frustrated and when famine becomes increasingly prevalent, it is most unrealistic to expect that warfare can be averted.

Running Faster

Is it really possible to provide for the increasing numbers of people in the world by technological methods—by "running faster"? Can the world's food supply be doubled or tripled in 30 years? Probably not. The "Green Revolution" (a combination of new plant strains, fertilizers, and pesticides) has produced substantial gains in some parts of the world but not enough to keep up with population growth. Furthermore, the more intensive agricultural practices become, the greater the ecological imbalances. As Paul Ehrlich puts it,

> The more we have manipulated our environment, the more we have been required to manipulate it. The more we have done with synthetic pesticides, the less we have been able to do without them. The more we have deforested, the more flood control dams we have had to build. The more farmland we have subdivided, the more pressure we have created to increase the yield on the land remaining under cultivation and to farm marginal land.[4]

Is food from the sea the answer? Probably not. It is more likely that food from the sea will decrease rather than increase. If nations persist in using the oceans as a free-for-all grab bag, fishery production will soon diminish—and there is no historically based reason to expect that ocean conservation methods will be adopted. Will Science find a way? Probably not. The best "way" we have found so far in the United States has been to import raw materials from abroad.

Suppose the foregoing judgments are incorrect and that ways can be found to feed seven billion people by 2000, what of the quality of life? Former Interior Secretary Stewart Udall considers this question in his essay "Population: Less Is More."

Even if the United States can solve its own problems of population, production, and pollution, what of the rest of the world? In Paul Ehrlich's words, we can't tell the developing countries, "Your end of the boat is sinking." We are all in the same boat, and that boat has a limited capacity. Wallace Stegner puts it this way:

> We may exercise our ingenuity in any way we please—colonize space, build floating continents for our surplus people, put half of them into deep freeze and let them drift around the Pacific on rafts until it comes their turn to thaw out and live again—but in the end all our ingenuities are mere delaying actions, as the discovery of the Americas was a delaying action. Sooner or later the weed must be controlled, or must control itself, in its most vital function; must have its capacity to breed limited, inhibited, cut away, or taxed away.[5]

Governmental Action to Reduce Population Growth

As late as 1959 President Eisenhower said he "could not imagine anything more emphatically a subject that is not a proper political or governmental activity or function or responsibility" than family planning. Ten years later President Nixon devoted an entire Presidential message to population problems, in which he proposed that adequate family planning services be made available "to all those who want them but cannot afford them." In the previous year a Gallup poll found that 76 percent of the Catholics and 75 percent of the Protestants polled believed that birth control information should be available to anyone who wanted it.

Beginning in 1966 Congress passed several laws relating to family planning: an Act (P.L. 89-749) providing grants to states for health service programs including family planning, 1966; an amendment to the Food for Peace Act (P.L. 89-808) allowing expenditure of funds for activities related to problems of population growth, 1966; an amendment to the foreign aid bill (P.L. 89-583) allowing expenditures for voluntary family planning programs in countries requesting such assistance, 1966; and the Social Security Amendments of 1967 (P.L. 90-248), stipulating that not less than 6 percent of funds for maternal and child health be spent for family planning services.

After these slow and hesitant starts (which apparently produced little political opposition), an expanded series of programs was initiated. A Commission on Population Growth and the American Future was established in 1970 (P.L. 91-213) with John D. Rockefeller III as its chairman. A Center for Population Research was established in 1968, and a new National Center for Family Planning was authorized in late 1969. The budget for fiscal year 1971 allocated $218 million for family planning services, research, and training as compared to $125 million the previous year. Funds were also contributed to some 30 foreign governments for birth control services.

A subject that was considered "political dynamite" a few years ago now appears to be almost taken for granted as a proper subject for governmental action.

* * *

Garrett Hardin leads off this series of selections on the population problem with "The Tragedy of the Commons," in which he writes of the dangers of the "commons approach" in resource use, pollution, and procreation. Wayne H. Davis is next with an essay on "Overpopulated America." The United States is worse off than India, Davis says, because we are exhausting our resources 25 to 30 times as fast. Next Stewart Udall describes what the American landscape will be like if our population continues to grow at its present rate. The basic question, Udall says, is the conservation of man.

If the population bomb is ticking away and ready to explode, as we have suggested in these pages, what do practicing politicians say about it? President Nixon and 1968 Presidential candidate Hubert Humphrey state their positions in the next two carefully worded selections.

Not all Americans agree that family planning services should be made easily accessible. In fact, some blacks maintain that such services are a deliberate attempt to reduce the number of black people in the United States. Ralph Z. Hallow explores this point of view in "The Blacks Cry Genocide."

Finally, in an article first published in 1963, Aldous Huxley, author of *Brave New World,* writes of "The Politics of Population."

The Tragedy of the Commons*
Garrett Hardin**

The Population problem has no technical solution; it requires a fundamental extension in morality.

It is fair to say that most people who anguish over the population problem are trying to find a way to avoid the evils of overpopulation without relinquishing any of the privileges they now enjoy. They think that farming the seas or developing new strains of wheat will solve the problem—technologically. I try to show here that the solution they seek cannot be found. The population problem cannot be solved in a technical way, any more than can the problem of winning the game of tick-tack-toe.

What Shall We Maximize?

Population, as Malthus said, naturally tends to grow "geometrically," or, as we would now say, exponentially. In a finite world this means that the per capita share of the world's goods must steadily decrease. Is ours a finite world?

*Science, CLXII (December 13, 1968), 1243-1248. Copyright 1968 by the American Association for the Advancement of Science. Reprinted by permission.
**Mr. Hardin is a Professor of Biology at the University of California, Santa Barbara. This article is based on a presidential address presented before the meeting of the Pacific Division of the American Association for the Advancement of Science at Utah State University, Logan, Utah, June 25, 1968.

A fair defense can be put forward for the view that the world is infinite; or that we do not know that it is not. But, in terms of the practical problems that we must face in the next few generations with the foreseeable technology, it is clear that we will greatly increase human misery if we do not, during the immediate future, assume that the world available to the terrestrial human population is finite. "Space" is no escape.[1]

* * *

We want the maximum good per person; but what is good? To one person it is wilderness, to another it is ski lodges for thousands. To one it is estuaries to nourish ducks for hunters to shoot; to another it is factory land. Comparing one good with another is, we usually say, impossible because goods are incommensurable. Incommensurables cannot be compared.

Theoretically this may be true; but in real life incommensurables *are* commensurable. Only a criterion of judgment and a system of weighting are needed. In nature the criterion is survival. Is it better for a species to be small and hideable, or large and powerful? Natural selection commensurates the incommensurables. The compromise achieved depends on a natural weighting of the values of the variables.

* * *

We can make little progress in working toward optimum population size until we explicitly exorcize the spirit of Adam Smith in the field of practical demography. In economic affairs, *The Wealth of Nations* (1776) popularized the "invisible hand," the idea that an individual who "intends only his own gain," is, as it were, "led by an invisible hand to promote . . . the public interest."[2]

Adam Smith did not assert that this was invariably true, and perhaps neither did any of his followers. But he contributed to a dominant tendency of thought that has ever since interfered with positive action based on rational analysis, namely, the tendency to assume that decisions reached individually will, in fact, be the best decisions for an entire society. If this assumption is correct it justifies the continuance of our present policy of laissez-faire in reproduction. If it is correct we can assume that men will control their individual fecundity so as to produce the optimum population. If the assumption is not correct, we need to reexamine our individual freedoms to see which ones are defensible.

Tragedy of Freedom in a Commons

The rebuttal to the invisible hand in population control is to be found in a scenario first sketched in a little-known pamphlet[3] in 1833 by a mathematical amateur named William Forster Lloyd (1794-1852). We may well call it "the tragedy of the commons," using the word "tragedy" as the philosopher Whitehead used it:[4] "The essence of dramatic tragedy is not unhappiness. It resides in the solemnity of the remorseless working of things." He then goes on to say, "This inevitableness of destiny can be only be illustrated in terms of human life by incidents which in fact involve unhappiness. For it is only by them that the futility of escape can be made evident in the drama."

The tragedy of the commons develops in this way. Picture a pasture open to all. It is to be expected that each herdsman will try to keep as many cattle as possible on the commons. Such an arrangement may work reasonably satisfactorily for centuries because tribal wars, poaching, and disease keep the numbers of both man and beast well below the carrying capacity of the land. Finally, however, comes the day of reckoning, that is, the day when the long-desired goal of social stability becomes a reality. At this point, the inherent logic of the commons remorselessly generates tragedy.

As a rational being, each herdsman seeks to maximize his gain. Explicitly or implicitly, more or less consciously, he asks, "What is the utility *to me* of adding one more animal to my herd?" This utility has one negative and one positive component.

1) The positive component is a function of the increment of one animal. Since the herdsman receives all the proceeds from the sale of the additional animal, the positive utility is nearly +1.

2) The negative component is a function of the additional overgrazing created by one more animal. Since, however, the effects of overgrazing are shared by all the herdsmen, the negative utility for any particular decision-making herdsman is only a fraction of −1.

Adding together the component partial utilities, the rational herdsman concludes that the only sensible course for him to pursue is to add another animal to his herd. And another; and another. . . . But this is the conclusion reached by each and every rational herdsman sharing a commons. Therein is the tragedy. Each man is locked into a system that compels him to increase his herd without limit—in a world that is limited. Ruin is the destination toward which all men rush, each pursuing his own best interest in a society that believes in the freedom of the commons. Freedom in a commons brings ruin to all.

* * *

Pollution

In a reverse way, the tragedy of the commons reappears in problems of pollution. Here it is not a question of taking something out of the commons, but of putting something in—sewage, or chemical, radioactive, and heat wastes into water; noxious and dangerous fumes into the air; and distracting and unpleasant advertising signs into the line of sight. The calculations of utility are much the same as before. The rational man finds that his share of the cost of the wastes he discharges into the commons is less than the cost of purifying his wastes before releasing them. Since this is true for everyone, we are locked into a system of "fouling our own nest," so long as we behave only as independent, rational, free-enterprisers.

The tragedy of the commons as a food basket is averted by private property, or something formally like it. But the air and waters surrounding us cannot readily be fenced, and so the tragedy of the commons as a cesspool must be prevented by different means, by coercive laws or taxing devices that make it cheaper for the polluter to treat his pollutants than to discharge them untreated. We have not progressed as far with the solution of this problem as we have with the first. Indeed, our particular concept of private property, which deters us from exhausting the positive resources of the earth, favors pollution. The owner of a factory on the bank of a stream—whose property extends to the middle of the stream—often has difficulty seeing why it is not his natural right to muddy the waters flowing past his door. The law, always behind the times, requires elaborate stitching and fitting to adapt it to this newly perceived aspect of the commons.

The pollution problem is a consequence of population. It did not much matter how a lonely American frontiersman disposed of his waste. "Flowing water purifies itself every 10 miles," my grandfather used to say, and the myth was near enough to the truth when he was a boy, for there were not too many people. But as population became denser, the natural chemical and biological recycling process became overloaded, calling for a redefinition of property rights.

* * *

Freedom to Breed Is Intolerable

The tragedy of the commons is involved in population problems in another way. In a world governed solely by the principle of "dog eat dog"—if indeed there ever was such a world—how many children a family had would not be a matter of public concern. Parents who bred too exuberantly would leave fewer descendants, not more, because they would be unable to care adequately for their children. David Lack and others have found that such a negative feedback demonstrably controls the fecundity of birds.[5] But men are not birds, and have not acted like them for millenniums, at least.

If each human family were dependent only on its own resources; *if* the children of improvident parents starved to death; *if,* thus, overbreeding brought its own "punishment" to the germ line—*then* there would be no public interest in controlling the breeding of families. But our society is deeply committed to the welfare state,[6] and hence is confronted with another aspect of the tragedy of the commons.

In a welfare state, how shall we deal with the family, the religion, the race, or the class (or indeed any distinguishable and cohesive group) that adopts overbreeding as a policy to secure its own aggrandizement?[7] To couple the concept of freedom to breed with the belief that everyone born has an equal right to the commons is to lock the world into a tragic course of action.

Unfortunately this is just the course of action that is being pursued by the United Nations. In late 1967, some 30 nations agreed to the following.[8]

The Universal Declaration of Human Rights describes the family as the natural and fundamental unit of society. It follows that any choice and decision with regard to the size of the family must irrevocably rest with the family itself, and cannot be made by anyone else.

It is painful to have to deny categorically the validity of this right; denying it, one feels as uncomfortable as a resident of Salem, Massachusetts, who denied the reality of witches in the 17th century. At the present time, in liberal quarters, something like a taboo acts to inhibit criticism of the United Nations.

There is a feeling that the United Nations is "our last and best hope," that we shouldn't find fault with it; we shouldn't play into the hands of the archconservatives. However, let us not forget what Robert Louis Stevenson said: "The truth that is suppressed by friends is the readiest weapon of the enemy." If we love the truth we must openly deny the validity of the Universal Declaration of Human Rights, even though it is promoted by the United Nations. We should also join with Kingsley Davis[9] in attempting to get Planned Parenthood-World Population to see the error of its ways in embracing the same tragic ideal.

Mutual Coercion Mutually Agreed Upon

The social arrangements that produce responsibility are arrangements that create coercion, of some sort. Consider bank-robbing. The man who takes money from a bank acts as if the bank were a commons. How do we prevent such action? Certainly not by trying to control his behavior solely by a verbal appeal to his sense of responsibility. Rather than rely on propaganda we follow Frankel's lead and insist that a bank is not a commons; we seek the definite social arrangements that will keep it from becoming a commons. That we thereby infringe on the freedom of would-be robbers we neither deny nor regret.

The morality of bank-robbing is particularly easy to understand because we accept complete prohibition of this activity. We are willing to say "Thou shalt not rob banks," without providing for exceptions. But temperance also can be created by coercion. Taxing is a good coercive device. To keep downtown shoppers temperate in their use of parking space we introduce parking meters for short periods, and traffic fines for longer ones. We need not actually forbid a citizen to park as long as he wants to; we need merely make it increasingly expensive for him to do so. Not prohibition, but carefully biased options are what we offer him. A Madison Avenue man might call this persuasion; I prefer the greater candor of the word coercion.

Coercion is a dirty word to most liberals now, but it need not forever be so. As with the four-letter words, its dirtiness can be cleansed away by exposure to the light, by saying it over and over without apology or embarrassment. To many, the word coercion implies arbitrary decisions of distant and irresponsible bureaucrats; but this is not a necessary part of its meaning. The only kind of coercion I recommend is mutual coercion, mutually agreed upon by the majority of the people affected.

To say that we mutually agree to coercion is not to say that we are required to enjoy it, or even to pretend we enjoy it. Who enjoys taxes? We all grumble about them. But we accept compulsory taxes because we recognize that voluntary taxes would favor the conscienceless. We institute and (grumblingly) support taxes and other coercive devices to escape the horror of the commons.

An alternative to the commons need not be perfectly just to be preferable.

* * *

We must admit that our legal system of private property plus inheritance is unjust—but we put up with it because we are not convinced, at the moment, that anyone has invented a better system. The alternative of the commons is too horrifying to contemplate. Injustice is preferable to total ruin.

* * *

Recognition of Necessity

Perhaps the simplest summary of this analysis of man's population problems is this: the commons, if justifiable at all, is justifiable only under conditions of low-population density. As the human population has increased, the commons has had to be abandoned in one aspect after another.

First we abandoned the commons in food gathering, enclosing farm land and restricting pastures and hunting and fishing areas. These restrictions are still not complete throughout the world.

Somewhat later we saw that the commons as a place for waste disposal would also have to be abandoned. Restrictions on the disposal of domestic sewage are widely accepted in the Western world; we are still struggling to close the commons to pollution by automobiles, factories, insecticide sprayers, fertilizing operations, and atomic energy installations.

In a still more embryonic state is our recognition of the evils of the commons in matters of pleasure. There is almost no restriction on the propagation of sound waves in the public medium. The shopping public is assaulted with mindless music, without its consent. Our government is paying out billions of dollars to create supersonic transport which will disturb 50,000 people for every one person who is whisked from coast to coast 3 hours faster. Advertisers muddy the airwaves of radio and television and pollute the view of travelers. We are a long way from outlawing the commons in matters of pleasure. Is this because our Puritan inheritance makes us view pleasure as something of a sin, and pain (that is, the pollution of advertising) as the sign of virtue?

Every new enclosure of the commons involves the infringement of somebody's personal liberty. Infringements made in the distant past are accepted because no contemporary complains of a loss. It is the newly proposed infringements that we vigorously oppose; cries of "rights" and "freedom" fill the air. But what does "freedom" mean? When men mutually agreed to pass laws against robbing, mankind became more free, not less so. Individuals locked into the logic of the commons are free only to bring on universal ruin; once they see the necessity of mutual coercion, they become free to pursue other goals. I believe it was Hegel who said, "Freedom is the recognition of necessity."

The most important aspect of necessity that we must now recognize is the necessity of abandoning the commons in breeding. No technical solution can rescue us from the misery of overpopulation. Freedom to breed will bring ruin to all. At the moment, to avoid hard decisions many of us are tempted to propagandize for conscience and responsible parenthood. The temptation must be resisted, because an appeal to independently acting consciences selects for the disappearance of all conscience in the long run, and an increase in anxiety in the short.

The only way we can preserve and nurture other and more precious freedoms is by relinquishing the freedom to breed, and that very soon.

"Freedom is the recognition of necessity"—and it is the role of education to reveal to all the necessity of abandoning the freedom to breed. Only so can we put an end to this aspect of the tragedy of the commons.

Overpopulated America*
Wayne H. Davis**

I define as most seriously overpopulated that nation whose people by virtue of their numbers and activities are most rapidly decreasing the ability of the land to support human life. With our large population, our affluence and our technological monstrosities the United States wins first place by a substantial margin.

Let's compare the US to India, for example. We have 203 million people, whereas she has 540 million on much less land. But look at the impact of people on the land.

The average Indian eats his daily few cups of rice (or perhaps wheat, whose production on American farms contributed to our one percent per year drain in quality of our active farmland), draws his bucket of water from the communal well and sleeps in a mud hut. In his daily rounds to gather cow dung to burn to cook his rice and warm his feet, his footsteps, along with those of millions of his countrymen, help bring about a slow deterioration of the ability of the land to support people. His contribution to the destruction of the land is minimal.

An American, on the other hand, can be expected to destroy a piece of land on which he builds a home, garage and driveway. He will contribute his share to the 142 million tons of smoke and fumes, seven million junked cars, 20 million tons of paper, 48 billion cans, and 26 billion bottles the overburdened environment must absorb each year. To run his air conditioner we will strip-mine a Kentucky hillside, push the dirt and slate down into the stream, and burn coal in a power generator, whose smokestack contributes to a plume of smoke massive enough to cause cloud seeding and premature precipitation from Gulf winds which should be irrigating the wheat farms of Minnesota.

In his lifetime he will personally pollute three million gallons of water, and industry and agriculture will use ten times this much water in his behalf. To provide these needs the US Army Corps of Engineers will build dams and flood farmland. He will also use 21,000 gallons of leaded gasoline containing boron, drink 28,000 pounds of milk and eat 10,000 pounds of meat. The latter is produced and squandered in a life pattern unknown to Asians. A steer on a Western range eats plants containing minerals necessary for plant life. Some of these are incorporated into the body of the steer which is later shipped for slaughter. After being eaten by man these nutrients are flushed down the toilet into the ocean or buried in the cemetery, the surface of which is cluttered with

---

*The New Republic, January 10, 1970, pp. 13-15. Reprinted by permission.
**Wayne H. Davis is a member of the Department of Zoology at the University of Kentucky.

boulders called tombstones and has been removed from productivity. The result is a continual drain on the productivity of range land. Add to this the erosion of overgrazed lands, and the effects of the falling water table as we mine Pleistocene deposits of groundwater to irrigate to produce food for more people, and we can see why our land is dying far more rapidly than did the great civilizations of the Middle East, which experienced the same cycle. The average Indian citizen, whose fecal material goes back to the land, has but a minute fraction of the destructive effect on the land that the affluent American does.

Thus I want to introduce a new term, which I suggest be used in future discussions of human population and ecology. We should speak of our numbers in "Indian equivalents". An Indian equivalent I define as the average number of Indian citizens required to have the same detrimental effect on the land's ability to support human life as would the average American. This value is difficult to determine, but let's take an extremely conservative working figure of 25. To see how conservative this is, imagine the addition of 1000 citizens to your town and 25,000 to an Indian village. Not only would the Americans destroy much more land for homes, highways and a shopping center, but they would contribute far more to environmental deterioration in hundreds of other ways as well. For example, their demand for steel for new autos might increase the daily pollution equivalent of 130,000 junk autos which *Life* tells us that US Steel Corp. dumps into Lake Michigan. Their demand for textiles would help the cotton industry destroy the life in the Black Warrior River in Alabama with endrin. And they would contribute to the massive industrial pollution of our oceans (we provide one third to one half the world's share) which has caused the precipitous downward trend in our commercial fisheries landings during the past seven years.

The per capita gross national product of the United States is 38 times that of India. Most of our goods and services contribute to the decline in the ability of the environment to support life. Thus it is clear that a figure of 25 for an Indian equivalent is conservative. It has been suggested to me that a more realistic figure would be 500.

In Indian equivalents, therefore, the population of the United States is at least four billion. And the rate of growth is even more alarming. We are growing at one percent per year, a rate which would double our numbers in 70 years. India is growing at 2.5 percent. Using the Indian equivalent of 25, our population growth becomes 10 times as serious as that of India. According to the Rienows in their recent book *Moment in the Sun,* just one year's crop of American babies can be expected to use up 25 billion pounds of beef, 200 million pounds of steel and 9.1 billion gallons of gasoline during their collective lifetime. And the demands on water and land for our growing population are expected to be far greater than the supply available in the year 2000. We are destroying our land at a rate of over a million acres a year. We now have only 2.6 agricultural acres per person. By 1975 this will be cut to 2.2, the critical point for the maintenance of what we consider a decent diet, and by the year 2000 we might expect to have 1.2.

You might object that I am playing with statistics in using the Indian equivalent on the rate of growth. I am making the assumption that today's American child will live 35 years (the average Indian life span) at today's level of affluence. If he lives an American 70 years, our rate of population growth would be 20 times as serious as India's.

But the assumption of continued affluence at today's level is unfounded. If our numbers continue to rise, our standard of living will fall so sharply that by the year 2000 any surviving Americans might consider today's average Asian to be well off. Our children's destructive effects on their environment will decline as they sink ever lower into poverty.

The United States is in serious economic trouble now. Nothing could be more misleading than today's affluence, which rests precariously on a crumbling foundation. Our productivity, which had been increasing steadily at about 3.2 percent a year since World War II, has been falling during 1969. Our export over import balance has been shrinking steadily from $7.1 billion in 1964 to $0.15 billion in the first half of 1969. Our balance of payments deficit for the second quarter was $3.7 billion, the largest in history. We are now importing iron ore, steel, oil, beef, textiles, cameras, radios and hundreds of other things.

Our economy is based upon the Keynesian concept of a continued growth in population and productivity. It worked in an underpopulated nation with excess resources. It could contine to work only if the earth and its resources were expanding at an annual rate of 4 to 5 percent. Yet neither the number of cars, the economy, the human population, nor anything else can expand indefinitely at an exponential rate in a finite world. We must face this fact *now*. The crisis is here. When Walter Heller says that our economy will expand by 4 percent annually through the latter 1970s he is dreaming. He is in a theoretical world totally unaware of the realities of human ecology. If the economists do not wake up and devise a new system for us now somebody else will have to do it for them.

A civilization is comparable to a living organism. Its longevity is a function of its metabolism. The higher the metabolism (affluence), the shorter the life. Keynesian economics has allowed us an affluent but shortened life span. We have now run our course.

The tragedy facing the United States is even greater and more imminent than that descending upon the hungry nations. The Paddock brothers in their book, *Famine 1975!*, say that India "cannot be saved" no matter how much food we ship her. But India will be here after the United States is gone. Many millions will die in the most colossal famines India has ever known, but the land will survive and she will come back as she always has before. The United States, on the other hand, will be a desolate tangle of concrete and ticky-tacky, of strip-mined moonscape and silt-choked reservoirs. The land and water will be so contaminated with pesticides, herbicides, mercury fungicides, lead, boron, nickel, arsenic and hundreds of other toxic substances, which have been approaching critical levels of concentration in our environment as a result of our numbers and affluence, that it may be unable to sustain human life.

Thus as the curtain gets ready to fall on man's civilization let it come as no surprise that it shall first fall on the United States. And let no one make the mistake of thinking we can save ourselves by "cleaning up the environment." Banning DDT is the equivalent of the physician's treating syphilis by putting a bandaid over the first chancre to appear. In either case you can be sure that more serious and widespread trouble will soon appear unless the disease itself is treated. We cannot survive by planning to treat the symptoms such as air pollution, water pollution, soil erosion, etc.

What can we do to slow the rate of destruction of the United States as a land capable of supporting human life? There are two approaches. First, we must reverse the population growth. We have far more people than we can continue to support at anything near today's level of affluence. American women average slightly over three children each. According to the *Population Bulletin* if we reduced this number to 2.5 there would still be 330 million people in the nation at the end of the century. And even if we reduced this to 1.5 we would have 57 million more people in the year 2000 than we have now. With our present longevity patterns it would take more than 30 years for the population to peak even when reproducing at this rate, which would eventually give us a net decrease in numbers.

Do not make the mistake of thinking that technology will solve our population problem by producing a better contraceptive. Our problem now is that people want too many children. Surveys show the average number of children wanted by the American family is 3.3. There is little difference between the poor and the wealthy, black and white, Catholic and Protestant. Production of children at this rate during the next 30 years would be so catastrophic in effect on our resources and the viability of the nation as to be beyond my ability to contemplate. To prevent this trend we must not only make contraceptives and abortion readily available to everyone, but we must establish a system to put severe economic pressure on those who produce children and reward those who do not. This can be done within our system of taxes and welfare.

The other thing we must do is to pare down our Indian equivalents. Individuals in American society vary tremendously in Indian equivalents. If we plot Indian equivalents versus their reciprocal, the percentage of land surviving a generation, we obtain a linear regression. We can then place individuals and occupation types on this graph. At one end would be the starving blacks of Mississippi; they would approach unity in Indian equivalents, and would have the least destructive effect on the land. At the other end of the graph would be the politicians slicing pork for the barrel, the highway contractors, strip-mine operators, real estate developers, and public enemy number one—the US Army Corps of Engineers.

We must halt land destruction. We must abandon the view of land and minerals as private property to be exploited in any way economically feasible for private financial gain. Land and minerals are resources upon which the very survival of the nation depends, and their use must be planned in the best interests of the people.

Rising expectations for the poor is a cruel joke foisted upon them by the Establishment. As our new economy of use-it-once-and-throw-it-away produces more and more products for the affluent, the share of our resources available for the poor declines. Blessed be the starving blacks of Mississippi with their out-door privies, for they are ecologically sound, and they shall inherit a nation. Although I hope that we will help these unfortunate people attain a decent standard of living by diverting war efforts to fertility control and job training, our most urgent task to assure this nation's survival during the next decade is to stop the affluent destroyers.

Population: Less Is More*
Stewart L. Udall**

An increasing gross national product has become the Holy Grail, and most of the economists who are its keepers have no concern for the economics of beauty. Those industrial indices of national well-being—auto output, steel production, heavy construction—have become the universal yardsticks of the American advance. We have had no environmental index, no census statistic to measure whether the country is more or less habitable from year to year. A tranquillity index or a cleanliness index might have told us something about the condition of man, but a fast-growing country preoccupied with making and acquiring material things has had no time for the amenities that are the very heart and substance of daily life.

Our environment has not been ruined by the errors or inroads of any single segment of society. Public outrage has been averted because the innumerable pollutants and defacements were not, taken one by one, outrageous. No floods or forest fires or great dust storms warned us of impending bankruptcy. It is hard to say just when San Francisco began to lose its bay, Los Angeles its salubrious air, or New York its lordly Hudson River. There was no cry of outrage. The reason was a spendthrift and subversive one: the common belief that the piecemeal blight of a green and pleasant land was the price we had to pay for progress.

"Progress" in the past was always conducted in an atmosphere of competitive speed. "Get it done!" was the universal American cry. The cost of the "Sooner" syndrome has caught up with us at last. Now the rule must be "Slow down and plan."

* * *

For a rational nation proud of its scientific prowess, we are remarkably fatalistic about the future. In regard to population there is a strong streak of passive determinism in our attitude. Will we permit the future just to happen, or will we choose the future we prefer? This is the fateful issue of public policy we tend to ignore. If we want a sustaining and vibrant environment, if we aspire to a social and physical setting that enlarges, not narrows, the choices of the individual, then it is clear that each thoughtless increment of population erodes the options of our tomorrows.

The democratic way is the way of rational choice. Yet men cannot really choose unless the consequences of unlimited growth are spelled out for them. The cures and comforts and scientific spectaculars of the postwar period have seemed to reinforce, perhaps incurably, our traditional optimism. "Life is better

*From *1976: Agenda For Tomorrow*, copyright © 1968 by Stewart L. Udall. Reprinted by permission of Harcourt Brace Jovanovich, Inc., pp. 48-49, 55-59.
**Mr. Udall is former Secretary of the U.S. Department of the Interior and the author of several books on the environment.

than ever" is by and large the current, complacent conviction. Before we are finally caught up in the anthill world dangled before us by the supertechnocrats and mechanistic planners, let us at least understand the implications of the environment they would thrust upon us. We can make room for five or ten billion Americans if that would serve either mankind or our national purpose. But the question is: Will it?

Let me offer a personal forecast of the conditions that will prevail in an America of a billion bodies—or a half-billion, for that matter.

An asphalt America will have overtaken and largely obliterated the green America we still know. Engineering will have overwhelmed nature. The design of this new man-made America will, at best, be more functional; at worst, it will be unattractive, overmechanized, and simply inhuman.

The everyday choices of the individual will have been diminished; his freedom of movement, his space for creative play and contemplation, the diversity of his milieu will have been lessened as his big-sky and open-continent freedoms are drastically reduced.

We will have become a glassed-in, domesticated people, and the outdoor ethos of so much of this country will have gradually disappeared.

The face of the land will be cluttered and unclean. Isolated, unspoiled farmlands and seascapes will be far between—and in California (that region so often reputed to be the precursor of all tomorrows), the farms and orchards and fields will be gone.

Genuine seemliness will be unattainable. Children will, by slow degrees, have learned to accept the noisy, the vulgar, the pretentious and the ugly; moreover, they will have come to countenance as natural conditions of life the shoddy, the crude, and the unkempt.

Silence will have almost expired. Only the hardy few who wander to the farthest shores or walk the paths of winter will find the serenity of the out-of-doors. There will be the ersatz quiet of soundproof rooms, and the solitude we still enjoy today (an elixir of space, aloneness, and the immanence of nature) will be the scarcest amenity and the most lamented of all the glories common to our lost past.

The Brooklyn, Texas, New England, Rocky Mountain, and other regional differences in our people will have disappeared, victims of the overpowering forces of an overregimented society. An overpopulated America will be, inevitably, a homogenized, lock-step, increasingly conformist country. Fewer and fewer people will really have the feeling of belonging to a special region, of loving a river or wood, or will know the joy of a kinship with the out-of-doors.

The countryside will be flat-faced. Stream valleys, swamps, and estuaries will be filled and paved over as the waste receptacles of an overpeopled land.

All forms of outdoor recreation will be rationed; the freedom to fish, to hunt, to boat, to walk the wilderness will be an occasional privilege, not an everyday right in a land where, paradoxically, leisure will have increased. Limits on outdoor opportunities will have slowly extinguished interest in wild things and open country. City-bound, house-oriented men and women will turn increasingly to glassed-in avocations and to a sedentary spectatorship greater that that which already poses physiological threats stemming from lack of exercise.

The national parks and all beaches and seashores will be severely rationed. The typical "park experience" will be equivalent to a visit to an oversized zoo. The pressure of people will have caused overdevelopment and overregulation, and in more fragile parks the wonders and regimens of nature will simply be trampled on and destroyed.

Unnumbered species of plants and animals, their habitats destroyed, will have disappeared. There will be little fruit left with the taste of the sun still in it, few lonely beaches with the cry of gulls overhead, few places where the call of wild geese still haunts the air. Overpopulation will have driven much wildlife to extinction. Because most larger animals must have a separate habitat, existence in close proximity with man is not possible. The eagle and the elk may have become memories, or rare phenomena of some remnant wilderness banned to man. But weeds will remain, and with them weedy birds and animals such as the rat, the roach, and the starling, who will thrive.

An America of a billion inhabitants will have lost other choices and amenities: there will be no clean rivers left, and few brooks where one can safely stoop and drink; there will be few mountain fastnesses where only a pine smell permeates the air; many will eat fish flour, but very few will know the taste of brook trout or fresh-caught salmon.

We will thus lose more than elbow room if we race ahead to the billion bodies and bulging cities the demographers passively predict. Experience tells us that life is cheap in China, dear in the deserts, and most ideal in the medium-peopled countries. Overpopulation means the impoverishment of life no matter what level a goods-and-gadgets standard of living attains.

It is impossible to overstate the case for elbow room. It has, in this country, given Presidents and planners a spacious outlook on life; it has given us room for trial and error; it has been an omnipresent wellspring of the vitality that is characteristically American. Thoreau said the land gave man "a larger margin for life"; it made Theodore Roosevelt a leader "with distance in his eyes." The vaunted American traits of independence and initiative have derived, in part, from the expansiveness of our setting. Individualism flourished wherever space gave play to a wide range of alternatives for action.

There is nothing mysterious about this mystique of space. All members of the animal kingdom—including man—thrive best in that milieu which is most life-giving. Pearl Buck may have indulged in overstatement when she observed that "Democracy is impossible in an overpopulated country." However, it is no overstatement to say that the full life, as we think of it today, or as we would like to shape it for tomorrow, is impossible in an overpopulated land.

The inhibitions of old cultures and outdated religious doctrines have slowed the forming of sound priorities for planetary planning. Despite the amazing advance of science, our current approach to human betterment is most unscientific. We have long since perfected the concept of the land's carrying capacity for animals, and we practice the principle of sustained yield in the management of trees and plants. Yet, strangely, we forget the law of a natural balance when we come to man. We have mastered the arts of animal husbandry, we know the life laws of crops and insects, we know how to plan high-yield growth for agriculture. In effect, we have enhanced the future of everything except the over-all future of the human race. We must now identify the carrying capacity of continents, and evolve an ecology for man in harmony with the unfolding ecology of other living things. If we want it, our engineers can double- and triple-deck our freeways and other public facilities and fill the urban sky line with high-rise apartments, but man can never double-deck a park, a marsh, or a seashore. If man is to be the prince, not the prisoner, of the system, he must evolve an optimum "sustained-yield" concept keyed to human fulfillment. Can we talk seriously of individual excellence in the long run unless we create environmental excellence as well?

The nightmares of overpopulation would subside if we applied the conservation concept to our own kind. What we call conservation is rooted in the needs of man's nature and the inner order of his universe. It puts the future first and expedience second. It makes the fullness of life the overriding objective of all social planning. The conservation of man now demands that we use this well-tested idea of earth stewardship for the betterment of our own species.

U.S. Should Set Example in Fighting Overpopulation*
Senator Hubert H. Humphrey**

As a nation, we are finally paying more attention to our environment. This concern seems to come from a growing feeling, especially among our young people, that the quality of life is more important than the quantity of material goods we produce.

Most of the current attention is centered on cleaning up our air and water. To win the war on pollution, we will have to invest more than a lot of people realize—about $10 billion to $15 billion a year of federal money plus a considerable investment by the states and private enterprise.

But we should also look beyond the five and ten-year programs to what continued population growth could do to our country and our planet.

India is adding people at the rate of one million a month. Latin America, the area of highest birth rate, will have gone from 60 million people at the beginning of the century to 600 million people at the end of the century.

It brings to mind a cartoon I saw in a newspaper several months ago. Two orbiting spacemen were looking down on the teeming planet Earth, and the caption was: "It's not a planet. It's an incubator."

But it's hard to smile about it. Two billion of the world's 3.5 billion people are underfed now.

Many ecologists think we are on the road to disaster, and that we cannot decide to do something about it in 10 or 20 years. To level off the world's population at the end of the century, nations have to take significant steps now.

Population planners say the growth rate can be reduced by about one-tenth of a per cent a year. This means that in Latin America, where the growth rate is 3%, it will take 30 years of effort to level off the population.

Ecologists say that to handle a world population of 7 billion (in the year 2000), we will have to invest much more money than we are now contemplating

---

*Hubert H. Humphrey, "U.S. Should Set Example in Fighting Overpopulation," *Los Angeles Times,* March 9, 1970, p. 3. (c) Register and Tribune Syndicate. Reprinted by permission of the author.

**Mr. Humphrey is a U.S. Senator from Minnesota. He was formerly Vice President of the United States and was the Democratic Party candidate for President in 1968.

to control pollution. Many resources, such as water, will have to be continually reused. We will have to drastically change the world's food distribution patterns. We will have to accept some austerity to be able to exist with one another.

The most serious problem may not be the impact on the world's standard of living or on the amount of cooperation that will be required between nations. What ecologists are really concerned about are the changes in the Earth's life system—its air, oceans, and land vegetation—that might result from the population explosion.

They point out that there is still very much we don't know about what we are doing to the planet. Concern is growing over the possible long-term effects of pesticides, of thermal pollution from nuclear power plants, of the growing level of carbon dioxide in the atmosphere.

There is an uneasy feeling among ecologists that we are taking part in a great experiment, and nobody is quite sure how it will come out. And it is the fear of overpopulation that fuels every other ecological fear.

One thing for certain: Population control programs won't spread spontaneously around the world. It will take leadership—from the United Nations and from many countries, including the United States.

Before we tell other nations how to develop population control programs, we ought to come up with one of our own.

The first step should be to see that family planning services are available to all people who want help. It is estimated that there are 6 million women in the United States who want family planning help but who cannot afford it.

Only about 700,000 of these 6 million women are now being helped through Planned Parenthood and public health clinics. We should see that every woman who wants help can get it.

With the increased concern over the side effects of the birth control pill, it is especially important that more research be done on it and on other methods of family planning.

To do these things, we will have to spend some five times more than the $30 million a year we are investing in family planning services and the $17 million a year we are spending for research.

Once we have set a population goal, we can adapt our economic policies, urban programs, tax schedules, health planning, and educational programs to it. Then the United States will be able to help more effectively the underdeveloped nations.

Much of our effort should be through the United Nations. An American task force headed by John D. Rockefeller III has suggested that a commissioner of population be named to coordinate and expand U.N. population control programs.

As of now, the U.N. spends only about $1.5 million a year on family planning with 10 advisers working in Asia, Africa, and Latin America. The task force says an annual U.N. budget of $100 million a year for family planning is needed now.

If the world is not willing to expand its population control efforts, there are only two other ways the number of people will be reduced: through epidemics or war.

Overpopulation, besides lowering our standard of living and polluting the environment, increases the chances of both.

We do not have to stay on this road to potential disaster. If we are willing to adjust our attitudes on family planning to what the world will be like at the end of the century, if we are willing to invest the necessary resources, we can defuse the population explosion.

This would give every child born on this Earth a much better chance at a decent life.

**Message from the President
of the United States
Relative to Population Growth***
Richard M. Nixon

To the Congress of the United States:

In 1830 there were one billion people on the planet earth. By 1930 there were two billion, and by 1960 there were three billion. Today the world population is three and one-half billion persons.

These statistics illustrate the dramatically increasing rate of population growth. It took many thousands of years to produce the first billion people; the next billion took a century; the third came after thirty years; the fourth will be produced in just fifteen.

If this rate of population growth continues, it is likely that the earth will contain over seven billion human beings by the end of this century. Over the next thirty years, in other words, the world's population could double. And at the end of that time, each new addition of one billion persons would not come over the millennia nor over a century nor even over a decade. If present trends were to continue until the year 2000, the eighth billion would be added in only five years and each additional billion in an even shorter period.

While there are a variety of opinions as to precisely how fast population will grow in the coming decades, most informed observers have a similar response to all such projections. They agree that population growth is among the most important issues we face. They agree that it can be met only if there is a great deal of advance planning. And they agree that the time for such planning is growing very short. It is for all these reasons that I address myself to the population problem in this message, first to its international dimensions and then to its domestic implications.

In the Developing Nations

It is in the developing nations of the world that population is growing most rapidly today. In these areas we often find rates of natural increase higher than any which have been experienced in all of human history. With their birth rates

*U.S. Congress, House, 91st Cong., 1st Sess., July 21, 1969, Doc. No. 91-139.

remaining high and with death rates dropping sharply, many countries of Latin America, Asia, and Africa now grow ten times as fast as they did a century ago. At present rates, many will double and some may even triple their present populations before the year 2000. This fact is in large measure a consequence of rising health standards and economic progress throughout the world, improvements which allow more people to live longer and more of their children to survive to maturity.

As a result, many already impoverished nations are struggling under a handicap of intense population increase which the industrialized nations never had to bear. Even though most of these countries have made rapid progress in total economic growth—faster in percentage terms than many of the more industrialized nations—their far greater rates of population growth have made development in per capita terms very slow. Their standards of living are not rising quickly, and the gap between life in the rich nations and life in the poor nations is not closing.

There are some respects, in fact, in which economic development threatens to fall behind population growth, so that the quality of life actually worsens. For example, despite considerable improvements in agricultural technology and some dramatic increases in grain production, it is still difficult to feed these added people at adequate levels of nutrition. Protein malnutrition is widespread. It is estimated that every day some 10,000 people—most of them children—are dying from diseases of which malnutrition has been at least a partial cause. Moreover, the physical and mental potential of millions of youngsters is not realized because of a lack of proper food. The promise for increased production and better distribution of food is great, but not great enough to counter these bleak realities.

The burden of population growth is also felt in the field of social progress. In many countries, despite increases in the number of schools and teachers, there are more and more children for whom there is no schooling. Despite construction of new homes, more and more families are without adequate shelter. Unemployment and underemployment are increasing and the situation could be aggravated as more young people grow up and seek to enter the work force.

Nor has development yet reached the stage where it brings with it diminished family size. Many parents in developing countries are still victimized by forces such as poverty and ignorance which make it difficult for them to exercise control over the size of their families. In sum, population growth is a world problem which no country can ignore, whether it is moved by the narrowest perception of national self-interest or the widest vision of a common humanity.

* * *

In the United States

For some time population growth has been seen as a problem for developing countries. Only recently has it come to be seen that pressing problems are also posed for advanced industrial countries when their populations increase at the rate that the United States, for example, must now anticipate. Food supplies may be ample in such nations, but social supplies—the capacity to educate youth, to provide privacy and living space, to maintain the processes of open, democratic government—may be grievously strained.

In the United States our rate of population growth is not as great as that of developing nations. In this country, in fact, the growth rate has generally declined since the eighteenth century. The present growth rate of about one percent per year is still significant, however. Moreover, current statistics indicate that the fertility rate may be approaching the end of its recent decline.

Several factors contribute to the yearly increase, including the large number of couples of childbearing age, the typical size of American families, and our increased longevity. We are rapidly reaching the point in this country where a family reunion, which has typically brought together children, parents, and grandparents, will instead gather family members from *four* generations. This is a development for which we are grateful and of which we can be proud. But we must also recognize that it will mean a far larger population if the number of children born to each set of parents remains the same.

In 1917 the total number of Americans passed 100 million, after three full centuries of steady growth. In 1967—just half a century later—the 200 million mark was passed. If the present rate of growth continues, the third hundred million persons will be added in roughly a thirty-year period. This means that by the year 2000, or shortly thereafter, there will be more than 300 million Americans.

This growth will produce serious challenges for our society. I believe that many of our present social problems may be related to the fact that we have had only fifty years in which to accommodate the second hundred million Americans. In fact, since 1945 alone some 90 million babies have been born in this country. We have thus had to accomplish in a very few decades an adjustment to population growth which was once spread over centuries. And it now appears that we will have to provide for a third hundred million Americans in a period of just 30 years.

The great majority of the next hundred million Americans will be born to families which looked forward to their birth and are prepared to love them and care for them as they grow up. The critical issue is whether social institutions will also plan for their arrival and be able to accommodate them in a humane and intelligent way. We can be sure that society will *not* be ready for this growth unless it begins its planning immediately. And adequate planning, in turn, requires that we ask ourselves a number of important questions.

Where, for example, will the next hundred million Americans live? If the patterns of the last few decades hold for the rest of the century, then at least three quarters of the next hundred million persons will locate in highly urbanized areas. Are our cities prepared for such an influx? The chaotic history of urban growth suggests that they are not and that many of their existing problems will be severely aggravated by a dramatic increase in numbers. Are there ways, then, of readying our cities? Alternatively, can the trend toward greater concentration of population be reversed? Is it a desirable thing, for example, that half of all the counties in the United States actually lost population in the 1950's, despite the growing number of inhabitants in the country as a whole? Are there ways of fostering a better distribution of the growing population?

Some have suggested that systems of satellite cities or completely new towns can accomplish this goal. The National Commission on Urban Growth has recently produced a stimulating report on this matter, one which recommends the creation of 100 new communities averaging 100,000 people each, and ten new communities averaging at least one million persons. But the total number of people who would be accommodated if even this bold plan were implemented is only twenty million—a mere-fifth of the expected thirty-year increase. If we were to accommodate the full 100 million persons in new communities, we would have to build a new city of 250,000 persons each month from now until the end of the century. That means constructing a city the size of Tulsa, Dayton, or Jersey City every thirty days for over thirty years. Clearly, the problem is enormous, and we must examine the alternative solutions very carefully.

Other questions also confront us. How, for example, will we house the next hundred million Americans? Already economical and attractive housing is in very short supply. New architectural forms, construction techniques, and financing strategies must be aggressively pioneered if we are to provide the needed dwellings.

What of our natural resources and the quality of our environment? Pure air and water are fundamental to life itself. Parks, recreational facilities, and an attractive countryside are essential to our emotional well-being. Plant and animal and mineral resources are also vital. A growing population will increase the demand for such resources. But in many cases their supply will not be increased and may even be endangered. The ecological system upon which we now depend may seriously deteriorate if our efforts to conserve and enhance the environment do not match the growth of the population.

How will we educate the employ such a large number of people? Will our transportation systems move them about as quickly and economically as necessary? How will we provide adequate health care when our population reaches 300 million? Will our political structures have to be reordered, too, when our society grows to such proportions? Many of our institutions are already under tremendous strain as they try to respond to the demands of 1969. Will they be swamped by a growing flood of people in the next thirty years? How easily can they be replaced or altered?

Finally, we must ask: how can we better assist American families so that they will have no more children than they wish to have? In my first message to Congress on domestic affairs, I called for a national commitment to provide a healthful and stimulating environment for all children during their first five years of life. One of the ways in which we can promote that goal is to provide assistance for more parents in effectively planning their families. We know that involuntary childbearing often results in poor physical and emotional health for all members of the family. It is one of the factors which contribute to our distressingly high infant mortality rate, the unacceptable level of malnutrition, and the disappointing performance of some children in our schools. Unwanted or untimely childbearing is one of several forces which are driving many families into poverty or keeping them in that condition. Its threat helps to produce the dangerous incidence of illegal abortion. And finally, of course, it needlessly adds to the burdens placed on all our resources by increasing population.

None of the questions I have raised here is new. But all of these questions must now be asked and answered with a new sense of urgency. The answers cannot be given by government alone, nor can government alone turn the answers into programs and policies. I believe, however, that the Federal

Government does have a special responsibility for defining these problems and for stimulating thoughtful responses.

Perhaps the most dangerous element in the present situation is the fact that so few people are examining these questions from the viewpoint of the whole society. Perceptive businessmen project the demand for their products many years into the future by studying population trends. Other private institutions develop sophisticated planning mechanisms which allow them to account for rapidly changing conditions. In the governmental sphere, however, there is virtually no machinery through which we can develop a detailed understanding of demographic changes and bring that understanding to bear on public policy. The federal government makes only a minimal effort in this area. The efforts of state and local governments are also inadequate. Most importantly, the planning which does take place at some levels is poorly understood at others and is often based on unexamined assumptions.

In short, the questions I have posed in this message too often go unasked, and when they are asked, they seldom are adequately answered.

Commission on Population Growth and the American Future

It is for all these reasons that I today propose the creation by Congress of a Commission on Population Growth and the American Future.

The Congress should give the Commission responsibility for inquiry and recommendations in three specific areas.

First, *the probable course of population growth, internal migration and related demographic developments between now and the year 2000.*

* * *

Second, *the resources in the public sector of the economy that will be required to deal with the anticipated growth in population.*

* * *

Third, *ways in which population growth may affect the activities of Federal, state and local government.*

* * *

For the Future

One of the most serious challenges to human destiny in the last third of this century will be the growth of the population. Whether man's response to that challenge will be a cause for pride or for despair in the year 2000 will depend very much on what we do today. If we now begin our work in an appropriate manner, and if we continue to devote a considerable amount of attention and energy to this problem, then mankind will be able to surmount this challenge as it has surmounted so many during the long march of civilization.

When future generations evaluate the record of our time, one of the most important factors in their judgment will be the way in which we respond to population growth. Let us act in such a way that those who come after us—even as they lift their eyes beyond earth's bounds—can do so with pride in the planet on which they live, with gratitude to those who lived on it in the past, and with continuing confidence in its future.

The Blacks Cry Genocide*
Ralph Z. Hallow**

Not long ago a family planning center in Cleveland was burned to the ground after militant Negroes had labeled its activities "black genocide." More recently, the antipoverty board of Pittsburgh became the first in the nation to vote down OEO appropriations to continue Planned Parenthood clinics in six of the city's eight poverty neighborhoods. The move resulted from intense pressure and threats of violence by blacks—all males—who have kept the genocide issue boiling since one of the clinics was threatened with fire bombing last fall. Although a coalition of women, black and white, has succeeded in rescuing the program, national officers of Planned Parenthood-World Population fear the Pittsburgh example may encourage black opponents to lay siege to similar programs in other cities. Organized opposition can be found in cities from California to New York, and summer could bring the violence which militant critics of the clinics have threatened.

Although concerted opposition to the Planned Parenthood Association (PPA) programs in the ghettos has centered in Pittsburgh, the issue has been gaining national currency through articles published in *Muhammed Speaks,* the newspaper of the Black Muslims. The author of the articles is Dr. Charles Greenlee, a respected black physician in Pittsburgh who first raised the issue nearly two years ago. Dr. Greenlee contends that the birth control information and "propaganda" of federally financed family planning programs are carried into the homes of poor blacks by "home visitors" and public assistance workers, who allegedly coerce indigent black women into visiting the clinics. Greenlee says, and welfare officials deny, that the intimidation takes the form of implicit or explicit threats that welfare payments will be cut off if the recipient has more children. Thus it is argued, the free clinics constitute "genocide," a conscious conspiracy by whites to effect a kind of Hitlerian solution to the "black problem" in the United States.

---

*The Nation, CCVIII, (April 26, 1969), 535-537. Figure deleted. Reprinted by permission.
**Mr. Hallow is an editorial writer for the Pittsburg Post-Gazette.

Dr. Greenlee's formula for leading his people out of white America's cul-de-sac is: black babies equal black votes equal Black Power. Recognizing this logic, he said recently on a local television panel discussion, the white power structure is using the neighborhood clinics to "decimate the black population in America within a generation." The Planned Parenthood national office sent a black representative to sit on the panel. The two top white executives of PPA in Pittsburgh decided their presence on the panel would only lend credence to Dr. Greenlee's charges. But, they point out, the neighborhood community action committees have representatives, including blacks, on the local PPA board.

Also arguing PPA's side of the question was Mrs. Frankie Pace, a resident of the city's largest black ghetto, the Hill District, where most of the "action" occurred during the civil disorders last April. Mrs. Pace believes that most black women in poor neighborhoods not only want the clinics but also desperately need such help because they are often ignorant of scientific methods of birth control. (Health department and welfare workers in nearly every U.S. city report that they still occasionally encounter indigent women who believe that urinating after intercourse prevents conception.)

The television panel illustrated the new alliances that have grown up over the "black genocide" issue. Seated next to Dr. Greenlee was Msgr. Charles Owen Rice, who for more than thirty years has enjoyed the reputation of being the liberal's liberal. Always a champion of the cause of labor and more recently of peace and an end to the war in Vietnam, he has nevertheless enunciated a position on birth control that is closer to that of the Vatican than to the more liberal one held by a significant number of priests and lay Catholics in America. He said during the panel discussion that the term "black genocide" is not too strong; for, he observed, it is "passing strange" that no clinics exist in the city's two mostly white poverty neighborhoods. Local PPA officials point out, however, that the predominantly Catholic populations in those neighborhoods have rejected the establishment of clinics in their communities.

PPA supporters also suggest it was no accident that William "Bouie" Haden was the only black leader to whom the Catholic diocese of Pittsburgh recently gave a $10,000 annual grant—to help run the United Movement for Progress, Haden's black self-help group. Haden, a fiery though not so young militant, was quick to pick up Dr. Greenlee's charges of "black genocide" and to force the temporary closing last summer of one of the clinics on his "turf," the city's Homewood-Brushton district. Although about seventy irate black women forced Haden to back off from the issue for a time, in early February he led the forces which, through skillful parliamentary maneuvering, got a divided and confused anti-poverty board to vote down an appropriation to continue the clinics. Although Haden's enemies flaunt his long criminal record, most observers recognize him as a sincere and effective leader who did much to keep Homewood-Brushton cool during the disorders last April.

In spite of his leadership abilities, Haden has only piecemeal support for his "black genocide" charges. Family planning supporters point out that it was the black women in the poverty neighborhoods who demanded that PPA set up a network of neighborhood clinics under the hegemony of the city's anti-poverty board. The women claimed that the PPA center in the downtown area was inaccessible to the indigent whose welfare allowances made no provision for baby-sitting fees and bus fares.

To complicate the issue still further, supporters of family planning programs in the ghettos include such eminent black men of the Left as Bayard Rustin and Dr. Nathan Wright, Jr., who was chairman of the Black Power conference. Writing on "Sexual Liberation" in the Newark *State-Ledger,* Dr. Wright said the poor—both black and white—are discriminated against sexually and should seek the help of Planned Parenthood.

The term "family planning" is slightly euphemistic; except in the states where it is prohibited, birth control counseling is offered even to unmarried girls under 18, provided there is parental consent and usually if the girl has had one child. Women in the 15-to-19-year age group account for the highest percentage of illegitimate births (40.2 percent for whites and 41.9 for blacks), according to U.S. Public Health Service figures for 1964. Here again, defenders of birth control argue that the clinics help to alleviate one of the grossest hypocrisies practiced by our male-dominated legislatures. Lawmakers, they say, hand down so-called moral standards for American women in defiance of the sexual practices actually prevailing in the society. If young women from enlightened middle-class families are still undergoing unwanted pregnancies and are forced to seek expensive or dangerous abortions, how much worse must it be for the teen-age daughters of the indigent?

Everywhere the statistics are on the side of family planning—at least for those who view them in unideological terms. In New Orleans, for example, where the largest family planning program in the United States has been operating, an indigent female population of 26 percent accounted for 56 percent of all births, 88 percent of illegitimate births and 72 percent of stillbirths. Nationally, the infant mortality rate of blacks is twice that of whites. The United States ranks fifteenth in the world in infant mortality, and there is a surfeit of evidence relating the problem directly to poverty. A study by the U.S. Department of Health, Education and Welfare found that the most effective way to reduce infant mortality is to offer family planning. Finally, of the 5.3 million indigent women in the United States, only 850,000 receive family planning services, and only 30 percent of those who do are nonwhite.

All this, however, means nothing to the black militant and his white allies who believe that Black Power and "poor" power (and the consequent redistribution of wealth they would bring) are threatened by free family planning clinics whose representatives actively seek out black women. Caught in the middle is the indigent American woman who wishes to have the same freedom to choose sex without conception that her middle-class counterpart enjoys.

The Politics of Population*
Aldous Huxley**

In politics, the central and fundamental problem is the problem of power. Who is to exercise power? And by what means, by what authority, with what purpose in view, and under what controls? Yes, under what controls? For, as history has made it abundantly clear, to possess power is *ipso facto* to be tempted to abuse it. In mere self-preservation we must create and maintain institutions that make it difficult for the powerful to be led into those temptations which, succumbed to, transform them into tyrants at home and imperialists abroad.

For this purpose what kind of institutions are effective? And, having created them, how then can we guarantee them against obsolescence? Circumstances change, and, as they change, the old, the once so admirably effective devices for controlling power cease to be adequate. What then? Specifically, when advancing science and acceleratingly progressive technology alter man's long-established relationship with the planet on which he lives, revolutionize his societies, and at the same time equip his rulers with new and immensely more powerful instruments of domination, what ought we to do? What *can* we do?

Very briefly let us review the situation in the light of present facts and hazard a few guesses about the future.

On the biological level, advancing science and technology have set going a revolutionary process that seems to be destined for the next century at least, perhaps for much longer, to exercise a decisive influence upon the destinies of all human societies and their individual members. In the course of the last fifty years extremely effective methods for lowering the prevailing rates of infant and adult mortality were developed by Western scientists. These methods were very simple and could be applied with the expenditure of very little money by very small numbers of not very highly trained technicians. For these reasons, and because everyone regards life as intrinsically good and death as intrinsically bad, they were in fact applied on a worldwide scale. The results were spectacular. In the past, high birthrates were balanced by high death rates. Thanks to science, death rates have been halved but, except in the most highly industrialized, contraceptive-using countries, birthrates remain as high as ever. An enormous and accelerating increase in human numbers has been the inevitable consequence.

At the beginning of the Christian era, so demographers assure us, our planet supported a human population of about two hundred and fifty millions. When the Pilgrim fathers stepped ashore, the figure had risen to about five hundred millions. We see, then, that in the relatively recent past it took sixteen hundred years for the human species to double its numbers. Today world population

*Aldous Huxley, "The Politics of Population," reprinted, by permission, from the March 1969 issue of *The Center Magazine,* a publication of The Center for the Study of Democratic Institutions in Santa Barbara, California, Vol. 2, No. 2, pp. 13-19.

**Aldous Huxley is the author of numerous books and articles. He is perhaps best known for his novel *Brave New World.*

stands at three thousand millions. By the year 2000, unless something appallingly bad or miraculously good should happen in the interval, six thousand millions of us will be sitting down to breakfast every morning. In a word, twelve times as many people are destined to double their numbers in one-fortieth of the time.

This is not the whole story. In many areas of the world human numbers are increasing at a rate much higher than the average for the whole species. In India, for example, the rate of increase is now 2.3 per cent per annum. By 1990 its four hundred and fifty million inhabitants will have become nine hundred million inhabitants. A comparable rate of increase will raise the population of China to the billion mark by 1980. In Ceylon, in Egypt, in many of the countries of South and Central America, human numbers are increasing at an annual rate of three per cent. The result will be a doubling of their present populations in about twenty-three years.

On the social, political, and economic levels, what is likely to happen in an underdeveloped country whose people double themselves in a single generation, or even less? An underdeveloped society is a society without adequate capital resources (for capital is what is left over after primary needs have been satisfied, and in underdeveloped countries most people never satisfy their primary needs); a society without a sufficient force of trained teachers, administrators, and technicians; a society with few or no industries and few or no developed sources of industrial power; a society, finally, with enormous arrears to be made good in food production, education, road building, housing, and sanitation. A quarter of a century from now, when there will be twice as many of them as there are today, what is the likelihood that the members of such a society will be better fed, housed, clothed, and schooled than at present? And what are the chances in such a society for the maintenance, if they already exist, or the creation, if they do not exist, of democratic institutions?

Mr. Eugene Black, the former president of the World Bank, once expressed the opinion that it would be extremely difficult, perhaps even impossible, for an underdeveloped country with a very rapid rate of population increase to achieve full industrialization. All its resources, he pointed out, would be absorbed year by year in the task of supplying, or not quite supplying, the primary needs of its new members. Merely to stand still, to maintain its current subhumanly inadequate standard of living, will require hard work and the expenditure of all the nation's available capital. Available capital may be increased by loans and gifts from abroad, but in a world where the industrialized nations are involved in power politics and an increasingly expensive armament race there will never be enough foreign aid to make much difference. And even if the loans and gifts to underdeveloped countries were to be substantially increased any resulting gains would be largely nullified by the uncontrolled population explosion.

The situation of these nations with such rapidly increasing populations reminds one of Lewis Carroll's parable in *Through the Looking Glass,* where Alice and the Red Queen start running at full speed and run for a long time until Alice is completely out of breath. When they stop, Alice is amazed to see that they are still at their starting point. In the looking glass world, if you wish to retain your present position, you must run as fast as you can. If you wish to get ahead, you must run at least twice as fast as you can.

If Mr. Black is correct (and there are plenty of economists and demographers who share his opinion), the outlook for most of the world's newly independent and economically non-viable nations is gloomy indeed. To those that have shall be given. Within the next ten or twenty years, if war can be avoided, poverty will almost have disappeared from the highly industrialized and contraceptive-using societies of the West. Meanwhile, in the underdeveloped and uncontrolled breeding societies of Asia, Africa, and Latin America the condition of the masses (twice as numerous, a generation from now, as they are today) will have become no better and may even be decidedly worse than it is at present. Such a decline is foreshadowed by current statistics of the Food and Agriculture Organization of the United Nations. In some underdeveloped regions of the world, we are told, people are somewhat less adequately fed, clothed, and housed than were their parents and grandparents thirty and forty years ago. And what of elementary education? UNESCO provided an answer. Since the end of World War II heroic efforts have been made to teach the whole world how to read. The population explosion has largely stultified these efforts. The absolute number of illiterates is greater now than at any time.

The contraceptive revolution which, thanks to advancing science and technology, has made it possible for the highly developed societies of the West to offset the consequences of death control by a planned control of births, has had as yet no effect upon the family life of people in underdeveloped countries. This is not surprising. Death control, as I have already remarked, is easy, cheap, and can be carried out by a small force of technicians. Birth control, on the other hand, is rather expensive, involves the whole adult population, and demands of those who practice it a good deal of forethought and directed will power. To persuade hundreds of millions of men and women to abandon their tradition-hallowed views of sexual morality, then to distribute and teach them to make use of contraceptive devices or fertility-controlling drugs—this is a huge and difficult task, so huge and so difficult that it seems very unlikely that it can be successfully carried out, within a sufficiently short space of time, in any of the countries where control of the birthrate is most urgently needed.

Extreme poverty, when combined with ignorance, breeds that lack of desire for better things which has been called "wantlessness"—the resigned acceptance of a subhuman lot. But extreme poverty, when it is combined with the knowledge that some societies are affluent, breeds envious desires and the expectation that these desires must of necessity, and very soon, be satisfied. By means of the mass media (those easily exportable products of advancing science and technology), some knowledge of what life is like in affluent societies has been widely disseminated throughout the world's underdeveloped regions. But, alas, the science and technology which have given the industrial West its cars, refrigerators, and contraceptives have given the people of Asia, Africa, and Latin America only movies and radio broadcasts, which they are too simpleminded to be able to criticize, together with a population explosion, which they are still too poor and too tradition-bound to be able to control through deliberate family planning.

In the context of a three, or even of a mere two per cent annual increase in numbers, high expectations are foredoomed to disappointment. From disappointment, through resentful frustration, to widespread social unrest the road is short. Shorter still is the road from social unrest, through chaos, to dictatorship, possibly of the Communist Party, more probably of generals and colonels. It would seem, then, that for two-thirds of the human race now suffering from the consequences of uncontrolled breeding in a context of industrial backwardness, poverty, and illiteracy, the prospects for democracy, during the next ten or twenty years, are very poor.

From underdeveloped societies and the probable political consequences of their explosive increase in numbers we now pass to the prospect for democracy in the fully industrialized, contraceptive-using societies of Europe and North America.

It used to be assumed that political freedom was a necessary precondition of scientific research. Ideological dogmatism and dictatorial institutions were supposed to be incompatible with the open-mindedness and the freedom of experimental action, in the absence of which discovery and invention are impossible. Recent history has proved these comforting assumptions to be completely unfounded. It was under Stalin that Russian scientists developed the A-bomb and, a few years later, the H-bomb. And it is under a more-than-Stalinist dictatorship that Chinese scientists are now in the process of performing the same feat.

Another disquieting lesson of recent history is that, in a developing society, science and technology can be used exclusively for the enhancement of military power, not at all for the benefit of the masses. Russia has demonstrated, and China is now doing its best to demonstrate, that poverty and primitive conditions of life for the overwhelming majority of the population are perfectly compatible with the wholesale production of the most advanced and sophisticated military hardware. Indeed, it is by deliberately imposing poverty on the masses that the rulers of developing industrial nations are able to create the capital necessary for building an armament industry and maintaining a well-equipped army with which to play their parts in the suicidal game of international power politics.

We see, then, that democratic institutions and libertarian traditions are not at all necessary to the progress of science and technology, and that such progress does not of itself make for human betterment at home and peace abroad. Only where democratic institutions already exist, only where the masses can vote their rulers out of office and so compel them to pay attention to the popular will, are science and technology used for the benefit of the majority as well as for increasing the power of the state. Most human beings prefer peace to war, and practically all of them would rather be alive than dead. But in every part of the world men and women have been brought up to regard nationalism as axiomatic and war between nations as something cosmically ordained by the Nature of Things. Prisoners of their culture, the masses, even when they are free to vote, are inhibited by the fundamental postulates of the frame of reference within which they do their thinking and their feeling from decreeing an end to the collective paranoia that governs international relations. As for the world's ruling minorities, by the very fact of their power they are chained even more closely to the current system of ideas and the prevailing political customs; for this reason they are even less capable than their subjects of expressing the simple human preference for life and peace.

Some day, let us hope, rulers and ruled will break out of the cultural prison in which they are now confined. Some day. And may that day come soon! For, thanks to our rapidly advancing science and technology, we have very little time at our disposal. The river of change flows ever faster, and somewhere downstream, perhaps only a few years ahead, we shall come to the rapids, shall hear, louder and ever louder, the roaring of a cataract.

Modern war is a product of advancing science and technology. Conversely, advancing science and technology are products of modern war. It was in order to wage war more effectively that first the United States, then Britain and the U.S.S.R., financed the crash programs that resulted so quickly in the harnessing of atomic forces. Again, it was primarily for military purposes that the techniques of automation, which are now in the process of revolutionizing industrial production and the whole system of administrative and bureaucratic control, were initially developed. "During World War II," writes Mr. John Diebold, "the theory and use of feedback was studied in great detail by a number of scientists both in this country and in Britain. The introduction of rapidly moving aircraft very quickly made traditional gun-laying techniques of anti-aircraft warfare obsolete. As a result, a large part of scientific manpower in this country was directed toward the development of self-regulating devices and systems to control our military equipment. It is out of this work that the technology of automation as we understand it today has developed."

The headlong rapidity with which scientific and technological changes, with all their disturbing consequences in the fields of politics and social relations, are taking place is due in large measure to the fact that, both in the U.S.A. and the U.S.S.R., research in pure and applied science is lavishly financed by military planners whose first concern is in the development of bigger and better weapons in the shortest possible time. In the frantic effort, on one side of the Iron Curtain, to keep up with the Joneses—on the other, to keep up with the Ivanovs—these military planners spend gigantic sums on research and development. The military revolution advances under forced draft, and as it goes forward it initiates an uninterrupted succession of industrial, social, and political revolutions. It is against this background of chronic upheaval that the members of a species, biologically and historically adapted to a slowly changing environment, must now live out their bewildered lives.

Old-fashioned war was incompatible, while it was being waged, with democracy. Nuclear war, if it is ever waged, will prove in all likelihood to be incompatible with civilization, perhaps with human survival. Meanwhile, what of all the preparations for nuclear war? If certain physicists and military planners had their way, democracy, where it exists, would be replaced by a system of regimentation centered upon the bomb shelter. The entire population would have to be systematically drilled in the ticklish operation of going underground at a moment's notice, systematically exercised in the art of living troglodytically under conditions resembling those in the hold of an eighteenth-century slave ship. The notion fills most of us with horror. But if we fail to break out of the ideological prison of our nationalistic and militaristic culture, we may find ourselves compelled by the military consequences of our science and technology to descend into the steel and concrete dungeons of total and totalitarian civil defense.

In the past, one of the most effective guarantees of liberty was governmental inefficiency. The spirit of tyranny was always willing, but its technical and organizational flesh was weak. Today the flesh is as strong as the spirit. Governmental organization is a fine art, based upon scientific principles and disposing of marvelously efficient equipment. Fifty years ago an armed revolution still had some chance of success. In the context of modern weaponry a popular uprising is foredoomed. Crowds armed with rifles and homemade grenades are no match for tanks. And it is not only to its armament that a modern government owes its overwhelming power. It also possesses the strength of superior knowledge derived from its communication systems, its stores of accumulated data, its batteries of computers, its network of inspection and administration.

Where democratic institutions exist and the masses can vote their rulers out of office, the enormous powers with which science, technology, and the arts of organization have endowed the ruling minority are used with discretion and a decent regard for civil and political liberty. Where the masses can exercise no control over their rulers, these powers are used without compunction to enforce ideological orthodoxy and to strengthen the dictatorial state. The nature of science and technology is such that it is peculiarly easy for a dictatorial government to use them for its own anti-democratic purposes. Well-financed, equipped, and organized, an astonishingly small number of scientists and technologists can achieve prodigious results. The crash program that produced the A-bomb and ushered in a new historical era was planned and directed by some four thousand theoreticians, experimenters, and engineers. To parody the words of Winston Churchill, never have so many been so completely at the mercy of so few.

Throughout the nineteenth century the state was relatively feeble, and its interest in, and influence upon, scientific research were negligible. In our day the state is everywhere exceedingly powerful and a lavish patron of basic and ad-hoc research. In western Europe and North America the relations between the state and its scientists on the one hand and individual citizens, professional organizations, and industrial, commercial, and educational institutions on the other are fairly satisfactory. Advancing science, the population explosion, the armament race, and the steady increase and centralization of political and economic power are still compatible, in countries that have a libertarian tradition, with democratic forms of government. To maintain this compatibility in a rapidly changing world, bearing less and less resemblance to the world in which these democratic institutions were developed—this, quite obviously, is going to be increasingly difficult.

A rapid and accelerating population increase that will nullify the best efforts of underdeveloped societies to better their lot and will keep two-thirds of the human race in a condition of misery in anarchy or of misery under dictatorship, and the intensive preparations for a new kind of war that, if it breaks out, may bring irretrievable ruin to the one-third of the human race now living prosperously in highly industrialized societies—these are the two main threats to democracy now confronting us. Can these threats be eliminated? Or, if not eliminated, at least reduced?

My own view is that only by shifting our collective attention from the merely political to the basic biological aspects of the human situation can we hope to mitigate and shorten the time of troubles into which, it would seem, we are now moving. We cannot do without politics; but we can no longer afford to indulge in bad, unrealistic politics. To work for the survival of the species as a whole and for the actualization in the greatest possible number of individual men and women of their potentialities for good will, intelligence, and creativity—this, in the world of today, is good, realistic politics. To cultivate the religion of idolatrous nationalism, to subordinate the interests of a single national state and its ruling minority—in the context of the population explosion, missiles, and atomic warheads, this is bad and thoroughly unrealistic politics. Unfortunately, it is to bad and unrealistic politics that our rulers are now committed.

Ecology is the science of the mutual relations of organisms with their environment and with one another. Only when we get it into our collective head that the basic problem confronting twentieth-century man is an ecological problem will our politics improve and become realistic. How does the human race propose to survive and, if possible, improve the lot and the intrinsic quality of its individual members? Do we propose to live on this planet in symbiotic harmony with our environment? Or, preferring to be wantonly stupid, shall we choose to live like murderous and suicidal parasites that kill their host and so destroy themselves?

Committing that sin of overweening bumptiousness which the Greeks called *hubris,* we behave as though we were not members of earth's ecological community, as though we were privileged and, in some sort, supernatural beings and could throw our weight around like gods. But in fact we are, among other things, animals—emergent parts of the natural order. If our politicians were realists, they would think rather less about missiles and the problem of landing astronauts on the moon, rather more about hunger and moral squalor and the problem of enabling three billion men, women, and children, who will soon be six billions, to lead a tolerably human existence without, in the process, ruining and befouling their planetary environment.

Animals have no souls; therefore, according to the most authoritative Christian theologians, they may be treated as though they were things. The truth, as we are now beginning to realize, is that even things ought not to be treated as *mere* things. They should be treated as though they were parts of a vast living organism. "Do as you would be done by." The Golden Rule applies to our dealings with nature no less than to our dealings with our fellowmen. If we hope to be well treated by nature, we must stop talking about "mere things" and start treating our planet with intelligence and consideration.

Power politics in the context of nationalism raises problems that, except by war, are practically insoluble. The problems of ecology, on the other hand, admit of a rational solution and can be tackled without the arousal of those violent passions always associated with dogmatic ideology and nationalistic idolatry. There may be arguments about the best way of raising wheat in a cold climate or of reforesting a denuded mountain. But such arguments never lead to organized slaughter. Organized slaughter is the result of arguments about such questions as: Which is the best nation? The best religion? The best political theory? The best form of government? Why are other people so stupid and wicked? Why can't they see how good and intelligent *we* are? Why do they resist our beneficient efforts to bring them under our control and make them like ourselves?

To questions of this kind the final answer has always been war. "War," said Clausewitz, "is not merely a political act but also a political instrument, a continuation of political relationships, a carrying out of the same by other means." This was true enough in the eighteen-thirties, when Clausewitz published his famous treatise, and it continued to be true until 1945. Now, obviously, nuclear weapons, long-range rockets, nerve gases, bacterial aerosols, and the laser (that highly promising addition to the world's military arsenals) have given the lie to Clausewitz. All-out war with modern weapons is no longer a continuation of previous policy; it is a complete and irreversible break with previous policy.

Power politics, nationalism, and dogmatic ideology are luxuries that the human race can no longer afford. Nor, as a species, can we afford the luxury of ignoring man's ecological situation. By shifting our attention from the now completely irrelevant and anachronistic politics of nationalism and military power to the problems of the human species and the still inchoate politics of human ecology we shall be killing two birds with one stone—reducing the threat of sudden destruction by scientific war and at the same time reducing the threat of more gradual biological disaster.

The beginnings of ecological politics are to be found in the special services of the United Nations Organization. UNESCO, the Food and Agriculture Organization, the World Health Organization, the various technical-aid services—all these are, partially or completely, concerned with the ecological problems of the human species. In a world where political problems are thought of and worked upon within a frame of reference whose coördinates are nationalism and military power, these ecology-oriented organizations are regarded as peripheral. If the problems of humanity could be thought about and acted upon within a frame of reference that has survival for the species, the well-being of individuals, and the actualization of man's desirable potentialities as its coördinates, these peripheral organizations would become central. The subordinate politics of survival, happiness, and personal fulfillment would take the place now occupied by the politics of power, ideology, nationalistic idolatry, and unrelieved misery.

In the process of reaching this kind of politics we shall find, no doubt, that we have done something, in President Wilson's prematurely optimistic words, "to make the world safe for democracy."

The Population Bomb

[1]Philip M. Hauser, *The Population Dilemma* (2nd ed.; Englewood Cliffs, N. J.: Prentice-Hall, Inc., (c) 1969), p. 13.

[2]See Philip Appleman, *The Silent Explosion* (Boston: Beacon Press, 1965), pp. 3-9.

[3]Robert Rienow and Leona Rienow, *Moment in the Sun* (New York: The Dial Press, Inc., 1967), p. 12.

[4]Paul R. Ehrlich, "Population, Food and Environment: Is the Battle Lost?" *The Texas Quarterly,* Summer 1968, p.74.

[5]Wallace Stegner, "What Ever Happened to the Great Outdoors?" *Saturday Review,* XLVIII, No. 21 (May 22, 1965), 38.

8

The Politics of Survival

Here, sir, the people rule.

Alexander Hamilton

We have previously asserted that the environment cannot be saved or restored except through governmental action. We cannot here examine the intricacies of the process by which governmental policy is formed, but it may be possible to set out some definitions and attempt some generalizations about the basic ingredients and the major actors in the policy-forming process.

Politics and Policy: Some Definitions

In its most basic sense, politics is the process of forming governmental policy. All the activities that we commonly associate with the term *politics* are carried on with the ultimate objective of influencing governmental policy. Campaigns and elections, for example, are mainly preliminaries to pick the players for the "policy game."

A governmental policy is an enforceable decision or set of decisions that determines who gets what, when, and how, and who pays for it.

"What" is not restricted to material things; it may include such intangibles as freedom or justice or an aesthetically pleasing environment.

"Who" may be a single individual, a group, a state, a section of the country, or "the general public." Most policy proposals are advanced for the "good of the public" or to "protect the public interest," but such proposals will ordinarily benefit one or a few groups more than the rest, and it will be these "high beneficiary" groups who are most active in supporting the proposal. The high beneficiary groups will ordinarily attempt to concentrate the benefits and diffuse the costs.

Policies are formed by people *for people.* There is really no such thing as environmental policy—there is only *people policy.* The effect of a policy on the environment is important mainly because of its effect on people.

Policy decisions are never neutral. Ordinarily somebody gains and somebody loses. Conceivably everyone might gain or everyone might lose as the result of a particular policy decision.

There can be no such thing as a "policy vacuum." There always exists some sort of policy. Such policies need not be articulated in laws, court decisions, executive directives, or administrative regulations. Thus the United States government permitted and encouraged the killing of buffalo for many years, even though there was no formal statement of this policy. Similarly it was our policy until very recent times to allow air pollution, with no penalties or restrictions placed on the polluter.

In general terms, the policy process is a continuum in which there are no final decisions. However, environmental policy decisions tend to have a greater degree of finality than do decisions in some other policy areas. In some cases the cost of reversing or changing a decision may be unacceptably high. We are not likely to destroy a multi-million dollar dam even though we may decide that its construction was a mistake. It may be economically impractical to rejuvenate Lake Erie. Furthermore, some environmental policy decisions may be ecologically irreversible. We cannot take back the DDT that has been deposited in the oceans. If the whooping crane is exterminated, there will be no more whooping cranes.

In the United States we solve most problems and reconcile or resolve most conflicts without any action by the government. It is only when such resolutions become unsatisfactory to a politically effective public that they come to the agenda of government. When a problem reaches the point of political resolution, the technical and economic considerations do not change, but new considerations are added and the weights of the original considerations may be changed. The infusion of these new inputs and the changing weights of the original considerations are likely to be frustrating to technologists who may believe that they have already solved the problem.

The Basic Ingredients of Policy Formation

The Physical Environment. The characteristics of the physical environment determine, in part, the kinds of policy problems that will arise, and influence the range of problem-resolving proposals that will be considered. Thus an arid condition gives rise to the problem of supplying adequate water, and the proximity of water determines whether irrigation will be considered as a method for resolving the problem. The observed deterioration of the physical environment has triggered recent public interest and concern.

Sustenance Patterns. The common, usual, or traditional methods by which individuals support themselves will similarly determine, in part, the kinds of policy problems that will arise. They will likewise influence the range of problem-resolving proposals that will be considered.

People of a lumbering community will consider forest fires and insect infestations to be major problems, but they will probably not consider the water pollution caused by a paper mill to be in that category. They will probably attempt to solve the problems of fires and insects, and thus protect their established sustenance pattern, rather than try to change the sustenance pattern through eliminating water pollution, stocking streams, and serving as guides, lodge-keepers, and the like.

Prevailing Ideologies. In every society there exists a congeries of prevailing value-laden beliefs of varying weights. The strength of these belief systems varies somewhat between localities, occupations, income levels, and so forth. The strength of such belief systems may also change with time. Such ideologies sometimes conflict, and indeed conflicting ideologies may be strongly held by the same individual. Whether or not such ideologies are true or valid is largely irrelevant as regards policy formation in the short run. What is relevant is the prevalence of the ideology and the strength with which it is held.

Current environmental policies are to a very considerable degree the consequence of a constellation of prevailing ideologies.

Policy decisions ordinarily will not be accepted unless they fit one or more prevailing ideologies. Furthermore, it is unlikely that possible solutions outside these prevailing ideologies will even occur to decision-makers or planners. Stated differently, it is unlikely that an unorthodox problem solution (lying outside a prevailing ideology) will arise in the minds of the planners. If one should arise, the planner will be reluctant to submit it, and if he does submit it, it will ordinarily not be seriously considered.

Organizations as Institutions. Some organizations have a high degree of stability (structural strength) and long tenure in the society. For most practical purposes, such organizations can be considered permanent institutions. Realistic policy must take into account the organizational framework of these institutions and tailor policy determinations to fit them.

Planners may wish to develop policies for entire river basins, but these basins may encompass such organizations as state, county, city, and special district governments, chambers of commerce, labor unions, and farm and business organizations. River basin policies must therefore be carried out through (and sometimes by) some of these groups.

In the case of government organizations, it does no good to bewail the artificiality of boundaries. Most such boundaries are fixed and can be considered as "given."

Ideologies and institutions change slowly, not only because of the inertia of habit and standardized operating procedure, but because change is expensive—in terms of both economic and psychic costs. Furthermore, the most successful (and influential) people in the society are least likely to recognize the need for change. They will usually be most interested in perpetuating the ideologies and institutions through which they became successful. We could not expect it to be otherwise.

Disaster. Many, possibly most, changes in environmental policies have come about as the consequence of publicized disaster. In such instances it is likely that the need for an action-policy was recognized some time before the disaster occurred. But often it takes a disaster to generate enough support and publicity to get action on a policy proposal.

Some examples of disasters which have influenced present environmental policies are: floods, forest fires, drought, dust storms, oil spills, pollution-caused fish kills, and deaths from smog.

The State of Technology. The stage of technological development limits the range of problem recognition and of problem-solving policy proposals. The use of technology to solve one problem is also likely to create other or additional problems. DDT was used to solve the malaria problem, but its use created other problems. The development of automobiles helped solve the transportation problem, but in so doing it created problems of smog, parking, highways, and suburbanization.

We should note in passing that when the status of technology ("science") is high, the proponents of particular policies which have a social or economic or political objective will attempt to explain or rationalize their objectives in technological terms. Thus persons who wish to place a dam at site A rather than site B for business or other reasons may advance their case in terms of the differing rates of evaporation between the two sites.

When technology disagrees as to methods or conclusions, interest groups with a stake in the outcome will choose that technology or technological process which will rebound to their benefit and will give it their support. Technological problems and technological conflicts are thus moved out of the realm of science and into the arena of politics, and the technological problems or conflicts are resolved through a political process.

Previous Policy Decisions. Policies are not isolated islands in time. The process of policy formation is a continuum in that each policy decision builds on, or is influenced by, previous policy decisions; and it, in turn, influences the course and direction of future policy decisions.

Of crucial importance is the fact that public policy decisions may affect all the other basic ingredients of public policy formation. It is commonly assumed that the ingredients listed above, with the possible exception of disaster, have a life of their own—that they exist independently of, and are unaffected by, public policies. But this is simply not true. Climates can be changed; topography can be changed; ideological systems can be changed; and all the other ingredients can be changed by policy decisions. So while these are the basic factors in the formation of policy, they, in turn, can be changed by public policy.

Policy Makers for the People

Who makes public policy? The general public does not make policy except in a negative sense. Someone else makes the shoe, but they wear it. Consequently they supposedly know best where the shoe pinches or whether it is wearable at all. If they are dissatisfied they exert a veto by refusing to comply, by voting out incumbent officials, and by similar methods. This veto power exists before as well as after the fact; before a decision is made, policy planners must take into account the anticipated limits of public tolerance.

If the general public does not make policy except in a negative sense, who does?

Interest Groups. An interest group is an organized body of persons which seeks to advance its objectives through governmental action. Such objectives may be selfish or they may be altogether altruistic.

Interest groups and interest group officials are the principal innovators, promoters, organizers, and fighters in the process of public policy formation. They originate most policy proposals and they furnish the energy to get them adopted as official public policy.

Administrative Agencies of Government. Governmental agencies are second only to interest groups in innovating, promoting, organizing, and fighting for the adoption of given policies.

Legislative Bodies. Congress and the state legislatures are generally assumed to be the policy-making organs of society. It seems likely, however, that legislatures act more as formalizers or "pronouncers" of policy than as its architects.

Legislative bodies would appear to function primarily in a negative sense as the representatives of the public. That is, the legislative body as a whole does not actively function in policy formation except to exercise a veto over the policy proposals of individual committees. Even in the committees there is little innovation of policy, but there *is* considerable organizing and promoting and some fighting. But the principal role of the committees seems to be that of judging the probable political reception of policy proposals and of negotiating among interest groups, administrative agencies, and other committees, as well as with individual legislators.

Some Congressional and legislative committees are specialized in one area that especially interests legislators from particular districts. Naturally legislators try to obtain assignments to the committees whose work deals most directly with the interests of their constituents. Thus the Senate Committee on Interior and Insular Affairs is composed primarily of Westerners. Such committees, then, tend to become small, specialized congresses that are *not* representative of Congress as a whole. But unless Congress uses its veto power over committee policy proposals, such proposals do become official policy.

It frequently happens that an influential interest group or groups, a government agency, and the members of a legislative committee may all represent the same special interest. Within certain broad limits, they make public policy for the United States in their area of primary interest. This phenomenon might be called a monopolitical system because of the absence of effective competition. Here there is no real competition unless the policies developed go so far as to outrage the general public and bring forth the "public veto."

It is sometimes held that while legislative bodies do not ordinarily innovate in policy matters, they do act as catalysts, synthesizers, and argument settlers; that they choose from among the claims of contending groups, or that they attempt to develop workable compromises among the contenders. There is undoubtedly much truth in this concept. However, there is also a strong tendency to avoid settling arguments and even to avoid compromise. Probably this is achieved principally by postponing decisions and by giving in to both or all the contenders. If sportsmen complain that insecticides are killing fish, it may be easier to restock the streams than to face up to the Bureau of Plant Pest Control and its supporting interest groups and Congressional committees.

Political Influentials. Quite frequently single individuals are influential in forming policy. Such persons obtain power because of income, social status, position in an organizational hierarchy, knowledge, hard work, experience, charisma, or, most likely, a combination of several of these factors. Governor Nelson Rockefeller, for example, may embody all of them.

The political influential is likely to be a symbol and a rallying point for one or more prevailing ideologies. He is also likely to be a "popularizer," explainer, and publicist for the ideology. He is frequently in the "inner circle" of the interest group—government agency—Congressional committee triumvirate.

The Courts. One definition of a law might be "a formal statement of public policy." The doctrine of *stare decisis* (the use of precedents) simply means that the courts interpret a given policy in terms of past interpretations of public policy decisions. But these interpretations are made in consideration of the basic ingredients previously listed. Furthermore, the courts are especially careful to choose precedents which point toward decisions that do not violate prevailing ideologies.

Finally, we are a legalistic people, so we frequently clothe policy problems with legal terminology and transfer them to the courts for policy decisions. These policy decisions are set forth as legal concepts or decisions by the courts and are then translated back into policy decisions. Such decisions have no more finality than other policy decisions and are a part of the continuum of policy formation.

Action to Improve the Environment

Measures to improve specific portions of the environment (air, water, and so forth) have been discussed in previous chapters. In addition, the United States has a long history of efforts to conserve or restore forests, grazing lands, wildlife, natural beauty, parklands, and soil.[1] However, none of these efforts has attempted to encompass the total physical environment.

During 1970 and 1971 some efforts were made to take an over-all view and to restructure government for better environmental management.

On January 1, 1970 the President signed the National Environmental Policy Act of 1969 (83 Stat. 852). In this landmark Act, Congress assumed responsibility to "assure for all Americans safe, healthful, productive, and esthetically and culturally pleasing surroundings" and to "attain the widest range of beneficial uses of the environment without degradation, risk to health or safety, or undesirable and unintended consequences." The Act also created a Council of Environmental Quality within the Executive Office of the President. Among other things the Council was instructed to review all programs and activities of the Federal government in terms of their environmental effects. On January 29, 1970 the President appointed Russell E. Train, Robert Cahn, and Gordon J. F. McDonald to comprise the Council, and in August 1970 the Council submitted its first annual report.[2]

In his State of the Union address on January 22, 1970, President Nixon gave considerable attention to environmental concerns, and the following February 10th he sent a message to Congress which set forth a 37-point program on the environment.

On July 9, 1970 the President submitted a reorganization plan to Congress which would create two new government agencies, mainly by consolidating certain functions then being carried on by several different departments. Both plans were accepted. A new "Environmental Protection Agency" (EPA) was established which included the functions formerly carried out by the Federal Water Quality Administration, the National Air Pollution Control Administration, and the Bureau of Solid Waste Management, as well as certain functions relating to pesticide control, radiation criteria and standards, and some other environmental protection activities. Clearly EPA was intended to be the principal Federal agency for environmental protection and enhancement. The budget request for fiscal year 1972—$2.45 billion—gives some indication of the size of the undertaking. William D. Ruckelshaus was appointed as the first EPA administrator.

The second new agency, the Oceanic and Atmospheric Administration, is composed of the old Environmental Science Services Administration (in the Department of Commerce) plus elements of the Bureau of Commercial Fisheries and the Bureau of Sport Fisheries and Wildlife, along with some other smaller marine research and survey organizations.

The first report of the Council on Environmental Quality (August 1970) called for a "national commitment" to resolve the nation's environmental problems. Perhaps its most significant recommendation was the formulation of a national land-use policy to direct the type, location, and timing of future land development. Other major recommendations called for the formulation of national policies on energy and transportation.

In his message to Congress on the environment dated February 8, 1971, President Nixon reminded Congress that he had recommended a 37-point program the previous year, and that most of that program had not been acted upon. He then went on to reiterate some of his previous recommendations and to add new ones. Of particular significance was a proposal to levy charges on sulphur oxide emissions and a proposal for an additional tax on leaded gasoline. The President's major proposals are summarized below.

1.   Measures to strengthen pollution-control programs.

Charges on sulfur oxides and a tax on lead in gasoline to supplement regulatory controls on air pollution.

More effective control of water pollution through a $12 billion national program and strengthened standard-setting and enforcement authorities.

Comprehensive improvement in pesticide control authority.

A Federal procurement program to encourage recycling of paper.

2.   Measures to control emerging problems.

Regulation of toxic substances.

Regulation of noise pollution.

Controls on ocean dumping.

3.   Measures to promote environmental quality in land-use decisions.

A national land-use policy.

A new and greatly expanded open space and recreation program, bringing parks to the people in urban areas.

Preservation of historic buildings through tax policy and other incentives.

Substantial expansion of the wilderness areas preservation system.

Advance public agency approval of power plant sites and transmission line routes.

Regulation of environmental effects of surface and underground mining.

The efforts listed above are only the beginning; they are not solutions. In facing up to the problems of environmental restoration, we can be sure that there are no simple solutions; there are no easy solutions; there are no final solutions; and there is no such thing as a free lunch.

**Adequacy of the Political
System to Solve Environmental
Problems**

Can environmental problems be resolved through the political system described above? Is our system adequate to cope with these new, complex, and difficult problems? President Nixon thinks it is, but in this excerpt from a message to Congress on February 10, 1970, he suggests that we need new philosophies (ideologies) of land, air, and water use.

Like those in the last century who tilled a plot of land to exhaustion and then moved on to another, we in this century have too casually and too long abused our natural environment. The time has come when we can wait no longer to repair the damage already done, and to establish new criteria to guide us in the future.

The fight against pollution, however, is not a search for villains. For the most part, the damage done to our environment has not been the work of evil men, nor has it been the inevitable by-product either of advancing technology or of growing population. It results not so much from choices made, as from choices neglected: not from malign intention, but from failure to take into account the full consequences of our actions.

Quite inadvertently, by ignoring environmental costs, we have given an economic advantage to the careless polluter over his more conscientious rival. While adopting laws prohibiting injury to person or property, we have freely allowed injury to our shared surroundings. Conditioned by an expanding frontier, we came only late to a recognition of how precious and how vulnerable our resources of land, water and air really are.

The tasks that need doing require money, resolve, and ingenuity— and they are too big to be done by government alone. They call for fundamentally new philosophies of land, air, and water use, for stricter regulation, for expanded government action, for greater citizen involvement, and for new programs to ensure that government, industry, and individuals all are called on to do their share of the job and to pay their share of the cost.

Throughout this book we have listed many governmental actions that have been taken to improve the environment. Perhaps most of them have been "too little and too late," but in general the "guys in the white hats" have been winning. One of the reasons they have achieved limited victories is that no one is in favor of dirty air, dirty water, and so forth. We are all in favor of a better environment in general terms. However, when specific actions are undertaken to advance general goals, we can expect that resistance will begin to develop.

* * *

Political scientists have extensively analyzed the process of policy formation. Acting on this information, and on their perception of the sequence of political events, a subcommittee of the House Committee on Science and Astronautics developed the first selection in this chapter, "Sequence of Events in Environmental Quality Issues." Readers may wish to evaluate the adequacy and accuracy of the Subcommittee's findings.

The second selection is the concluding chapter of the first annual report of the Council on Environmental Quality. The Council, naturally, has to assume that problems of the environment can be solved, but it sets out a long "agenda for urgent action," and it concludes by saying, "If a better environment is passed down to future generations, it will be because of the values and actions of people—all of us—today." This is not an overly optimistic statement.

Standard Oil Company Chairman John E. Swearingen next presents an article on "Environmental Pollution" which may represent the views of a substantial portion of the business community. Swearingen is optimistic about our chance for success in solving environmental problems. They are nothing new, he says, and we have the technology to solve them. From his point of view, what is most necessary is to face up to the problems and get on with the job.

Political scientist Lynton K. Caldwell proposes a new approach to land-use policy based on ecological principles. Caldwell proposes that all land (both public and private) be managed as part of the eco-system rather than being considered as simply another commodity. Since practically every human activity involves the use of land, either directly or indirectly, ecologically based land management could provide the "handle" which would allow us to get hold of the environmental problems. Caldwell recognizes that such a basic change would cause large scale dislocations throughout the economy, so he is probably not very optimistic about the chance of his recommendations being adopted.

Next political scientists Straayer and Meek point out the difficulties involved in accomplishing environmental improvement through the political process. In a closely reasoned essay they analyze the capacity of the political system "to meet the growing expectations for the development of effective programs for environmental control." They first set out the "requisites for successful environmental control through the process of collective decision making." Secondly, they consider the factors which limit our capacity to plan and control the environment. They conclude that environmental improvement is likely to occur incrementally and on a limited scale. In their words, "the dominant pattern of environmental decision making will remain incremental muddling." Comprehensive environmental control will remain, they say, the dream of anti-pluralistic planners.

Finally, journalist Barry Weisberg asserts that the present system "sustains itself through the systematic destruction of man and his physical world." Weisberg argues that the environment cannot be saved unless there are "very basic and very revolutionary" changes in the system. While he does not directly advocate such action, he suggests that we can expect "the bombing of more corporate headquarters, sabotage to the industrial machinery that pollutes, and obstruction at airports and other transportation corridors."

Sequence of Events in Environmental Quality Issues*

The subcommittee has noted a sequence of public opinion, political action, and corrective measures which is common to most pollution problems. The same sequence may be expected in many other instances of technological impact on society. Because of the long-term goal of achieving a technology assessment capability for the Congress, the sequence is described here, insofar as it is understood.

1. Apathy

The subtle nature of environmental quality problems makes it possible for effects to become quite advanced before the public becomes aware of them. Despite the fact that billions of dollars have been spent for waste treatment in the past five decades, the average citizen is not aware of the effort. Sanitary sewerage, garbage, and trash collection are designed to remove the wastes from view. In this same period the life expectancy has risen continuously, mortality is at its lowest point in history and the public health must be considered as good. Therefore, the current, rather sophisticated concern with environmental hazards does not gain immediate attention.

---

*U.S. Congress, House, Committee on Science and Astronautics, *Report of the Subcommittee on Science, Research, and Development: Managing the Environment* (Washington, D.C.: U.S. Government Printing Office, 1968), pp. 9-12.

The slow degradations of air, water, and landscape are difficult to detect in the busy atmosphere of day-to-day living.

2. View with Alarm

The early stages of quality loss often are noticed by naturalists, recreation enthusiasts, resort operators, and scientists who work in the outdoors. Also there are technologists who recognize very sensitive ecological situations which may be easily upset. Depending on their ability to communicate, and their access to mass media, an early warning can be obtained. Often, the alarm is exaggerated (purposely or not) and a negative response is obtained from other observers who do not view the trend as serious. There is a peculiar receptivity in the public for forecasts of natural or manmade disasters. But curiosity is often limited to a "Sunday supplement" treatment and if the date of the cataclysm is more than a few years ahead, then apathy prevails.

The public information system of scientists, media, and officials can not always produce an objective report. A scientist may find an obscure, little-understood anomaly in a highly sensitive, delicate eco-system. He proceeds to speculate imaginatively that irreversible, disastrous results might occur. Antipollution agencies and private groups sponsor studies on "what would happen if—" or "assuming a set of conditions, then—", extrapolating observations as if no corrective action is possible or would be taken. The mass media remove whatever limitations or caveats which may have been attached to these speculations and hypotheses so that they are published as "predictions of things to come." Officials then use the press reports to argue for new authority and to defend present programs.

3. Episodes Occur

A real disturbance in the environment may be manifested by local or short term episodes. An air pollution "attack" resulting from a rare coincidence of meterological and pollutant emission conditions will reveal the degree of contamination in an airshed in a dramatic way. Mysterious fish kills in rivers and estuaries may have origins in up-stream waste disposal inadequacies or in natural biological infections. The interpretation of these serious episodes brings scientists into the problem and gains the attention of the public. This attention can then be used to elaborate on the long term possibilities and to cultivate a desire for control of the environmental hazard.

4. Monitoring and Source Identification

The public officials and scientists who become interested in the problem want to understand cause and effect. Monitoring in the environment is usually inadequate as to number of stations, length of time covered, and accuracy of measurement. The contamination may be sporadic. Many sources, large and small, may be involved.

Contaminants may change chemically in the biosphere before they do their damage. The eye irritating property of Los Angeles smog is not found in automobile exhaust, but is formed from exhaust hydrocarbons under the influence of sunlight as the gases stagnate in the geographical basin. Long and ingenious laboratory studies were necessary to relate eye irritation to reactive hydrocarbons.

5. Human Health Effects

While the effects of environmental contamination on human health are often extremely difficult to qualify, it is not at all difficult to reach the conclusion that pollution "can't be good for you." Proceeding from that dogma, the obvious goal becomes one of returning to a pristine environment, free of any trace of manmade influence.

6. Public Cry for Action

Public opinion is now aroused and there is a thirst for information and explantion which often cannot be met with the facts at hand. The political potency of these issues lies in the fact that since society has created the situation which threatens environmental quality values, society can correct its actions— and the leadership of the Nation is called upon to do so. There is a great pressure for immediate implementation of abatement.

Pollution affecting one local jurisdiction often originates in another which may not choose to take abatement action. Local authorities are sometimes intimidated by the fear that offending industries may move out, rather than control emissions. (Actually such threats have seldom been verified.) Within a single jurisdiction, there may be great resistance to the location of an incinerator or sewage treatment plant. These problems escalate the call for action to higher levels of authority and finally to the Federal Government.

7. Stringent Target Abatement Goals
   Are Set

With relatively little information available on causes, sources, abatement technology, or benefits and costs, but with a growing pressure for correction, ambient air and water standards are set. These target numbers are, of necessity, hasty and arbitrary; and depend, for their enforcement, on nuisance laws or existing public health regulations. In a circular process, some industrial pollution goes uncorrected, leading to precipitous action by government which brings recalcitrance and controversy which obstruct progress and prevent a cooperative atmosphere from developing.

8. Reaction from Polluters

Those regulations made in an atmosphere of emotional clamor and in the absence of sufficient and pertinent facts are apt to be restrictive enough to bring immediate reaction from discharging industries and municipalities. Tough regulations mean large capital expenditures or drastic operational revisions. It is unlikely that any abatement practices which could pay for themselves (in waste recycle, etc.) have already been employed, or result from considerations other than abatement. Faced with investments which yield no return, the attitude becomes one of questioning the proof of an alleged health effect, and whether the indicted emission source is the only offender, and whether all other sources will be restricted also. A delaying action is fought to avoid, if possible, the unproductive investments and expenditures for abatement. Personal freedom is restricted (e.g., leaf burning, choice of fuels, auto maintenance requirements, etc.). Thus industry, local government, and individuals begin to react against control.

9. Response to the Need for Abatement

As more and better cause-and-effect data are accumulated, a new phase of response from polluters is entered. Where the case for abatement is made, ambient quality standards are set, the available technology is installed and the costs are passed on to the consumer in higher prices, or the stockholder in lower dividends or to the taxpayer. Accompanying this acceptance of abatement is an intense effort to find out more about what actually occurs in the local airshed or river basin and to reexamine manufacturing processes for waste eliminating changes. Industry is forced into research in order to know as much about their pollution problem as does the abatement agency.

10. Reviews and Second Thoughts

As research on cause-and-effect relationships proceeds and as the monitoring of the actual environment is improved, the quality issue gains a deeper perspective. It is probable that noticeable improvements will have been made in the gross and obvious contaminants. New abatement techniques and devices which are less costly to install and to operate will change the economic feasibility situation. Older plants and obsolete equipment will be replaced by new machinery which is intrinsically less polluting or damaging to the environment, or the operations close down. Goals will be reexpressed in a more realistic way, taking into account the assimilative capacity of air and water, and the local variations of terrain and weather.

11. Negotiation for Long-Term Management

As the climate for discussion becomes less emotional, less polarized, and based on greater knowledge, society begins to accept commonsense tradeoffs. Environmental quality values are compared with benefits of resource use in the standard of living. The data and mechanisms for cost effectiveness are improved to the point where complex ecosystems can be managed for optimum yield to civilization.

An ethic for the environment—a notion of the right thing to do—is accepted as fundamental policy for the Nation. Increased public understanding of human ecology changes personal and collective habits to favor a perpetuation of high environmental quality.

12. The Status Today

Each particular environmental quality issue may be at a different stage in the above sequence as of today. A pessimist would say that each new problem will necessarily travel the same path. An optimist hopes that a general increase in scientific research and technological development can short circuit the early stages of apathy, emotion, demagoguery, overreaction and gross neglect.

Present and Future Environmental Needs*

This report has looked closely at particular environmental problems. It has looked at what is being done now to combat them. And it has looked at what might be done in the days, months, and years ahead. The agenda for urgent action is long. Much has already been done, but much more must still be done with current management tools wielded by existing institutions. Moreover, the pace of change in programs underway promises, over the next few years, to brake even further what has seemed a headlong careening toward environmental decay.

The pressing need for tomorrow is to know much more than we do today. We lack scientific data about how natural forces work on our environment and how pollutants alter our natural world. We lack experience in innovating solutions. We lack tools to tell us whether our environment is improving or deteriorating. And most of all, we lack an agreed upon basic concept from which to look at environmental problems and then to solve them.

---

*The First Annual Report of the Council on Environmental Quality, *Environmental Quality* (Washington, D.C.: U.S. Government Printing Office, 1970), pp. 231-241.

Needed—A Conceptual Framework

A problem is said to exist when our view of what conditions are does not square with our view of what they should be. Problems, in short, are products of our values. People agree—for example, that a river should not be polluted. And when they see that it is, water pollution becomes a problem. But some of the values dealt with in this report are not unanimously agreed upon. The chapter on land use is critical of urban sprawl; yet many Americans choose to live in dwellings which abet such sprawl. This uncertainty about what values are relevant to environmental questions and how widely or strongly they are held throws up a major obstacle to conceiving environmental problems. How much value do Americans place on the natural environment as against the man-made environment of cities? How much do people value esthetics? Do they agree about what is esthetically desirable? These and a host of similar questions must be raised when trying to align priorities for coping with environmental decline.

Our ignorance of the interrelationship of separate pollution problems is a handicap in devising control strategies. Is pollution directly related to population or to land use or to resources? If so, how? Indeed, does it do any good to talk about pollution in general, or must we deal with a series of particular pollution problems—radiation, pesticides, solid waste? A systems approach is needed, but what kind of system? The pollution system, the materials and resources use system, the land use system, the water resources or atmospheric system? In this report the Council has suggested tentative answers to some of these questions. But much more thought is necessary before we can be confident that we have the intellectual tools necessary to delineate accurately the problems and long-range strategies for action.

Experience will help resolve some of the conceptual problems. We already know what problems are most pressing. Clearly we need stronger institutions and financing. We need to examine alternative approaches to pollution control. We need better monitoring and research. And we need to establish priorities and comprehensive policies.

Needed—Stronger Institutions

Most of the burden for dealing with environmental problems falls to governments at all levels. And the Nation's ability to strengthen these institutions is central to the struggle for environmental quality. To make them stronger, fundamental changes are necessary at Federal, State, and local levels of government. Chapter II of this report treats in detail the President's proposed improvements in the Federal Government for better environmental policy development and management. Although these changes will not be the final answer, they do lay the base for a comprehensive and coordinated Federal attack on environmental problems.

States play a key role in environmental management because of their geographic scope and broad legal powers. Many have reorganized to focus comprehensively on environmental problems. Many are helping municipalities build sewage treatment plants; some are planning statewide treatment authorities to construct and operate plants. And California has led the Nation in trying to curb automobile air pollution since the 1950's. In land use control many States are carving out larger responsibilities for land use decisions of regional scope.

In many respects local government, of all the levels, most needs institutional improvement. It has suffered from fragmentation, from skyrocketing demands and costs for public services, and from generally inelastic tax sources. The financial burden of environmental improvement staggers local governments. Most of the costs of water pollution control, both capital and operating expenses, come from their budgets. In some cities, efforts to deal with combined sewer overflows raise almost insuperable financial and technical hardships. Solid waste disposal is a major expense for most local governments, and the costs grow as disposal techniques are upgraded, as land grows scarcer, and as wages spiral. On top of its financial headaches, local government is caught in a tangled web of overlapping and conflicting jurisdictions that hamstring solutions to land use and air pollution.

Existing institutions must be made better and, in some cases, new institutions created to deal with the environment. Occasionally more funds, personnel, and public support are all that is necessary. Other cases call for a more fundamental restructuring. This may mean extending geographic coverage and operational capabilities. Air and water pollution, for example, do not respect political boundaries, so institutions covering entire watersheds or airsheds may be necessary to cope with them. Important aspects of land use planning, review, and control may need to be shifted to regional or State levels as the only way to tie land use needs together over wide areas. And new forms of land use criteria may be necessary to reverse the current myopia of local government zoning.

Many environmental problems cross not only local, state, and regional boundaries, but international boundaries as well. Control of pollution of the seas and the atmosphere requires new forms of international cooperation—for monitoring, research, and regulation.

Needed—Financial Reform

Financing for environmental quality is in need of dramatic overhaul. Liquid and solid waste collection and disposal by local governments represent an indispensible service—not unlike electricity and water. Yet rarely do the users of these services, industry and homeowners, bear the full costs of operation and amortization. Rather, financially beleaguered local governments subsidize these services. The current method of financing, therefore, is not only inequitable; it encourages a greater accumulation of waste by industries because they do not bear the full costs of disposal. It deprives local governments of needed funds to operate and maintain waste disposal facilities properly. In short, it contributes to the sorry performance of facilities in the United States in treating sewage and disposing of solid wastes. If future demands for environmental improvement are to be funded adequately, better methods of financing must be developed.

Needed—Pollution Control Curbs

This report discusses many tools for curbing pollution. Most have been regulatory. For centuries authority to regulate has been wielded to a limited extent—more broadly by the middle of the 20th century. But there is considerable debate whether regulation represents the best course of action. Economic incentives have won increasing support as a pollution control weapon. Charges or taxes on the volume of pollutants—say, 10 cents a pound on oxygen-demanding material—are another lever that might spur industry to reduce wastes. The charge system, some say, would not only be more economic but also more effective compared to the traditionally cumbersome enforcement process.

In this report the Council urges stricter and more systematic enforcement of air and water standards. That cannot be done, however, without better monitoring and data—as well as clear-cut enforcement policies that will leave no doubt of responsibilities on the part of the private sector.

The Council believes that economic incentives offer promise, especially if backed up by regulatory power. It believes that they should be selectively demonstrated. And it believes that effluent or emission charges should be evaluated as a supplementary method of stimulating abatement measures.

Needed—Monitoring and Research

Effective strategy for national environmental quality requires a foundation of information on the current status of the environment, on changes and trends in its condition, and on what these changes mean to man. Without such information, we can only react to environmental problems after they become serious enough for us to see. But we cannot develop a long-term strategy to prevent them, to anticipate them, and to deal with them before they become serious. For example, we became aware of the mercury problem only after it had become critical in some areas and had probably done environmental damage. Yet we still do not know the extent or significance of that damage. Our attack on the problem can now be but a cure or a cleanup. It has already happened. However, if we had possessed an adequate environmental early warning system, we would have been able to anticipate mercury pollution and take early action to stop it at its sources.

We do not know what low-level exposure to most pollutants does to man's health over the long term. Nor do we know how people react to changes in their environment. The challenge to the social sciences is to develop entirely new gauges to measure environmental stress. What do crowding, urban noise, and automation do to man? These are critical questions. We do not understand enough about the interactions of different environmental forces such as urbanization, land use, and pollution. We do not even understand many of the natural processes that play critical roles in environmental well being—such as changes in world climate.

To obtain such information, a comprehensive program is required. It involves nationwide environmental monitoring, collection, analysis, and—finally—effective use of the information. In the case of some pollution, such monitoring should be international.

The first step is to identify the environmental parameters—things in the environment which are or should be measured. These range from substances such as DDT, sulfur dioxide, and lead to percentages of open space in the cities, visitor use of parks, and survival of species. Once identified, the parameters must be monitored—measured on a regular, repeated, continuing basis. In this way, baselines of the present status can be determined and changes from that base detected.

Environmental indices can be developed from these data. Indices are data aggregated to provide a picture of some aspect of environmental quality—for example, the quality of air as it affects human health. They are not unlike the cost of living index by which economists measure the status of the economy and by which housewives measure their budgets. Some environmental indices—and the parameters on which they are based—are easily identified and measured. For example, conditions that clearly affect human health in air or drinking water can be easily detected. Other indices and parameters are based on value judgments and are much more difficult to deal with. The quality of National Parks and scenic beauty are examples. To develop indices, the information from monitoring must be collected, translated into a usable form, and analyzed. Good indices do two important things. They inform the general public of the quality of the environment, and they inform the government and other decision-makers who can take action. Good indices show the current environmental quality on a national or local scale and whether this condition is improving or degrading.

At present no nationwide environmental monitoring and information system exists. Federal, State, and local agencies now collect a variety of data. Many of these data, however, are obtained for limited program purposes or for scientific understanding. They are fragmentary and not comparable on a nationwide basis. Although it may be possible to use some of these in the comprehensive system which is needed, at present they do not provide the type of information or coverage necessary to evaluate the condition of the Nation's environment or to chart changes in its quality and trace their causes.

Therefore, a major national objective must be to develop a comprehensive nationwide system of environmental monitoring, information, and analysis. The Council has initiated a study of the nature and requirements for the early development of such a system. However, even after we have developed a system, we must then have additional knowledge to enable us to understand and interpret the data we get. We are not yet in a position to understand the significance of the monitoring results to man and to natural systems. More research is needed on how the environmental systems operate and on the impact of man on the environment and its impact on him. Consequently, augmenting such research must take a high national priority.

Needed—A System for Priorities

It is difficult, given the current state of environmental knowledge, to set long-term priorities for the future. Relevant measures of environmental quality are often not available or, if available, are inadequate. These difficulties are compounded by great regional differences. For the present we can use our limited current data to identify pressing problems for immediate attention. In the future, the difficult task of deciding the Nation's environmental priorities, however, must be faced. Resources for combating environmental blight and decay are limited. Choices will have to be made on which problems have first claim on these resources. Four main criteria should determine this priority:

The intrinsic importance of the problems—the harm caused by failing to solve them.

The rate at which the problems are going to increase in magnitude and intensity over the next few years.

The irreversibility of the damage if immediate action is not taken.

The measure of the benefits to society compared to the cost of taking action.

The process of setting priorities is difficult. There is deep conflict over which problems are most important. And the inertia of on-going activities is a major obstacle. There are conflicts between the needs of industry and the needs of the environment. And the public yearning for more conveniences clashes often with the best interests of the ecology. Nor will the priorities of the Federal Government always coincide with those of State and local governments. The Federal priorities will be broad and national. States and localities, however, will often give higher priority to other aspects of environmental quality. As long as these other levels of government at least meet national standards, the imposition of higher standards in some areas is welcome. Whatever the divergences, diligent application of priorities will be necessary to make any real progress toward a high quality environment.

Needed—Comprehensive Policies

As priorities are developed, policies must be devised to translate them into action. These policies may consist of a mix of activities aimed at a particular goal. Dealing with many environmental problems will require a battery of economic incentives, regulations, research, and assistance programs. In some areas, policies cannot be developed until more information is available. In other areas, they can and should be developed now.

For example, the need for a national energy policy is clear. As the demand for power increases rapidly, new power facilities have to be built. Power plants will pollute the air with oxides of sulfur and nitrogen, the water with heat, and the landscape with mammoth towers and obtrusive power lines.

This environmental harm cannot be wholly averted now, but it can be limited. For the short term, the design and siting of power generating facilities and transmission lines must be better planned and controlled. But for the longer run, a national energy policy should be developed. It would require a comprehensive analysis of energy resources and actual needs. It would provide for wise use of fuels, both conserving them for the future and lessening environmental damage. For example, wider use of nuclear fuel, natural gas, or low sulfur coal and oil would lower sulfur oxide levels in critical areas.

As national transportation policies are shaped, air pollution is one among several critical environmental factors that must be considered. Although air pollution can be abated by enforcing emission standards, control devices for individual vehicles and other technological solutions may not be enough in the long run to keep air pollution from worsening as population and the number of automobiles continue to increase in the cities. One part of a transportation policy should be the continued examination of alternative means of curbing auto emissions, such as the development and use of systems combining the flexibility of the individual automobile with the speed of modern mass transportation.

Control over land use, a critical need of the seventies, is lodged for the most part in local governments. And often local solutions are piecemeal and haphazard. The local property tax favors the single-family residence on a large lot over types of housing less wasteful of land. Planning often fails to take into account the impact of development on the natural surroundings and often is not heeded by local governments. All these factors together lead to a series of local zoning decisions and regulatory action that perpetuate urban sprawl.

The State role in land use control has traditionally been small because most of the authority has been delegated to local governments. And direct Federal control over local land use is smaller still. However, the Federal Government can influence how land is used through planning and capital grants. Under existing programs the Federal Government, by its actions, could spur more modern land use methods. It could encourage cluster zoning and timed development. It could identify natural areas for preservation and encourage channeling of future growth in more rational patterns.

The problems of land use are complicated and diffuse. And the challenge is to center all the capabilities of all levels of government in a coordinated attack on them. The problems and the challenge together argue for a national land use policy.

Population growth and economic growth are potential wellsprings of environmental decay. They increase the demands upon limited natural resources. The U.S. population will continue to grow for the next few decades. But environmental quality is difficult to achieve if population growth continues. The President has appointed a commission on Population Growth and the American Future, headed by John D. Rockefeller III, which will explore the policy implications of future population growth.

The development of knowledge will doubtless indicate many new areas in which national policies are appropriate. And as these policies are developed, specific programs for implementation must then be formulated.

Conclusions

The year 1970 represents a pivotal year in our battle for a clean environment. The Nation is committing resources at all levels of government and in the private sector. Public support is at an all-time high. And the President's proposal for consolidation of anti-pollution programs, coupled with the

Council's policy advisory and coordinating role, provide an opportunity to look at environmental quality in new ways.

This report emphasizes the need to move aggressively now to deal with problems that can be dealt with within existing knowledge and by existing institutions. For the long term, we need much more knowledge of values; the scope and nature of environmental problems; status and trends in the environment; the workings of natural processes; and the effects of pollutants on man, animals, vegetation, and materials. As we gain this knowledge, we will need to develop the institutions and financing mechanisms, the priorities, the policies, and finally, the programs for implementation. Without such a systematic approach, the current piecemeal, unrelated efforts will achieve only partial and unsatisfactory progress in meeting environmental problems of tomorrow.

This report emphasizes that changes in one part of the environment inevitably trigger changes in other parts. These complex interactions of environmental processes must be looked at as a whole. While keeping in mind the indivisibility of the environment and its intricate interrelationships, it is also necessary that some segments be treated separately when attacking environmental decay. Water pollution caused by a specific source may affect an entire ecosystem. But enforcement action must be taken against the particular source, not against the ecosystem. The major portion of this report has dealt separately with interrelated environmental problems, but only because of the inadequacy of our current framework for considering the environment and the need to focus attention on particular problem areas.

The National Environmental Policy Act of 1969 clearly stresses the necessity of approaching environmental problems as a totality. The act requires that Federal decision making incorporate environmental values along with technical and economic values; that both short- and long-term effects be given careful consideration; and that irreversible actions and commitments be carefully weighed.

National environmental goals must be developed and pursued in the realization that the human environment is global in nature, and that international cooperation must be a principal ingredient to effective environmental management.

All levels of government should function in two distinct ways: Within their geographic scope and needs, they must consider and plan for the environment as an interrelated system. But at the same time they must make specific decisions and take specific actions to remedy environmental problems. These two levels apply to action by individual citizens and private institutions as well. Our view of the environment and its value is changing and will continue to change. But these changes have effect only as they relate to specific choices by local communities, by particular industries, and by individuals. People in the end shape the environment. If a better environment is passed down to future generations, it will be because of the values and actions of people—all of us—today.

Environmental Pollution*
John E. Swearingen**

As we enter the concluding chapters of the 20th Century, we find the United States in a mood of uncertainty and self-doubt which has few parallels in our history. While the Civil War was the high water mark of our national division, it was at least division into two broad camps, each of which was convinced of the eternal rightness of its position.

Today, however, nearly every aspect of our national life is under attack for one reason or another. Considerable numbers of the young appear convinced that our whole society is rotten to the core, and in need of rebuilding from the ground up. At the other end of the age spectrum are eminent adults who are equally convinced that fatal threats to our wellbeing lie in the conduct of foreign policy, defense, taxation and spending, or some other policy area. In between we are confronted by a host of crusaders for various causes, enthusiastically abetted by the mass media, reminding us of an endless list of deficiencies demanding immediate correction if the nation is to survive. Many of the crusaders have drastic, and sometimes peculiar, solutions to the problems which have caught their attention.

In the course of this national psychoanalysis, we have rediscovered a number of problems—such as poverty, inferior education, inequality of opportunity, and urban decay—which are as old as civilization itself. The scale of this self-criticism has reached such proportions that it threatens to turn us into a nation of hypochondriacs—along with giving aid and comfort to our enemies, who delight in the deliberate exaggeration of anything which puts the United States in an unfavorable light.

A good deal of the hand-wringing that is going on is unproductive of anything but a mood of fatalism and despair. Certainly we have a formidable list of very real problems crying for solution. As I have suggested, however, none of these is new, and all of them happen to exist to a greater degree outside the United States than they do here.

In addition, the heat and extent of the debate going on—whether the subject is pot in the schools or the war in Vietnam—is ample evidence of vitality within our society. It is also a daily reminder that our system allows considerably more room for dissent than is to be found in the systems erected by the followers of Marx, Lenin, Che Guevara, Comrade Mao and the other heroes of the militant Left.

More to the point is the fact that we are trying to eradicate some of these age-old evils. This is clearly in the pioneering and egalitarian tradition of America. Thanks to the tremendous productive capacity of our economy, such a goal may indeed be within our reach. No other sizeable country in the world

---

*Vital Speeches of the Day, XXXVI, No. 4 (December 1, 1969), 118-121. Reprinted by permission.
**John E. Swearingen is Chairman, Standard Oil Company (Indiana). This speech was delivered at the Annual Meeting of the Indiana State Chamber of Commerce, Indianapolis, Indiana on November 6, 1969.

could seriously begin to consider such an undertaking, on economic grounds alone.

There is hardly a problem area you can name which has not been the target of increasing expenditures and efforts in recent years, and—measured by historical standards—considerable progress has been registered on many fronts. With our characteristic impatience, however, we want to see the job done tomorrow, and more attention gets focused on the shortcomings than on the gains.

Along the way, we have made the painful discovery that some of these problems are a good deal more complex and intractable than had been generally realized. It has also been discovered that it takes more than grants of money, however large, and the enactment of legislation, however well-intended, to bring about the desired changes.

The most recent of our problems to assume national priority—and the one to which I am going to address my remarks today—is air and water pollution. I think this is an appropriate forum in which to raise the subject, since we have represented here the principal elements of our society which are currently engaged in the effort to arrest pollution. While individuals and groups of every persuasion have an interest in cleaner air and water, the assignment of doing something about the matter is in the hands of the governmental and business leadership of which this audience is composed.

While pollution has been a subject of concern in many quarters for some time, it is only in recent years that the public has given it real note. However, according to national opinion surveys, over 50 per cent of the public now considers air and water pollution to have reached serious levels. The concern of the forward-looking conservationist has been communicated to the public, and has provided the leverage for legislation and other action to combat the problem.

Within the past few years, approximately 500 bills and amendments dealing with pollution control have been introduced in Congress. Even admitting the sure-fire political appeal of standing foursquare on the side of clean air and water, this is a truly remarkable concentration of Congressional attention in so short a period.

The most significant outcome of this concentration to date has been the Air Quality Act of 1967, a blueprint for dealing with air pollution on a regional basis by establishing concurrent state and federal jurisdictions and enforcement requirements. In turn, this act has provided a springboard for corollary legislation at the state and local levels. Equally far-reaching proposals to deal with water pollution are nearing approval.

Running through the bills and amendments at the national level is a determined effort to extend federal jurisdiction into many areas traditionally reserved to the states. The basis of the demand by federal agencies for a greater role in decision making is the contention that the states have not been vigorous enough in using their control authority, and that many state programs are either nominal or inadequate, or both. Friction and jurisdictional disputes extending down to local governmental levels have been among the byproducts of this process, and more can be expected. Meanwhile, business and industry are called upon to devote increasing amounts of time and money to comply with progressively stricter standards applying to their operations.

Apart from the question of who's in charge, there is no mistaking the gravity of the challenge posed by pollution. Individually and collectively, we have defied the laws of intelligent housekeeping for so long as to impair the quality of our environment to a serious degree. Before the situation is further compounded by the projected new waves of population about to crash down upon us, concerted action is imperative.

One of the accomplishments of the space program has been to give us a better perspective of our situation here on earth. Scientists have been pointing out for years the relative frailty of the envelope of atmosphere and water which sustains life on this planet. Now that we have had a closer look at the desolate landscapes of some of our neighbors in the solar system—along with a view of this lush earth from outside—the importance of preserving our environmental heritage has been driven forcibly home.

However, there is a danger that national concern over arresting pollution is going to lead us into repeating some of the same mistakes that have hobbled efforts to combat problems in other social areas. Lesson number one is that you can't successfully solve a problem unless you understand it—and there is considerable evidence that we have not yet reached this point.

The rhetoric, the television shows, the magazine and newspaper articles, the campaign speeches, the committees and the demonstrations that have awakened the public to the spread of pollution have made a positive contribution by calling attention to a situation in need of correction. To the extent that this barrage has tended to concentrate on industrial pollution, on the other hand, it has been somewhat misleading.

There is a danger that the public is being led into a belief that most of the problem can be eliminated simply by imposing strict controls on industry. Unfortunately, the problem is far too complex to be legislated out of existence, and crash programs aimed at symptoms rather than underlying causes are more likely to lead to economic waste than to environmental improvement.

We are not likely to make much headway in the fight against pollution unless we recognize that:

Environmental pollution is both a social and an economic problem.

It must be approached and solved on a practical basis—in terms of costs versus benefits.

In one manner or another, the costs must inevitably be borne by the consuming public—which means all of us.

A rational and effective approach to pollution control is impossible without genuine understanding of what the problem is, why it has developed, and what the roles of industry, government, and the individual should be in meeting the problem. In short, there is urgent need for an overall perspective—a philosophy of pollution control.

The central question is not whether we should have cleaner air and water, but how clean, at what cost, and how long to take to do the job.

The fact that these considerations are frequently ignored in popular discussions of the problem does not diminish their validity. No one can argue with the premise that wherever pollution can be scientifically demonstrated to be a genuine hazard to human health, it should be eliminated immediately and regardless of expense.

Beyond question, pollution has increased hand in hand with growth and concentration of population and with the introduction of technology. Some degree of pollution is part of the cost involved in achieving the benefits made possible in a technological society. Our challenge is to identify the complex sources of pollution and keep them within socially and economically tolerable limits.

There are a good number of people around who are convinced the curses of technology outweigh its blessings. My own view is closer to that expressed in the findings of a major study of the progress of technological societies, whose authors concluded: "Without its progress since the 19th Century, most men alive today would not have been born; those alive would have been sentenced to disease, filth, and even greater misery than exists in the world today. We are in better shape because of it."

Another long study of technology and society by a different group of scholars has concluded that the effect of technology has been to promote individualism—to give Americans a greater range of personal choice, wider experience, and a more highly developed sense of self-worth than any people in history.

Even the detractors of modern technology are hard put to portray it as the source of all our difficulties. Both air and water pollution have been around for a long time. Strong complaints were lodged by the patricians of ancient Rome because soot was smudging their white wool togas. Residents of the Los Angeles Basin who may think smog is a recent local invention might be interested to know that early Spanish explorers noted the haze from Indian campfires already hanging over the area.

As for water pollution, the battle against silt—which is still the leading pollutant—began some 8,000 years ago in Mesopotamia not long after the Sumerians invented irrigation. Babylon and Ninevah were brought down primarily because silt overcame the irrigation system on which the first great civilization was built. The same problem ruined Rome's famed sewer system and created the disease-breeding Pontine Marshes.

Our present situation is largely a function of ancient forces at work in an urban society of unprecedented size, and in which insufficient attention has been given to the changes this combination was bringing about in our environment.

Now that we are belatedly aware that the supply of pure air over a number of our cities is diminishing and that contamination of our water supplies has risen alarmingly, we are setting out to do something about the threat. Laws have been passed, new regulatory bodies have been established, funds appropriated, and research accelerated.

But the prospects for successful action to arrest pollution cannot be ranked very high until there is greater awareness that all members of society have created the problem and that all will have to be parties to the solution. Any serious examination of the situation indicates that there are three major sources of pollution: the public, governmental agencies, and industry. Of these three, I might note, responsible elements of industry were the first to recognize their contributions to pollution and to initiate remedial measures.

However, public criticism is levelled chiefly at industry as the major cause of both air and water pollution. The contributions to air pollution of public incinerators, garbage dumps, and the heating of homes and buildings are largely disregarded. When it comes to water pollution, the public singles out factory and plant wastes as the major offender, and assigns only a minor role to the silting of rivers and streams, to private septic tanks, or to wastes from other private sources such as power boats. In addition, the surveys also suggest that public enthusiasm for pollution control is matched by a reluctance to pay even a modest share of the cost.

This attitude will have to change. While industry presents one identifiable source of pollution, the unhappy fact remains that a problem of national magnitude would still be with us if pollution were somehow completely eliminated from all industrial operations. As one leading government enforcement official has noted, an underlying cause of water pollution is that all over the country we have municipal sewage systems that are inadequate for the loads imposed on them in the past few years. The cost of providing adequate municipal sewage treatment facilities has, by itself, been estimated at over $30 billion through the year 2000.

Or let us consider agriculture. Agriculture withdraws twice as much water from streams and wells as public water utilities and manufacturing industry combined. Much of this water finds its way back into rivers and streams, and we really know very little about the condition in which it is returned—although there are grounds for definite concern.

Any public illusions that the problem will be solved simply by applying strict controls on industry, and at little public cost, are going to be shattered before very long. The public can recognize its direct financial involvement when called upon to vote on a local bond issue or tax increase to underwrite improved sewage treatment or incineration facilities. But the same principle applies when it comes to pollution-control expenditures by industry. These are merely an additional cost of doing business, and—like all other costs—must ultimately be passed on to the customer. As for government grants to control pollution, that bill will be rendered to us all by the Internal Revenue Service.

Along with many others, the petroleum industry is making strenuous efforts to minimize its contributions to the problem. Oil company expenditures for air and water conservation last year reached an estimated $382 million, as against $271 million two years earlier, and are expected to continue to increase. More than half of these pollution control expenditures are being devoted to capital equipment.

In arriving at decisions in this area, I should note that any corporate management faces a dual responsibility—to conserve not only natural resources, but also social and economic resources, such as capital. Even in designing a new facility, it usually becomes apparent at an early stage that, while significant improvement in pollution control can be made at reasonably modest cost, further additional investments will achieve smaller and smaller improvements.

Finally one reaches a point beyond which prohibitive incremental investments are required for small incremental improvements. Some place along the line, economic penalties outweigh social benefits, and management—along with society at large—must determine where that occurs in evaluating the cost and benefits involved.

In arriving at proper solutions to environmental control problems, it is essential that decisions be based on facts, not on suppositions or suspicion. Urgent situations create a responsibility to develop facts speedily, but not the responsibility to act before facts are determined. In its planning for conservation, industry needs reasonable assurance that a proposed solution is not motivated solely by a desire to solve the problem, but is backed up by enough facts to insure that it is the best solution available.

The only sound bases for legislation and regulation are scientific knowledge and a sense of social responsibility, along with a series of definite goals. Without clear objectives, crash programs rather than planned ones are likely to result. This leads to a situation in which everyone is sure to lose, but not at all certain to win.

In our attempts to find the best available solution, I think it is clear from experience that pollution problems are not monolithic; they vary widely according to geographical conditions. There are, for example, different types of smog. London-type smog occurs chiefly where coal is the principal fuel used, and blankets the area at night or on cold foggy days when the air is stagnant. Photochemical smog, on the other hand, is prevalent around Los Angeles and some other sunny, poorly ventilated urban centers—and remains a big city, rather than a nationwide, problem. The same is true in regard to water pollution. Watersheds are defined by nature, and different geographical and ecological conditions call for different solutions.

When it comes to regulatory responsibility, the soundest principle is to place responsibility to take the necessary action on the level of government best able to cope with specific conservation problems. Such action should be tailored to local conditions. Mere copying of regulations adopted by other governmental units fails to recognize the diversity of local needs—and it is part of industry's responsibility to work to help clarify these local needs.

I think it is clear that the responsibility to act in defense of our essential natural resources, such as air and water, extends across the entire social structure of the nation—individuals, industry, plus local, state, and federal governments. In addition to its internal efforts to minimize pollution stemming from its operations, and research to improve conservation technology, industry has a responsibility to cooperate actively with government.

It is equally important that the public understands its role in the process, and comes to recognize the importance of balancing the inevitably large costs involved. The range of cost-versus-benefit choices is already extremely wide, and will grow wider as federal, state, and municipal programs for pollution control are put into effect. Only if the economic facts are widely understood can the public make an informed decision in each case, based on its willingness to pay for a stated degree of environmental cleanliness.

The cost-versus-benefit approach will not result in a Utopia, with an environment as pure as our first pioneers found it; rather, it points toward air and water quality that is acceptable, and compatible with the multiple needs of a technology-centered society.

In conclusion let me suggest that it is time we left the stage of fingerpointing, reciting past sins, and viewing with alarm and moved on to the vastly more difficult matter of solving some of our pollution problems. If a problem could be talked to death, pollution would have long since been lowered into its final resting place.

In today's climate, there are probably more people who are against pollution than are for motherhood, and a number of them are extremely vocal about where they stand. In their zeal, some of them verge on fanaticism. Just as in other areas, true fanatics at least merit our understanding. In my judgment, there is not much to be said for a much larger group of people who have been cynically and systematically using public concern over pollution as another platform from which to attack the business community and its motives.

Despite the positive harm these people do through fogging the issues, however, the best course appears to be to ignore them and to try to get on with the job.

In the words of John W. Gardner, "We have plenty of debaters, plenty of blamers, plenty of provocateurs, plenty of people who treat public affairs as an opportunity for personal catharsis or glorification. We don't have plenty of problem-solvers."

American industry at least has a high percentage of people in its ranks who have experience in solving problems, and, as I have noted, responsible segments of industry were the first to recognize their contribution to pollution and to launch costly and extensive measures to try to remedy the situation. That these efforts are going to accelerate is unquestionable, and they are one of the most promising signs on the horizon that something concrete is going to get done about our collective problem.

The roadblocks in our path lie more in the realm of sociology than technology. A society capable of interplanetary travel can surely devise the technology to control its own wastes. But broad public support of the necessary steps and a willingness to share the costs are indispensable. This is one more counter at which no free lunch is available, and the sooner the public faces up to that fact the sooner we will be on our way.

**An Ecosystems Approach to Public
Land Policy***
Lynton K. Caldwell**

A public lands policy restricted to lands in government ownership has been politically expedient but ecologically unrealistic. The natural processes of physical and biological systems that comprise the land do not necessarily accomodate themselves to the artificial boundaries and restrictions that law and political economy impose upon them. The stress of human demands upon the land tends to displace natural processes throughout its ecosystems and to impair its capacity for self-renewal. American public land policy, however, is based upon a set of historically derived assumptions—legal, economic, and political—that provide no means for taking the fundamental ecological context of land use into account. It is, of course, necessary to cope with land problems within the conventional context of public attitudes, laws, and economic arrangements, inadequate though they may be. But it is also important to know that there is a larger context for policy with which man must ultimately reckon:

---

*Lynton K. Caldwell, "An Ecosystems Approach to Public Land Policy," in *Public Land Policy*, ed. Phillip O. Foss (Boulder, Colo.: Colorado Associated University Press, 1970), pp. 43-50, 51-54. Reprinted by permission.
**Mr. Caldwell is a professor of political science at Indiana University.

it is the condition of the land as the physical basis for human welfare and survival. If human demands upon the natural environment continue to mount, it will become necessary as a matter of welfare and survival to abandon present land policy assumptions for a policy of public management of human environment on ecologically valid principles. Under this eventuality, public land policy would be public policy for all land, and traditional rights of ownership would be greatly modified, although the enjoyment of privacy within socially approved uses of the land might be enhanced.

How would a public land policy based upon ecosystems concepts differ from policies based upon other considerations?

Public land policies here and abroad have traditionally been based on juridic, economic, or demographic concepts. Ecological considerations, although not always by that name, have sometimes influenced land policies, but an ecosystems approach to public land policy has seldom been attempted on national or regional scales. The reason does not lie in the complexity and infinitude of ecosystems, although these are deterring factors. Failure to apply ecological concepts to land use policies is primarily the consequence of two related causes. The first is the inability of society, because of inadequacy of knowledge, insufficiency of wealth, or inappropriateness of institutions, to build ecologically based land policies into a general system of environmental management. The second, and more obvious, is incompatibility of interests among competing land users.

An ecosystems approach to land policy encounters resistance to the degree that it is inconsistent with the values, assumptions, institutions, and practices that shape the prevailing social arrangements affecting the custody and care of the land. Ecological considerations may, in themselves, be compatible with specific aspects of traditional land use arrangements. Incompatibility often derives as much from the structuring of the arrangements, from the way their components are put together, as it does from contradictions among the components themselves. Thus the factors involved in banking, money-lending, taxation, insurance, and laws of title and trespass, when woven into a nonecological matrix of public land policy, afford a very resistant barrier to an ecosystems approach. To establish an ecological land policy would require that the conventional matrix be raveled out and rewoven into a new pattern.

In addition, the context of land policy changes when the ecosystems concept is introduced. The discourse can no longer be confined realistically to lands in government ownership, but must take into account whatever lands are included in particular ecosystems, regardless of who holds title to them. This broadening of the policy context may be opposed by persons who are committed to the sanctity of private landownership, or those who are primarily concerned with specific problems of policy on government-owned lands. It is true that ecological principles can be and often are applied to the management of government lands. But if the management of whole ecosystems becomes a matter of public policy, then the scope of public land policy must be revised upon the basis of the proposition that all land is in some degree public.

To conceive an ecosystems approach to public land policy one must have first arrived at an ecological viewpoint toward the world of man and nature. But this is not the viewpoint from which pioneers, land speculators, farmers, miners, stockmen, lawyers, bankers, or local government officials have commonly seen the land. To institute an ecosystems approach to public land policy a great many other things besides land must be considered. An ecosystems approach is essentially a total systems approach. It therefore includes in its purview many things omitted in less comprehensive systems. And it would impose constraints upon single-purpose approaches to the environment and would arouse hostility among individuals whose single-purpose pursuits would thereby be constrained.

Implications of an Ecosystems
Land Policy

Before examining more closely the ecosystem concept and the opposition to its implied modification of rights of landownership, the scope of public land policy must itself be identified, since it is basic to the question: What approach to land policy is best? The word *best* arouses a multitude of subsidiary questions. It is certain to arouse objections among persons unwilling or unable to think critically about normative concepts. It may fail to interest persons who believe that the only practical focus of public policy is upon the operation of things as they are. Nevertheless, goals and values are implicit in the concept of "policy," and scholars are at liberty to examine, if they wish, the relevance of public policies to changes in the condition of society and to its future stability and welfare. Not all approaches to policy afford equally effective means to their specified ends. Moreover, not all goals or objectives serve equally well the general or long-term interests of society. For example, land policy that permitted massive and continuing loss of top soil or encouraged price-escalating speculation would not be a good *public* land policy under any criteria, however beneficial it might appear to be to the immediate interests of particular land users or owners.

In the United States, and particularly in the West, ambiguity can easily occur in the use of the expression "public land policy." Does the expression connote a public policy for land generally, all land? Or does it refer only to policies regarding lands in public ownership? Conventional American assumptions and word usage take the latter as the practical definition. Yet public exercise of eminent domain, of land-use zoning, and of the expropriation of land for tax delinquency makes it clear that public jurisdiction over land is general and not confined to land in public ownership.

An ecosystems approach to public land policy assumes a scope of policy that embraces all land regardless of its ownership or custody under law. The metes and bounds of ecosystems are determined by physical and biological forces. Men may impose their own arrangements on natural systems, but engineers, surveyors, and lawyers neither amend nor repeal the so-called laws of nature. Ecosystems form a complex unity embracing the entire earth. And although men have never been able to deal with the ultimate unity of the ecosphere, they have been learning more and more about its interrelated workings. As more has been learned, the practicality of introducing ecological concepts into land use policy is enhanced. But the word *practicality* may be given two different interpretations. There is a conventional short-run practicality of socially sanctioned arrangements, and there is also a long-run practicality that takes account of ecological trends and the consequences of their unmodified continuation into the future.

Implicit in the ecosystems concept is recognition that maintenance of the system depends upon the consistency of man-made standards, laws, and boundaries with those that have evolved through natural processes. But what of goals? Does an ecosystems concept impute some teleological design to nature? Is man required to seek out nature's purposes and adapt his laws and practices to nature's ends regardless of his own needs and purposes? The ancient Christian, substituting God's purposes for nature's, could have affirmed this proposition. Adherents to concepts of natural law might still do so. But to the man of technoscientific age, mastery, or at the very least manipulation, of nature has become a goal that sometimes approaches a secular religion. Nature, if she has purposes, does not reveal them in language that science-directed man understands. Man, however, has defined and developed his own purposes in relation to nature. These purposes basically require the obtaining of food, clothing, and shelter from nature, and to this end man has organized his relationships with his environment on the basis of the uses he makes of particular components of the natural world. These components are the familiar "natural resources."

As long as man's numbers were few, his technology simple, and his demands upon the natural world limited, it was feasible to deal with the land and its products as if they were no more than discrete resources. Man was unable simultaneously to make rapid and far-reaching changes in the ecosystem. Major ecological changes, such as deforestation or the spread of cultivation by hoe and plow over the grasslands, required time, measured in the histories of Europe and Asia by centuries. Some of these changes, as in the brittle, subarid ecosystems of the Middle East, were cumulatively destructive. Other changes, as in the clearing of forests for agriculture in Western Europe, largely substituted one ecological system for another of comparable stability and productivity. But science permitted man to upset long-standing ecological balances. His numbers multiplied without restraint, his technology became powerful and complex with unpredictable side effects, and his demands upon his environment became inordinate. Competition for resources rapidly increased and conflicts among resource users became a major phenomenon of politics.

If the categorizing of the products of nature into "natural resources" had been based upon a conscious, utilitarian subdividing of the ecosystem, the larger concept, the ecosystem, would have been available as a source for principles or considerations by which conflicts over specific resource uses might be mediated. But the ecosystem as a working hypothesis has followed, not preceded, the natural resources concept of man—environment relationships. As a consequence, public land policy has shared in the contentiousness associated with the politics of natural resources and the ecosystem concept has, as yet, had little effect upon the degree of conflict. Neither in politics nor in administration has there been a generally accepted body of knowledge or doctrine by which conflicts over resource uses can readily be resolved. In the absence of an ordering or organizing concept, efforts to coordinate natural resources policies have been largely unavailing, or have been used as covers either to impose one use over others or to prevent such imposition. A substantial part of the recent history of coordinative efforts in water policy, for example, may be accounted as efforts to restrain the autonomous and arbitrary exercise of power by the U.S. Army Corps of Engineers.

Public policy for land use, as for resources use generally, has been decided chiefly through trial by combat. Conservation as a concept has been helpful principally as an intermediary proposition, midway between unrestricted competition among resource users and an ecologically based view of public responsibility for the self-renewing capabilities of the ecosystem. Aphorisms such as "conservation means wise use" are of little help in the absence of objective criteria for wisdom. An ecosystems approach to public land policy implies the possibility of public decisions based upon empirically demonstrable principles of public interest.

Availability of an objectively rational basis for land policy decisions (if such a basis is actually possible) does not imply as a matter of course that the option to be guided by this knowledge will be accepted or acted upon. Human beings may be expected to act more often on a subjective level of rationality than upon more general and enduring principles. But until the ecosystems concept has been made articulate and its amenability to practical application has been demonstrated, it is unavailable as a basis for policy. Yet, although the ecosystems approach to land policy remains on the theoretical level, it is nevertheless available for practical application whenever it is perceived as a means toward coping with the ecological predicament into which man has blundered.

To understand the ecological predicament of modern man is to begin to understand why an ecosystems approach may ultimately become necessary to human well-being and even to survival. Unfortunately, understanding of the circumstances, now often described as the "ecological crisis," carries no automatic insight into how to correct or prevent conditions that are almost universally conceded to be harmful. If, as we shall presently contend, application of the ecosystems concept implies a wholly new way of organizing man's relations with the natural world, an ecosystems approach to public land policy implies fundamental changes in the rights and responsibilities of individuals and corporations in the possession and use of land.

It may not be too much to say that ecologically based public policies imply a thoroughgoing transformation of the nation's political economy. The nature and scope of a public land policy based on ecological principles would be comprehensive and coordinative. The individual landowner would lose certain rights and gain certain protections. Controversies over land use would be more often settled by administrative than by judicial means, and the criteria for settlement more often ecological facts than statutory laws.

Drastic changes could be expected in land economics. Application of ecological concepts to land use would find their major obstacle in the treatment of land as a commodity. Private possession of land under ecological ground rules could be made consistent with an ecosystems approach to land policy, but the freedom to buy, sell, or transfer land without regard to the ecological consequences of the action would not be consistent with an ecosystems approach. Laissez-faire land economics, although deeply rooted in American folkways, is becoming increasingly inconsistent with the interests of the vast majority of citizens, who live in great cities, who own no land, and for whom the needs and amenities of life in land are becoming increasingly costly and difficult of access.

The Substance of an
Ecosystems Approach

The ecosystems approach has been advanced as a new basis for determining public land policy. What would be novel about it?

First of all it is wholistic, in a pluralistic political economy that has generally eschewed wholistic thinking. Secondly, it is based on scientific knowledge, although science does not offer answers to all its problems. Public land policies now are not notably based on scientific considerations; to enlist science in determining the goals of domestic policy is a departure from tradition, although science has often been invoked on behalf of policies otherwise decided. For example, the Bureau of Land Management applies many scientific concepts in its administration of federal public lands; but there is much less science in the laws under which the total public land system operates. Thirdly, an ecosystems approach uses administrative means to resolve conflicts in preference to adjudication. This becomes possible to the extent that laws and policies are based on scientifically ascertainable facts. Questions of fact become more important than questions of law, and numerous issues now litigated in the courts cease to be issues when certain rights or practices associated with land ownership are modified or extinguished.

The substance of an ecosystems approach is simple, although ecosystems themselves are infinitely complex. The approach begins with an assumption derived from scientific inquiry: the natural world is a composite of interrelating life-systems subsisting in a highly improbable terrestrial environment. This environment—the ecosphere—is finite. Some of the components are naturally renewable; others are not. Of its renewable components (or resources) some are capable of restoration within a time dimension meaningful to man. But others—fossil fuels, for example—are incapable of renewal, although for some of these, substitutes may be found.

The ultimate necessity of an ecosystems approach to environmental policy, including land policy, follows from the finite amount of land, water, air, and other substances upon which the human economy depends, and the infinite character of human demands upon these substances. The heavier the stress of human demands upon the environment, the greater the degree to which those demands must be coordinated and policed in order that the economy may continue to function. In an economy of scarce essentials and pressing demands, either the strong preempt the resources and deprive the weak, or where democratic collectivism prevails, socialization, rationing, licensing, and summary police action are instituted to ensure fair shares. Political laissez faire in relation to the environment is feasible only when the demands that man makes upon that environment are relatively light and when natural ecological processes are permitted to operate, continually renewing the ecosystem so that what man uses today is replaced for his use tomorrow.

Throughout nearly all human history man appears to have enjoyed generally favorable ecological equilibrium. There were, of course, exceptional circumstances in which natural disasters or human errors disrupted a localized part of the ecosystem. Earthquakes, floods, droughts, epidemics, and famines have occurred, but the ecosphere as a whole has maintained its stability over thousands of years, even though suffering and death have resulted from its localized oscillations. Technology and science have enabled man to cope more effectively with natural disasters and in some measure to prevent them. But the very success of the human enterprise has created its greatest danger. Technoscience has now given man free rein to increase his numbers and his demands. The result has been a runaway increase in human populations and unremitting pressure on all resources, including land.

This rapid inflation of people and their demands has already impaired the quality of the human environment over large areas of the earth and threatens more serious damage in the years ahead. But at the present stage of human affairs, contemplation of the almost certain consequences of ecological folly is less painful than undergoing the changes that would be required to bring man-environment relationships into ecological balance. There may yet be time to preserve a margin of personal freedom, of environmental variety, and of unforeclosed opportunities that would be comparable to what man has experienced in the past, but the prospect of this possibility's surviving into the next century is every day lessened. Science fiction, which often assumes a role of prophecy, presents in the main the bleakest of prospects for human freedom and variety. The triumphs of science and technology do not seem to include the timely mastery by man of the cybernetics of his ecosystems. To accomplish this, he would first have to bring his impulses under control and to exercise a collective self-restraint that has not yet become one of man's strongly marked characteristics.

The idea of instituting lesser controls now to protect basic values and to avoid more drastic measures later has little contemporary appeal. It is the American way, indeed the human way, to react to crises rather than to forestall them. For who can be sure that the threatened crisis will actually materialize? There is no end to conventional wisdom on behalf of procrastination. What candidate for elective public office would advocate action in the face of uncertain dangers that, if real, could only be prevented by an inconvenient rearrangement of present institutions and relationships and by measures that would cost prospective voters the happy prospect of future profits?

* * *

Unwise policies are breeders of unwisdom. When human society works itself into an ecological straitjacket, the ecosystem itself may be destroyed in efforts to break out of self-induced deprivations and constraints. Ecologically overstressed societies are impelled to further intensification of pressure on their environments in an effort to survive. Political leaders of overpopulated, ecologically impoverished nations are seldom apt pupils in the school of resources conservation. For them survival often means getting from the environment whatever can be got today regardless of the consequences for tomorrow. An ecosystems approach to land policy thus also implies a policy of population control. Unless population pressure is manageable, no other aspect of the ecosystem can be freely managed indefinitely. Ultimately the pressure of sheer numbers and the attendant demands upon the ecosystem would force all environmental policies into serving the one overpowering objective of maintaining a minimal existence for the human masses.

There is an alternative to such a course of constrained futility. It should perhaps be classed under the heading of unthinkable thoughts. The alternate course would be for a tough-minded and ecologically sophisticated elite to impose ecological order on their less perceptive or less self-disciplined brethren. Compulsory population control through biomedical science if possible, or Malthusian control if all other means fail, could very well be the outcome of the present unwillingness of human societies to assess their ecological predicament realistically. Hopefully Americans will have the intelligence to avoid the grim consequence of ecological ignorance and optimistic procrastination.

Among the contradictions of our future-oriented technoscientific society is its fragmented treatment of time. The relativity of time has become commonplace, and for certain purposes—as in space flight, atomic technology, and medicine—very refined concepts of time are employed. With respect to the dynamics of the ecosystem, however, the time perceptions of modern man are perhaps less developed than those that characterized his agrarian ancestors. Modern man in the aggregate has not learned to perceive the world as a complex of dynamic interrelated systems. His behavior suggests that he believes the world to be an infinitely open system. Within this imagined open system, time and change have a different meaning than they have when the system is closed, when there is no escape from mistakes, and when the consequences of a chain reaction once started in time cannot be avoided by interplanetary flight. Space exploration has reinforced the illusion that the infinity of the cosmos offers a way out for earthbound man. The reality for human society in the ascertainable future is that the earth must be considered a closed system even though, in a physical sense, it is in continuing interaction with the galaxy.

Within this essentially closed terrestrial system, change goes on continuously. Man's future is inextricably involved with changes in the air, the water, and the land, which are the gross elements of the ecosphere. He has himself become a principal agent of change. His numbers and technologies have the effect of accelerating changes in time, of wearing down land forms, of increasing the salinity of the sea, of altering the chemistry of the atmosphere. Only the most comprehensive surveillance of the side effects of technology, and the most carefully evaluated application of science and technology to the ecosystem can prevent inadvertent damage to its self-regenerating capabilities. And to be effective, management of the ecosystem must conform to the appropriate time table of nature, not merely to the convenience of man. To illustrate: A dollar crisis or a Far Eastern war may offer politically defensible but ecologically invalid arguments for delaying efforts to save the Great Lakes from death by pollution. Politically there may be higher priorities today, but ecologically tomorrow may be too late.

In Defense of an Ecosystems Land Policy

The intention in this essay is not to describe the content of an actual ecosystems public land policy. To attempt this without reference to specific places, times, and circumstances would be to contradict the very thesis that has been developed. It is the ecosystems *approach* to policy that has been introduced. It was conceded at the outset that no such comprehensive approach to land policy exists in the United States today, and that if such a policy, based on ecological concepts, were to be adopted, some major changes would also have to occur in the laws, expectations, and governmental arrangements in American society. And these changes are not of the kind that has been of primary concern to the Public Land Law Review Commission or the responsibility of the Division of Lands and Natural Resources of the United States Department of Justice. But if they are not the practical problems of the present, they may well be the compelling problems of the future. If the implications of this essay are correct, American society—indeed mankind generally—will eventually be forced into something like ecosystems land policy.

In essence this essay asserts that man's predicament is that of passengers on a space ship whose destination is unknown, whose numbers and appetites are increasing, and who have been long accustomed to quarrelsome and improvident conduct. The passengers assume that the builders of the space ship endowed it with self-renewing parts so that they need take little thought for its maintenance. Moreover, because the ship is very large, they act as though it were infinite, although they are quite capable of calculating its carrying capacity and they know that there may come a day when its resources are taxed beyond capacity. But they are also possessed by the optimistic thought that before the day of disaster arrives they will land on some habitable planet. And so there is doubt among them as to the practical necessity for restraint now.

This is the paradigm of Spaceship Earth, whose passengers are only now beginning to realize where they are. Only the ecologically informed among them are aware of the growing precariousness of their condition. Unfortunately the practical men who are the leaders and managers of the enterprise, although well informed in many important ways, are generally uninformed or misinformed in this important respect. Their attention is on the lesser mechanics of the enterprise and on the mediation of quarrels among the passengers that might destroy the ship prematurely. Is it then to be conceded that the outcome of the voyage is hopeless, that the passengers are unteachable, and that the officers and crew are unwilling to learn? No incontrovertible evidence compels this conclusion. It is equally plausible to assume, because human civilization is in itself a highly improbable phenomenon, that the limits of its improbability have not yet been reached. Unlikely as it may be, it is possible that American society, if not mankind generally, may reassess its circumstances with sufficient realism and insight to avoid ecological foreclosure. It is conceivable that people may voluntarily adopt changed ways of organizing their economy and of behaving in relation to the natural environment so as to bring the economy and the ecosystem into a dynamic self-sustaining equilibrium.

The Political Parameters of Environmental Control*
John A. Straayer and R. L. Meek**

Concern with environmental preservation and control is not new either in the United States or internationally. Individual conservationists, preservationist oriented interest groups, political leaders, and governmental agencies have promoted these goals for many years. The use and abuse of natural resources, the development of parks, wildlife preserves and recreation areas, and land use planning have been matters of public interest and governmental policy for decades. The national government has established and maintained parks, monuments, preserves, and seashores; it has sought to control and in some cases to encourage mineral and timber exploitation; it has exercised extensive control over the development and use of waterways, reclaimed land from deserts and swamps; and it has supported the development of nuclear energy. The states have devoted considerable attention and resources to parks, to the control of hunting and fishing, and to the supervision of land and water use within their jurisdictions. Local governments have long attempted to effectively utilize land use planning, to establish and maintain parks, to promote neighborhood beautification programs, and to develop sanitary means of disposing of human and solid wastes. And such international bodies as the United Nations have had an abiding concern for environment and resources.

What is relatively new, however, is the increased publicity given to environmental problems and the explosion of articulated concern for the condition of the entire ecological system, and indeed, for man's capacity to survive. Alarmists are forecasting the "end of oceans," uncontrollable population growth, massive epidemics, famine, pestilence, and even more calamitous and horrible states of affairs in the not too distant future.[1] The interest in the ecological balance and in human survival is no longer the unique concern of a few academicians, planners, or novelists; it has attracted the attention and concern of a substantial and growing portion of the general public. The "new visibility" of the ecology issue has brought increasing pressure upon governments at all levels to act positively to develop plans and to create programs of environmental control so as to avoid ecological destruction.†

The paper analyzes the potential capacity of the political system to meet the growing expectations for the development of effective programs of environmental control. More specifically, it identifies some of the major

---

*This paper was prepared for delivery at the meeting of the Southwestern and Rocky Mountain Division of the American Association for the Advancement of Science and the Arizona Academy of Science, Tempe, Arizona, April 21-24, 1971. It draws upon a larger work by the same authors entitled *The Politics of Neglect* (Boston: Houghton-Mifflin Company, 1971). This selection is reprinted here with the permission of the authors.
**Professors Straayer and Meek are members of the Department of Political Science at Colorado State University.
†We speak of the "visibility" of the environment issue because, as we will imply later, we are not sanguine about the depth and staying power of the widespread expressed concern when the chips are down and when talk must be replaced by planning, control and finance.

problems and complexities which inhere in the making of the collective decisions needed for the achievement of the desired pattern of environmental control. Although the emphasis is upon the limits of collective decision making, this paper is not purposely pessimistic. Rather, it represents an attempt at a realistic appraisal of what government can, or cannot do. Such an appraisal requires, at a minimum, the identification of the nature of the expectations of governmental action, the determination of the primary requisites of successful collective decision making in the environmental area, and the specification of the major constraints upon such collective decision making. While its focus is the United States, the points made have tremendous implications internationally.

Environmental Control as a Public Problem

The combination of a large number of physical conditions, technological innovations, and individual values and their attendent life styles have resulted in the environmental destruction which has created the contemporary threat to the ecological balance. These factors interact to form a system of behavior as complex as the ecological system itself. Any attempts to rectify the current state of affairs and guide the future into more acceptable channels must take into account the relationships within and between these two highly complex systems.

There is growing consensus in the society that much of the blame for the current state of affairs must be placed upon a pattern of uncoordinated private decisions which, in the aggregate, have resulted in substantial environmental destruction.* Similarly, there is growing recognition that the problems associated with environmental control are too large, complex, interrelated, and immediate to be attacked successfully by individual efforts alone, that they are problems for the entire society, and that they must be challenged by organized power. There is broad agreement that environmental planning is necessary and a recognition of the inability of the private sector to plan and maintain a quality environment. These developments have brought the environmental problem to the agenda of government, and have made environmental control an issue for collective decision making through the institutionalized processes of the political system.

Neither cataclysmic prediction nor abstract concern for the environment are enough to guide intendedly remedial public policy. There must be careful definition of the dimensions of specific problems, their causes and their consequences. Manageable segments of problems must be identified and decisions must be made as to which segments can be solved by feasible policy choices. Careful problem definition, while always difficult, presents a much greater challenge when collective societal choices are involved than is the case

---

*This has happened in one area after another—including the economy, health systems, transit, and others. The "Smithian" invisible hand which failed to emerge to save us from our economic troubles fails to appear in area after area as society becomes more technical and "mass" in nature.

with simple individual decisions. Public problems are not equally self-evident to all persons. Conditions which one individual or group believes to be deserving of public attention may be of absolutely no concern to others. Much of the apparent broad consensus on the importance of environmental concerns may dissolve when attempts are made to identify the individual components to be given priority for public action, and when questions are raised as to the allocation of benefits and costs. The relative importance of clean air, clean water, natural beauty, and population control will become bases of serious conflict; and externalities, such as policy effects on consumption and employment, will become part of the problems themselves. These and many other factors tend to make for hazy and loose problem definition. Any attempts to solve the problems are sure to suffer from the lack of accurate and clear problem definition.

Requisites for Successful Environmental Control

The process of collective decision making in the area of environmental control, like in other public problem areas, can be characterized as a four step process. These are: (1) undesirable states of affairs (problems) are identified and defined; (2) alternatives are hypothesized and their consequences assessed; (3) public choices are made (policy is formed), and (4) public policy is implemented. Environmental control is not, of course, as simple or orderly a process as this suggests. But like public problem solving efforts generally, environmental control does involve these activities in some form.

The chances of success in environmental planning and control, like the chances of success in public problem solving generally, are significantly increased by the presence of several factors. These include: (1) a clear specification of the problem and its boundaries; (2) institutional development; (3) the development and maintenance of political support; (4) adequate resources; and (5) goal maintenance.

First, until the object area for environmental control is specified, and the problem well defined, effective action is difficult. Progress in land use planning, improvements in air or water quality, the regulation of pesticide use cannot be expected to produce desired results unless the target area is clear and the nature of the problem is well defined. This is more difficult to achieve than it first appears. For example, the mere identification of a county or set of counties as the target area for a "clean air program" has little chance of success unless: (1) provision is made for the control of intrusions into the area by federally funded expressways, automobiles from Detroit and drifting pollutants from adjacent counties; and (2) the types and levels of pollutants to be controlled are clearly identified. Likewise, the general goal of a "quality environment" will forever remain an unattainable ideal unless operational meaning is given to the term "quality," unless the "environment" of concern is specifically delineated, and unless action programs are designed which account for the intrusion of factors physically external to the target area, e.g., the control of an upstream polluting paper mill.

Second, the fate of environmental planning and control efforts hinges in part upon the development of institutions capable of identifying problems and developing alternatives and intendedly remedial programs. These may include official bodies such as municipalities, counties, special districts, consortia of governments and commissions, or political parties, interest groups and concerned "publics." Some form of official governmental apparatus must exist, of course, to legitimize and implement control programs. But secondly, institutions must exist which are capable of bringing problems to the public agenda and providing support for remedial efforts. As suggested earlier, problems do not bring themselves to public attention and policy does not create and implement itself—people and institutions do.*

A third requisite for effective environmental control, and one which is closely related to the one above, is the development and maintenance of political support. As Norton Long has articulately pointed out, a policy wrung from a reluctant coalition of relatively ineffective agencies and clientele groups which themselves have but half-hearted interest in the problem is certain to be less than wildly successful. On the other hand, a policy which results from a vigorous drive by a strong coalition of stable and resourceful agencies and groups and which has broad support with the general public will, in all probability, prove rather effective. Thus, both the formulation and the implementation of policy for environmental control is dependent for success upon a base of political power; political power in the form of public support, the support of organized lobbies, and the support of stable, secure and firmly rooted administrative agencies.[2]

A fourth requisite for effective environmental planning and control has to do with the obvious need for sufficient financial and human resources. Environmental programs must constantly compete with programs in other areas for public attention and resources. Existing programs in education, defense, health and welfare, for example, command large portions of the annual supply of public resources, and environmental efforts must compete not only with these, but with such spectacular and attention-getting events as space exploration and Indo-Chinese crises. Thus, environmental programs, like most others, are apt to be chronically underfunded—in the eyes of their supporters at least.

Fifth, the success of environmental control efforts will be enhanced by the consistency and stability of goals through time and space. Conversely, environmental control will be more difficult if (1) the nature of the "desired future" changes with any degree of frequency, or (2) if different policies seek to create a variety of futures. Where this is the case, programs will be abandoned long before they achieve their intended effect, or a multiplicity of programs may work at cross purposes.

Finally, there is the obvious point that man's ability to plan and shape his future is closely tied to what he knows. The possession of knowledge permits more accurate problem identification, more alternatives, more insight into possible consequences of various courses of action, and an increased ability to avoid purposeful actions which produce unanticipated and unwanted results.

---

*This point is made by a number of writers, including Robert Dahl, *A Preface To Democratic Theory* (Chicago: University of Chicago Press, 1956).

Constraints on Effective
Environmental Control

There are a number of factors which act to limit our capacity to plan and control the environment, many of which are closely related to the factors discussed above. This list includes, but is not limited to: (1) jurisdictional fragmentation; (2) the diffusion of negative externalities; (3) the frequent distribution of both the benefits and costs of environmental abuse to the same parties (with a consequent reduction in public support for intendedly remedial programs); (4) differential value patterning throughout most communities; (5) the need for environmental control programs to compete for attention and resources with many other issues; (6) shifts in individual and collective preferences through time; (7) the restriction of decisional options through such factors as sunk costs, established procedure and behavior patterns, as well as lack of information; and (8) the development of unanticipated and unwanted consequences of purposeful action resulting from inadequate knowledge.

First, the extensive atomization of the American political system, in urban areas especially, creates numerous problems for environmental control.* Environmental problems do not obligingly respect legal boundaries. Dirty air and water move freely from one city, county or state to another. And in many of our metropolitan areas, where we have literally hundreds of governments, there may well be hundreds of land use programs existing in totally uncoordinated fashion. Thus there are typically no political units capable of unilateral and effective planning and control. Intergovernmental coordination and cooperation is always possible, of course, and in a few cases it has proven effective. But the fact of jurisdictional chaos remains to complicate environmental control efforts.

A second and closely related constraint on environmental control is the extensive diffusion of the negative effects of many environmentally related problems. Decisions made—or not made—in one decision center often result in negative consequences for people totally unable to affect that decision. Air pollution generated in one city or state may move freely to plague people in neighboring cities or states. Waste poured into a stream by a paper mill may befoul a nice lake area a hundred or more miles away. Decisions made in Washington, D.C. to encourage suburban tract housing development or expand the expressway system may result in haphazard land use in some metropolitan area, or contribute to the slow death of rural towns. Where the negative externalities of some purposeful activity fall to people beyond those who make the decision or where profit can be made through actions detrimental to *others,* the incentive to cooperate in comprehensive environmental improvement is diminished.

Third, it is frequently the case that benefits and the costs of environmental abuse are distributed to essentially the same parties with the result that the likelihood of stable widespread public support for planning and control are diminished. The millions of individuals who drive the automobiles which pollute

---

*The most recent census of governments lists over 80,000 units of government in the United States. Most of these are concentrated in metropolitan areas, and, in most, decision making power is further dispersed through separation of powers, boards and commissions and the development of semi-autonomous subsystems characteristic of large organizations.

the air in our metropolitan areas, and who likewise have to breathe that air, are the same millions who enjoy the freedom and mobility which the automobile provides. Further, many of them depend upon the automobile or related industries for employment. Likewise, as haphazard as much of our suburban land use has been, it has provided comfortable single-unit housing for millions, and jobs or tremendous profit for certain others. And the high standard of living which most of us enjoy comes at a cost in terms of resource depletion, solid waste production and air and water pollution. None of this obviates public concern for pollution or for man's future; but it does dampen support for many possible environmental programs. When we are asked to pay more taxes, re-locate, or take a bus to work, our enthusiasm for the environment often declines. Without strong and constant support, from both the general public and organized interests, effective environmental planning and control is all but impossible.

Fourth, it is one of the more elementary facts of political life that in nearly any given community, different people and groups will want and value different things. At a very general or abstract level, value variations are not so great. For example, few people actually like pollution, poor land use or the rape of the landscape. But as we move from the general to the more specific, differences begin to appear and multiply. How rigidly should land use be controlled? How rapidly should polluting industries be forced to comply with anti-pollution legislation when the rate of pollution reduction will affect the viability of the subject corporation? Should auto manufacturers be forced to build cleaner engines, or should the public be forced, through extremely high gasoline, license and toll charges, to go to mass transit? Again, when one moves from the general to the specific, variations in public preferences become an increasing problem for the development of any sort of consensus for effective and long term planning.

A fifth constraint results from the fact that issues, problems and programs must compete for public attention and resources in a manner that approximates a zero-sum game. Public attention can be rather rapidly diverted from one issue to another. An example of such a shift was the sudden intrusion of the Cambodian issue, in the spring of 1970, into the limelight then enjoyed by the "environmental crisis." True, concern for the environment did not die in 1970, but the enthusiasm did diminish for a time.

Fluctuations in public concern for problems generally transfer into shifts in the flow of related legislation and financial commitment. If concern for a problem comes and goes in a faddish manner, the problem is not apt to be attacked with sustained vigor. And the level of public concern for a particular problem through time is not solely dependent upon the intrinsic merits of the problem; it varies as well with the competition it faces from other problems. Thus, the success of environmental control programs hinges in part upon their visibility and saliency vis-a-vis other real or imagined problems and crises.

A sixth problem, and one which is related to the above, involves shifts in public preferences through time. As noted above, real or perceived crises can occasionally intrude to divert both public attention and political support from one problem to another. In addition, democratic ideology and its related systems of periodic elections and turnover in public office invite reversal, or at least re-direction, of public policy. The result is simply that it is difficult to maintain the primacy of a defined set of goals and set of programs through extended periods of time, whether the goal is environmental control or any other set of major goals.

Seventh, impediments to effective environmental planning and control often result from "sunk costs." Sunk costs may exist in the form of physical plant, ongoing programs, trained manpower, or habit and patterned behavior.* Efforts to reduce air pollution through the development of mass transit systems may run counter to the habits and preferences of the average auto owner and to the goals of the taxi, trucking, petroleum and automobile industries. Likewise, attempts to relocate a noisy airport which has, through time, become surrounded by commercial and residential development, may well meet with fatal resistance as a result of financial, physical, and behavioral sunk costs. Relocation would create losses in terms of the disruption of normal patterns of activity. And it would meet with resistance from those who would be affected by the new location.[3]

Sunk costs take a toll within organizations as well, because habit and patterned behavior may restrict the options available to top level decision makers. They may, upon occasion, be unable to elicit from their organization the performance they want. Bureaucracy fosters routine and habit and, to a certain extent, it does so by design. Individuals become accustomed to doing things in a given manner and, indeed, risk trouble by deviant behavior. Also, it is psychically more comfortable to keep the boat from rocking, for change can bring about new organizational behavior patterns into which the employee may not comfortably fit. Thus, the collective result of financial, physical and behavioral sunk costs is to restrict the operational latitude of future oriented decision making in the environmental area as in all others.

A final constraint on environmental planning and control has to do with information gaps and unanticipated consequences. If we knew everything about everything, we might have outstanding success planning a utopian future. But we don't. We have built expressways and public housing only to find expressways contributing to the development of ghettos in inner-cities, and the slow death of small towns; and public housing transforms itself into tall cement jungles. We have used DDT and other chemicals to control insects and pests and to increase agricultural production only to discover serious negative spin-off results, decades later.

If we could delay problem oriented decision-making indefinitely we could reduce the frequency of unanticipated consequences in the area of environmental control as in most others. But we can't. Decisions must be made constantly, and must be made on the basis of available information. Thus, we invariably base decisions upon some combination of hard data and hunch. Of course the more research we do, the better our decisions should be. But in the foreseeable future, the effectiveness of environmental planning and control will be restricted by our cognitive limits and the supply of available knowledge.†

---

*For discussions of sunk costs and resistance to change, see almost any public administration text. For a particularly succinct statement of these and related problems see Anthony Downs, *Inside Bureaucracy* (Boston: Little, Brown and Co., 1967).

†For an old but rather good discussion of the relation between knowledge and unanticipated consequences see Robert Merton, "The Unanticipated Consequences of Purposeful Action," *American Sociological Review,* December 1936. See also Herbert Simon, *Administrative Behavior* (New York: The Free Press edition, 1965).

The Prospects for Environmental Control

There are at least two broad sets of conditions which facilitate effective environmental control—crisis and consensus. Regarding the former, the record of public policy formation and implementation in the United States suggests that major policy efforts, particularly those of a redirecting or innovative nature, come about mainly in times of real or perceived crisis.* Between 1850 and the 1930's technology and industry profoundly altered the shape of the American economic system. Yet governmental response to these changes remained incremental and minimal until, in the 1930's, crises of major and national proportions struck. Then, rather sweeping and redirecting public policy responses were made and popular attitudes *vis-a-vis* the government-economy relationship underwent fundamental change. Since the 1930's we have, by comparison, faced only minor economic crises (the 1957-58 recession and the 1968-71 inflationary spiral) and, predictably, no major policy changes have occurred.

A similar pattern of response-to-crisis tells the story of much of the American space effort. We plodded along into the mid-1950's slowly refining and expanding upon the left-over technology of the Second World War. But in 1957 Russia's Sputnik I changed our approach to space exploration suddenly and fundamentally. Sputnik I appeared as a serious Communist threat to American safety and virility, and talk of all sorts of "gaps" began. In response, we adopted elaborate public programs to "close the gaps." Money was poured into the education of thousands of young "scientists-to-be," through National Defense Education Act programs. The National Aeronautics and Space Council and National Aeronautics and Space Administration were formed (1958), and a crash program for placing men and machinery in space was developed.

A third example of action and reaction only after crisis involves the passage of both the poverty program and the 1964 Civil Rights Act following the death of President John Kennedy. Both poverty and racial discrimination have existed in the United States since its founding, and while they have not historically been matters of total unconcern, the climate and circumstances preceding and succeeding the Kennedy death provided tremendous impetus for new policy.

Collective environmental planning and control efforts appear to be following the same pattern which is evidenced in the cases cited above. The quasi-polemics of people like Ehrlich and Commoner and the increasing unattractiveness of big city life have created a sense of urgency about the environment with the general public and leadership alike. But progress has been slow; in fact, to the extent that anything at all has been done, one might argue that it has been the result of actual crisis. For example, the creation of the Environmental Protection Agency and the rigidified stance of the Secretary of the Interior on environmental protection matters were preceded by the Santa Barbara oil spill.

The environment "problem" has many dimensions, including air and water pollution, land use, resource use and depletion and solid waste, and on many of these fronts almost nothing has been done. Land use decisions in most communities continue to be governed by short run, localized economic factors,

---

*The late Professor John Gaus made this point as well as any point can be made.

and while some communities are a little more leery of polluting industries than they were in the past, there has been no dramatic shift away from concern for economic vitality and growth.

If crisis relates closely to public policy development, so does consensus; in fact they relate to one another. It is an elementary political fact that it is much more difficult to arrive at collective decisions—and, of course, to implement them, in the absence of fairly widespread agreement as to what should be done, and how it should be accomplished. Totalitarian states attempt to create consensus through the control of education and communication systems and by the harassment of such potential sources of deviant belief systems as churches, professional organizations and the arts. We make no such overt attempts at consensus building in the United States and, in fact, elements of both the democratic and individualist myth systems encourage the reverse. Thus there is no automatic guarantee of consensus on the why and how of environmental control, and governmental attempts to create one are apt to be met with cries of foul play while similar private efforts may be viewed as narrow-interest propaganda programs.

The kind of consensus which can provide a base for massive environmental control is apt to develop slowly, if at all, and in an atmosphere of varying degrees of crisis. It will involve the perception by more and more people that the advancement of their self-interest depends on some form of effective collective action. This may come about slowly as increasing numbers of people identify their self-interest with clean air and water and recreational opportunities rather than with occupational promotion, pay raises, prestige or community growth. Or it may occur suddenly, with the highly visible threat of ecological disaster.

Until consensus spreads through crisis or some other mechanism, the dominant pattern of environmental decision-making will remain incremental "muddling." That is, what control we exercise over the environment, or what peace we make with it, will continue to come in the form of a haphazard aggregation of often conflicting decisions based upon short-run and non-comprehensive considerations. Comprehensive environmental control, at a global, national or even state or regional level will remain the dream of certain anti-pluralistic planners. To be sure there has been and will continue to be some cooperative planning. Municipalities, counties, special districts and states will continue to carry on dialogue on land use, transit systems and cooperative police and fire protection programs. But the shape of the environment, the metropolitan environment especially, is almost sure to remain the product of market decision-making.

This does not mean, however, that man has not, cannot or will not influence his environment and his future. He has, he can, and he does—but typically on a limited scale and incrementally, and not on a grandiose spatial basis.

It is often tempting to embrace one or two polar positions on the question of environmental control. The first is to assume that all we need to do is make the same commitment to social and environmental concern as we have to the space programs and bridge construction and, presto, we shall solve our problems. Many magicians on the luncheon speaking circuit put out this sort of "information" and evidence an incredible lack of knowledge of the complexities of accomodating a wide variety of preference in decision-making in a democracy. The second tempting position is more realistic, but discouragingly pessimistic; it concludes that there is an "iron law of environmental disorder" in operation, and to plan is to waste time and energy.[4] Our society and our own psychic well-being require something in between, namely—the combination of healthy skepticism and naive hope upon which scientific inquiry rests.

The Politics of Ecology*
Barry Weisberg**

The critical importance of ecology as a developing source of political opposition in America stems from the realization that politics in our age has acquired an absolute character. While political decision making and control is steadily concentrated in the hands of a very few—the arena of control is steadily expanding. Fewer and fewer people control more and more—so that the very conditions which support life on this planet: the land we walk upon, the air we breathe, and the water we drink, are now the subjects of political management on a scale beyond normal comprehension. The politics of ecology must start from the premise that present-day reality is increasingly the product of a structure of economic and political power that consolidates and sustains itself through the systematic destruction of man and his physical world. The exploitation of man by man and nature by man are merely two sides of the same coin.

It is then folly to think that the destruction of our global life support systems under advanced industrial capitalism or communism is merely a by-product of progress, a case of bad management, the result of insufficient esthetic sensibilities on the part of business and engineers, or simply a matter of who owns the means of production. In an historical sense, we have reached the point where we can totally violate the processes and structures of the natural world; hence our relationship to nature is no longer determined by the forces of nature but by the rule of political management. The deterioration of the natural environment all around us is therefore clearly a product of the nature of production and consumption, of cultural values and social relationships that today hold sway over industrial technological society—American or Soviet.

In short, our present technical manipulation of the life-support capacity of the planet now threatens the totality of physical conditions which nurture life itself. The oxygen content in the atmosphere, the metabolism of our own bodies, food chains and the relationship between populations and the resources needed to support them, conditions upon which the existence of all plant and animal life today depends, are the products of evolutionary processes extending over billions of years. Our industrial civilization is now destroying them in a matter of decades. We are talking about processes which may well have worked their irrevocable consequences within a decade or two—after which there will be nothing within the human potential to restore their life-giving capacity.

---

*Liberation, January 1970, pp. 20-25. Reprinted by permission.
**Barry Weisberg is a free-lance writer and co-director of the Bay Area Institute, San Francisco, California.

The culture itself is aware of the explosive potential of the imbalances between society and nature. Government and industry through the media have begun to manage these issues on a daily basis. Scientists speak out, reports are called for and committees created. In fact, the pattern of action and language emerging around pollution parallels exactly the failures of civil rights and poverty—"a war on pollution," the calling for a "pollution pentagon." Even new bureaucratic offices to replace the Department of Interior are suggested. What such proposals miss is that it is not the control of the land, air and water that is at stake but the control of man.

The obvious question resulting from this brief survey is whether or not these are matters of bad management, disfunction or the like, as mentioned earlier. The origins of our present destruction of the life-support capacity of this planet are rooted in the very fabric of our civilization, reaching their most insane dimensions in the present corporate America. The Greek rationalism of Aristotle, the Roman engineering mentality, the biblical anthropomorphic injunctions to "have dominion over the land and subdue every creeping thing," the post-Enlightenment notions of growth and progress, the present technical corporate economic systems motivated by competition—all dominate the Western mentality of man against nature. Where nature works toward harmony, cooperation and interdependence, advanced industrial society works toward growth, competition and independence. The advanced nation state works in direct opposition to those basic life giving instincts which have nourished our billion year evolution. To repeat, the domination of man by man and man over nature are two sides of the same coin. The precondition for our survival requires the most basic transformation of the cultural, social, political and economic mentalities and structures which dominate the developed nations and hang as a carrot over the never-to-be-developed nations.

In view of the sudden flurry of government-initiated programs (including the spate of officially endorsed campus "teach-ins" planned for next April), it is especially chilling to contemplate the performance of government, industry and their conservationist junior partners. Here's a rundown:

Government

The proportion of the National Budget spent on all natural resource programs has declined steadily since 1959.

1965	2.3%
1966	2.2%
1967	2.0%
1968	1.9%
1969	1.9% est.
1970	1.8% est.

In other words, for fiscal 1969, we spent only 3.6 billion on all natural resource programs, of some 202 billion dollars, spending more (4 billion) to reach outer space than to make the earth habitable. The gap between authorization and appropriation on programs such as air and water pollution has widened every year. This is merely to demonstrate the inability of the Congress to achieve its own stated objectives—not that those objectives would have successfully dealt with any major issue. In fact, there is every reason to believe that more spending would have produced merely more pollution. Add to this a government which at the same time subsidizes the supersonic transport, maintains the depletion allowance for continued off-shore drilling, undermines efforts at consumer protection—and one begins to understand the meaning of federal efforts. While there are more committees, more reports, more research and more attention, less and less is actually done. The frightening conclusion, however, is not that government should do more, for the more it does the worse our ecological systems get.

Industry

What are we to make of the flurry of industrial ads depicting everything from Standard Oil to Dow Chemical to the American Rifle Association as conservation-minded people? Of the recent Business of Pollution Control Technology? Of the investment of industry in conservation organization? The answer I think is to be found, for instance, in the words of Robert O'Anderson, chairman of the board of Atlantic Richfield. In a recent address before a State Department-sponsored conference on Man and His Environment, Anderson argued that the costs of pollution control should be passed on to the consumer and that oil should remain the base of energy supply. In short, industry has made of the environmental crisis a commodity. Recent financial reports indicate that the business of pollution control will in fact make a profit out of pollution while at the same time generating more pollution: more growth will be the remedy applied to the perils of growth. In short, that advertising will continue to cost more for business than research, that the consumers will be passed on any costs of "pollution control," and that federal agencies, new or old, will continue to operate as captives of the industry they are to regulate.

Conservation

More than any single element of the present collage of conservation activity, the conservation organizations themselves, to varying degrees, lead the public to believe that the Emperor has no clothes when in fact they serve as clothes for the Emperor. Such organizations act in the most fragmentary ways, attacking isolated problems and not complex patterns of social and political behavior. They save a nature area and fail to address the entire land use patterns of that region. They save a seashore from development when that seashore is threatened with the biological destruction of its wildlife. As such, their victories are at best stop gaps, always provisional. They foster the existence of centralized forms of authority through the support they lend to present elective procedures—"get the good guys in office." They have virtually no critical understanding of the governments of oil, agri-business, public utilities or chemicals. The conservation ists frequently violence-bait the Left or shun it as revolutionary. "The country is tired of SDS and ready to see someone like us come to the forefront," a young conservationist recently noted. Increasingly motivated and supported by various governmental machinations, these people work in total isolation to the civil rights and peace movements, with no relationship to the varied forces of opposition and liberation in the society today—the revolutionary young, women's liberation, labor, and oppressed minorities. They seek private solutions to what more correctly are public issues—picking up litter rather than attacking the production of junk, refusing to use autos rather than struggling against oil and the auto manufacturers, to be merely suggestive.

But most important, the "new breed of young conservationists" fail to see that the crisis of the environment truly is but a reflective of the crisis of this culture itself, of the values, institutions, and procedures which have for some 200 years systematically guided the slaughter of human and all other forms of life at home and abroad. These tendencies were demonstrated too well by a recent selection of "youth" hand-picked by the Department of State to participate in the US Commission for UNESCO Conference on Man and His Environment in San Francisco last month. Virtually all "programs" suggested by these participants lent credence to the status quo by advocating "better" candidates, new ecology colleges, yet additional "research," and more jobs for conservation-minded college kids.

The barrage of petitions and letters to the President was greeted by the conference "adults" with adulation, for the kids turned out to be "reasonable men" just as their parents. The popular press billed their performance as revolutionary—defined as "non-violent," get-your-man-in-office, and increased student participation. But the role of our benign media goes much further.

By and large, the media has purposely obscured the political and social content of the environmental crisis by confining problems as well as solutions solely to the realm of science and technology. The result is that blind faith in the omnipotence of expertise and technocracy wholly dominates current thinking on ecological issues. Technological innovation and more reasonable methods of resource allocation cannot possibly reverse the present logic of the environment unless the overriding political, social and economic framework which has actually generated that trend is radically rebuilt. Such a transformation cannot reside solely in the realm of culture and values—as most often proposed by the youthful elites of conservation. The critical task today is to raise the issue of pollution/destruction, imperialistic styles of consumption, and of over-population to a political status in order to reveal an arena of political opposition in America which the Left has hitherto ignored. That is not to say that the Left can simply absorb the ecological crisis into its own kind of "business as usual" behavior. For the patterns of life in which most of us partake are not much different than those of the ruling class. This is not to say that true solutions reside in private action, but that public transformation without an entirely different style of life is futile. Thus the development of an ecological politics on a practical level may provide the only framework in which the alienated and oppressed can achieve true liberation.

That potential for liberation doesn't lie in the Save the Bay Campaigns, the protection of a redwood grove or planned parenthood. It does not reside alone in the culturally symbolic acts of many ecology action groups around the country. The true origin of what has yet to become an authentic movement is in the People's Park episode, in militant actions against corporate despoilers (including sabotage) and in the private as well as public attempts to create ecologically sound lives.

While the traditional conservationists have made no imaginative attempt to understand what our cities would look like without autos, with decentralized agriculture or power, with neighborhood control and rationed resources, save for few scant efforts, the Left, with few exceptions, has been equally derelict. "Radical" economists still contemplate growth-motivated economies grounded in false notions of affluence and unlimited resources.

The New Left has at this point made little serious effort to understand or relate to the politics of ecology. While the battles in the streets appear more pressing and more direct, it ought to be understood that unless something very basic and very revolutionary is done about the continued destruction of our life support systems, there may well be no wind to weather in the near future.

Dismissing over-population as simply a matter of genocide, efforts to take back the land as bourgeois or the necessity for clean air and water as a luxury completely fails to grasp what can only properly be understood as a matter of life or death.

The task of ecological radicals is to continually raise those issues which sort those which would seek to patch up the status quo from those who struggle for basic transformation. The polarization of the rulers and the ruled is the authentic growth of any true movement for liberation. When conservationists argue that everyone is in the same boat (or on the same raft), that everyone must work together, tempering their actions to suit the imperatives of coalition, they are in fact arguing for the further consolidation of power and profit in the hands of those responsible for the present dilemma.

There is no easy way to summarize exactly how the Movement must respond to the growing politics of ecology. Publishing special magazine editions and flimsy attacks on "sewermen" will not do. Few models exist to lend direction to organizing efforts. Already throughout the country people have been organized around industrial accidents and health hazards, consumer boycotts, women's liberation and the nuclear family, the extinction of animal species or the struggle against a new highway. This is just the beginning. This winter and spring we can expect a series of radical ecological actions: the bombing of more corporate headquarters, sabotage to the industrial machinery that pollutes and obstruction at airports and other transportation corridors.

It is safe to suggest that organizing around environment issues that fails immediately to lead to the political causes and implications of that peril is misguided. For too long eco news and reports have begun and ended with nature—without understanding that nature itself is today the product of manipulation by man. We should have learned from the Peoples' Park that the road ahead will be perilous and paved with a life and death struggle. If the State of California would defend a parking lot with the life of one person and the shooting of another 150, imagine the cost of taking back a forest, preventing an off-shore drilling rig from being placed, blocking the construction of a nuclear power plant or tampering with the power/communication/food/transport systems which make America grow. But the sooner this happens the better. The sooner the spirit of the Peoples' Park infuses every ecological action, the brighter will be our chances to insure the conditions for our survival and, beyond that, a decent society.

Educating "the people about the impending ecological disaster" without pointing to possible forms of action available is at this point a disservice to the Movement. As people engage in direct struggle against the Con Edisons, the Standard Oils, the pollution control agencies, and the United Fruit companies of the world, more and more new insights for strategy will develop. What has been happening to poor whites and blacks for several hundred years, what America has done to the Vietnamese, America is now doing to its own population, en masse. The organizing implications of this single fact may be profound. In a world of total biological slavery, liberation is the very condition of Life itself. To fail does not mean growing up absurd, but not growing up at all.

The Politics of Survival

[1]See Phillip O. Foss, *Recreation* (New York: Van Nostrand Reinhold Co., 1971).

[2]*Environmental Quality,* The First Annual Report of the Council on Environmental Quality (Washington, D.C.: U.S. Government Printing Office, 1970).

The Political Parameters of Environmental Control

[1]See, for example, Paul R. Ehrlich, *The Population Bomb* (New York: Ballantine Books, 1969); and Barry Commoner, *Science and Survival* (New York: The Viking Press, Inc., 1968).

[2]Norton Long, "Power and Administration," *Public Administration Review,* IX, No. 4 (1949), 257-64.

[3]See, for example, The National Academy of Sciences, *Jamaica Bay and Kennedy Airport,* Washington, D.C., 1971.

[4]See John A. Straayer and R. L. Meek, "The Iron Law of Disorder," in *The Politics of Neglect,* eds. Meek and Straayer (Boston: Houghton-Mifflin Company, 1971).

9   Epilogue

> Man has lost the capacity to foresee and to forestall. He will end by
> destroying the earth.
>
> Albert Schweitzer

It is altogether possible that we will be unable to solve the environmental problems described in this book. It is altogether possible that the world will experience an ecological breakdown of catastrophic proportions.

During his short time on this planet man has exploited the natural environment without considering the ecological consequences of his acts. This behavior cannot be ascribed to ignorance because even in primitive times man could see and understand the more obvious consequences of his behavior. During the short period of recorded history a succession of civilizations have disintegrated because they disregarded ecological principles—but these clear lessons of history apparently have had little effect on the policies of succeeding civilizations. In the light of historical evidence there would appear to be no reason to expect a drastic change in the ecological behavior of mankind at this time. There is no historical reason to expect men to behave differently today than they have in the past.

We have been told that self-preservation is the first law of nature. We have also been told that men commonly destroy resources and disrupt ecological systems for selfish, short term gains. In the long run these two concepts are basically inconsistent, but in the short run (one lifetime) they are entirely consistent. The instinct for self-preservation will cause men to attempt to maximize their satisfactions; to "cut out and get out"; to "get what we can while the getting is good." Moreover, the concept of selfish, short term gains encompasses a wide variety of actions and responses. Trying to stay alive by using DDT to control malaria might be one example of a selfish, short term gain. The so-called "vandal ideology" is simply an exaggeration of the self-preservation instinct. There appears to be no reason to expect a radical change in this elemental human drive. Ironically, the instinct for individual self-preservation could result in the annihilation of the human species.

Much lip service is given to the idea of planning for posterity or of leaving a better world for generations yet unborn. In actuality, most people can only think in terms of the futures of their own children—and many of them not that far ahead. As Abraham Lincoln once said,

> Few can be induced to labor exclusively for posterity; and none will do it enthusiastically. Posterity has done nothing for us; and theorize on it as we may, practically we shall do very little for it, unless we are made to think we are at the same time doing something for ourselves.

"Boosterism," the idea that more is better, is not restricted to the United States. The apparent success of the United States and the U.S.S.R. has caused other cultures to jettison age-old customs and mores in favor of industrial growth. Unless adequate countervailing forces are employed, the more rapid the growth the greater the ecological disturbance. On balance, boosterism is probably on the rise throughout the world.

The belief that nature exists to be exploited by man is not peculiar to the Western world. Notwithstanding the emphasis given to the ecologically disastrous effects of Judeo-Christian ideologies, the drive to exploit nature is common to most cultures. Americans may be the most efficient exploiters in the world, but they have no monopoly on the urge to exploit natural resources.

Even if the United States can make substantial progress towards resolving its own environmental problems, it seems most unlikely that international ecological order can be achieved in an anarchic world of highly nationalistic states. And the actions of one or a few nations can have ecological effects on the rest of the world. So we cannot guarantee our survival simply by putting our own house in order.

Finally, there are no possible solutions as long as population growth remains unchecked. Growing populations will cancel out any possible technological innovations. During the last few decades the United States has had a modest growth rate as compared with some countries, but we have been losing ground in environmental terms. We have spent millions on water pollution control, but water quality has deteriorated. We have spent additional millions on air pollution abatement, but air quality is worse than ever. We have attempted to regulate the use of pesticides since 1947, but the hazards have sharply accelerated. So far we have not been able to run fast enough to stay in the same place. The developing countries, with their rapid growth rates and already inadequate economic base, are headed for certain disaster. There is no possible way out for them unless their birth rate goes down.

* * *

These kinds of considerations prompted Paul Ehrlich to write the following scenario, which sets forth his predictions for the decade of the Seventies if the present course of environmental destruction continues throughout the world.

Eco-Catastrophe!*
Dr. Paul R. Ehrlich**

I.

The end of the ocean came late in the summer of 1979, and it came even more rapidly than the biologists had expected. There had been signs for more than a decade, commencing with the discovery in 1968 that DDT slows down photosynthesis in marine plant life. It was announced in a short paper in the technical journal, *Science,* but to ecologists it smacked of doomsday. They knew that all life in the sea depends on photosynthesis, the chemical process by which green plants bind the sun's energy and make it available to living things. And they knew that DDT and similar chlorinated hydrocarbons had polluted the entire surface of the earth, including the sea.

But that was only the first of many signs. There had been the final gasp of the whaling industry in 1973, and the end of the Peruvian anchovy fishery in 1975. Indeed, a score of other fisheries had disappeared quietly from over-exploitation and various eco-catastrophes by 1977. The term "eco-catastrophe" was coined by a California ecologist in 1969 to describe the most spectacular of man's attacks on the systems which sustain his life. He drew his inspiration from the Santa Barbara offshore oil disaster of that year, and from the news which spread among naturalists that virtually all of the Golden State's seashore bird life was doomed because of chlorinated hydrocarbon interference with its reproduction. Eco-catastrophes in the sea became increasingly common in the early 1970's. Mysterious "blooms" of previously rare microorganisms began to appear in offshore waters. Red tides—killer outbreaks of a minute single-celled plant—returned to the Florida Gulf coast and were sometimes accompanied by tides of other exotic hues.

It was clear by 1975 that the entire ecology of the ocean was changing. A few types of phytoplankton were becoming resistant to chlorinated hydro-carbons and were gaining the upper hand. Changes in the phytoplankton community led inevitably to changes in the community of zooplankton, the tiny animals which eat the phytoplankton. These changes were passed on up the chains of life in the ocean to the herring, plaice, cod and tuna. As the diversity of life in the ocean diminished, its stability also decreased.

Other changes had taken place by 1975. Most ocean fishes that returned to fresh water to breed, like the salmon, had become extinct, their breeding streams so dammed up and polluted that their powerful homing instinct only resulted in suicide. Many fishes and shellfishes that bred in restricted areas along the coasts followed them as onshore pollution escalated.

By 1977 the annual yield of fish from the sea was down to 30 million

Ramparts, VII, No. 3 (September 1969), 24-28. Reprinted by permission of Paul R. Ehrlich and the Editors of *Ramparts.*

**Paul Ehrlich is a professor of biology at Stanford University. He is the author of *The Population Bomb* and has written extensively on the environmental problem.

metric tons, less than one-half the per capita catch of a decade earlier. This helped malnutrition to escalate sharply in a world where an estimated 50 million people per year were already dying of starvation. The United Nations attempted to get all chlorinated hydrocarbon insecticides banned on a worldwide basis, but the move was defeated by the United States. This opposition was generated primarily by the American petrochemical industry, operating hand in glove with its subsidiary, the United States Department of Agriculture. Together they persuaded the government to oppose the U.N. move—which was not difficult since most Americans believed that Russia and China were more in need of fish products than was the United States. The United Nations also attempted to get fishing nations to adopt strict and enforced catch limits to preserve dwindling stocks. This move was blocked by Russia, who, with the most modern electronic equipment, was in the best position to glean what was left in the sea. It was, curiously, on the very day in 1977 when the Soviet Union announced its refusal that another ominous article appeared in *Science*. It announced that incident solar radiation had been so reduced by worldwide air pollution that serious effects on the world's vegetation could be expected.

II.

Apparently it was a combination of ecosystem destabilization, sunlight reduction, and a rapid escalation in chlorinated hydrocarbon pollution from massive Thanodrin applications which triggered the ultimate catastrophe. Seventeen huge Soviet-financed Thanodrin plants were operating in underdeveloped countries by 1978. They had been part of a massive Russian "aid offensive" designed to fill the gap caused by the collapse of America's ballyhooed "Green Revolution."

It became apparent in the early '70s that the "Green Revolution" was more talk than substance. Distribution of high yield "miracle" grain seeds had caused temporary local spurts in agricultural production. Simultaneously, excellent weather had produced record harvests. The combination permitted bureaucrats, especially in the United States Department of Agriculture and the Agency for International Development (AID), to reverse their previous pessimism and indulge in an outburst of optimistic propaganda about staving off famine. They raved about the approaching transformation of agriculture in the underdeveloped countries (UDCs). The reason for the propaganda reversal was never made clear. Most historians agree that a combination of utter ignorance of ecology, a desire to justify past errors, and pressure from agro-industry (which was eager to sell pesticides, fertilizers, and farm machinery to the UDCs and agencies helping the UDCs) was behind the campaign. Whatever the motivation, the results were clear. Many concerned people, lacking the expertise to see through the Green Revolution drivel, relaxed. The population-food crisis was "solved."

But reality was not long in showing itself. Local famine persisted in northern India even after good weather brought an end to the ghastly Bihar famine of the mid-'60s. East Pakistan was next, followed by a resurgence of general famine in northern India. Other foci of famine rapidly developed in

Indonesia, the Philippines, Malawi, the Congo, Egypt, Colombia, Ecuador, Honduras, the Dominican Republic, and Mexico.

Everywhere hard realities destroyed the illusion of the Green Revolution. Yields dropped as the progress farmers who had first accepted the new seeds found that their higher yields brought lower prices—effective demand (hunger plus cash) was not sufficient in poor countries to keep prices up. Less progressive farmers, observing this, refused to make the extra effort required to cultivate the "miracle" grains. Transport systems proved inadequate to bring the necessary fertilizer to the fields where the new and extremely fertilizer-sensitive grains were being grown. The same systems were also inadequate to move produce to markets. Fertilizer plants were not built fast enough, and most of the underdeveloped countries could not scrape together funds to purchase supplies, even on concessional terms. Finally, the inevitable happened, and pests began to reduce yields in even the most carefully cultivated fields. Among the first were the famous "miracle rats" which invaded Philippine "miracle rice" fields early in 1969. They were quickly followed by many insects and viruses, thriving on the relatively pest-susceptible new grains, encouraged by the vast and dense plantings, and rapidly acquiring resistance to the chemicals used against them. As chaos spread until even the most obtuse agriculturists and economists realized that the Green Revolution had turned brown, the Russians stepped in.

In retrospect it seems incredible that the Russians, with the American mistakes known to them, could launch an even more incompetent program of aid to the underdeveloped world. Indeed, in the early 1970's there were cynics in the United States who claimed that outdoing the stupidity of American foreign aid would be physically impossible. Those critics were, however, obviously unaware that the Russians had been busily destroying their own environment for many years. The virtual disappearance of sturgeon from Russian rivers caused a great shortage of caviar by 1970. A standard joke among Russisn scientists at that time was that they had created an artificial caviar which was indistinguishable from the real thing—except by taste. At any rate the Soviet Union, observing with interest the progressive deterioration of relations between the UDCs and the United States, came up with a solution. It had recently developed what it claimed was the ideal insecticide, a highly lethal chlorinated hydrocarbon complexed with a special agent for penetrating the external skeletal armor of insects. Announcing that the new pesticide, called Thanodrin, would truly produce a Green Revolution, the Soviets entered into negotiations with various UDCs for the construction of massive Thanodrin factories. The USSR would bear all the costs; all it wanted in return were certain trade and military concessions.

It is interesting now, with the perspective of years, to examine in some detail the reasons why the UDCs welcomed the Thanodrin plan with such open arms. Government officials in these countries ignored the protests of their own scientists that Thanodrin would not solve the problems which plagued them. The governments now knew that the basic cause of their problems was over-population, and that these problems had been exacerbated by the dullness, daydreaming, and cupidity endemic to all governments. They knew that only population control and limited development aimed primarily at agriculture could have spared them the horrors they now faced. They knew it, but they were not about to admit it. How much easier it was simply to accuse the Americans of failing to give them proper aid; how much simpler to accept the Russian panacea.

And then there was the general worsening of relations between the United States and the UDCs. Many things had contributed to this. The situation in America in the first half of the 1970's deserves our close scrutiny. Being more dependent on imports for raw materials than the Soviet Union, the United States had, in the early 1970's, adopted more and more heavy-handed policies in order to insure continuing supplies. Military adventures in Asia and Latin America had further lessened the international credibility of the United States as a great defender of freedom—an image which had begun to deteriorate rapidly during the pointless and fruitless Viet-Nam conflict. At home, acceptance of the carefully manufactured image lessened dramatically, as even the more romantic and chauvinistic citizens began to understand the role of the military and the industrial system in what John Kenneth Galbraith had aptly named "The New Industrial State."

At home in the USA the early '70s were traumatic times. Racial violence grew and the habitability of the cities diminished, as nothing substantial was done to ameliorate either racial inequities or urban blight. Welfare rolls grew as automation and general technological progress forced more and more people into the category of "unemployable." Simultaneously a taxpayers' revolt occurred. Although there was not enough money to build the schools, roads, water systems, sewage systems, jails, hospitals, urban transit lines, and all the other amenities needed to support a burgeoning population, Americans refused to tax themselves more heavily. Starting in Youngstown, Ohio in 1969 and followed closely by Richmond, California, community after community was forced to close its schools or curtail educational operations for lack of funds. Water supplies, already marginal in quality and quantity in many places by 1970, deteriorated quickly. Water rationing occurred in 1723 municipalities in the summer of 1974, and hepatitis and epidemic dysentery rates climbed about 500 per cent between 1970-1974.

III.

Air pollution continued to be the most obvious manifestation of environmental deterioration. It was, by 1972, quite literally in the eyes of all Americans. The year 1973 saw not only the New York and Los Angeles smog disasters, but also the publication of the Surgeon General's massive report on air pollution and health. The public had been partially prepared for the worst by the publicity given to the U.N. pollution conference held in 1972. Deaths in the late '60s caused by smog were well known to scientists, but the public had ignored them because they mostly involved the early demise of the old and sick rather than people dropping dead on the freeways. But suddenly our citizens were faced with nearly 200,000 corpses and massive documentation that they could be the next to die from respiratory disease. They were not ready for that scale of disaster. After all, the U.N. conference had not predicted that accumulated air pollution would make the planet uninhabitable until almost 1990. The population was terrorized as TV screens became filled with scenes of horror from the disaster areas. Especially vivid was NBC's coverage of hundreds of unattended people choking out their lives outside of New York's hospitals. Terms like nitrogen oxide, acute bronchitis and cardiac arrest began to have real meaning for most Americans.

The ultimate horror was the announcement that chlorinated hydrocarbons were now a major constituent of air pollution in all American cities. Autopsies of smog disaster victims revealed an average chlorinated hydrocarbon load in fatty tissue equivalent to 26 parts per million of DDT. In October, 1973, the Department of Health, Education and Welfare announced studies which showed unequivocally that increasing death rates from hypertension, cirrhosis of the liver, liver cancer and a series of other diseases had resulted from the chlorinated hydrocarbon load. They estimated that Americans born since 1946 (when DDT usage began) now had a life expectancy of only 49 years, and predicted that if current patterns continued, this expectancy would reach 42 years by 1980, when it might level out. Plunging insurance stocks triggered a stock market panic. The president of Velsicol, Inc., a major pesticide producer, went on television to "publicly eat a teaspoonful of DDT" (it was really powdered milk) and announce that HEW had been infiltrated by Communists. Other giants of the petro-chemical industry, attempting to dispute the indisputable evidence, launched a massive pressure campaign on Congress to force HEW to "get out of agriculture's business." They were aided by the agro-chemical journals, which had decades of experience in misleading the public about the benefits and dangers of pesticides. But by now the public realized that it had been duped. The Nobel Prize for medicine and physiology was given to Drs. J. L. Radomski and W. B. Deichmann, who in the late 1960's had pioneered in the documentation of the long-term lethal effects of chlorinated hydrocarbons. A Presidential Commission with unimpeachable credentials directly accused the agro-chemical complex of "condemning many millions of Americans to an early death." The year 1973 was the year in which Americans finally came to understand the direct threat to their existence posed by environmental deterioration.

And 1973 was also the year in which most people finally comprehended the indirect threat. Even the president of Union Oil Company and several other industrialists publicly stated their concern over the reduction of bird populations which had resulted from pollution by DDT and other chlorinated hydrocarbons. Insect populations boomed because they were resistant to most pesticides and had been freed, by the incompetent use of those pesticides, from most of their natural enemies. Rodents swarmed over crops, multiplying rapidly in the absence of predatory birds. The effect of pests on the wheat crop was especially disastrous in the summer of 1973, since that was also the year of the great drought. Most of us can remember the shock which greeted the announcement by atmospheric physicists that the shift of jet stream which had caused the drought was probably permanent. It signalled the birth of the Midwestern desert. Man's air-polluting activities had by then caused gross changes in climatic patterns. The news, of course, played hell with commodity and stock markets. Food prices skyrocketed, as savings were poured into hoarded canned goods. Official assurances that food supplies would remain ample fell on deaf ears, and even the government showed signs of nervousness when California migrant field workers went out on strike again in protest against the continued use of pesticides by growers. The strike burgeoned into farm burning and riots. The workers, calling themselves "The Walking Dead," demanded immediate compensation for their shortened lives, and crash research programs to attempt to lengthen them.

It was in the same speech in which President Edward Kennedy, after much delay, finally declared a national emergency and called out the National Guard to harvest California's crops, that the first mention of population control was made. Kennedy pointed out that the United States would no longer be able to offer any food aid to other nations and was likely to suffer food shortages herself. He suggested that, in view of the manifest failure of the Green Revolution, the only hope of the UDCs lay in population control. His statement, you will recall, created an uproar in the underdeveloped countries. Newspaper editorials accused the United States of wishing to prevent small countries from becoming large nations and thus threatening American hegemony. Politicians asserted that President Kennedy was a "creature of the giant drug combine" that wished to shove its pill down every woman's throat.

Among Americans, religious opposition to population control was very slight. Industry in general also backed the idea. Increasing poverty in the UDCs was both destroying markets and threatening supplies of raw materials. The seriousness of the raw material situation had been brought home during the Congressional Hard Resources hearings in 1971. The exposure of the ignorance of the cornucopian economists had been quite a spectacle—a spectacle brought into virtually every American's home in living color. Few would forget the distinguished geologist from the University of California who suggested that economists be legally required to learn at least the most elementary facts of geology. Fewer still would forget that an equally distinguished Harvard economist added that they might be required to learn some economics, too. The overall message was clear: America's resource situation was bad and bound to get worse. The hearings had led to a bill requiring the Departments of State, Interior, and Commerce to set up a joint resource procurement council with the express purpose of "insuring that proper consideration of American resource needs to be an integral part of American foreign policy."

Suddenly the United States discovered that it had a national consensus: population control was the only possible salvation of the underdeveloped world. But that same consensus led to heated debate. How could the UDCs be persuaded to limit their populations, and should not the United States lead the way by limiting its own? Members of the intellectual community wanted America to set an example. They pointed out that the United States was in the midst of a new baby boom: her birth rate, well over 20 per thousand per year, and her growth rate of over one per cent per annum were among the very highest of the developed countries. They detailed the deterioration of the American physical and psychic environments, the growing health threats, the impending food shortages, and the insufficiency of funds for desperately needed public works. They contended that the nation was clearly unable or unwilling to properly care for the people it already had. What possible reason could there be, they queried, for adding any more? Besides, who would listen to requests by the United States for population control when that nation did not control her own profligate reproduction?

Those who opposed population controls for the U.S. were equally vociferous. The military-industrial complex, with its all-too-human mixture of ignorance and avarice, still saw strength and prosperity in numbers. Baby food magnates, already worried by the growing nitrate pollution of their products, saw their market disappearing. Steel manufacturers saw a decrease in aggregate demand and slippage for that holy of holies, the Gross National Product. And military men saw, in the growing population-food-environment crisis, a serious threat to their carefully nurtured Cold War. In the end, of course, economic arguments held sway, and the "inalienable right of every American couple to determine the size of its family," a freedom invented for the occasion in the early '70s, was not compromised.

The population control bill, which was passed by Congress early in 1974, was quite a document, nevertheless. On the domestic front, it authorized an increase from 100 to 150 million dollars in funds for "family planning" activities. This was made possible by a general feeling in the country that the growing army on welfare needed family planning. But the gist of the bill was a series of measures designed to impress the need for population control on the UDCs. All American aid to countries with overpopulation problems was required by law to consist in part of population control assistance. In order to receive any assistance each nation was required not only to accept the population control aid, but also to match it according to a complex formula. "Overpopulation" itself was defined by a formula based on U.N. statistics, and the UDCs were required not only to accept aid, but also to show progress in reducing birth rates. Every five years the status of the aid program for each nation was to be re-evaluated.

The reaction to the announcement of this program dwarfed the response to President Kennedy's speech. A coalition of UDCs attempted to get the U.N. General Assembly to condemn the United States as a "genetic aggressor." Most damaging of all to the American cause was the famous "25 Indians and a dog" speech by Mr. Shankarnarayan, Indian ambassador to the U.N. Shankarnarayan pointed out that for several decades the United States, with less than six per cent of the people of the world, had consumed roughly 50 per cent of the raw materials used every year. He described vividly America's contribution to worldwide environmental deterioration, and he scathingly denounced the miserly record of United States foreign aid as "unworthy of a fourth-rate power, let alone the most powerful nation on earth."

It was the climax of his speech, however, which most historians claim once and for all destroyed the image of the United States. Shankarnarayan informed the assembly that the average American family dog was fed more animal protein per week than the average Indian got in a month. "How do you justify taking fish from protein-starved Peruvians and feeding them to your animals?" he asked. "I contend," he concluded, "that the birth of an American baby is a greater disaster for the world than that of 25 Indian babies." When the applause had died away, Mr. Sorensen, the American representative, made a speech which said essentially that "other countries look after their own self-interest, too." When the vote came, the United States was condemned.

IV.

This condemnation set the tone of U.S.-UDC relations at the time the Russian Thanodrin proposal was made. The proposal seemed to offer the masses in the UDCs an opportunity to save themselves and humiliate the United States at the same time; and in human affairs, as we all know, biological realities could never interfere with such an opportunity. The scientists were silenced, the politicians said yes, the Thanodrin plants were built, and the results were what any beginning ecology student could have predicted. At first Thanodrin seemed to offer excellent control of many pests. True, there was a rash of human fatalities from improper use of the lethal chemical, but, as Russian technical advisors were prone to note, these were more than compensated for by increased yields. Thanodrin use skyrocketed throughout the underdeveloped world. The Mikoyan design group developed a dependable, cheap agricultural aircraft which the Soviets donated to the effort in large numbers. MIG sprayers became even more common in UDCs than MIG interceptors.

Then the troubles began. Insect strains with cuticles resistant to Thanodrin penetration began to appear. And as streams, rivers, fish culture ponds and onshore waters became rich in Thanodrin, more fisheries began to disappear. Bird populations were decimated. The sequence of events was standard for broadcast use of a synthetic pesticide: great success at first, followed by removal of natural enemies and development of resistance by the pest. Populations of crop-eating insects in areas treated with Thanodrin made steady comebacks and soon became more abundant than ever. Yields plunged, while farmers in their desperation increased the Thanodrin dose and shortened the time between treatments. Death from Thanodrin poisoning became common. The first violent incident occurred in the Canete Valley of Peru, where farmers had suffered a similar chlorinated hydrocarbon disaster in the mid-'50s. A Russian advisor serving as an agricultural pilot was assaulted and killed by a mob of enraged farmers in January, 1978. Trouble spread rapidly during 1978, especially after the word got out that two years earlier Russia herself had banned the use of Thanodrin at home because of its serious effect on ecological systems. Suddenly Russia, and not the United States, was the *bête noir* in the UDCs. "Thanodrin parties" became epidemic, with farmers, in their ignorance, dumping carloads of Thanodrin concentrate into the sea. Russian advisors fled, and four of the Thanodrin plants were leveled to the ground. Destruction of the plants in Rio and Calcutta led to hundreds of thousands of gallons of Thanodrin concentrate being dumped directly into the sea.

Mr. Shankarnarayan again rose to address the U.N., but this time it was Mr. Potemkin, representative of the Soviet Union, who was on the hot seat. Mr. Potemkin heard his nation described as the mass killer of all time as Shankarnarayan predicted at least 30 million deaths from crop failures due to overdependence on Thanodrin. Russia was accused of "chemical aggression," and the General Assembly, after a weak reply by Potemkin, passed a vote of censure.

It was in January, 1979, that huge blooms of a previously unknown variety of diatom were reported off the coast of Peru. The blooms were accompanied by a massive die-off of sea life and of the pathetic remainder of the birds which had once feasted on the anchovies of the area. Almost immediately another huge bloom was reported in the Indian ocean, centering around the Seychelles, and then a third in the South Atlantic off the African coast. Both of these were accompanied by spectacular die-offs of marine animals. Even more ominous were growing reports of fish and bird kills at oceanic points where there were no spectacular blooms. Biologists were soon able to explain the phenomena: the diatom had evolved an enzyme which broke down Thanodrin; that enzyme also produced a breakdown product which interfered with the transmission of nerve impulses, and was therefore lethal to animals. Unfortunately, the biologists could suggest no way of repressing the poisonous diatom bloom in time. By

September, 1979, all important animal life in the sea was extinct. Large areas of coastline had to be evacuated, as windrows of dead fish created a monumental stench.

But stench was the least of man's problems. Japan and China were faced with almost instant starvation from a total loss of the seafood on which they were so dependent. Both blamed Russia for their situation and demanded immediate mass shipments of food. Russia had none to send. On October 13, Chinese armies attacked Russia on a broad front. . . .

Selected Additional Readings

Bibliographies

Caldwell, Lynton K., *Science, Technology, and Public Policy: A Selected and Annotated Bibliography.* Bloomington, Ind.: Department of Government, Indiana University, 1968.

Durrenberger, Robert W., *Environment and Man: A Bibliography.* Palo Alto, Calif: National Press Books, 1970.

Henning, Daniel H., *A Selected Bibliography on Public Environmental Policy and Administration.* Albuquerque, N.M.: Natural Resources Journal, University of New Mexico Law School, 1971.

Paulsen, David F., *Natural Resources in the Governmental Process.* Tucson, Arizona: University of Arizona Press, 1970.

General Studies

Anderson, Walt, ed., *Politics and Environment.* Pacific Palisades, Calif.: Goodyear Publishing Co., 1970.

Caldwell, Lynton K., *Environment: A Challenge for Modern Society.* Garden City, N.Y.: The Natural History Press, 1970.

_____, ed., *Environmental Studies: Papers on the Politics and Public Administration of Man-Environment Relationships.* 4 vols. Bloomington, Indiana: Institute of Public Administration, Indiana University, 1967.

Congressional Quarterly, *Man's Control of the Environment.* Washington, D.C., 1970.

Cooley, Richard A. and Geoffrey Wandesforde-Smith, *Congress and the Environment.* Seattle: University of Washington Press, 1970.

Davies, J. Clarence, III, *The Politics of Pollution.* New York: Pegasus, 1970.

Doherty, William T., Jr., *Minerals.* New York: Van Nostrand Reinhold, 1971.

Foss, Phillip O., *Recreation.* New York: Van Nostrand Reinhold Co., 1971.

Helfrich, Harold W., Jr., ed., *Agenda for Survival.* New Haven: Yale University Press, 1971.

Johnson, Huey D., ed., *No Deposit—No Return.* Reading, Mass.: Addison-Wesley Publishing Company, Inc., 1970.

Marine, Gene, *American the Raped.* New York: Avon Books, 1970.

McEvoy, James, III, *The American Public's Concern with the Environment.* Davis, California: Institute of Government Affairs, University of California, 1971.

Meek, Roy L. and John A. Straayer, *The Politics of Neglect.* Boston: Houghton-Mifflin Company, 1971.

Editors of *Ramparts, Eco-Catastrophe.* San Francisco: Canfield Press, 1970.

Roos, Leslie L., Jr., *The Politics of Ecosuicide.* New York: Holt, Rinehart and Winston, Inc., 1971.

Smith, Frank E., *The Politics of Conservation.* New York: Pantheon Books, 1966.

Udall, Stewart L., *1976: Agenda for Tomorrow.* New York: Harcourt, Brace Jovanovich, Inc., 1968.

_____, *The Quiet Crisis.* New York: Avon Books, 1963.

Prologue

"A Giant Step—Or a Springtime Skip?" *Newsweek,* LXXVI, No. 18 (May 7, 1970), 26-28.

Boulding, Kenneth E., "No Second Chance for Man," *The Progressive,* XXXIV, No. 4 (April, 1970), 40-43.

_____, "The Economics of the Coming Spaceship Earth," in *Environmental Quality in a Growing Economy,* ed. Henry Jarrett. New York: Johns Hopkins Press, 1966.

Caldwell, Lynton K., "Achieving Environmental Quality: Is Our Present Governmental Organization Adequate?" in *No Deposit—No Return,* ed. Huey D. Johnson. Reading, Mass.: Addison-Wesley Publishing Company, Inc., 1970.

_____, "Biopolitics: Science, Ethics, and Public Policy," *The Yale Review,* LIV, No. 1 (October, 1964), 1-16.

Commoner, Barry, "Nature under Attack," *Columbia Forum,* XI, No. 1 (Spring, 1968), 17-22.

Ehrlich, Paul R., "The Biological Revolution," *The Center Magazine,* II, No. 6 (November, 1969), 28-31.

Iseminger, Gordon L., "Environmental Abuse and Neglect: Precursors of Civilizations' Doom?" *North Dakota Quarterly,* XXXVII, No. 1 (Winter, 1969), 29-48.

Margolis, Jon, "Our Country 'Tis of Thee, Land of Ecology . . .," *Esquire,* LXXIII, No. 3 (March, 1970), 124ff.

Mitchell, John G., "On the Spoor of the Slide Rule," in *Ecotactics: The Sierra Club Handbook for Environment Activists.* New York: Simon and Schuster, Inc., 1970.

Oppenheimer, Jack C. and Leonard A. Miller, "Environmental Problems and Legislative Responses," *Annals of the American Academy of Political and Social Sciences,* CCCLXXXIX (May, 1970), 77-86.

Rienow, Robert and Leona Rienow, "Conservation for Survival," *Nation,* CCVII, No. 5 (August 26, 1968), 138-142.

Sutherland, Thomas C., "The Battle over America's Environment," *University,* XLIII, (Winter, 1969-1970), 3-12.

"The Ravaged Environment," *Newsweek,* LXXVI, No. 4 (January 26, 1970), 30-47.

U.S. Department of the Interior, *The Third Wave.* Washington, D.C.: U.S. Government Printing Office, 1966.

Ways, Max, "How to Think about the Environment," *Fortune,* LXXXI, No. 2 (February, 1970), 98ff.

Wengert, Norman, "The Ideological Basis of Conservation and Natural Resources Policies and Programs," *The Annals of the American Academy of Political and Social Sciences,* November, 1962, pp. 65-75.

What's the Problem?

Bliss, L. C., "Why We Must Plan Now to Protect the Arctic," *Bulletin of the Atomic Scientists,* XXVI, No. 8 (October, 1970), 34-38.

Cain, Stanley A., "Man and His Environment," *Ekistics,* XXIV, No. 137 (April, 1967), 203-207.

Caulfield, Henry, "Planning the Earth's Surface," in *No Deposit—No Return,* ed. Huey Johnson. Reading, Mass. Addison-Wesley Publishing Company, Inc., 1970.

Commoner, Barry, Michael Corr, and Paul J. Stamler, "The Causes of Pollution," *Environment,* XIII, No. 3 (April, 1971), 2-19.

"Fighting to Save the Earth from Man," *Time,* February 2, 1970, pp. 56-63.

Galbraith, John Kenneth, "The Polipollutionists," *The Atlantic,* CCXIX, No. 1 (January, 1967), 52-54.

Gaus, John Merriman, *Reflections on Public Administration.* University, Alabama: University of Alabama Press, 1947.

Godfrey, Arthur, "A View Toward Survival," in *No Deposit—No Return,* ed. Huey D. Johnson. Reading, Mass. Addison-Wesley Publishing Company, Inc., 1970.

Harrison, Gordon, "An Ecological Primer," *Sierra Club Bulletin,* LIV, No. 10 (October-November, 1969), 18-19.

Lieber, Harvey, "Public Administration and Environmental Quality," *Public Administration Review,* XXX, No. 3 (May, 1970), 277-286.

Mayda, Jaro, "Conservation, 'New Conservation' and Ecomanagement," *Wisconsin Law Review,* MCMLXIX, No. 3 (1969), 788-799.

Means, Richard L., "Why Worry about Nature?" *Saturday Review,* L, No. 48 (December 2, 1967), 13-15.

Murdoch, William and Joseph Connell, "All about Ecology," *The Center Magazine,* III, No. 1 (January-February, 1970), 56-63.

Nelson, C. N., "Call to Action," *North Dakota Quarterly,* XXXVII, No. 1 (Winter, 1969), 5-9.

Pfaltzgraff, Robert L., Jr., "Ecology and the Political System," *American Behavioral Scientist,* XI, No. 6 (July-August, 1968), 3-6.

Pinchot, Gifford, *Breaking New Ground.* New York: Harcourt, Brace Jovanovich, Inc., 1947.

Rienow, Robert and Leona Train Rienow, *Man against His Environment.* New York: Ballantine Books, 1970.

Ritchie-Calder, Lord Peter, "Polluting the Environment," *The Center Magazine,* II, No. 3 (May, 1969), 7-12.

Weisberg, Barry, "Raping Alaska," *Ramparts,* VIII, No. 7 (January, 1970), 26-33.

The Effluent Society

Bryan, Edward H., "Water Supply and Pollution Control Aspects of Urbanization," *Law and Contemporary Problems,* XXX, No. 1 (Winter, 1965), 176-192.

Carmichael, Donald M., "Forty Years of Water Pollution Control in Wisconsin, A Case Study," *Wisconsin Law Review,* MCMLXVII, No. 2 (Spring, 1967), 350-419.

Carr, Donald E., *Death of the Sweet Waters.* New York: Berkeley Publishing Corp. by arrangement with W. W. Norton and Company, Inc., 1971.

Cleary, Edward J., "Institutional Innovations for Water Quality Management," *Journal of the Water Pollution Control Federation,* XLII, No. 2, Pt. 1 (February, 1970), 157-164.

Drew, Elizabeth, "Dam Outrage: The Story of the Army Engineers," *The Atlantic,* CCXXV, No. 4 (April, 1970), 51-62.

Dworsky, Leonard B., *Water and Air Pollution.* New York: Van Nostrand Reinhold, 1971.

Gianelli, William R., *The Engineer and His Environment.* A Report to the Pacific Southwest Conference of the American Society of Civil Engineers, Sacramento, California, March 23, 1970.

Hill, Gladwin, "The Great and Dirty Lakes," *Saturday Review,* XLVII, No. 43 (October 23, 1965), 32-34.

Kneese, Allen V., "New Directions in Water Management," *Bulletin of the Atomic Scientists,* XXI, No. 5 (May, 1965), 2-8.

Marine, Gene, "The California Water Plan: The Most Expensive Faucet in the World," *Ramparts,* VIII, No. 11 (May, 1970), 36-41.

Marsh, George P., *The Earth as Modified by Human Action.* New York: Charles Scribner's Sons, 1864.

Middleton, John T., "Man and His Habitat: Problems of Pollution," *Bulletin of the Atomic Scientist,* XXI, No. 3 (March, 1965), 18-22.

Moss, Frank E., *The Water Crisis.* New York: Frederick A. Praeger, 1967.

Muskie, Edmund S., "Fresh Water: A Diminishing Supply," *Current History,* LVIII, No. 346 (June, 1970), 329ff.

Rienow, Robert and Leona Train Rienow, "Last Chance for the Nation's Waterways," *Saturday Review,* XLVIII, No. 21 (May 22, 1965), 35ff.

Rivers, William L., "The Politics of Pollution," *The Reporter,* XXIV, No. 7 (March 31, 1961), 34-36.

Roalman, A. R., "A Bounty on Water Polluters," *Water Resources Bulletin,* V, No. 2 (June, 1969), 62-65.

Schrag, Peter, "Life on a Dying Lake," *Saturday Review,* LII, No. 38 (September 20, 1969), 19ff.

Smith, Frank E., *Land and Water.* 2 vols. New York: Van Nostrand Reinhold, 1971.

Stevens, Leonard A., "Every Drop Counts," *National Civic Review,* LVI, No. 3 (March, 1967), 142-155.

Still, Henry, *Will the Human Race Survive?* New York: Hawthorn Books, Inc., 1966.

Warne, William E., "The Water Crisis Is Present," *Natural Resources Journal,* IX, No. 1 (January, 1969), 53-62.

The Garbage in the Sky

Behle, Calvin A., "Industry—The Views of the Regulated," *Arizona Law Review,* X, No. 1 (Summer, 1968), 74-80.

Berry, Stephen R., "Perspectives on Polluted Air—1970," *Bulletin of the Atomic Scientists,* XXVI, No. 4 (April, 1970), 2ff.

Carr, Donald E., *The Breath of Life.* New York: Berkeley Publishing Corp. by arrangement with W. W. Norton and Company, Inc., 1970.

"Con Ed and the Good Life, A Question of Power," *Newsweek,* LXXVI, No. 28 (July 13, 1970), 76ff.

Cousins, Norman, "There's Something in the Air," *Saturday Review,* L, No. 4 (January 28, 1967), 28-29.

Dixon, James P., "For Air Conservation," *Bulletin of the Atomic Scientists,* XXI, No. 6 (June, 1965), 7-12.

Dworsky, Leonard B., *Water and Air Pollution.* New York: Van Nostrand Reinhold, 1971.

Esposito, John C., *Vanishing Air.* New York: Grossman Publishers, Inc., 1970.

Griffin, C. W., Jr., "America's Airborne Garbage," *Saturday Review,* XLVIII, No. 21 (May 22, 1965), 32ff.

Haydel, Doug, "Regional Control of Air and Water Pollution in the San Francisco Bay Area," *California Law Review,* LV, No. 3 (August, 1967), 702-727.

Kennedy, Harold W., "Introduction—Some Legal Ramifications of Air Pollution Control and a Review of Current Control of Automotive Emissions," *Arizona Law Review,* X, No. 1 (Summer, 1968), 1-9.

Lovell, Bernard, "The Pollution of Space," *Bulletin of the Atomic Scientists,* XIV, No. 10 (December, 1968), 42-45.

Muskie, Edmund S., "Setting Goals for Clean Air," in *Proceedings: The Third National Conference on Air Pollution.* Washington, D.C.: U.S. Government Printing Office, 1967.

Nelson, Gaylord, "A Congressional View of the Problem," in *Proceedings: The Third National Conference on Air Pollution.* Washington, D.C.: U.S. Government Printing Office, 1967.

Ramsey, Norman F., "We Need a Pollution Tax," *Bulletin of the Atomic Scientists,* XXVI, No. 4 (April, 1970), 3ff.

Rydell, C. Peter and Gretchen Schwarz, "Air Pollution and Urban Form: A Review of Current Literature," *Ekistics,* XXVI, No. 153 (August, 1968), 209-214.

Seaborg, Glenn T., "Development of National Policy with Respect to Nuclear and Other New Sources of Power," in *Proceedings: The Third National Conference on Air Pollution.* Washington, D.C.: U.S. Government Printing Office, 1967.

Seymour, Whitney North, "Cleaning Up Our City Air," *Urban Affairs Quarterly,* III, No. 1 (September, 1967), 34-45.

The Politics of Poison

"Agricultural Pesticides: The Need for Improved Control Legislation," *Minnesota Law Review,* LII, No. 6 (June, 1968), 1242-1260.

Beck, Robert E., "Pesticides and the Law," *North Dakota Quarterly,* XXXVII, No. 1 (Winter, 1969), 49-64.

Carson, Rachel, *Silent Spring.* Boston: Houghton Mifflin Company, 1962.

Graham, Frank, Jr., *Since Silent Spring.* Boston: Houghton Mifflin Company, 1970.

Whiteside, Thomas, *Defoliation.* New York: Ballantine Books, 1970.

Whitten, Jamie L., *That We May Live.* Princeton, N.J.: D. Van Nostrand Company, Inc., 1966.

Governing the Ocean Environment

Alexander, Lewis M., "National Jurisdiction and the Use of the Sea," *Natural Resources Journal,* VIII, No. 3 (July, 1968), 373-400.

Borgese, Elisabeth Mann, "The Republic of the Deep Seas," *The Center Magazine,* I, No. 4 (May, 1968), 18-27.

Cheever, Daniel S., "Marine Science and Ocean Politics," *Bulletin of the Atomic Scientists,* XXVI, No. 2 (February, 1970), 22ff.

Christy, Francis T., Jr., "Marine Resources and the Freedom of the Seas," *Natural Resources Journal,* VIII, No. 3 (July, 1968), 424-433.

Ehrlich, Paul R. and Anne H. Ehrlich, "The Food-from-the-Sea Myth," *Saturday Review,* LIII, No. 14 (April 4, 1970), 53ff.

Hirdman, Sven, "Weapons in the Deep Sea," *Environment,* XIII, No. 3 (April, 1970), 28-42.

Jones, Galen E., "The Living Economy of the Sea," *Bulletin of the Atomic Scientists,* XXI, No. 4 (March, 1965), 13-17.

Kennan, George F., "To Prevent a World Wasteland," *Foreign Affairs,* XLVIII, No. 3 (April, 1970), 401-413.

Marx, Wesley, *The Frail Ocean.* New York: Ballantine Books, 1967.

Miles, Edward, "Technology, Ocean Management, and the Law of the Sea: Some Current History," *Denver Law Journal,* XLVI, No. 2 (Spring, 1969), 240-260.

Molotch, Harvey, "Santa Barbara: Oil in the Velvet Playground," *Ramparts,* VIII, No. 5 (November, 1969), 44-51.

O'Connell, Dennis M., "Continental Shelf Oil Disasters: Challenge to International Pollution Control," *Cornell Law Review,* LV, No. 1 (November, 1969), 113-128.

————, "Reflections on Brussels: IMCO and the 1969 Pollution Conventions," *Cornell International Law Journal,* III, No. 2 (Spring, 1970), 161-188.

"The Dirty Dilemma of Oil Spills," *Life,* LXVIII, No. 8 (March 6, 1970), 28ff.

The Population Bomb

"Abortion and the Changing Law," *Newsweek,* LXXVI, No. 15 (April 13, 1970), 53-61.

"Abortion Comes out of the Shadows," *Life,* LXIII, No. 7 (February 27, 1970), 20B-29.

Appleman, Philip, *The Silent Explosion.* Boston: Beacon Press, 1965.

Dubos, Rene Jules, "Man Adapting: His Limitations and Potentialities," in *Environment for Man,* ed. William R. Ewald, Jr. Bloomington, Ind.: Indiana University Press, 1967.

Durand, John D., "A Long-Range View of World Population Growth," *The Annals of the American Academy of Political and Social Sciences,* CCCLXIX (January, 1967), 1-8.

Ehrlich, Paul, "Population," *The Texas Quarterly,* XI, No. 2 (Summer, 1968), 71-77.

————, *The Population Bomb.* New York: Ballantine Books, 1968.

————, "The Population Explosion: Facts and Fiction," *Sierra Club Bulletin,* LIII, No. 10 (October, 1968), 11-14.

———— and Anne H. Ehrlich, *Population, Resources, Environment: Issues in Human Ecology.* San Francisco: W. H. Freeman and Co., 1970.

Hardin, Garrett, "The Tragedy of the Commons," *Ekistics,* XXVII, No. 160 (March, 1969), 168-170.

Hauser, Philip M., ed., *The Population Dilemma.* Englewood Cliffs, N.J.: Prentice-Hall, Inc., 1969.

Lamanna, Richard A., "Population and Pollution," *The Scholastic,* III, No. 18 (March 20, 1970), 30-31.

Lyle, David, "The Human Race Has, Maybe, Thirty-Five Years Left," *Esquire,* LXIII, No. 3 (September, 1967), 116ff.

Paddock, William and Paul Paddock, *Famine, 1975.* Boston: Little, Brown and Company, 1967.

Sax, Karl, *Standing Room Only: The World's Exploding Population.* Boston: Beacon Press, 1955.

Wald, George, "A Better World for Fewer Children," *Progressive,* XXXIV, No. 4 (April, 1970), 26-28.

The Politics of Survival

Caldwell, Lynton K., "Authority and Responsibility for Environmental Administration," *Annals of the American Academy of Political and Social Sciences,* CCCLXXXIX (May, 1970), 107-115.

————, "Environment: A New Focus for Public Policy?" *Public Administration Review,* XXIV, No. 3 (September, 1963), 132-139.

_____, ed., *Political Dynamics of Environmental Control*. No. 1 of Environmental Studies Series. Bloomington, Ind.: Institute of Public Administration, University of Indiana, January 30, 1967.

Commoner, Barry, *Science and Survival*. New York: The Viking Press, Inc., 1966.

D'Amato, Anthony A., "Environmental Degradation and Legal Action," *Bulletin of the Atomic Scientists*, XXVI, No. 3 (March, 1970), 24-26.

Diamond, Robert S., "What Business Thinks," *Fortune*, LXXXI, No. 2 (February, 1970), 188ff.

Gellen, Martin, "The Making of a Pollution-Industrial Complex," *Ramparts*, VIII, No. 11 (May, 1970), 22-27.

Hardin, Garrett, "To Trouble a Star: The Cost of Intervention in Nature," *Bulletin of the Atomic Scientists*, XXVI, No. 1 (January, 1970), 17-20.

Landsberg, Hans H., "Villains Obscure Some Real Keys to Pollution," *The Washington Post*, April 26, 1970, p. B3.

Lindsay, John V., "The Plight of the Cities," *The Progressive*, XXXIV, No. 4 (April, 1970), 29-31.

Maiken, Peter, "Hysterics Won't Clean Up Pollution," *Chicago Tribune Magazine*, April 12, 1970, pp. 69ff.

Mitchell, John G. and John Stallings, eds., *Ecotactics, The Sierra Club Handbook for Environment Activists*. New York: Simon and Schuster, 1970.

Murphy, Earl Finbar, "A Law for Life," *Wisconsin Law Review*, MCMLXIX, No. 3 (1969), 773-787.

Nelson, Gaylord A., "The 'New Citizenship' for Survival," *The Progressive*, XXXIV, No. 4 (April, 1970), 32-37.

Possony, Stephen, "Technology and the Human Condition," *American Behavioral Scientist*, XI, No. 6 (July-August, 1968), 43-48.

Potter, Frank M., Jr., "Everyone Wants to Save the Environment but No One Knows Quite What to Do," *The Center Magazine*, III, No. 2 (March-April, 1970), 35-40.

Reitze, Arnold W., Jr., "Pollution Control: Why Has It Failed?" *American Bar Association Journal*, LV, No. 10 (October, 1969), 923-927.

Sax, Joseph L., "Emerging Legal Strategies: Judicial Intervention," *Annals of the American Academy of Political and Social Sciences*, CCCLXXIX, (May, 1970), 71-76.

Smith, Frank E., *Improving the Southern Environment*. A Report to the Symposium on the Emerging South, Memphis, Tennessee, April 18, 1970.

Stockmar, J. Brian, "Pollution: The Capitalist Response," *Logres*, I, No. 1 (May, 1970), 11-13.

Warne, William, "Virulent Environmentalism," *Public Administration Review*, XXX, No. 3 (May/June, 1970), 327-328.

Wengert, Norman, *Natural Resources and the Political Struggle*. New York: Doubleday & Company, Inc., 1955.

White, Theodore H., "How Do We Get from Here to There?" *Life*, LXVIII, No. 24 (June 26, 1970), 36-44.

Zurhorst, Charles, *The Conservation Fraud*. New York: Cowles Book Company, Inc., 1970.